PELOUBET'S
NOTES
1975-1976

PELOUBET'S NOTES

1975 - 1976

Based on the International Bible

Lessons for Christian Living

Uniform Series

by

RALPH EARLE

102nd ANNUAL VOLUME

Founded by Francis N. Peloubet

BAKER BOOK HOUSE ● GRAND RAPIDS, MICHIGAN

ISBN: 08010-3345-4

Copyright 1975 by
Baker Book House Company

Printed in the United States of America

PREFACE

The state of world affairs causes many people concern about the future. Does the Bible tell us anything that can help us face an uncertain future with confidence?

This volume of *Peloubet's Notes* demonstrates that this is not the first time in history that God's people have faced an uncertain future. And it assures the Sunday school student that God rules and overrules for the good of His chosen people. After presenting man as God's creation—a free, yet accountable creature—the history of the patriarchs is traced as they followed God's leading into an uncharted way of life.

In the second and third quarters the Messiah is presented—the God-Man who saves us from sin and sets an example of suffering through which one learns obedience.

The lessons of the fourth quarter introduce the Bible student to the Word of God and Church History: The Apostolic Era, the Medieval Era, the Modern Era.

For the fourth year Dr. Ralph Earle, Professor of New Testament at Nazarene Theological Seminary, Kansas City, Missouri, presents the lessons in a way that applies Scripture knowledge to living the Christian life in the seventies. His detailed outlines make the lessons easy to follow. He quotes extensively from a wide field of commentators in order to present several points of view, then applies the lesson with a personal application and questions that lead to class discussion. The Suggested Introduction for Adults and Suggested Introduction for Youth set the stage for each lesson for a particular age group, as does the Concepts for Children.

Baker Book House proudly presents this volume in a series that has for over a century been cherished in church schools of many denominations.

CONTENTS

FOURTH QUARTER

The Bible and Church History

Unit I: The Bible and the Church: Apostolic Era

Unit II: The Bible and the Church: Medieval Era

Unit III: The Bible and the Church: Modern Era

GENESIS: MAN'S QUEST FOR IDENTITY

THE IMAGE OF GOD

.DEVOTIONAL READING	Acts 17:22-31

ADULTS

Topic: *The Image of God*

Background Scripture: Genesis 1–2

Scripture Lesson: Genesis 1:26-27; 2:7, 18-25

Memory Verse: *Then the Lord God formed man of dust from the ground, and breathed into his nostrils the breath of life; and man became a living being.* Genesis 2:7

YOUTH

Topic: *In the Image of God*

Background Scripture: Genesis 1–2

Scripture Lesson: Genesis 1:26-27; 2:7, 18-25

Memory Verse: *Then the Lord God formed man of dust from the ground, and breathed into his nostrils the breath of life; and man became a living being.* Genesis 2:7

CHILDREN

Topic: *In God's Likeness*

Background Scripture: Genesis 1–2

Scripture Lesson: Genesis 1:26-31

Memory Verse: *Yet thou hast made him little less than God, and dost crown him with glory and honor.* Psalm 8:5

DAILY BIBLE READINGS

Mon., Sept. 1: Creation of Living Creatures, Genesis 1:20-25.
Tues., Sept. 2: God Is Our Creator, Isaiah 45:7-12.
Wed., Sept. 3: Always in God's Presence, Psalm 139:7-18.
Thurs., Sept. 4: Crowned with Glory and Honor, Psalm 8.
Fri., Sept. 5: Union of Husband and Wife, Matthew 19:3-12.
Sat., Sept. 6: God Dwells Within All Men, Acts 17:22-31.
Sun., Sept. 7: Put on This Image, Colossians 3:5-12.

LESSON AIM

To help us see who we are and what we as human beings are.

LESSON SETTING

Time: The date of man's creation is uncertain. In the margin of many Bibles one finds 4004 B.C. This date was fixed by Archbishop Ussher (1581–1656), who derived it from a careful study of Old Testament data. Many evangelicals today would place the creation of man between 4000 and 8000 B.C.

11

Place: The exact location of the Garden of Eden is unknown. It has been placed anywhere from Armenia to Southern Mesopotamia. The latter is favored by E. A. Speiser (*Anchor Bible*, I, 20).

The Image of God

SUGGESTED INTRODUCTION FOR ADULTS

The story of creation is beautifully told in the first two chapters of Genesis. The book opens with the magnificent statement: "In the beginning God created the heaven and the earth." The term "heaven" here does not apply to the eternal abode of God but to what we call "the sky," with all its "heavenly bodies"—sun, moon, planets, and stars.

The process of creation is spelled out in periods of days—six in all. Some conservative scholars feel that these were literal twenty-four-hour days. Other evangelical scholars prefer to think of them as long periods of time, the geological ages. It should be recognized that the Bible says nothing about the age of the earth, though it does give definite indications about the age of man.

On the first day God created light and made a division between night and day. The second day saw the separation between the cloudy firmament above and the waters below. The third day there was a separation between the dry land and the seas. Also plant life sprang forth. On the fourth day the sun, moon, and stars appeared. The fifth day saw the emergence of fish and birds from the waters. On the sixth day animal life appeared. God's crowning creation was man. That man is distinct from all other created beings is indicated in the opening verses of our printed lesson for today.

SUGGESTED INTRODUCTION FOR YOUTH

Who am I? Where did I come from? Where am I going? These are pertinent questions that young people are asking—and should ask. A cynical age asserts that there are no answers to these questions. So we read Jean Paul Sartre and lead meaningless, purposeless lives. This breeds violence, murder, suicide.

Authentic, authoritative answers to these questions can be found only in the Bible. It tells us that we were created in the image of God, to have fellowship with Him. It informs us that we came from His hand of love and that if we believe and obey Him we will some day live with Him forever. This gives meaning to life and provides us with goal and purpose.

Who am I? Today's lesson tells us. It is a beautiful and challenging story.

CONCEPTS FOR CHILDREN

1. God created man in His own image.
2. This does not mean the shape of the body, for God is spirit.
3. It means the image of moral and spiritual likeness.
4. So we are to take care of our souls as well as our bodies.
5. Our duty is to love God and obey Him.

THE LESSON COMMENTARY

I. MAN'S SOUL IN THE IMAGE OF GOD:
Genesis 1:26-27

The doctrine of the Trinity is not spelled out clearly in any passage in the Old Testament. But there are many hints of it. We find in verse 2 that the Spirit of God brooded over the face of the waters. The very name for God is the Hebrew *Elohim*, which is plural. This could be the plural of majesty, a feature of ancient languages. But it may also suggest plurality of persons.

Here in verse 26 we find a more definite disclosure of the Trinity. God said, "Let us make." This implies a conference of Father, Son, and Holy Spirit—as they are identified clearly in the New Testament. Some scholars have suggested a council with angels, but Isaiah 40:13 definitely rules this out.

The decision was: "Let us make man in our image, after our likeness." It is generally held today that there is no basic difference between "image" and "likeness"; the terms are synonymous. The repetition emphasizes the significance of this important truth of divine revelation.

God ordained that man should rule over all animal creation—fish, birds, domestic animals ("cattle"), and reptiles ("every creeping thing"). Because of sin, man has not exercised this dominion as fully as was intended. But his rulership is still valid. The use of "them" shows that "man" means mankind.

Many scholars feel that "all the earth" (after "cattle") means "all wild animals on earth" (NEB). The Jerusalem Bible translates it "all the wild beasts" (from the Syriac). This would supplement "cattle," the domesticated animals.

"So God created man in his own image, in the image of God created he him" (v. 27). This is one of the most significant statements that we can contemplate. In a day when too many people are living mostly on the animal level, we need to be reminded again and again that we were created in God's image, to be like Him.

What is meant by the image of God? George L. Livingston says: "God created man to be a person who possessed self-consciousness, self-determination, and inward holiness (Eccles. 7:29; Eph. 4:24; Col. 3:10)" (*Beacon Bible Commentary*, I, 35). Lee Haines puts it this way: "The likeness is thus one of nature and involves man's spirituality, intelligence, sensibilities or emotional nature and will, with the consciousness of moral responsibility" (*Wesleyan Bible Commentary*, I, Part I, 29). The last point is especially important. Animals have a certain amount of intelligence and volition. But they are not morally responsible for what they do.

Whitelaw suggests that the image of God "consisted (1) in the spirituality of his being, as an intelligent and free agent; (2) in the moral integrity and holiness of his nature; and (3) in his dominion over the creatures" (*Pulpit Commentary*, I, "Genesis," p. 30).

The repeated use of "created" in verse 27 underscores an important fact—the unique creation of man. The verb *bara* occurs in the first verse, which describes the general creation of the material universe. It is found again in verse 21 (once). With regard to its emphasis here Whitelaw writes: "The threefold repetition of the term 'created' should be observed as a significant negation of modern evolution theories as to the descent of man, and an emphatic proclamation of his Divine original. The threefold parallelism of the members of this verse is likewise suggestive . . . of the jubilation with which the writer contemplates the crowning work of Elohim's creative word" ("Genesis").

The last clause of verse 27 summarizes the creation of man and woman. The creation of the latter is described in detail in 2:21-22.

The verb "replenish" in verse 28 has sometimes been used as support for the idea that the earth had been previously inhabited by another race of intelligent beings, prior to the creation of the human race. But this is an unfortunate mistranslation in the King James Version. The Hebrew verb is exactly the same as in verse 22, where it is rendered "fill," and that is the way it should be translated here. There is no hint here of refilling.

II. MAN'S BODY FROM THE DUST OF THE GROUND:
Genesis 2:7

In this verse we find a new name for Deity. Throughout the first chapter and the first three verses of the second chapter we have a summary account of creation. In all of this section the designation of Deity is "God" (*Elohim*). At 1:4 it changes to "Lord God" (*Yahweh Elohim*), and this continues through chapter 3. It is obvious that the first chapter should end with the third verse of the second chapter.

Yahweh is a more personal name than Elohim. The latter word is plural in form, as we have noted, and is used for the heathen "gods." But Yahweh is used only for the true God, the God of Israel. It is sometimes explained as indicating the covenant-keeping God, that is, God in His personal relationship to His people.

Man's spirit was a fresh, unique creation from God (1:27). But his body was "formed," or "fashioned" from the ground. The Hebrew word for "man" is *adam*, translated as a proper name in 2:19-23. The word for "ground" is *adamah*. Man, as far as his body is concerned, is "of the earth, earthy."

When God had fashioned man's body from the dust of the ground, He "breathed into his nostrils the breath of life; and man became a living soul." Of no other creature is it said that God breathed into him. This inbreathing is often assumed as indicating the impartation of immortality, which may well be true. It must be recognized, however, that "living soul" does not mean immortal spirit, for the same Hebrew expression is translated "living creature" and is applied to all kinds of animals (1:20-21, 24, 30; 2:19; 9:12, 15-16).

When we compare 2:7 with 1:27 we realize that man is a combination of dust and deity. That is his problem. He seems pulled up and pulled down at the same time.

The *Anchor Bible* translates "dust of the ground" as "clods in the soil." That reminds one of Francis Thompson's statement: "Man is kin to clod and cherubim." Blaise Pascal said that he is "the glory and scum of the universe." It is true that man can rise higher than the angels or become lower than the animals.

Lee Haines has written beautifully on 2:7: "This verse explains at once the frailty of man and the infinite potential of man. In him is both time and eternity. In him the world and heaven meet. He is at once a part of the lowest order of God's creation and also the image of God Himself. Man is only true man as he makes the best possible use of both parts of his nature, disciplining the earthy, enjoying its pleasures only within the divinely appointed bounds, making it the tool of the heavenly, and so committing himself to the pursuit of heaven and the service of its King as to fulfill the divine purpose in an exquisite and eternal fellowship" (*Wesleyan*, p. 32).

There has been much debate as to whether man lost the image of God when he fell. It would seem correct to say that he lost the image of holiness but retained the image of moral responsibility.

III. WOMAN'S BODY FROM MAN'S SIDE:
Genesis 2:18-25

A. The Need for a Companion: v. 18

The Lord prepared a beautiful place for man to live in—the garden of Eden (v. 8). It was well watered and was filled with fruit trees. Adam was given the task of tilling and tending the garden (v. 15). Some people have thought that work and toil came as a result of man's sin (cf. 3:17-19). But here it is plainly indicated that Adam was to be busy taking care of this large garden before the Fall.

The truth is that work is one of God's greatest blessings to mankind. It is the idle who most frequently get into trouble. Useful employment is one of the best ways to keep from being bored. It is work that acts as a safeguard to keep most people out of jail, the hospital, or the mental institution. We should thank God for it and appreciate the privilege of working.

Though man was surrounded by beauty and every material comfort, there was one thing he lacked—a companion. The Lord said: "It is not good that the man should be alone; I will

make him an help meet for him." The Jerusalem Bible says, "I will make him a helpmate." The New English Bible uses a bit more modern terms: "I will provide a partner for him." Man is normally a social creature and needs companionship. Whitelaw comments: "All that Adam's nature demanded for its completion, physically, intellectually, socially, was to be included in this *altera ego* who was soon to stand by his side" ("Genesis," p. 50).

"Meet for him" is literally "alongside him" or "corresponding to him." The Berkeley Version has "a suitable helper, completing him." There is a real sense in which man without woman is incomplete. God intended that one should complement the other.

B. No Helpmate Among the Animals: vv. 19-20

The first part of verse 19 does not mean that God at this point formed the beasts and birds. He made them before He created man (1:24-27). But He now brought them to Adam to have him assign names to the various species.

In verse 20 we are told that Adam gave names "to all cattle [domestic animals] and to the fowl [birds] of the air, and to every beast of the field." This shows a high order of intelligence on his part. R. Payne Smith says that this passage "sets him before us as a keen observer of nature; and as he pursues his occupations in the garden, new animals and birds from time to time come under his notice, and these he studies, and observes their ways and habits, and so at length gives them appellations" (Ellicott's *Commentary on the Whole Bible*, I, 21). Adam doubtless had a perfect intellect.

Whitelaw points out one implication of this. He writes: "The portrait here delineated of the first man is something widely different from that of an infantile savage slowly groping his way towards the possession of articulate speech and intelligible language by imitation of the sounds of animals. Speech and language both spring full-formed, though not completely matured, from the *primus homo* of the Bible" ("Genesis," p. 51).

The last clause of verse 20 is particularly important. All the various kinds of animals passed before Adam, but not a single one of them could fill the role of being a companion to him. This underscores the impassable gulf between the highest species of animals and the human species. Man is more than the most developed animal. He is a human being made in the image of God.

The King James Version has "Adam" twice in verse 19, twice in verse 20 and once in verse 21. The New American Standard Bible has it only once, in the last clause of verse 20. The reason for this is that in this one place *adam* occurs without the article and so is treated by some scholars as a proper name. In the other four places it is "the man," because the Hebrew has the definite article, as in verse 8.

C. The Creation of Woman: vv. 21-22

The Lord put Adam to sleep, opened his side, and from a part of man's body He made a woman. About the Hebrew word for "rib," Smith has this to say: "The word is never translated *rib* except in this place, but al-

---

DISCUSSION QUESTIONS

1. Why is God's creation of man the most reasonable explanation of human origins?
2. What are the alternatives?
3. How have current concepts of biology, psychology and sociology affected society?
4. In what ways is man like the higher animals and in what ways is he different?
5. How may marriage be strengthened?
6. What did Jesus say about it?

---

ways *side, flank.* . . . Woman was not formed out of one of man's many ribs, of which he would not feel the loss. She is one side of man; and though he may have several sides to his nature and character, yet without woman one integral portion of him is wanting" (Ellicott's, p. 22).

The verb "made" in verse 22 translates a strong Hebrew term: He *built up* into a woman. Again Smith has a helpful comment: "Her formation is described as requiring both time and care on the heavenly artificer's part. This woman is no casual or hasty production of nature, but is the finished result of labour and skill. Finally, she is brought with special honour to the man as the Creator's last and most perfect work. Every step and stage in this description is intended for the ennoblement of marriage. Woman is not made from the *adamah* [ground], but from the *adam*. She is something that he once had, but has lost; and while for Adam there is simply the closing of the cavity caused by her withdrawal, she is moulded and re-fashioned, and built up into man's counterpart" (Ellicott's).

These two verses give us a beautiful concept of marriage, which ought to be recognized by both husband and wife. Someone has put it this way: "Woman was not taken from man's head, to be above him; nor from his feet, to be beneath him; but from his side, to be equal to him; and from near his heart to be dear to him." When this principle is accepted by both, it makes for a happy marriage.

D. The Man and the Woman Together: vv. 23-25

In verse 23 "Man" is *ish* and "Woman" is *ishshah* (feminine). Adam realized that his wife was a part of himself.

And so we find the divine concept of marriage—one man and one woman becoming united into one flesh. A man must *leave* his father and mother and *cleave* ("be glued" by love) to his wife.

Verse 25 gives a picture of the primitive innocence of the first pair. Unfortunately sin has spoiled the picture.

CONTEMPORARY APPLICATION

A popular philosophy of life today is this: "It doesn't make any difference what you believe; it's what you do that's important."

Only a shallow thinker could accept this confusion of logic. For what you believe governs what you do. People who believe that man is descended from animals are apt to live an animal existence. If we are going to die like an animal, we might as well live like one.

To believe that man was created in the image of God puts nobility into life. We sorely need it today.

A FREE, YET ACCOUNTABLE, CREATURE

DEVOTIONAL READING	Galatians 5:13-25

ADULTS

Topic: *A Free, Yet Accountable, Creature*

Background Scripture: Genesis 2:15-17; 3

Scripture Lesson: Genesis 3:1-13

Memory Verse: *For you were called to freedom, brethren; only do not use your freedom as an opportunity for the flesh, but through love be servants of one another.* Galatians 5:13

YOUTH

Topic: *Free, Yet Accountable*

Background Scripture: Genesis 2:15-17; 3

Scripture Lesson: Genesis 3:1-13

Memory Verse: *For you were called to freedom, brethren; only do not use your freedom as an opportunity for the flesh, but through love be servants of one another.* Galatians 5:13

CHILDREN

Topic: *Free to Choose*

Background Scripture: Genesis 2:15-17; 3

Scripture Lesson: Genesis 3:1-6, 8-9

Memory Verse: *He has showed you, O man, what is good; and what does the Lord require of you but to do justice, and to love kindness, and to walk humbly with your God?* Micah 6:8

DAILY BIBLE READINGS

Mon., Sept. 8: Called as God's People, Exodus 19:1-6.
Tues., Sept. 9: Respect Your Body, I Corinthians 6:12-20.
Wed., Sept. 10: Free to Love, Galatians 5:13-25.
Thurs., Sept. 11: Go Beyond Freedom, I Corinthians 9:19-23.
Fri., Sept. 12: Seek Forgiveness, I Samuel 15:22-31.
Sat., Sept. 13: Disobedience Brings Judgment, Deuteronomy 28:15-21.
Sun., Sept. 14: Obedience Is Rewarded with Love, John 14:15-24.

LESSON AIM

To show the tragic consequences of disobedience, and also the relationship of freedom and responsiblity.

LESSON SETTING

Time: Uncertain

18

Place: The Garden of Eden

A Free, Yet Accountable Creature

LESSON OUTLINE

SUGGESTED INTRODUCTION FOR ADULTS

It has been well said that we are free to choose but we are not free to choose the consequences of our choice. We can choose right or wrong, but the consequences are already built in.

We choose our own destiny. Someone has described Election this way: God, at Calvary, voted for my salvation. (Christ died for all.) Satan is voting for my condemnation. I cast the deciding ballot. If I decide to accept God's free offer of salvation through faith in Christ, I will be saved. If I reject it, I will be lost forever.

The choice of Adam and Eve was not predetermined. They were free to choose. That is clearly the Biblical view. To say that God decreed they should sin would be to make Him an immoral monster. We cannot blame God if we are finally lost. The whole thrust of the Bible is that of redemption provided by God and freely offered to all who will accept it.

SUGGESTED INTRODUCTION FOR YOUTH

Freedom—that's what we want! But we need to face up to the fact that freedom carries a high price tag. For freedom involves responsibility. If we are going to live in a free nation we must discharge our responsibilies as free citizens. As has often been said, to fail to exercise the privilege of voting is finally to lose it.

But freedom has its limitations. Freedom without law

would be chaos. Without any traffic regulations, freedom to drive my car would result in accident and death. So we must operate our lives within the limits of divine law. If we do not, we pay a tragic price for it. We must choose to be what God wants us to be.

CONCEPTS FOR
CHILDREN

1. Adam and Eve were given everything they needed, but they wanted more.
2. It is easy to want what is forbidden.
3. We must think of the results of our choice.
4. The right to choose involves the responsibility to choose the right.

THE LESSON COMMENTARY

I. THE SINGLE PROHIBITION: Genesis 2:15-17

A. The Blessing of Work: v. 15

"And the Lord God took the man, and put him into the garden of Eden to dress it, and to keep it"—"to till and tend it" (*Anchor Bible*). The word for "put" literally means "made him rest." That is, God gave Adam the garden of Eden as his permanent home and settled dwelling place. It was a real paradise, which he could have enjoyed all his life if he had remained obedient.

The garden was a place of rest, but it was also a place of work. As we noted in the previous lesson, work is a blessing, not a curse. Sidney Hillman says, "God gave man work, not to burden him, but to bless him." Since it is God's will that man should work, we should work, we should do it joyfully. Whitelaw writes: "Even in a state of innocence it was impossible that man could be suffered to live in indolence; his endowments and capacities were fitted for activity. His happiness and safety (against temptation) required him to be employed. And if God who made him was ever working, why should he be idle? The same arguments forbid idleness today. Christianity with emphasis condemns it. 'If a man will not work, neither shall he eat' " (*Pulpit Commentary*, I, "Genesis," p. 47).

B. The Abundance of Food: v. 16

Adam was told that he could eat freely whatever grew on the trees in the garden. We may assume that before the curse on nature, as a result of man's sin, there were no poisonous foods. Adam could enjoy all the vast variety of fruits and nuts that abounded in "paradise" (the Persian word for "park"). Everything was delicious and nutritious.

Lee Haines writes: "Adam was surrounded with all the beauty and bounty which a God of infinite power and love could provide. But for all of His careful provision, He did not overindulge His child and impose upon him a boredom which would have destroyed his happiness. . . . While labor became extremely hard and grueling after the fall, it was not in itself outside the divine plan for man. It was rather part of his original destiny and will probably be involved in some form in his eternal destiny" (*Wesleyan Bible Commentary*, Vol. I, Part I, p. 33).

How long did Adam enjoy this delightful experience, before and after a companion was given him? Our answer must simply be, "We don't know." There is no indication as to whether it involved a few days, weeks, months, or years. But the implication of verse 15 seems to be that it was a considerable period of time.

C. The Command and Warning: v. 17

God put only one restriction on man's freedom: Adam was not to eat from the tree of the knowledge of good and evil. We are not told what kind of a tree it was. All talk about Eve eating the forbidden apple is of course just childish nonsense—and an insult to the innocent apple!

The thing that we need to realize is that this tree was a symbol. Whitelaw makes this helpful suggestion: "The prohibition laid on Adam was for the time being a summary of the Divine law. Hence the tree was a sign and symbol of what that law required. And in this, doubtless, lies the explanation of its name. It was a concrete representation of that fundamental distinction between right and wrong, duty and sin, which lies at the basis of all responsibility. It interpreted for the first pair those great moral intuitions which had been implanted in their natures, and by which it was intended they should regulate their lives" ("Genesis," p. 46).

With the command came the solemn warning: "For in the day that thou eatest thereof thou shalt surely die"—literally, "dying, thou shalt die" (a typical intensive Hebraism). What kind of death is meant? Apparently 3:19 indicates that it was first of all physical death. Man's body would return to the dust from which it was made.

It is useless to speculate as to what would have happened with an endless succession of human births and no human deaths. Rather than wasting our time on profitless speculations, we should be concerned about what actually happened and the consequences. All else we can leave to an all-knowing, all-powerful, all-loving God. What we have to face is the fact that man did sin, that he thereby was rendered mortal, and that "in Adam all die" (I Corinthians 15:22). We should spend our time preparing for the future, not speculating about the past.

But "thou shalt surely die" means more than physical death. It means spiritual death. This is the greater tragedy. It was not only the separation of the soul from the body, but the separation of the soul from God. For Adam, physical death did not take place immediately. But spiritual death did. This is shown in the next chapter by man's act of hiding from God.

Actually the death which results from sin is threefold: spiritual, natural, and eternal. Every sinner is separated from God and so is spiritually dead. His body is mortal, subject to death. And if he refuses to accept God's provision of salvation and continues in disobedience, he will die eternally—that is, be forever separated from God. That is ultimate tragedy.

Someone has said: "Think, how great, how abounding was the provision for Adam; how narrow the prohibition. It was a small thing that God demanded; but a great ruin was involved in the withholding of obedience. We wonder to see how slight was the thread to which a world's destinies were suspended. Blind fools we are, slow to learn the lesson taught in every page of the Bible, and in every dispensation of personal providence, that there is nothing trivial with God" (*Biblical Illustrator*, I, 172).

II. THE TEMPTATION OF EVE: Genesis 3:1-5

A. Satan's Subtle Question: v. 1

Satan appeared to Eve in the form of a serpent. In Revelation 12:9 (cf. 20:2) he is described as "that old serpent, called the Devil and Satan, which deceiveth the whole world"—as he originally deceived Eve. The Greek word for "devil" (*diabolos*) means "slanderer." The term *Satan*, taken over by the Greek from the Hebrew, means "adversary." The old serpent is both. Here the serpent is called the sliest of all creatures God had made.

Now he approached Eve and said: "Yea, hath God said, Ye shall not eat of every tree of the garden?" R. Payne Smith writes: "There is a tone of surprise in these words, as if the tempter could not bring himself to believe that such a command had been given. Can it really be true, he asks, that Elohim has subjected you to such a prohibition? How unworthy and wrong of Him!" Smith adds this observation: "Neither the serpent nor the woman use the title—common through this section—of Jehovah-Elohim. . . . It is the impersonal God of creation to whom the tempter refers, and the woman follows his guidance, forgetting that it was Jehovah, the loving personal Being in covenant with them, who had really given them the command" (Ellicott's *Commentary on the Whole Bible*, I, 23).

B. Eve's Answer: vv. 2-3

The woman's first mistake was in listening to the serpent. She should have sensed his deceitful purpose and turned away from him. Conversations with Satan can have serious consequences!

Eve correctly replied that they could eat freely what grew on the trees in the garden. But of a certain tree in the midst of the garden, God had said: "Ye shall not eat of it, neither shall ye touch it, lest ye die." If the command of God is taken as complete in 2:17, then Eve added the middle clause, "neither shall ye touch it." This would seem to imply that God was especially unreasonable. We should be careful not to add something to the Word of God.

C. Satan's Denial: . 4

Probably the tempter's words in verse 1 were intended to inject doubt. But now we find an outright denial of God's Word. This is typical of progress in temptation. The subtle foe begins with insinuation and moves on to slander. Flatly he declares here, "Ye shall not surely die."

D. Impugning God's Motive: v. 5

Waxing bolder by the moment, the serpent charged God with an ulterior motive. It was because God did not want these creatures of His to know as much as He knew that He had forbidden them to eat from the tree of the knowledge of good and evil. It was fear and jealousy that had caused Him to give the unreasonable command. And the warning that went with it was completely false. Thus Satan, the arch-liar, accused the holy God of being a liar. It was the most blasphemous charge that he could have brought against Deity.

"Gods" in this verse is a translation of *Elohim*. We have already noted that this is the Hebrew word for "God" in these chapters, as throughout the Old Testament. So probably the correct translation here is, "You will be as God"—that is, in the understanding of good and evil.

In itself this should have been an adequate warning to Eve not to listen any longer to the serpent. The supreme wickedness of the human heart is wanting to take the place of God, refusing to let Him be supreme.

Haines gives this brief summary of the temptation: "The tempter's words show a three-step progression. (1) His first recorded speech seems to express incredulity: Has God really forbidden you to eat of one of the trees? . . . (2) He followed this with a flat denial of the divine warning. . . . (3) Then to the insidiousness of doubt and the sacrilege of attempting to rob God of His truthfulness, he added the blasphemy of suggesting that God's command was due to ulterior and selfish motives" (*Wesleyan*, p. 35).

III. THE DISOBEDIENCE OF ADAM AND EVE: Genesis 3:6

Doubt (v. 1) and denial (v. 4) were followed by deed (v. 6). When we begin to listen to Satan's suggestions we are already on the path to destruction. The only safe way to treat temptation is to turn away from it immediately, as Joseph did when tempted by Potiphar's wife (39:12).

Three things brought Eve's temptation to a tragic climax. She saw that the tree was (1) "good for food," (2) "pleasant to the eyes," and (3) "a tree to be desired to make one wise." It has often been pointed out that there is a striking parallel between this and the description of temptation in I John 2:16 as consisting of "the lust of the flesh, the lust of the eyes, and the pride of life." Eve got into trouble first by listening to Satan and then by looking at the tree. It is still true that most temptations to evil come through eye-gate and ear-gate. If we guard these two carefully it will save us a lot of tragedy.

Led on by the serpent's suggestion and her own lingering contemplation of the tree, the woman finally "took of the fruit thereof, and did eat, and gave also unto her husband with her; and he did eat." As Haines notes, "Satan had won a double victory: Eve had yielded to his temptation, and Eve in turn had become the instrument of temptation for Adam" (*Wesleyan*, p. 36).

The woman has often been blamed for the Fall and the consequent degradation of the human race. It is true that she was deceived first (I Timothy 2:14). But Haines comments: "The actual taking of the fruit, however, must have been nearly simultaneous. Such is indicated by the close connection of *did eat* and *gave*, the words *with her*, and the fact that the awareness of guilt was experienced together" (v. 7). And whatever Eve's choice may have been, it was to Adam that God had directly given the commandment and it was on Adam's choice that the destiny of all mankind rested (Romans 5:12), and it was Adam who must accept the final responsibility for his own fall and that of the entire human race" (*Wesleyan*).

IV. THE RESULTS OF DISOBEDIENCE:
Genesis 3:7-8

A. Guilt: v. 7

Satan was correct on one point: He said that if they ate the fruit of the tree of the knowledge of good and evil their eyes would be opened. This now took place. But the results were not what they anticipated. Instead of blessing there came the curse.

In the pure innocence of the first pair, no clothing was needed. But now, having disobeyed, Adam and Eve saw themselves and each other in a new light. They tried to cover their nakedness by sewing fig leaves together and making themselves "aprons"—rather, "loincloths." Haines remarks that their shame had nothing to do with sex. "Rather, the nakedness which caused their frantic invention of clothing was their sudden awareness that they had lost the divine glory which had previously enshrouded them" (*Wesleyan*, p. 37).

B. Fear: v. 8

Guilt brought fear, as it always does. We have here first the beautiful picture of God walking in the garden of Eden in "the cool of the day"— literally "the wind," or the breezy time of the day. This would be about sundown, when a cool breeze would

DISCUSSION QUESTIONS

1. Why did God test man by giving him a prohibition?
2. Can there be positive character without human probation?
3. What temptations are most dangerous for Christians today?
4. How can we avoid temptation?
5. How should we respond to temptation when it does confront us?
6. What is the proper attitude to take when we are conscious that we have done wrong?

invite one to walk around. The implication is that God normally walked and talked with His crown of creation each evening. He had made man (including woman) in His own image as rational, responsible beings so that He might have intelligent, spiritual fellowship with them. What a privilege for Adam and Eve! And what a calamity that they forfeited this fellowship through disobedience. This was indeed a *fall.*

But this time the appointed tryst turned into a tragedy. As Adam and Eve heard the voice of the Lord God—notice the introduction of the personal name Yahweh again—they hid themselves from His presence by slipping behind the trees out of sight.

V. THE DIVINE ENCOUNTER: Genesis 3:9-13

A. God Seeking Man: v. 9

Liberal writers have often described religion as man's search for God. But this is not at all the Biblical picture. In the Scriptures we find God seeking man.

"Where art thou?" God wants us first of all to locate ourselves in relation to Him. Where are we spiritually? That is the first question we must face. It confronts each one of us today.

B. Man Confessing His Fear: v. 10

God always takes the initial step. But we must respond. And our response must first of all be in the form of confession. This is our first step toward God.

C. God Questioning Man: v. 11

When Adam answered that he had hidden from God's presence because of his own nakedness, the Lord abruptly asked: "Who told you that you were naked? Did you eat from the tree that I commanded you to leave alone?" There was no escaping the divine interrogation.

D. Man and Woman Confessing Sin: vv. 12-13

Verse 12 reveals a pathetic human trait—that of putting the blame on someone else. As still happens today, the man blamed his wife! But he also came blasphemously near blaming God when he said, "It was the woman you gave me." This habit of throwing the blame on others, instead of honestly accepting it ourselves, can sometimes lead to dangerous consequences.

When the Lord God asked the woman what she had done, she in turn put the blame on the serpent—one of God's creatures. But it does no good for us to try to shift the blame. Each one of us is morally responsible for what we do, regardless of the influence or pressure from others. That is one of the most important lessons we must learn.

CONTEMPORARY APPLICATION

There is no use for us to blame others, much less to blame God, for our failure and sin. Modern behavioristic psychology—too often based on experimentation with animals—has done away pretty much with all moral responsibility. Those who do wrong—we shouldn't call it "sin"!—are the victims of circumstances. The logical conclusion is that criminals should not be punished for their crimes. This sociological point of view has turned dangerous criminals loose in society to be protected repeaters. We need to get the Biblical view.

September 21, 1975

MY BROTHER'S BROTHER

DEVOTIONAL READING	I John 4:7–21

ADULTS

Topic: *My Brother's Brother*

Background Scripture: Genesis 4

Scripture Lesson: Genesis 4:1-15

Memory Verse: *If anyone says, "I love God," and hates his brother, he is a liar; for he who does not love his brother whom he has seen, cannot love God whom he has not seen.* 1 John 4:20

YOUTH

Topic: *My Brother's Brother*

Background Scripture: Genesis 4

Scripture Lesson: Genesis 4:1-15

Memory Verse: *If anyone says, "I love God," and hates his brother, he is a liar; for he who does not love his brother whom he has seen, cannot love God whom he has not seen.* I John 4:20

CHILDREN

Topic: *My Feelings for Others*

Background Scripture: Genesis 4

Scripture Lesson: Genesis 4:8-15

Memory Verse: *And this commandment we have from him, that he who loves God should love his brother also.* I John 4:21

DAILY BIBLE READINGS

Mon., Sept. 15: Causes of Strife Between Men, James 4:1-12.
Tues., Sept. 16: Judge Not Your Brothers, Matthew 7:1-5.
Wed., Sept. 17: Care for Your Brethren, Leviticus 25:35-42.
Thurs., Sept. 18: Accept a Servant's Role, John 13:3-17.
Fri., Sept. 19: Live as Members of One Another, Romans 12:3-18.
Sat., Sept. 20: God Dwells in Those Who Love, I John 4:7-12.
Sun., Sept. 21: Righteousness Requires Brotherhood, I John 4:13-21.

LESSON AIM | To see our responsibility to our brothers around us.

LESSON SETTING | Time: Uncertain

25

Place: Probably east of the garden of Eden

LESSON OUTLINE

I. **Two Brothers:** Genesis 4:1-2
   A. Cain: v. 1
   B. Abel: v. 2

II. **Two Offerings:** Genesis 4:3-5
   A. Cain's Offering: v. 3
   B. Abel's Offering: v. 4a
   C. God's Appraisal: vv. 4b-5

III. **God's Challenge to Cain:** Genesis 4:6-7

IV. **The First Murder:** Genesis 4:8

V. **My Brother's Keeper:** Genesis 4:9-10
   A. Cain's Protest: v. 9
   B. God's Accusation: v. 10

VI. **The Curse on Cain:** Genesis 4:11-12

VII. **The Divine Compassion:** Genesis 4:13-15

SUGGESTED INTRODUCTION FOR ADULTS

One of the curses of society has always been that people do not want to feel responsible for others. But in spite of an understandable objection to the twofold phrase "the universal fatherhood of God and the universal brotherhood of man," there is a true sense in which every man is my brother and I have some responsibility for him. We were all made by the one creator, God. We are all descended from Adam and Eve. The basic oneness of the human race is a fact which we cannot deny and should not ignore. Before God I am my brother's keeper.

SUGGESTED INTRODUCTION FOR YOUTH

What is to be our attitude toward those we don't like? Cain's was that of anger and murder. Ours must be that of love and helpfulness.

We are not doing our duty by our schoolmates and acquaintances when we simply ignore them. There must be an attitude of trying to find some way of pointing them to Christ.

CONCEPTS FOR CHILDREN

1. We live in a world of hate and violence.
2. As Christians we must love everybody.
3. We should seek to show this love in all our relationships with others.
4. We should be especially careful not to be jealous of others.

THE LESSON COMMENTARY

I. TWO BROTHERS:
Genesis 4:1-2

A. Cain: v. 1

We are told that Adam "knew Eve his wife. " This is a euphemism, found in both the Old and New Testament, for sexual union.

As a result Eve bore a son, the first human being born into this world. She called him "Cain," saying, "I have gotten a man from the Lord." ("Cain" means "gotten.") Lee Haines points out the significance of this: "Eve looked upon her first-born son as a gift from God. Certainly the wonder of childbirth, especially since Cain was the first ever born, and the joy of any mother over her baby would prompt such an expression of praise and gratitude. She may also have seen in him further evidence that God had not abandoned them, but that His somewhat veiled promises concerning the future were going to be worked out" (*Wesleyan Bible Commentary*, Vol. I, Part I, p. 39).

In keeping with this, R. Payne Smith writes: "It has been said that Eve, in the birth of this child, saw the remedy for death. Death might slay the individual, but the existence of the race was secured. Her words therefore might be paraphrased: 'I have gained a man, who is the pledge of future existence'" (Ellicott's *Commentary on the Whole Bible*, I, 27).

In 3:15—often called the Protoevangelium, or "first gospel"—the Lord God declared that the seed of the woman (Christ, the Messiah) would bruise the serpent's (Satan's) head. In the light of this Whitelaw suggests that "Eve's utterance was the dictate of faith. In Cain's birth she recognized the earnest and guarantee of the promised seed, and in token of her faith gave her child a name (cf. ch. iii. 20), which may also explain her use of the Divine name *Jehovah* instead of *Elohim*, which she employed when conversing with the serpent" (*Pulpit Commentary*, I, "Genesis," p. 77).

B. Abel: v. 2

The Hebrew is *Hebel*, which means "a thing *unstable, not abiding*, like a breath or vapour" (Smith, Ellicott's, p. 28). We do not know why this name was given him. Did his mother have a presentiment of his early death or was she guided to do this prophetically?

As is often the case with two brothers, these two boys chose different vocations. "Abel was a keeper of sheep," a shepherd, but "Cain was a tiller of the ground," a farmer. Perhaps Cain was more rough and rugged by nature, while Abel was more gentle and meditative.

II. TWO OFFERINGS:
Genesis 4:3-5

A. Cain's Offering: v. 3

"In the process of time" is literally "at the end of days." Some have thought that this simply indicates an indefinite period of time. But the rest of the verse would seem to suggest the time of harvest, at the end of the summer season. For Cain brought "of the fruit of the ground an offering unto the Lord." That is, he gave an offering consisting of a portion of the crops he had raised. The word for "offering" means "a thank-offering" or "a gift." It is used for the "meat offering" (KJV)—rather "meal offering"—consisting of wheat flour mixed with olive oil (Leviticus 2:1-11).

B. Abel's Offering: v. 4a

Abel brought "the firstlings of his flock and of the fat thereof." The "firstlings" would be the firstborn, which God afterward required (Exodus 13:12). "The fat thereof" is literally "the fatness of them." This probably means the fattest of the firstlings.

Abel brought the best he had as an offering to God.

C. God's Appraisal: vv. 4b-5

"The Lord had respect unto"— literally, "looked upon" (with favor)— Abel and his offering. But he did not look with favor on Cain's offering. The result was that "Cain was very wroth" —literally, "it burned with Cain exceedingly." His heart was filled with hot resentment.

There has been much speculation as to why God approved Abel's offering and disapproved Cain's. It has sometimes been said that Abel brought the best while Cain did not. But there is nothing in the Biblical narrative to support this.

The New Testament often interprets the Old. So we turn to the Epistle to the Hebrews and find the true reason. There we read: "By faith Abel offered unto God a more excellent sacrifice than Cain" (11:4). As Smith says, "It was the state of their hearts that made the difference" (Ellicott's, p. 28).

But we feel that the Hebrews passage conveys a further suggestion. In Romans 10:17 we read: "So then faith cometh by hearing, and hearing by the word of God." Faith is acting in obedience to God's Word. How does this apply to Abel? None of the Bible had yet been given.

To find the answer to this question we need to go back to the previous chapter in Genesis. There we find that Adam and Eve tried to cover their nakedness with fig-leaf loincloths (3:7), a type of our own righteousness, which the Bible says is only "filthy rags" (Isaiah 64:6). The fact that this covering was not adequate is shown by the action of Adam and Eve in hiding in the garden from the Lord.

What did the Lord God do about it? He killed animals and used their skins to make modest garments for the sinful pair (3:21). It does not seem unreasonable to hold that in connection with this He revealed to Adam and Eve one of the central truths of redemption: "Without shedding of blood is no remission" (Hebrews 9: 22)—that is, no forgiveness of sins. And we may well assume that these parents passed on this essential teaching to their two sons.

If so, Abel was offering in faith because he was obeying God's command to present animal sacrifices as an atonement for his sins. Cain, on the other hand, was the first Modernist, rejecting the blood atonement.

III. GOD'S CHALLENGE TO CAIN: Genesis 4:6-7

The Lord asked Cain why he was angry, "and why is thy countenance fallen" (v. 6). Then He said, "If thou doest well, shall it not be lifted up?" (ASV). Whitelaw paraphrases this: "Instead, then, of thy present gloomy despondent mood, in which thou goest about with downcast look, thou shalt lift up thy head, and have peace and good temper beaming in thine eyes as the result of a quiet conscience" ("Genesis," pp. 28-29).

The rest of verse 7 is the most difficult part of this lesson to interpret. Whitelaw favors this meaning: "If thou doest not well, sin croucheth at the door, that is, lies dangerously near thee, and puts thee in peril. Beware, therefore, and stand on thy guard; and then *his* desire shall be unto thee, and thou shall rule over *him*" ("Genesis," p. 29). Cain was jealous of his brother for having God's favor and being blessed. The Lord told him that if he would do right, Abel would submit to him as the older brother.

The American Standard Version takes the "his" and "him" as referring to the sin that was crouching, like a wild animal, at the door of Cain's heart. So it translates the last part of the verse this way: "And unto thee shall be its desire"—to hurt you; "but do thou rule over it." That is, you can get the best of this sin of jealousy that is threatening to destroy you.

There is still another interpretation that seems to us to deserve some recognition. The word for "sin" can be translated "sin offering." In this case the Lord would be saying: "There is an animal lying at your door that you should sacrifice for your sins." The main objection to this interpretation is that it does not seem to fit in so well with the last part of the verse. But this could be taken as meaning that the sacrificial animal was ready to be offered and Cain could take it out and use it.

IV. THE FIRST MURDER:
Genesis 4:8

It is a shattering thing to realize that the first man born into this world became a murderer. But jealousy breeds hatred that too often leads to homicide—in this case, fratricide. This incident is a startling commentary on how fast and how far sin moves in the lives of those who give it a place. It also underscores the serious consequences of disobedience. Adam and Eve disobeyed God's single negative command. One result was that their first-born son murdered his own brother. What a heartbreaking experience this must have been for them!

V. MY BROTHER'S KEEPER:
Genesis 4:9-10

A. Cain's Protest: v. 9

The Lord said to Cain: "Where is your brother Abel?" We should note the emphasis on "your brother." Evidently Cain caught it, for he answered, perhaps in a surly tone: "I don't know. Am I my brother's keeper?"

The answer is Yes—emphatically! We cannot escape our responsibility to others, and especially to those of our own immediate family.

This truth has many daily applications. To have a rather close acquaintance with someone, fail ever to speak to him about his soul, and then have him suddenly cut off in his sins—this can be a shaking, sobering experience. We need to ask the Holy Spirit to help us witness to those whom He knows

can be helped. Obviously it is impossible for us to witness to everybody. But we should be prayerfully concerned to speak the word where it is needed.

In regard to Cain's protest, Haines comments: "The quick, downward progression of sin is revealed in Cain's answer. . . . Neither Adam nor Eve had dared to deny their sin completely. But now Cain follows murder with lying and adds to both a blasphemous insolence to God Himself" (*Wesleyan*, p. 41).

B. God's Accusation: v. 10

Instead of coming out with a flat charge, God countered with another question: "What have you done?" But it must have shaken Cain with the force of an outright accusation of murder. And his worst fears were immediately confirmed, for the Lord added: "The voice of thy brother's blood crieth unto me from the ground." Evidently Cain had buried his brother's dead body. But sin cannot be hidden from God's sight. The old saying "Murder will out" was strikingly true in this case.

VI. THE CURSE ON CAIN:
Genesis 4:11-12

It would seem that Adam and Eve were not directly cursed for their sin of disobedience. God did curse the serpent for tempting them (3:14) and He cursed the ground for Adam's sake (3:17). But He did not curse the culprits. So Cain was the first man to be cursed for his crime.

The unrepentant sinner was told that the very soil would wreak vengeance on him for his sin. Worse still, he would be "a fugitive and a vagabond"—banished and homeless—on the earth. Smith comments: "Restless and uneasy, and haunted by the remembrance of his crime, he shall become a wanderer, not merely in the *adamah*, his native soil, but in the earth. Poverty must necessarily be the lot of one thus roaming, not in search of a better lot, but under the compulsion of an evil conscience" (Ellicott's, p. 30).

Three times in three verses (9, 10, 11) we hear God saying, "thy brother." How those words must have haunted the memory of Cain. He had killed his own brother! How are we treating our brother?

VII. THE DIVINE COMPASSION: Genesis 4:13-15

These verses give us a sad picture of Cain. Instead of confessing his sin, he began to whimper and complain: "My punishment is greater than I can bear." He didn't feel sorry for his sin; he felt sorry for himself. Haines writes: "The tragedy is that Cain did not break down under his punishment. The grace of God was sufficient to have forgiven and redeemed Cain, had he been willing to appropriate it, but all he sought was some alleviation of his punishment: how typical this is of the convinced but rebellious sinful man" (*Wesleyan*, p. 41).

There is an alternative translation that some prefer: "My iniquity is greater than can be forgiven." But the context seems to indicate that Cain was primarily concerned with the severe punishment rather than with the heinousness of his sin. Smith, perhaps wisely, suggests that the full meaning is "My sin is past forgiveness, and its result is an intolerable punishment" (Ellicott's, p. 30). We would favor this both/and solution.

DISCUSSION QUESTIONS

1. Does one's sin ever affect himself alone?
2. What were some of the characteristics of these two brothers?
3. What are some of the essentials of true worship?
4. What should we do when we know that we have displeased God?
5. What are the causes of jealousy?
6. What responsibilities do we have to others?

At any rate, Cain continues to talk about the consequences of his sin, rather than about the sin itself. He says that God has driven him "from the face of the earth" (v. 14). This does not mean from "the earth" as we think of it, the globe on which we live. By the word *adamah* he meant his own plot of ground, where he raised his crops and where he felt at home. Away from here he felt that he would be hidden from the face of God, "a fugitive and a vagabond."

The last part of verse 14 poses a problem. Who would be the ones that would find Cain and kill him? The answer is that many years had passed by since Adam and Eve had been driven out of the garden of Eden. Some think that more than a century had passed and that many more children had been born, as well as grandchildren. We are told that Adam lived to be 930 years old. The first pair of human beings had been told to be fruitful and multiply and fill the earth (1:28). So we may assume that the population was increasing.

The same thing goes for a favorite cynical question of the "infidels" of a few generations ago: "Where did Cain get his wife?" (4:17). The obvious answer is that he married his sister. Archaeological discoveries have shown that the marriage of sisters was a common custom in the ancient world.

When the Israelites had conquered the land of Canaan, God told them to set aside "cities of refuge," where a person who had killed another accidentally could be kept safe from "the avenger of blood" (Joshua 20:2-3). It was held in that day that if a man was murdered, his closest brother was obligated to avenge the crime by seeking out and killing the murderer. Tribal revenge, a similar custom, is still in force in some primitive areas of the world. So Cain was afraid that some of his younger brothers would feel it their duty to put him to death. He was afraid for his life.

In spite of the seriousness of Cain's sin, God acted in mercy. He said that if anyone slew Cain, "vengeance will be taken on him sevenfold" (v. 15)—that is, completely, seven being the number of perfection. Smith gives the probable significance of this: "Cain's punishment was severe, because his crime was the result of bad and violent passions, but his life was not taken because the act was not premeditated. Murder was more than he had meant. But as any one killing him would mean murder, therefore the vengeance would be *sevenfold*" (Ellicott's, p. 30).

We are then told that the Lord set a mark upon Cain lest any finding him should kill him. There has been much useless speculation as to what kind of a "mark" this was. But in the other seventy-five times where the Hebrew word *oth* occurs in the Old Testament it is not translated "mark" but "sign." What the Hebrew suggests is that God appointed a sign to Cain, like the sign of the rainbow that He gave to Noah (9:12-15). Or it could possibly have been just an inward assurance. In any case, it was not a sign of divine forgiveness but a pledge of divine protection.

Why did God grant this special privilege and protection to Cain? Whitelaw suggests three reasons: "1. To show that 'Vengeance is mine; I will repay, saith the Lord.' 2. To prove

the riches of the divine clemency to sinful men. 3. To serve as a warning against the crime of murder" ("Genesis," p. 82). It would seem that Cain and Abel had had an argument about the offerings—"Cain talked with Abel his brother" (v. 8). In the altercations that followed, Cain became so furious that he killed his brother in a fit of anger. The Lord did not want this avenged by a deliberate murder of Cain. So He assured him of His protection.

Cain "went out from the presence of the Lord" (v. 16). This is what happens to every unrepentant sinner. He was banished for his sin. It must be realized that sin always brings separation. It separates us from God's presence and blessing in this life. If unconfessed, and so unforgiven, it will separate us forever from His presence. This is the greatest tragedy of eternal punishment. Outer darkness, forever separated from the Light of the world—this is the real hell of eternal torment.

Cain lived in the land of "Nod"—that is, "of wandering." For the sinner there is no place of rest. He is always a fugitive from God. No wonder that people live such restless lives! They are running away from God and trying to run away from themselves.

CONTEMPORARY APPLICATION

The memory selection for today is: "If anyone says, 'I love God,' yet hates his brother, he is a liar. For anyone who does not love his brother, whom he has seen, cannot love God, whom he has not seen" (I John 4:20, NIV). The next verse says: "And he has given us this command: Whoever loves God must also love his brother."

A man came home from his office one day. As he opened the front door and stepped into the living room he discovered a battle going on in full swing. The little lad of the home had his younger sister on the floor and was pummeling her in great anger.

Daddy quickly rescued his darling

daughter from her vicious assailant, picking her up in his arms. She hugged him tightly and showered him with grateful kisses.

But then, out of the corner of his eye, he saw that she was sticking out her tongue at her frustrated brother, who had been robbed of his prey. Immediately he held her out at arms length, looked her squarely in the eye and said sternly: "Daughter, you can't love your father and hate your brother at the same time."

That is what God says to us. If we say that we love God, we must prove it by loving our brother.

AN AGENT OF GOD'S GRACE

DEVOTIONAL READING | Isaiah 49:1-6

ADULTS

Topic: *An Agent of God's Grace*

Background Scripture: Genesis 6–9:17

Scripture Lesson: Genesis 6:13, 18-22; 9:8-13

Memory Verse: *By faith Noah, being warned by God concerning events as yet unseen, took heed and constructed an ark for the saving of his household.* Hebrews 11:7

YOUTH

Topic: *God's Agent*

Background Scripture: Genesis 6–9:17

Scripture Lesson: Genesis 6:13, 18-22; 9:8-13

Memory Verse: *By faith Noah, being warned by God concerning events as yet unseen, took heed and constructed an ark for the saving of his household.* Hebrews 11:7

CHILDREN

Topic: *A Man in God's Plan*

Background Scripture: Genesis 6–9:17

Scripture Lesson: Genesis 9:8-17

Memory Verse: *Bless the Lord, O my soul;
And all that is within me, bless his holy name!* Psalm 103:1

DAILY BIBLE READINGS

Mon., Sept. 22: God's Judgment Is Now, Deuteronomy 28:58-68.
Tues., Sept. 23: Jesus Is Our Judge, John 5:22-29.
Wed., Sept. 24: Go and Become Teachers, Matthew 28: 16-20.
Thurs., Sept. 25: Agents of Reconciliation, II Corinthians 5:17-21.
Fri., Sept. 26: Called to Serve the Nations, Isaiah 49:1-6.
Sat., Sept. 27: Be Persistent, II Timothy 4:1-5.
Sun., Sept. 28: God's Suffering Servant, Isaiah 53.

LESSON AIM | To see how God can use one man to save the future, and so how important it is for each individual to obey God fully.

LESSON SETTING | Time: The traditional date of the Flood is somewhere around 3000 B.C.

Place: Probably the Mesopotamian region. Mount Ararat is in ancient Armenia, modern Turkey.

An Agent of God's Grace

I. Conditions Before the Flood: Genesis 6:1-12
   A. Only Evil Continually: vv. 1-7
   B. Noah the Upright Man: vv. 8-10
   C. Corruption and Violence: vv. 11-12

II. Pronouncement of Judgment: Genesis 6:13

III. The Ark as a Place of Refuge: Genesis 6:14-22
   A. Description of the Ark: vv. 14-17
   B. A Refuge for Noah's Family and All Creatures: vv. 18-21
   C. Noah's Obedience: v. 22

IV. The Flood: Genesis 7

V. Leaving the Ark: Genesis 8

VI. A New Beginning: Genesis 9:1-7

VII. A New Covenant: Genesis 9:8-13
   A. A Covenant with All Creatures: vv. 8-10
   B. No More Flood: v. 11
   C. The Sign of the Covenant: vv. 12-13

LESSON OUTLINE

The first eleven chapters of Genesis are usually referred to by liberal scholars as prehistory. Nothing here is to be treated as having actually taken place historically. Everything is to be understood and interpreted as symbolical. The narrative is purely allegorical.

In contrast to this, conservative scholars have normally accepted the stories of Creation, the Fall, and the Flood as actual happenings. What we have here is history.

The both/and approach is helpful in this instance, as in most cases. We believe that we have in Genesis 1–11 a divine revelation of the beginnings of material creation, the human race, sin, judgment on sinners, and the scattering of mankind over the earth. But these events are also highly symbolical. They have permanent significance for us in our understanding of God's dealings with men.

It might be well to summarize the contents of these first eleven chapters of Genesis. We have: (1) Creation, chaps. 1–2; (2) the Fall, chap. 3; (3) the First Murder, chap. 4; (4) the First Genealogy, chap. 5; (5) the Flood, chaps. 6–9; (6) the Descendants of Noah, chap. 10; (7) the Tower of Babel, 11:1-9; (8) the Descendants of Shem, 11:10-32.

SUGGESTED INTRODUCTION FOR ADULTS

In a very real sense it may be said that with God the most important thing in the world is a single individual

SUGGESTED INTRODUCTION FOR YOUTH

human being. To a great extent history is a recital of the accomplishments of a few men who changed the course of human affairs. One thinks of Alexander the Great, of Martin Luther, of John Wesley, of Napoleon. And of course the supreme example is Jesus Christ, the God-man, who was willing to go to the cross and make an atonement for the sins of all mankind. What if He had failed?

God may want to use some of us to fill a strategic role. Are we willing to let Him do with us whatever He wants?

CONCEPTS FOR CHILDREN

1. It seemed that everything depended on one man obeying God.
2. We are glad that Noah obeyed, and saved the human race as well as the animals.
3. Noah obeyed even though he did not fully understand.
4. We should thank God for His mercies to us.

THE LESSON COMMENTARY

I. CONDITIONS BEFORE THE FLOOD:
Genesis 6:1-12

A. Only Evil Continually: vv. 1-7

The human race was multiplying (v. 1). Then we read that "the sons of God saw the daughters of men" and married them (v. 2). Who were these "sons of God"?

The *Anchor Bible* identifies them as "divine beings." More specifically, a number of the church fathers, plus Luther and some modern commentators, take this phrase as meaning "angels." But this seems farfetched. Jesus certainly implied that the angels are sexless (Matthew 22:30).

The Jewish expositors held that the "sons of God" were men of high rank, who married maidens of humble birth. But this view is usually rejected today.

R. Payne Smith writes: "The third, and most generally accepted interpretation in modern times, is that the sons of the Elohim were the Sethites, and that when they married for mere lust of beauty, universal corruption soon ensued" (Ellicott's *Commentary on the Whole Bible*, I, 35). Adam's third son was Seth (5:3), from whom Noah was descended (5:6-29). It is assumed that the male descendants of

Seth married the female descendants of Cain. Smith strangely reverses the two, identifying "the sons of God" ("mighty ones") as the descendants of Cain, and "the daughters of men" as the descendants of Seth.

Verse 3 is often quoted: "My spirit shall not always strive with man ... his days shall be an hundred and twenty years." The second statement can be taken in two ways. The first would interpret it as a shortening of man's life span to 120 years. But chapter 11 seems to contradict this. More likely it means that man's further period of probation would now be limited to 120 years, and then the Flood would come and most people would be destroyed. This fits better with the first clause. That generation was having its last chance.

Verse 5 puts in brief, vivid form the reason for the Flood: "And God saw that the wickedness of man was great in the earth, and that every imagination of the thoughts of his heart was only evil continually"—literally, "every day" or "all the day," from morning until night. The Hebrew word for "imagination" is perhaps better translated "purpose." It has been well said, "If this is not total depravity, how can language express it?"

God "repented" or "regretted" (*Anchor Bible*) that He had made man

(v. 6). The Hebrew verb suggests the idea of panting or groaning and so is close to the last statement of this verse: "and it grieved him at his heart." God was brokenhearted over the sin of man, as He proved eloquently at Calvary.

Many people have a problem with this verse. How can it be harmonized with the doctrine of the immutability (unchangeableness) of God? The answer is that God always acts in love. "God is love" (I John 4:8, 16) and He cannot be other than that. But it was a loving act of God to destroy sinful man (v. 7), so that generations of babies would not be born into such a sinful society and perish forever in torment.

B. Noah the Upright Man: vv. 8-10

"But Noah found grace in the eyes of the Lord" (v. 8). Why? Because he was "a just man and perfect [upright] in his generations ["without blame in that age" (*Anchor Bible*)]" and "walked with God" (v. 9). Here for the first time in the Bible we find the beautiful word "grace," which becomes the keynote of Scripture. It means God's undeserved favor.

C. Corruption and Violence: vv. 11-12

We read that the earth "was corrupt before God" and "filled with violence," or "lawlessness." The term "corrupt" is used again twice in verse 12. This is a tragic contrast with the reiterated statement in chapter 1 that God created everything "good."

II. PRONOUNCEMENT OF JUDGMENT:
Genesis 6:13

God told Noah, "I have decided to put an end to all flesh" (*Anchor Bible*), that is, to all mankind, with the exception of Noah's family. The reason was that men had filled the earth with violence. The verb translated "destroy" is the same as that which is translated "corrupted" in verse 12. It means "destroyed, wrecked, ruined, overthrown." The connection stresses the fact of a fitting divine retribution for human sin. God is always just and fair in returning to us what we have given out.

III. THE ARK AS A PLACE OF REFUGE:
Genesis 6:14-22

A. Description of the Ark: vv. 14-17

Having told Noah that He was going to destroy "all flesh" (all mankind), God now instructed Noah to build an "ark"—something in the nature of an oblong houseboat. It was to be made of "gopher" wood, probably cypress, and with "rooms," or compartments. This would tend to give it greater structural strength. Also Noah was to "pitch it within and without with pitch," or bitumen. This would make it more seaworthy.

The ark was to be three hundred cubits long (450 feet), fifty cubits wide (75 feet) and thirty cubits high (45 feet). It was a large-sized vessel!

The word "window" (v. 16) literally means "light." The reference seems to be to an opening a cubit wide (18 inches), perhaps running all the way around the ark right under the eaves (for protection from rain). Its purpose, as suggested by the literal meaning, was to give light and also probably ventilation—which would surely be needed in an ark full of animals! It will be noted that the word "stories" is in italics, indicating that it is not in the original Hebrew. But it appears that this is the logical word to supply in order to complete the sense.

The Lord then told Noah specifically how He was going to destroy the inhabitants of the earth. A flood of waters would wipe out "everything that is in the earth" (v. 17). The ensuing narrative shows that an exception was made in the case of those who entered the ark.

B. A Refuge for Noah's Family and All Creatures: vv. 18-21

The Lord said that He would establish His covenant with Noah (v. 18). This is apparently defined in the rest of the verse. Noah, his sons, his wife and his sons' wives—note the typical ancient oriental custom of mentioning all the men first—were to enter the ark. There they would be saved from the destructive waters of the Flood.

But not only were eight human beings (cf. 5:32) to be saved. God instructed Noah to take into the ark one pair, a male and a female, of each species of animals, birds and reptiles (vv. 19-20). He was to stock the ark with food sufficient for all (v. 21).

C. Noah's Obedience: v. 22

Noah did "according to all that God commanded him." This is the kind of obedience that God demands of all of us.

One trembles to think of what the result would have been if Noah had been unwilling to cooperate with God. The whole human race would conceivably have become extinct.

The question has sometimes been raised as to how Noah and his sons could have built such a large ship. We should note that mention is made of working with iron (4:22). So they probably had adequate tools. Furthermore, we are told that Noah was about five hundred years old when his three sons—Shem, Ham and Japheth—were born and that he was six hundred years old when the Flood came (7:6). Even allowing time for his sons to grow up and get married—they apparently had no children as yet—there were many years left in which to build this massive boat.

IV. THE FLOOD: Genesis 7

When all was finished, the Lord said to Noah, "Come thou and all thy house into the ark" (v. 1). He did not say "Go," but "Come." God's presence was to be there in the ark with Noah and his family.

A new note is sounded in verse 2: Clean animals were to be taken into the ark "by sevens, the male and his female." This probably means seven pairs of each species of clean animals, such as sheep and oxen, though many commentators think that seven individuals is the correct interpretation. In any case, the reason for this special provision is obvious. As soon as Noah emerged from the ark he offered to the Lord a burnt offering "of every clean beast, and of every clean fowl" (8:20). These species would have become extinct right away if he had not sheltered the extra number in the ark.

The Lord informed Noah that at the end of seven days He would "cause it to rain upon the earth forty days and forty nights" (v. 4). So Noah got his family and the prescribed creatures into the ark. At the end of the seven days the Flood came (v. 10). We are not told how much of this week was spent in loading the ark, which would take some time, and how much of it was spent inside the ark. But the natural inference would be that the Lord was giving him a week to make final preparations and get all the animals safely inside.

Sure enough, it rained for forty days (v. 12). But the Lord had shut Noah in (v. 16). Finally the ark was water borne (v. 17) and then floating on deep water (v. 18). The waters rose fifteen cubits (22½ feet), "and the mountains were covered" (v. 20). Obviously "hills" is the correct translation in line with this figure.

The result was that "all flesh died that moved upon the earth, both of fowl, and of cattle, and of beast, and of creeping thing that creepeth upon the earth, and every man" (v. 21)—that is, all except those who were in the ark (v. 23). It was a total devastation. We are told that the waters prevailed upon the earth an hundred and fifty days (v. 24). This would include the forty days of rain.

V. LEAVING THE ARK:
Genesis 8

At the end of the five months, the ark came to rest on "the mountains of Ararat" (v. 4). Forty days later Noah opened the hatch of the ark and let loose a raven (v. 7). This scavenger bird roamed the surface of the waters, feeding on floating bodies. He also sent out a dove. But this gentle creature found no resting place and returned to the ark (vv. 8-9). A week later he released the dove again. This time it returned with an olive leaf in its beak (vv. 10-11). So Noah knew that the waters were down to the tree tops. He waited another week and sent out the dove again. This time it found enough dry land, or at least trees, so that it did not come back (v. 12). Still he waited a few days until the ground was dry (vv. 13-14).

Finally, after slightly over a year in the ark, Noah was told by the Lord that he and his family, together with all the creatures with them, could leave the ark (vv. 16-17). It must have been a great procession as they all filed out (vv. 18-19).

The first thing that Noah did was to build an altar and offer thanksgiving to the Lord for His preservation (v. 20). This was most appropriate, and it pleased God. The Lord pledged that as long as the earth lasted He would never send another flood to destroy its inhabitants (vv. 21-22). Noah had been God's agent to save creation.

VI. A NEW BEGINNING:
Genesis 9:1-7

In Genesis 1:28 we read: "And God blessed them [Adam and Eve] and God said unto them, Be fruitful and multiply and replenish [rather, "fill"] the earth." Here we have the same words, only addressed this time to "Noah and his sons" (9:1). The last part of 1:28 is also closely paralleled here. Man was to have dominion over the animal kingdom.

The human race began with one couple, Adam and Eve, who had three sons. Now we find human history making a new beginning with Noah, his wife, and their three sons and their wives. It was almost as small a group. The important point is that Noah was willing to be God's agent for this new beginning. Instead of the entire human race being wiped out, there was one godly man and his family to carry it on. Never in all of history did more depend on one man's obedience—outside of Christ—than here with Noah.

In the beginning man was told that he might eat all "herbs" and the fruit of every tree (1:29). But now a new stipulation is made: "Every moving thing that liveth shall be meat for you; even as the green herb have I given you all things" (v. 3). Only one restriction was made: no blood was to be eaten (v. 4). Also God gave a solemn warning against murder (vv. 5-6).

VII. A NEW COVENANT:
Genesis 9:8-13

A. A Covenant with All Creatures: vv. 8-10

God told Noah that He would establish His covenant not only with him and his descendants ("seed") but also with all the living creatures that had been in the ark. A covenant is a solemn pledge or agreement.

DISCUSSION QUESTIONS

1. Why did God permit the Flood to come?
2. Why did God use human means instead of a divine miracle to save Noah?
3. In what way are conditions today similar to those in Noah's day?
4. Why does God withhold judgment?
5. What did Jesus say about the days of Noah?
6. How can we be God's agents in the world today?

B. No More Flood: v. 11

The covenant was that there would never be another flood of universal proportions such as would threaten the whole human race. There have been many devastating local floods since then, but none of worldwide extent.

C. The Sign of the Covenant: vv. 12-13

The Lord knew that the next time it began to rain hard the people would probably be filled with fear. Was another flood about to come? So He gave them "a token" of His covenant.

He would set His rainbow on the clouds as an assurance of His promise. Whenever the black clouds appeared and threatened to terrify them, they would see the rainbow on the cloud and know that all was well (v. 14). This beautiful truth is asserted and repeated through several verses (12-17), showing the great importance it held for the people of that time.

In this "token"—better, "sign"—we see the evidence of God's infinite love. He does not want His children to be afraid. He wants them to trust in Him implicitly. And so He graciously gives us His promise to support our faith.

CONTEMPORARY APPLICATION

Do we sometimes fail God because we do not realize the importance of a decision we are making? Perhaps more depends on what we do in some situations and under certain circumstances than we can possibly imagine.

The only requirement is that we always obey when God speaks. If we obey His commands, then the responsibility is with Him to guide us and to use us as His agent whenever He so desires.

GOING WHERE GOD LEADS

DEVOTIONAL READING	Hebrews 11:8-16

ADULTS

Topic: *Going Where God Leads*

Background Scripture: Genesis 11:26–12:20

Scripture Lesson: Genesis 12:1-9

Memory Verse: *By faith Abraham obeyed when he was called to go out to a place which he was to receive as an inheritance; and he went out, not knowing where he was to go.* Hebrews 11:8

YOUTH

Topic: *Going Willingly*

Background Scripture: Genesis 11:26–12:20

Scripture Lesson: Genesis 12:1-9

Memory Verse: *By faith Abraham obeyed when he was called to go out to a place which he was to receive as an inheritance; and he went out, not knowing where he was to go.* Hebrews 11:8

CHILDREN

Topic: *Going Where God Leads*

Background Scripture: Genesis 12; Hebrews 11:8-10

Scripture Lesson: Genesis 12:1-9

Memory Verse: *Now faith is the assurance of things hoped for, the conviction of things not seen.* Hebrews 11:1

DAILY BIBLE READINGS

Mon., Sept. 29: Moving into the Unknown, Hebrews 11:8-16

Tues., Sept. 30: Finding Closed and Opened Doorways, Acts 16:6-10.

Wed., Oct. 1: Extending One's Witness, Acts 11:1-14.

Thurs., Oct. 2: Specific Directions from God, Acts 8:26-31.

Fri., Oct. 3: Get Equipped Before You Go, Acts 1:3-8

Sat., Oct. 4: Be Ready to Leave Immediately, Luke 9:57-62.

Sun., Oct. 5: Don't Worry About Others, John 21:15-22.

LESSON AIM

To show the importance of answering God's call and going where God leads.

LESSON SETTING

Time: Soon after 2000 B.C.

Place: Ur of the Chaldees was in the southern part of Mesopotamia, about 140 miles southeast of ancient Babylon. Haran was in northern Mesopotamia. Shechem ("Sichem") was in central Palestine, near Mount Gerizim. Bethel was about twelve miles north of Jerusalem, and Ai was east of Bethel.

Going Where God Leads

LESSON OUTLINE

I. Terah and His Family: Genesis 11:26-32

II. Abraham's Call: Genesis 12:1-3
   A. The Command: v. 1
   B. The Promise: vv. 2-3

III. Abraham's Obedience: Genesis 12:4-5
   A. Departure from Haran: v. 4
   B. Arrival in Canaan: v. 5

IV. Stopping Places in the Land: Genesis 12:6-9
   A. Shechem: vv. 6-7
   B. Bethel: v. 8
   C. Journeying South: v. 9

SUGGESTED INTRODUCTION FOR ADULTS

To a considerable extent, history revolves around outstanding individuals. For Old Testament times we think of Adam, Noah, Abraham, Moses, Joshua, Samuel, David, Solomon, Isaiah, Jeremiah, and Daniel. These were some of the men who made history.

Today we begin a unit of three lessons on Abraham, under the topic: "God's Call: Our Pilgrimage of Faith." Abraham is the greatest example in history of a man obeying God's call, with results that have affected the world ever since. It is not such a spectacular case as that of Noah, but just as important for the future of mankind. Conceivably the human race might have again descended into moral depths and deserved destruction, if Abraham had not stepped out under the stars with God. We don't know the future, but God does. All He asks of us is that we obey Him and follow where He leads.

SUGGESTED INTRODUCTION FOR YOUTH

Youth is the period of crucial decisions that affect all of later life. Most missionaries and preachers felt the call of God while they were still young. Obedience to that call often brought profound results, sometimes worldwide.

The greatest thing that any young person can do is to say to the Lord: "Here is my life. Take it and make of it whatever you will. Lead me wherever you want me to go, and I will follow you."

CONCEPTS FOR CHILDREN

1. God promised to bless Abraham if he would follow and obey Him.

2. We learn God's will for us by reading His Word.
3. He also speaks in our hearts for specific guidance.
4. When we obey God we know He is with us.

THE LESSON COMMENTARY

I. TERAH AND HIS FAMILY: Genesis 11:26-32

It is interesting to note that we have the names of three sons of Adam (Cain, Abel, Seth), three sons of Noah (Shem, Ham, Japheth), and now three sons of Terah (Abram, Nahor, Haran). The name Abram, meaning "exalted father," was later changed to Abraham (17:5).

Probably the correct meaning of verse 26 is expressed in the *Anchor Bible:* "And when Terah reached the age of 70, he had begotten Abram, Nahor, and Haran." We have a similar construction in 5:32. Abram is mentioned first among the three sons because he became the most prominent in the redemptive history. Haran means "tarrying" and may possibly have a symbolical connection with the fact that Abram tarried at Haran for awhile before going on to Canaan. The city was named for the man. Archaeology has also found reference to a city named Nahor.

Verse 28 gives the first instance of a man dying while his father was still living. We are not told the cause of Haran's death, but we are told that he died in his native land, "in Ur of the Chaldees" (or, Chaldeans). Modern archaeology has excavated the ruins of Ur and discovered that it was a magnificent city with a very high culture. "Education was well developed at Ur, for a school was found there with its array of clay tablets. Students learned to read, write, and do varied forms of arithmetic" (Zondervan's *Pictorial Bible Dictionary,* p. 876). They not only had multiplication and division tables but went on to square root and cube root (Joseph Free, *Archaeology and Bible History,* pp. 49-50). Ur was also a great commercial center, with ships bringing expensive goods from far-off countries. The average upper middle-class home had from ten to twenty rooms.

So Abraham came from a city with a highly developed culture and great wealth. But it was also a center for the worship of the moon god, Nanna. So Abraham grew up in an atmosphere of idolatry.

Abram and Nahor both married (v. 29). Abram's wife's name was Sarai, meaning "my princess." But she was "barren; she had no child" (v. 30). In those days that was considered a great calamity. Every man wanted a son, to carry on the family line.

As head of the family clan, Terah took Abram his son, Lot his grandson, and Sarai his daughter-in-law and moved from Ur to Haran. This was about six hundred miles northwest of Ur, on the way to "the land of Canaan" (v. 31). But Terah never reached Canaan, for he died in Haran (v. 32). That left Abram alone with his wife and his nephew Lot (cf. 11:27).

II. ABRAHAM'S CALL: Genesis 12:1-3

A. The Command: v. 1

The succession of narrative at this point seems to place the call of Abraham in Haran. But Stephen told the Sanhedrin—which would have corrected him if he was thought to be wrong—that the call came at Ur. Here are Stephen's words: "The God of glory appeared unto our father Abraham, when he was in Mesopotamia, before he dwelt in Charran"—Greek spelling of Haran—"and he said unto him, Get thee out of thy country, and from thy kindred, and come into the land which I shall shew thee" (Acts 7:2-3). The words of the call are almost identical with those in Genesis 12:1.

Negative critics have labeled this an obvious contradiction. But such a conclusion is unnecessary. A very reasonable explanation would be that the call first came to Abraham in Ur and that he told his father about it. Terah may have then insisted that, as head of the house, he must lead the way. And so Terah "took" Abram, Sarai, and Lot and headed for Canaan (Genesis 11: 31). But that was as far as he went and he died there. Then the call was renewed to Abraham and he moved on to Canaan. ("Had said," KJV, cannot be stressed, as the Hebrew simply means "said.")

If we accept this reconstruction, two or three observations might be in order. The first would be that Abraham failed to carry out fully God's call and command when he left Ur. For the Lord told him to leave not only his country but also his relatives. Was he delayed at Haran because he failed to go out alone with his wife? In the second place, Lot accompanied his uncle, not only to Haran but also to Canaan. And Lot was certainly a hindrance rather than a help to Abram (chaps. 13–14). There may be a hint here that if we do not obey God's commands precisely, we cause complications for the worse.

The implication of the last clause of the first verse is that Abram did not know his destination when he left Ur or Haran. This is confirmed by the Epistle to the Hebrews, where we read: "By faith Abraham, when he was called to go out into a place which he should after receive for an inheritance, obeyed; and he went out, not knowing whither he went" (11:8). This has justifiably been cited thousands of times as a striking example of faith and obedience. We often hear the erroneous epigram, "Seeing is believing." But it is not! Faith operates in the realm of the unseen (Hebrews 11:1). Real faith is not at all dependent on observable circumstances.

B. The Promise: vv. 2-3

"Going where God leads" is not always easy. Often it involves sacrifice. But ultimately it always has glorious consequences.

And so, with the command God gave a magnificent promise. If Abram obeyed, God would make of him a great nation. In view of the fact that Sarai had not been able to give birth to a single child, this is a startling prediction. It didn't seem to be fulfilled very fast! Actually, another twenty-five years went by before Sarah bore a son to Abraham (compare v. 4 with 21:5).

Abraham did become the father of a great nation. The fulfillment of this promise was especially true in the time of David and Solomon, who ruled over a wide territory. Solomon was called the wisest man among all rulers of the world, and he reigned over an extensive empire.

The Lord also promised: "I will bless thee, and make thy name great." This has been fulfilled beyond any of Abram's wildest dreams. Three great world religions—Judaism, Christianity and Islam—revere Abraham's name and think of him as one of the greatest men who ever lived. He is not only held up in the eleventh chapter of Hebrews as a great hero of faith, but Paul describes him as the father of the faithful.

"And thou shalt be a blessing" can also be translated "that it may be a blessing" (*Anchor Bible*), or "and be thou a blessing" (ASV). R. Payne Smith favors the last. He writes: "But in the command to 'be' or 'become a blessing,' we reach a higher level, and it is the glory of Abram's faith that it was not selfish, and in return for his consenting to lead the life of a stranger, he was the means of procuring religious privileges, not only for his own descendants, but also 'for all families of the earth' " (Ellicott's *Commentary on the Whole Bible*, I, 57).

God so identifies Himself with Abraham that He says: "I will bless them that bless thee, and curse him that curseth thee" (v. 3). The change from the plural to the singular may suggest that more people would bless Abraham than would curse him—which, of course, has been true.

In recent years some versions have translated the last clause of this verse: "And by you all the families of the earth will bless themselves" (RSV)—taking the verb as middle rather than passive. But the traditional rendering is preferable. Taken this way it is a beautiful Messianic promise. Through Christ, the greatest "son of Abraham" (Matthew 1:1), all the "families" (nations) of the earth have been blessed and are being blessed. Even before Christ came the Israelites were a blessing to many people in pointing them to the true God.

III. ABRAHAM'S OBEDIENCE:
Genesis 12:4-5

A. Departure from Haran: v. 4

When Abram left Haran, Lot naturally went with him, for otherwise he would have been all alone. In 13:5 we read: "And Lot also, which went with Abram." Lot was a hanger-on, one who just went along. This is reflected in his later selfishness and weakness, shown by his choosing the best land and then moving into Sodom. He lacked that ruggedness of character that made Abraham a great man.

There are many today who belong to the tribe of Lot. They grow up in church and follow the lead of parents, pastors, and people. Outwardly they conform at first. But when the time comes that they have to make their own decisions, they are too weak to take the way of obedience and sacrifice.

We read that Abram was seventy-five years old when he left Haran, the half-way point. But he was only beginning his great career, for he lived another hundred years (25:7). We do not know how long Abram stayed in Haran. But we do know that it was until his father died. This was in keeping with the custom of that day, still followed rigidly in countries like India,

that the oldest surviving son must care for his father in the latter's old age and see that he had a proper burial.

B. Arrival in Canaan: v. 5

Abram took with him not only his wife and nephew but also "all their substance that they had gathered and the souls that they had gotten in Haran." Many caravans passed through Haran, and Abram had obviously made the most of his opportunity to gain by trading. He apparently had acquired considerable wealth during his stay at Haran.

But he also had gotten "souls"—that is, persons. These would doubtless be servants, or slaves, that he had purchased while there. In those days a man's wealth was often measured by the number of animals and slaves that he owned. Abram had a large retinue as he left Haran and slowly moved, with his flocks and herds, across the three hundred miles to the land of Canaan. But they finally arrived.

IV. STOPPING PLACES IN THE LAND:
Genesis 12:6-9

A. Shechem: vv. 6-7

Coming from the north through Galilee, Abram reached "Sichem," better known as Shechem (see Gen. 37:12). The site of Shechem has been excavated in the last few years. It

---

DISCUSSION QUESTIONS

1. Why did God choose Abraham?
2. What place does Abraham hold in Old Testament history?
3. What is his importance for us as Christians?
4. What does Paul say about Abraham?
5. Can you think of someone in recent years whose obedience has had great consequences?
6. What is the greatest evidence of faith?

is near the modern city of Nablus, close by mounts Gerizim and Ebal.

Abram came to "the plain of Moreh"—rather, "the terebinth of Moreh." The terebinth was a large evergreen tree that grows in Palestine. "Moreh" means "teacher." So this may well have been a famous tree under which a noted wise man had dispensed wisdom. Perhaps that celebrity was now dead, and Abram chose the place as a suitable site for the time being. There is an interesting statement: "And the Canaanite was in the land." This may be intended to remind the reader that Canaan was at that time a pagan country, dominated by the low, sensuous religion of the Canaanites.

Because Abram had obeyed the divine command, the Lord appeared to him. The faithful pilgrim had now arrived in the appointed place. So the Lord said to him: "Unto thy seed [descendants] will I give this land." Now he knew that at last he had arrived in the land to which the Lord had directed him and where the Lord could bless him. It was to this land that the Messiah-Savior would later come and where He would sacrifice Himself for the sins of the whole world.

In response to the divine disclosure, Abram "built an altar unto the Lord." The path of Abraham's progress was always after this to be marked by the erection of altars. Someone has said of a great British preacher that wherever he went he carried a shrine in his heart. We must have an altar of prayer and worship in our lives every day, no matter where we are.

The Hebrew name Shechem means "shoulder." It probably referred first to the ridge which connects Mount Ebal and Mount Gerizim, whose summits are about two miles apart.

B. Bethel: v. 8

From Shechem Abram moved southward a few miles to Bethel, which is twelve miles north of Jerusalem. Here he pitched his tent on a mountain, with Bethel to the west and Ai to the east. There he again built an altar to the Lord. Abram had the right sense of priority. We nowhere read of his building a house, but everywhere erecting altars. He put God first in his life, and God prospered him.

Ai, which means "ruin," was the second city (after Jericho) taken by the Israelites under Joshua, after they had entered Canaan (Joshua 7–8).

Bethel is composed of two Hebrew words, beth, "house," and el, "God." So it means "house of God." This is what Jacob called it after his ladder-vision there (Genesis 28:10-22). And Abram found it to be a true "house of God" as he worshiped there.

By building these altars Abram was taking possession of the Promised Land and dedicating it to the Lord. Noah did the same with the ground after it had been washed by the Flood.

C. Journeying South: v. 9

Again Abram "journeyed"—literally, "broke up" camp—and continued his southern trek. We read here that he went toward the "south." The Hebrew word is Negeb, which means "dry." This is a reference to the desert in the southern part of Palestine (Israel) which is still called the Negeb (or Negev).

CONTEMPORARY APPLICATION

One can think of many young people who have heard God's call to go out from home and loved ones to some far-off land. They have obeyed and thus have brought salvation and blessing to many people.

The will of God and the salvation of the lost depend on obedience to such calls. It was such a call that came to William Carey, the father of modern missions. The spiritual welfare of the world is in a very real sense in our hands. We are all called to a life of obedience, wherever we may be led to work in the Kingdom.

STRUGGLING WITH DOUBT

DEVOTIONAL READING	Exodus 16:2-12

ADULTS

Topic: *Struggling with Doubt*

Background Scripture: Genesis 15—18:15

Scripture Lesson: Genesis 17:1-8, 15-19

Memory Verse: *My grace is sufficient for you, for my power is made perfect in weakness.* II Corinthians 12:9

YOUTH

Topic: *Struggling with Doubt*

Background Scripture: Genesis 15—18:15

Scripture Lesson: Genesis 17:1-8, 15-19

Memory Verse: *My grace is sufficient for you, for my power is made perfect in weakness.* II Corinthians 12:9

CHILDREN

Topic: *Receiving What God Gives*

Background Scripture: Genesis 15—18

Scripture Lesson: Genesis 17:1-9

Memory Verse: *Praise the Lord! O give thanks to the Lord, for he is good; for his steadfast love endures forever!* Psalm 106:1

DAILY BIBLE READINGS

Mon., Oct. 6: Abraham Has Some Doubts, Genesis 15:1-6.
Tues., Oct. 7: Abraham Is Afraid, Genesis 15:7-16.
Wed., Oct. 8: Sarah Doubts God, Genesis 18:9-15.
Thurs., Oct. 9: Depressed by Problems, Exodus 16:2-12.
Fri., Oct. 10: Disciples Doubt Resurrection, Luke 24:1-12.
Sat., Oct. 11: Thomas Seeks Personal Proof, John 20:24-29.
Sun., Oct. 12: God Honors Faith, Romans 7:13-25.

LESSON AIM

To see how we may overcome doubt by taking God at His word.

LESSON SETTING

Time: Around 1900 B.C.

Place: Near Hebron, twenty miles south of Jerusalem

LESSON OUTLINE

Struggling with Doubt

I. God's Covenant: Genesis 15
  A. The Promise of a Seed: vv. 1-6
  B. The Solemn Covenant: vv. 7-21

45

    II. **Sarah's Plot:** Genesis 16
       A. A Son by a Servant Girl: vv. 1-7
       B. The Lord and Hagar: vv. 8-14
       ·C. The Birth of Ishmael: vv. 15-16

    III. **The Covenant Confirmed:** Genesis 17:1-8
       A. The Covenant Renewed: vv. 1-2
       B. A Father of Many Nations: vv. 3-6
       C. An Everlasting Covenant: vv. 7-8

    IV. **The Sign of the Covenant:** Genesis 17:9-14

    V. **The Promise Concerning Sarah:** Genesis 17:15-19
       A. A Mother of Nations: vv. 15-16
       B. Abraham's Unbelief: vv. 17-18
       C. The Promise of a Son by Sarah: v. 19

    VI. **Sarah's Unbelief:** Genesis 18:9-15

SUGGESTED INTRODUCTION FOR ADULTS

Honest doubt is not sinful. It is what we do with our doubts, or what our doubts do to us, that can get us into trouble.

Everyone who is alert and awake to life about him or who thinks deeply is confronted with doubts at times. We live in a complicated world. Things don't always go the way we think they should. We become perplexed. We wonder why God doesn't do something about it.

One thing we need to realize is that God doesn't operate on our time clock. A thousand years with Him is as one day (II Peter 3:8). We get in a hurry. But God is never hurried. He knows what He is going to do.

We overcome doubt by faith, and faith is taking God at His word. Regardless of how impossible the circumstances look, we know that God will keep His promise. And so we relax in trust in Him.

SUGGESTED INTRODUCTION FOR YOUTH

Do you have doubts? Cheer up, all thinking people do! Doubts usually come through lack of understanding. And none of us has a perfect knowledge of life. We often don't understand what is going on around us.

We doubt things. We sometimes are forced to doubt people. But we must never doubt God. His integrity is absolute. And His knowledge is perfect. Some people, through no fault of their own, may not be able to carry out their promises made in good faith. But God is never caught in this "bind." He has all knowledge and all power. "What He says, He will do." And the fact that He is all love guarantees the performance of what He has promised. So let's trust Him completely.

CONCEPTS FOR CHILDREN

1. Sometimes people don't keep their promises, but God always does.
2. We should be thankful for God's gifts of life and health and happiness.

3. We are secure in God's love and care.
4. Just as God cared for Noah and Abraham, He can care for us.

THE LESSON COMMENTARY

I. GOD'S COVENANT:
Genesis 15

A. The Promise of a Seed: vv. 1-6

Here we meet for the first time the Biblical expression "the word of the Lord came" to someone. It occurs frequently in the Pentateuch, the Historical Books, the Psalms and especially the Prophets—in every part of the Old Testament. In this instance it came to Abram.

It would seem that this bold pioneer of faith may have been feeling a bit dejected. He had followed God's call to this new land. Perhaps some of the natives resented Abram's prosperity and may have been showing unfriendly attitudes. He might have been a little uneasy about his future.

But the Lord revealed Himself to Abram in a vision with these assuring words: "Fear not, Abram: I am thy shield, and thy exceeding great reward." The Lord promised him that He would protect him—and what better protection could anyone have! He also said that His presence would be the greatest reward that Abraham could have for obeying His command.

One thing apparently was preying on Abram's mind. God had promised to "make of thee a great nation" (12: 2). But he was getting old and he didn't even have a single child. How could God's promise be fulfilled? So he said, "Lord God, what wilt thou give me, seeing I go childless, and the steward of my house is this Eliezer of Damascus? . . . Behold to me thou hast given no seed: and, lo, one born in mine house is mine heir" (vv. 2-3). Rather plaintively Abram was saying, "Lord, I'd like to have a child of my own."

God's answer was prompt and satisfying: "This man will not be your heir, but one who shall come forth from your own body, he shall be your heir" (v. 4, NASB). This must have gladdened Abram's heart immeasurably.

Then the Lord brought him outside his tent and told him: "Now look toward the heavens, and count the stars, if you are able to count them." As Abram gazed at the stars in the sky, overwhelmed by their vast number, God declared, "So shall your descendants be" (v. 5, NASB).

What was Abram's reaction? Doubt? Incredulity? No, it says: "And he believed in the Lord; and he counted it to him for righteousness" (v. 6). This striking statement is cited in Romans 4:3 and James 2:23.

B. The Solemn Covenant: vv. 7-21

The Lord then reminded Abram that He was the One who had brought him out of Ur, to give him this land as his inheritance. But again Abram was plagued by doubts. He asked, "Lord God, whereby shall I know that I shall inherit it?" (v. 8). He wanted some token of assurance. It is interesting to note that right after the magnificent display of faith (v. 6) Abram was again struggling with doubt. It is often that way in our lives.

In reply the Lord told Abram to take three animals, each three years old, plus two sacrificial birds, divide the animals in two and lay the pieces opposite each other. In the darkness of the night God gave Abram a bit of preview of the coming Egyptian oppression of the Israelites (vv. 12-13). But He assured him that his descendants would finally be delivered and would return to Canaan.

Then a burning lamp passed between the pieces of the animals. This was a manifestation of God's presence as a pledge that He would keep His covenant with Abram. All this was in keeping with the custom of that day, when a covenant was sealed by the person walking between the pieces of divided animals.

II. SARAH'S PLOT:
Genesis 16

A. A Son by a Servant Girl: vv. 1-7

It is rather clear that Abram got out of the will of the Lord when, because of a famine in Canaan, he went down to Egypt (12:10-20). He got into trouble there and compromised his integrity. There was evidently another unfortunate result: Sarai "had an handmaid, an Egyptian, whose name was Hagar" (v. 1). So Sarai said to Abram: "Behold now, the Lord hath restrained me from bearing: I pray thee, go in unto my maid; it may be that I may obtain children by her" (v. 2).

Archaeological research has shown that this was according to the customs of the day. In the Nuzi tablets we find a striking parallel: "If Gilimninu bears children, Shennima shall not take another wife. But if Gilimninu fails to bear children, Gilimninu shall get for Shennima a woman from the Lullu country (i.e., a slave girl) as concubine. In that case Gilimninu herself shall have authority over the offspring" (quoted in *Anchor Bible*, I, 120).

Abram and Sarai had now been ten years in the Promised Land without any child (v. 3). So Sarai gave Hagar to her husband as a concubine. But when Hagar saw that she was going to have a child, she felt very superior to her mistress and despised her (v. 4).

This was more than Sarai could take. She said to her husband: "This outrage against me is your fault! I myself put my maid in your lap. But from the moment she found she had conceived, she has been looking at me with contempt. Yahweh decide between you and me!" (v. 5, *Anchor Bible*). Abram told her to do what she wished. Thereupon Sarai treated her maid so harshly that she ran away. Although Sarai's attitude was bad, it must be recognized that she was acting within her legal rights. "The Code of Hammurabi states explicitly that a slave girl who was elevated to the status of concubine must not claim equality with her mistress" (*Anchor Bible*, I, 117).

B. The Lord and Hagar: vv. 8-14

The angel of the Lord found Hagar out in the desert by a spring of water (v. 7). He told her to go back to her mistress and submit to her authority. But she was warned that her coming son, Ishmael ("father of a great multitude"), would be like a wild colt; "his hand will be against every man, and every man's hand against him" (v. 12).

C. The Birth of Ishmael: v. 15-16

And so Ishmael was born when Abram was eighty-six years old (v. 16). But the whole affair, though legal, was very unwise. Abram should have waited in faith for God to fulfill His promise in His own way.

III. THE COVENANT CONFIRMED:
Genesis 17:1-8

A. The Covenant Renewed: vv. 1-2

Thirteen years later, when Abram was ninety-nine years old, the Lord appeared to him and said: "I am the Almighty God; walk before me, and be thou perfect." Abram needed to recognize that God was the "Almighty God"—"possessing the power to realize His promises, even when the order of nature presented no prospect of their fulfillment, and the powers of nature were insufficient to secure it" (Keil, quoted in *Pulpit Bible*, I, "Genesis," p. 232).

What is meant by "perfect"? Some would reduce it to "blameless" (NASB). But Whitelaw says that it "indicates that absolute standard of moral attainment, viz., completeness of being in respect of purity, which the supreme Lawgiver sets before his intelligent creatures" ("Genesis"). God wants no impurity in our lives.

Then God promised: "And I will make my covenant between me and thee, and will multiply thee exceedingly." The expression "my covenant" is the key to this chapter, occurring no less than nine times (vv. 2, 4, 7, 9, 10, 13, 14, 19, 21), plus the word "covenant" alone three other times (vv. 7, 11, 19).

The word "covenant" means an agreement made between two parties. But in the case of God's covenant with man it is always unilateral rather than bilateral; that is, God sets the conditions, which are binding on man. At the same time, God binds Himself to keep His side of the agreement.

B. A Father of Many Nations: v. 3-6

Reverently Abram threw himself on his face. Then God assured him that he would be "a father of many nations." No longer would he be called Abram, "high father," but Abraham, "father of a multitude." This, of course, is what he became not only in his physical descendants but also in his spiritual descendants in this age.

C. An Everlasting Covenant: v. 7-8

God promised to make Abraham "exceeding fruitful." This man who had no child at all until he was eighty-six years old became the father of many nations—Israel, Edom, and the descendants of his later wife Keturah (25:1-4). God's covenant was fulfilled literally as well as spiritually.

IV. THE SIGN OF THE COVENANT: Genesis 17:9-14

Now the Lord discloses the sign of the covenant that Abram must observe. It was the rite of "circumcision," which means "a cutting around." God ordered: "Every man child among you shall be circumcised"

(v. 10). That would be a "token" (sign) of the covenant between God and man (v. 11). The circumcision was to take place when the baby boy was eight days old (v. 12). The parents of Jesus fulfilled this requirement for Him (Luke 2:21). Any male child that was not circumcised would be cut off from the people of the covenant.

V. THE PROMISE CONCERNING SARAH: Genesis 17:15-19

A. A Mother of Nations: vv. 15-16

Abram's wife's name was likewise changed—from Sarai, "my princess," to Sarah, "a princess." Whereas she had formerly been Abram's princess, now she was to be a princess in general. The rabbis held that the letter *h* added to both their names was taken from Yahweh, showing that they now belonged to the Lord in a special way.

Then the Lord made the startling announcement that Sarah would bear a son to Abraham (v. 16). She herself would become a mother of nations, with kings among her descendants. This was fulfilled in the kingdom period of Israel and Judah.

B. Abraham's Unbelief: vv. 17-18

The venerable patriarch again "fell upon his face" (cf. v. 3). But this time

---

DISCUSSION QUESTIONS

1. What is the covenant God has made with us?
2. What are the conditions we have to meet?
3. How may we hinder God's will by our plans?
4. What mistakes did Abraham and Sarah make?
5. How may we avoid such mistakes?
6. How did God treat their unbelief?

he laughed incredulously, saying in his heart: "Shall a child be born unto him that is a hundred years old? and shall Sarah, that is ninety years old, bear?" Humanly speaking, it was impossible.

So Abraham suggested an alternative: "O that Ishmael might live before thee!" (v. 18). It looked to Abraham as though this was the easiest and simplest way for God's promises to be fulfilled.

C. The Promise of a Son by Sarah: v. 19

The Lord said in effect: "No, not Ishmael. Sarah will bear a son, whom you will call Isaac. The promised seed will come through him." The word "Isaac" means "he laughs." Says Smith, "The name was to be a perpetual memorial that Isaac's birth was naturally such an impossibility as to excite ridicule" (Ellicott's *Commentary on the Whole Bible*, I, 73).

In this verse we find again the expression "everlasting covenant," which occurred in verse 7. When God makes a covenant with His people, it is in force forever.

Picking up Abraham's mention of Ishmael in verse 18, the Lord now assures the patriarch that He will bless Ishmael and that his descendants will become a great nation. But His special covenant will be with Isaac.

In obedience to God's command, Abraham circumcised all the male members of his household, including himself (vv. 23-24). Ishmael was thus thirteen years old when he was circumcised. For this reason the Muslims defer circumcision until a boy is thirteen.

VI. SARAH'S UNBELIEF: Genesis 18:9-15

One day Abraham was visited by three strangers. One of them was evidently "the Lord" appearing in human form (v. 1). Such theophanies are mentioned a number of times in the Old Testament. The other two were angels on an errand to Sodom (v. 22).

While the three "men" were enjoying Abraham's hospitality, they asked, "Where is Sarah thy wife?" (v. 9). He replied that she was in the tent (keeping herself out of sight, as women were supposed to do in that culture).

Then the Lord told Abraham that at the end of nine months Sarah would have a son (v. 10). Because of the advanced age of the couple, this seemed impossible. So "Sarah laughed within herself" (v. 12), as Abraham had done (17:17). But the Lord reproved her for laughing, and then asked the rhetorical question: "Is anything too hard for the Lord?" (v. 14). Admittedly such a birth was a physical impossibility. But with God all things are possible. And all things are possible to the one who believes. Then the Lord reiterated His statement that nine months later Sarah would have a son.

Sarah was fearful of these strangers, perhaps sensing the fact that it was actually the Lord who was speaking. So she denied that she had laughed. But the Lord corrected her (v. 15).

We have to recognize that these heroes of faith (Hebrews 11:8-12) were very human, as well as spiritual. And they lived in the pioneer days of the Old Testament, not in the light of nineteen centuries of Christian history.

CONTEMPORARY APPLICATION

Some great men of God in modern times have had severe struggles with doubt. But they emerged from it with a stronger faith because of the struggle.

Many Christians go through three stages in relation to faith. First they have a rather naive faith, largely inherited from their parents, pastors, and friends. Then, often in the teens or early twenties, they go through a period of questioning, of being plagued with doubts. From this they come into a strong faith such as they would not have had without the struggle.

October 19, 1975

GIVING WHAT GOD ASKS

DEVOTIONAL READING | Luke 20:45–21:4

ADULTS

Topic: *Giving What God Asks*

Background Scripture: Genesis 22:1-19

Scripture Lesson: Genesis 22:1-13

Memory Verse: *By faith Abraham, when he was tested, offered up Isaac, and he who had received the promises was ready to offer up his only son.* Hebrews 11:17

YOUTH

Topic: *Giving What God Asks*

Background Scripture: Genesis 22:1-19

Scripture Lesson: Genesis 22:1-13

Memory Verse: *By faith Abraham, when he was tested, offered up Isaac, and he who had received the promises was ready to offer up his only son.* Hebrews 11:17

CHILDREN

Topic: *Following God's Plan*

Background Scripture: Genesis 22:1-19

Scripture Lesson: Genesis 22:17-19

Memory Verse: *In all your ways acknowledge him, and he will make straight your paths.* Proverbs 3:6

DAILY BIBLE READINGS

Mon., Oct. 13: Giving Is Not Easy, Matthew 19:16-24.
Tues., Oct. 14: God Wants Your Life, Mark 8:34-38.
Wed., Oct. 15: Give God Your Thanks, Psalm 105:1-5.
Thurs., Oct. 16: Give God His Due Glory, Psalm 96:1-9.
Fri., Oct. 17: Give God Goodness and Justice, Isaiah 1:10-17.
Sat., Oct. 18: Offer Your Most Prized Possession, Hebrews 11:17-22.
Sun., Oct. 19: Give God Your All, Luke 20:45–21:4.

LESSON AIM | To see that whenever God asks us for anything, it is for our best good, and that He always gives us back more than we gave.

LESSON SETTING

Time: When Abraham was over a hundred years old

Place: Mount Moriah, at Jerusalem

LESSON OUTLINE | Giving What God Asks
   I. The Test: Genesis 22:1-2

51

A. God's Call: v. 1
B. God's Command: v. 2

II. The Obedience: Genesis 22:3-8
A. The Journey: v. 3
B. Abraham's Faith: vv. 4-5
C. Isaac's Question: vv. 6-7
D. Abraham's Answer: v. 8

III. The Sacrifice: Genesis 22:9-10
A. Preparing the Altar: v. 9
B. Preparing to Slay His Son: v. 10

IV. The Divine Substitute: Genesis 22:11-13
A. The Test Completed: v. 11-12
B. The Ram as a Substitute: v. 13

V. The Divine Blessing: Genesis 22:14-19

SUGGESTED INTRODUCTION FOR ADULTS

When we left Abraham at the end of the last lesson he was in Hebron, or Mamre, about twenty miles south of Jerusalem (18:1). In the nineteenth chapter we find the story of Lot's deliverance from Sodom, in answer to his uncle's plea (18:23-33).

Chapter 20 tells how Abraham journeyed south from Hebron and came to Gerar. There he told the people that Sarah was his sister (v. 2). He had already done the same thing in Egypt and had been reproved by Pharaoh (12:10-20). Actually, it was a half-lie that he told, for Sarah was his half-sister (20:12). But in God's sight it was nothing but a lie, for Abraham's intention was to deceive—and that's what a lie is.

Why this man of faith would repeat this sad performance is hard to understand. He should have believed that God would protect him and his beautiful wife. But both of these events took place when he went too far south and got out of God's appointed place for him. Whenever we get out of God's will we get into trouble. Faith operates within the boundaries of the divine will for our lives.

SUGGESTED INTRODUCTION FOR YOUTH

Severe testing is one of the inevitable requirements for building strong character. Those who have an easy time in life are not apt to amount to much in the service of the Lord. For the great tasks of the Kingdom God can only use those who have been tested and proved.

Jesus Himself "suffered being tempted" (Hebrews 2:18). If we follow in His footsteps we shall experience this also.

CONCEPTS FOR CHILDREN

1. God knows what is best in our lives.
2. All that He asks is that we cooperate with Him.
3. When we do so He works everything out for our best good.
4. Our duty is to obey, whatever He asks.

THE LESSON COMMENTARY

I. THE TEST:
Genesis 22:1-2

A. God's Call: v. 1

In chapter 21 we read of the birth of Isaac, the son of promise. Abraham was a hundred years old when this took place (v. 5).

When Isaac was weaned, his father made a great feast in his honor (v. 8). The boy was probably about three years old, according to the custom of that time (compare I Samuel 1:22-24 with II Chronicles 31:16). This would make Ishmael about seventeen years old (16:16).

At the celebration Sarah saw the older boy "mocking" her young child (v. 9). The margin of the New American Standard Bible has "playing." The *Anchor Bible* translates it "playing with her son Isaac." E. A. Speiser comments: "There is nothing in the text to suggest that he was abusing him, a motive deduced by many troubled readers in their effort to account for Sarah's anger" (*Anchor Bible*, I, 155).

At any rate, Sarah asked Abraham to "cast out this bondwoman and her son: for the son of this bondwoman shall not be heir with my son, even with Isaac" (v. 10; cf. Galatians 4:30). Though Abraham hated to do it, the Lord told him to comply with Sarah's request, "for in Isaac shall thy seed be called" (v. 12). It was God's will that from Isaac the chosen people of Israel would come. So Abraham carried out his orders—from his wife and from the Lord!

All this gives a poignant background for what we now find in chapter 22. "After these things"—all the many and varied experiences of the previous ten chapters—"God did tempt Abraham." A better translation is: "God tested Abraham" (NASB). We are specifically told that God does not tempt any man (James 1:13). That is Satan's main business. But God tests His children, to make them stronger in faith and character.

When God called, "Abraham," the patriarch answered, "Behold, *here* I *am*." It will be noted that both "here" and "am" are in italics, indicating that they are not in the Hebrew text. For Abraham's answer the *Anchor Bible* has simply, "Ready." Abraham was always ready to answer God's call and carry out His will. This serves as a constant challenge to us who have so much more light than this man of long ago.

B. God's Command: v. 2

How shocked and stunned Abraham must have been by what God told him to do! He was to take "thy son, thine only son Isaac, whom thou lovest"—note the accumulation of emphasis—and sacrifice him as a burnt offering to God. Incredible! Abraham had been through many crises in his life, but this was the most crucial one of all. We, too, find that the lesser crises prepare us for greater ones. Thus we grow in grace.

God told Abraham to go to "the land of Moriah" for this awesome sacrifice. The name "Moriah" occurs only here and in II Chronicles 3:1. We are told there that Solomon built "the house of the Lord," the temple, at Jerusalem on Mount Moriah. Evidently the Lord wanted this attempted sacrifice of Abraham's son to be done in the same place where His own Son would later be sacrificed for the sins of the world. The whole incident here is highly symbolical.

II. THE OBEDIENCE:
Genesis 22:3-8

A. The Journey: v. 3

"Abraham rose up early in the morning." He not only obeyed, but he obeyed promptly. This is always the safest course. If we put off doing something hard, the difficulty simply increases, and we are more in danger of failing finally to do it. But if we obey without hesitation, we usually find that the unpleasant task is easier than we thought, and it is soon over with.

Nevertheless, we can imagine what a traumatic experience that must have been for Abraham. Did he sleep any the previous night? Perhaps not. What thoughts must have gone through his mind as he lay there, saying to himself: "How can this be? I don't understand it." Yet he did not protest against God's command.

Had not God promised that his descendants ("seed") would be as the stars of the sky (15:5)? And had not the Lord told him, "In Isaac shall thy seed be called" (21:12)? And then there was the promise at the beginning: "In thee shall all families of the earth be blessed" (12:3). How could all this take place if he now sacrificed his son?

But Abraham did not hesitate. It was his business to obey and God's business to work out the results. It is the same with us today.

When Abraham rose early the next morning he saddled his donkey, took two of his servant boys along with Isaac, split wood for the burnt offering, and set out for Mount Moriah. He did everything in an orderly way.

B. Abraham's Faith: vv. 4-5

It was a three days' journey. At that time the average travel per day was twenty miles.

When Abraham saw Mount Moriah in the distance, he dismounted, turned his donkey over to the two servant boys and told them to stay there. Then he said: "I and the lad will go yonder and worship, and come again to you" (v. 5).

One is amazed at Abraham's faith as revealed in these words. What he said was: "We"—not "I"— 'will return." If he was going to sacrifice his son on the altar, how could he say that his son was coming back with him?

Fortunately we are given the answer to this question. In Hebrews 11:17-19 we read: "By faith Abraham, when he was tried [tested], offered up Isaac: and he that had received the promises offered up his only begotten son, of whom it was said, That in Isaac shall thy seed be called; accounting that God was able to raise him up, even from the dead; from whence also he received him in a figure." The Greek word for "figure" is *parabole* (meaning "comparison"), from which we get "parable." So the slated death and actual deliverance of Isaac were a parable of Jesus' death and resurrection.

It is clear that Abraham fully expected to sacrifice his son as a burnt offering on the altar—a pagan custom, which must have perplexed Abraham! But he also believed that God would restore his son to him, so that the divine promises could be kept. That is real faith!

C. Isaac's Question: vv. 6-7

Abraham placed the split wood for the burnt offering on his son's shoulder. He himself took a "knife"—the Hebrew word means a "cleaver," or butcher knife—and the "fire." It must be remembered that in those days they had no modern matches for lighting a fire. On such a long journey it seems doubtful that they could have kept a torch burning. So the true meaning may be "a firestone" (*Anchor Bible*); that is, a stone which could be rubbed by another stone so as to create a spark and ignite some kindling.

"And they went both of them together" is a dramatic statement. Probably they walked on in silence for some time. What thoughts were going through each of their minds as they plodded on toward Mount Moriah? The boy would be wondering, the father maintaining a solemn silence.

Finally Isaac revealed what he was thinking about. He broke the heavy silence with a question: "Behold the fire and the wood: but where is the lamb for a burnt offering?" (v. 7). He had been accustomed to seeing his father offer sacrifices frequently. But where was the animal this time?

D. Abraham's Answer: v. 8

The first word from the father's heart and lips was, "My son." The same expression is found in the middle of the previous verse. We may be sure that it was a spontaneous reflection of tender love from the heart of a concerned father.

Abraham's reply was, "God will provide himself a lamb for a burnt offering." He didn't know how the Lord would do it, but he was confident that the Lord knew. What a man of faith!

E. A. Speiser has caught well the atmosphere of this incident. He writes: "Each successive moment in that seemingly interminable interval of time is charged with drama that is all the more intense for not being spelled out: the saddling of the pack animal; the unarticulated orders to the servants; the splitting of the wood for the sacrificial fire; the long, wordless trip to the spot from which the chosen site can first be seen; the forced matter-of-factness of Abraham's parting instructions to the attendants. As father and son go off by themselves on the last stage of that melancholy pilgrimage—the boy burdened with the wood for his own sacrificial pyre, and the father fidgeting with the flint and the cleaver—the unwary victim asks but a single question. The father's answer is tender but evasive, and the boy must have sensed the truth. The short and simple sentence, 'And the two of them walked on together' (8), covers what is perhaps the most poignant and eloquent silence in all literature" ("Genesis," *Anchor Bible*, I, 164-65).

III. THE SACRIFICE: Genesis 22:9-10

A. Preparing the Altar: v. 9

Finally they reached the hilltop where God had told Abraham to go. There he built an altar and laid the wood in orderly fashion on it. Then he "bound Isaac his son, and laid him on the altar upon the wood."

Isaac was now practically full-grown. As has often been pointed out, his aged father could not have bound the boy and put him on the altar without his complete cooperation. As Smith says, "Meekly, as befitted the type of Christ, he submitted to his father's will, and the life restored to him was henceforth dedicated to God" (Ellicott's *Commentary on the Whole Bible*, I, 86).

The whole of Isaac's life shows him as a man who was gentle and obedient. In this particular incident he is one of the outstanding types of Christ in the Old Testament.

B. Preparing to Slay His Son: v. 10

Abraham reached out his hand and took the knife to slay his son. What a dramatic moment! The loyal patriarch was carrying out God's command literally. But what conflicting emotions must have almost torn his heart in two. This was obedience with a supreme price. But Abraham was prepared to pay it.

IV. THE DIVINE SUBSTITUTE: Genesis 22:11-13

A. The Test Completed: vv. 11-12

At that very moment, before he plunged the knife into his son's chest, the angel of the Lord intervened. "Abraham, Abraham," he called in a

---

DISCUSSION QUESTIONS

1. What is the main lesson we can learn from this incident?
2. Why do we need to be tested?
3. What are some ways that God tests us today?
4. Does God ever ask us to do something that is ultimately unreasonable?
5. What are some of the benefits that come from obedience?
6. What lessons can we learn from Isaac's role in this incident?

commanding, urgent voice. The father paused with the knife poised in his hand. Promptly and reverently he replied, "Here am I." The expression "the angel of the Lord" seems to refer often, as here, to the Lord himself speaking to man.

The voice commanded him not to harm his son nor carry out the planned slaying. Now Abraham had demonstrated conclusively that he feared God; that is, was totally dedicated to God in obedience and trust. He had taken the hardest test that anyone could imagine, and he had passed it with flying colors. There was no question about his complete loyalty to God. He had not held back his most precious possession, his own son.

B. The Ram as a Substitute: v. 13

Having been kept from offering his son as a sacrifice, Abraham looked around for a substitute. Sure enough, right there in front of him was a ram caught by its horns in a thicket. We can imagine with what tremendous relief and overflowing joy he took the ram and offered it in place of his son.

It takes both Isaac and the ram to give a full-orbed picture of the atonement. Isaac, the "only" (v. 2) and beloved son of Abraham, is a type of Christ, God's only begotten, beloved son, whom He offered as a sacrifice for our sins. At the same time, the ram brings in the idea of substitution. Jesus said in Mark 10:45: "For even the Son of man came not to be ministered unto, but to minister"—not to be served, but to serve—"and to give his life a ransom for many"—the Greek says "instead of many." Christ took our place on the cross and died in our stead. This is the miracle of divine grace that took place at Calvary. So Jesus is "the Lamb of God, which taketh away the sin of the world" (John 1:29). He is the substitute sacrifice for us.

V. THE DIVINE BLESSING: Genesis 22:14-19

Abraham renamed the spot "Jehovah-jireh." The exact meaning of this expression is debated. But perhaps the best translation is: "The Lord Will Provide . . . in the mount of the Lord it will be provided." Here, on Mount Moriah, God would later provide a place of sacrifice for sin in the temple to be erected at that place. There may also be a reference to the provision of the great Sacrifice for our sins, who died in this vicinity.

The previous promise to Abraham (12:2-3; 15:5) is now renewed and expanded. Because he had not withheld his son, "in blessing I will bless thee, and in multiplying I will multiply thy seed as the stars of the heaven, and as the sand which is upon the sea shore . . . and in thy seed shall all nations be blessed" (vv. 17-18). It had paid Abraham to obey.

CONTEMPORARY APPLICATION

The young pastor of a small church felt that he should give a hundred dollars in a special offering for world missions. But he didn't have the money. So he went to the bank to borrow it. When the banker asked the purpose of the loan, the pastor told him.

Result? The banker was so impressed that he gave one hundred acres of land on which to build a new Christian college, plus an initial gift of $100,000. Today that obedient, self-sacrificing young man finds himself pastor of the college church, speaking each Sunday morning to a congregation that overflows the twelve-hundred-seat sanctuary. Paul Cunningham found that it paid to obey the Lord, "giving what God asks," even when that asking seemed completely unreasonable. Our only duty is to obey; God will provide.

ATTEMPTING SELF-SUFFICIENCY

DEVOTIONAL READING	Philippians 2:1-11

ADULTS

Topic: *Attempting Self-Sufficiency*

Background Scripture: Genesis 25:19-34; 27; 29

Scripture Lesson: Genesis 25:29-34; 29:21-30.

Memory Verse: *Trust in the Lord with all your heart and do not rely on your own insight.* Proverbs 3:5

YOUTH

Topic: *Wanting One's Own Way*

Background Scripture: Genesis 25:19-34; 27; 29

Scripture Lesson: Genesis 25:29-34; 29:21-30

Memory Verse: *Trust in the Lord with all your heart and do not rely on your own insight.* Proverbs 3:5

CHILDREN

Topic: *A Boy Who Cheated His Brother*

Background Scripture: Genesis 25:19-34; 27; 29

Scripture Lesson: Genesis 27:18-27

Memory Verse: *So then, as we have opportunity, let us do good to all men. . . .* Galatians 6:10

DAILY BIBLE READINGS

Mon., Oct. 20: A Plot of Deceit, Genesis 27:1-10.
Tues., Oct. 21: Steps in Deceit, Genesis 27:11-17.
Wed., Oct. 22: The Act of Deceit, Genesis 27:18-29.
Thurs., Oct. 23: The Crime Is Uncovered, Genesis 27:30-40.
Fri., Oct. 24: The Family Is Split, Genesis 27:41-46.
Sat., Oct. 25: The Deceiver Is Deceived, Genesis 29:15-30.
Sun., Oct. 26: Assume the Role of a Servant, Philippians 2:1-11.

LESSON AIM

To show that it is best to let God have His way, rather than trying to work out our own way.

LESSON SETTING

Time: Somewhere around 1800 B.C. (All dates before 1000 B.C. are uncertain.)

Place: Isaac lived near Hebron. Jacob went to Padan-Aram (another name for Haran).

LESSON OUTLINE

Attempting Self-Sufficiency

I. Isaac and Rebekah: Genesis 25:19-23

57

II. Jacob and Esau: Genesis 25:24-28

III. Jacob Acquiring the Birthright: Genesis 25:29-34
    A. A Hungry Man: vv. 29-30
    B. A Hard Trader: v. 31
    C. A Foolish Exchange: vv. 32-34

IV. Jacob Acquiring the Blessing: Genesis 27

V. Jacob Acquiring a Wife: Genesis 29
    A. Meeting His Wife: vv. 1-14
    B. Working to Get His Wife: vv. 15-20
    C. Getting the Wrong Wife: vv. 21-26
    D. Getting the Wife He Loved: vv. 27-30

SUGGESTED INTRODUCTION FOR ADULTS

Today we begin the third and last unit of this quarter, which is entitled, "God's Will: Our Acceptance of Servanthood." The study centers mainly around two interesting characters—Jacob and Joseph. The first one had many faults and acted in very unwise and even questionable ways. But we do not find a single instance in which Joseph did wrong. Yet God blessed and used both of them.

Both men succeeded as they learned to accept God's role as Sovereign Lord and their own role as submissive servant. That is the lesson we all must learn if we are going to be truly successful in life.

In the first part of chapter 25 we have Abraham's marriage to Keturah, after Sarah had died. But the patriarch now realized that Isaac was God's choice, the miracle son of divine promise. So he gave gifts to the other sons and sent them eastward, away from Isaac, before he himself died (25:1-5).

SUGGESTED INTRODUCTION FOR YOUTH

This lesson is basically the story of twin brothers. They differed greatly in taste and temperament, as twins often do. One was more aggressive and covetous than the other. But he had to learn that his sufficiency was not enough. Jacob paid a high price for trying to work things out himself, rather than letting God work them out for him.

Too many young people today fail to profit by Jacob's bad example. Instead they have to learn the lesson the hard way, by following the same course he did. It's a smart thing to let God work out His will in His own way in our lives!

CONCEPTS FOR CHILDREN

1. Jacob twice tried to get the best of his brother.
2. By cheating his brother he really cheated himself.
3. Because he mistreated his brother he had to leave home.
4. We should be open and honest with everybody.

THE LESSON COMMENTARY

I. ISAAC AND REBEKAH:
Genesis 25:19-23

The longest and one of the most beautiful chapters in Genesis is the twenty-fourth. It tells how Abraham in his old age had become concerned about getting a wife for his son. So he called his trusted senior servant, his steward, and made him swear an oath that he would not take a wife for Isaac from among the Canaanitish women, who were pagans. Instead he was to go back to Abraham's relatives and get a bride there. But he was not to take Isaac back (v. 6).

The servant took ten of his master's camels, heavily loaded with provisions and gifts, and headed toward Mesopotamia, to the city of Nahor (v. 10; cf. 11:29), named after Abraham's brother.

As we read chapter 24 it will have more meaning and beauty if we keep in mind the obvious typology in it. Abraham is a type of God the Father, Isaac of Christ His Son, and the servant of the Holy Spirit. The Father has sent the Holy Spirit into the world to seek out a bride for His Son.

When the servant arrived at the city of Nahor he had his camels kneel by a well outside. It was evening, and soon the women would be coming to draw water.

The servant prayed for guidance. The girl who offered not only to give him a drink of water but also to supply the ten thirsty camels—that would be the bride for Isaac.

Sure enough, the girl who fulfilled these conditions turned out to be the daughter of Abraham's nephew. The servant had been divinely guided to the right home.

The result was that Rebekah made her free decision, "I will go" (v. 58), after the servant had showered her with gifts from Isaac. She evidently felt that this was the family to which she wanted to belong.

We may well imagine that on the long month's journey back to Canaan the servant cheered Rebekah with enthusiastic reports about Abraham's wealth and glowing descriptions of Isaac. So the Holy Spirit takes of the things of Christ and reveals them to us (John 16:14-15).

When they neared their destination, they found Isaac walking out in the field in the cool of the evening. The servant introduced the bride and groom. Isaac brought Rebekah into his mother's tent and she became his wife. He loved her and was now comforted over the death of his mother (v. 67).

If we accept the Spirit's invitation to give our hearts to Christ and if we then let the Holy Spirit lead us through life, He will some day bring us safely home to Him. Then we shall live forever with our heavenly Bridegroom.

We now turn to 25:19 to pick up the story of Isaac. He was forty years old when he married his relative Rebekah.

Like Sarah, Rebekah was childless. But finally the Lord answered Isaac's prayers for his wife (v. 21). However, all was not easy. As twins struggled within her, Rebekah cried out: "If this is how it is to be, why do I go on living?" (v. 22, *Anchor Bible*).

When she went to the Lord about it, He gave her a glimpse into the future:

"Two nations are in your womb;
And two peoples shall be separated from your body;
And one people shall be stronger than the other;
And the older shall serve the younger" (v. 23, NASB).
It was a preview of the history of Jacob and Esau, two radically different twin brothers.

II. JACOB AND ESAU:
Genesis 25:24-28

The first of the twins to be born was Esau. He became the father of the Edomites. Then came Jacob, the heel-grabber. Later his name was changed to Israel, and he became the father of the Israelites. Isaac was sixty years old when his sons were born (v. 26).

From the beginning, the boys differed greatly in personality and preferences. Esau was a skillful hunter, a man of the out-of-doors. Jacob was a peaceful man who kept close to the tents (v. 27).

Unfortunately, the parents had their preferences and prejudices. Isaac loved Esau, because he enjoyed the wild game he brought in. But Rebekah loved Jacob.

III. JACOB ACQUIRING THE BIRTH-RIGHT:
Genesis 25:29-34

A. A Hungry Man: vv. 29-30

One day Jacob, who loved household work, was cooking a stew. About that time Esau came in from the field, famished with hunger. When he saw and smelled what Jacob had on the fire, he said, "Please let me have a swallow of that red stuff there, for I am famished" (v. 30, NASB). That was one reason he was nicknamed Edom ("Red").

B. A Hard Trader: v. 31

Jacob was always the kind who would drive a hard bargain. So he said to his hungry brother: "First sell me your birthright" (NASB). That was the oldest son's legal right to inherit a double portion of the family estate—which in this case was very large. Jacob was a clever schemer!

C. A Foolish Exchange: vv. 32-34

The shallowness of Esau's character is revealed in his next remark. Instead of rebuking his brother's greedy covetousness, he moaned: "Behold, I am about to die; so of what use then is the birthright to me?" (v. 32, NASB).

Jacob was not taking any chances on his brother changing his mind later. So he demanded, "Swear to me this day" (v. 33). Esau complied and le-

gally transferred the privileges of his birthright to Jacob. It was a stupid thing to do.

Having secured legal title to the birthright, Jacob began dishing up the stew (v. 34). But he was to find himself later "in a stew" because of his selfish action in robbing his brother of the birthright. And robbery it was! The birthright was thousands of times as valuable as the single meal that Esau got in exchange for it.

In the Epistle to the Hebrews we read the warning: "Lest there be any fornicator, or profane person, as Esau, who for one morsel of meat sold his birthright" (12:16). "Profane" here does not have its modern connotation of one who uses "profane" language. Rather, it is used in its original sense of "secular," as in "profane literature." Esau was a secular person. He put no value on spiritual things. There was a time when atheism and infidelity were the great enemies of the church. But today the worst "-ism" is secularism. It pervades society everywhere. People will do almost anything to get a few dollars, selling their souls for a mess of pottage.

So "Jacob gave Esau bread and pottage of lentiles"—that is, "lentil stew" (NASB), what we today would call "vegetable stew." The fact that it was red (v. 30) shows that it had in it red peppers, beets, or red beans. In any case, it was a foolish exchange that Esau made.

When Esau finished eating and drinking what Jacob served him, he got up "and went his way"—his same old selfish way, with no reference to God. "Thus Esau despised his birthright." He would rather enjoy a little material substance than exercise the spiritual privileges of the firstborn son succeeding his father as the head of the family. He lived only for this world.

IV. JACOB ACQUIRING THE BLESSING:
Genesis 27

Chapter 26 deals with Isaac again. We find that in a time of famine he moved out of God's will, as Abraham had done. Following in the footsteps of his father, he went down to Gerar and told the same lie—that his wife was his sister (v. 7; cf. 20:2).

In spite of all this, "the Lord blessed him. And the man waxed great and went forward, and grew until he became very great," or "wealthy" (vv. 12-13). Yet Esau passed up his privilege of getting two-thirds of the family estate—just for a bowl of stew. He also grieved his parents by marrying two pagan wives (vv. 34-35).

We turn now to chapter 27 and see Jacob again cheating his brother, this time practicing outright deception. Jacob was by nature an inveterate schemer. But he had enough spiritual insight and appetite that God could bless him.

Isaac was getting old and losing his eyesight. One day he called his son and asked him to take his bow and his quiver of arrows, go out into the fields, and hunt some game for him (v. 3). ("Venison" does not necessarily mean deer meat, as now, but the meat of any wild animal.) Esau was then to prepare a "savoury" dish, such as his father loved, and bring it to him, "that my soul may bless thee before I die" (v. 4). This was according to the patriarchal custom of that day.

Rebekah, the mother of the two boys, heard her husband say this to Esau. But she had God's prophetic promise: "the elder shall serve the younger" (25:23). So she set out to help God fulfill His word!

With Esau gone to the fields to hunt game, Rebekah told Jacob what was taking place. He must hurry and do exactly what she ordered him to, before his brother got back. Rebekah, too, was a schemer.

She told Jacob to go to the flock and bring "two good kids of the goats" (v. 9). She would then make a savory dish, such as Isaac loved—"and thou shalt bring it to thy father, that he may eat, and that he may bless thee before his death" (v. 10). This mother was determined that her favorite son

should get the special blessing that belonged to the oldest brother.

It would seem that this overly concerned mother was trying to do God's business in her own way. We don't know whether Isaac was unaware of God's choice of Jacob, or whether his strong preference for Esau (25:28) led him to ignore it. At any rate, Rebekah was determined to get the best of her husband in this deal!

But Jacob protested that he had smooth skin, while Esau was a hairy man. His father might discover the deception (vv. 11-12).

His mother said, "I'll take care of that." But she was unwise when she said, "Upon me be thy curse, my son" (v. 13). She did suffer the curse of being deprived of the comfort and companionship of her beloved son during the last years of her life, because Jacob had to flee from Esau.

Two lessons we can learn from this. The first is that the end does not justify the means. The second is that when we take matters into our own hands, instead of prayerfully seeking God's guidance, we often bring sorrow and suffering to ourselves and others.

Jacob followed through on his mother's instructions and finally got the coveted blessing (vv. 28-29). But he had a few tense moments. His father was surprised that his son (Esau) had so quickly found some game, and Jacob told a lie to cover up (v. 20). Then Isaac asked to feel him. Fortunately, the goat skins that Rebekah had put on his hands and neck did the trick, but Jacob must have trembled as his father said, "The voice is Jacob's voice, but the hands are the hands of Esau" (v. 22). Isaac is the great example of a man who went by feeling, and he was fooled!

Sin always brings punishment. Jacob obtained the blessing, as he had previously secured the birthright. But he paid a high price for his cheating, for supplanting his brother twice (v. 36). Esau hated Jacob and said to himself: "The days of mourning for my father are at hand; then I will slay my brother Jacob" (v. 41).

When Rebekah heard this, she had to do some more scheming. (How much better if she had let the Lord work things out in His own way!) So she called Jacob and told him to flee to her brother Laban in Haran, to allow Esau to cool off (vv. 42-45).

Then she went to work on Isaac. Telling him what a trial to her were the two wives of Esau, she said that if Jacob married one of the pagan women of Canaan she was ready to give up (v. 46).

Isaac agreed. He called Jacob, ordered him not to marry a Canaanitish woman and instructed him to go to Haran and marry one of his mother's relatives there (28:1-2). Then he pronounced a special blessing on Jacob and his descendants (vv. 3-4). Jacob obeyed and left for Haran (Padanaram).

V. JACOB ACQUIRING A WIFE: Genesis 29

A. Meeting His Wife: vv. 1-14

The opening scene is somewhat parallel to 24:10-27. At the well near Haran, Jacob met Rachel and immediately fell in love with her (v. 11). Her father, Laban, was glad to see his sister's son (cf. 27:43) and welcomed him into the home.

DISCUSSION QUESTIONS

1. What were some of Isaac's good points and bad points?
2. What were the good and bad points of Esau and Jacob?
3. What was Jacob's greatest mistake in his thinking?
4. How would you characterize Rebekah?
5. What is the best way to cooperate with God in helping to carry out His will?
6. What lessons have you learned from the study today?

B. Working to Get His Wife: vv. 15-20

After a month Laban asked Jacob what he wanted for wages. The young man had been appraising Laban's two daughters: "Leah's eyes were weak, but Rachel was beautiful of form and face" (v. 17, NASB). Jacob made his choice: "I will serve you seven years for your youngest daughter Rachel" (v. 18, NASB). So much did he love her that the seven years seemed but a few days to him (v. 20).

C. Getting the Wrong Wife: vv. 21-26

At the end of the agreed period, Jacob asked for his wife. Laban gathered in the people and made a great feast, in keeping with the customs of that time and place.

Jacob had been a great schemer, plotting and conniving to get what he wanted. It had worked successfully on his brother and father. But now he found his match: Laban outwitted him! He took his older daughter Leah that evening and gave her to Jacob, who there upon consummated the marriage.

How could Jacob have been deceived? The answer is that the bride was brought in fully veiled. Jacob had to "take her by faith," and this time he missed it.

Whitelaw makes a relevant comment here. He writes: "The conduct of Laban is perfectly intelligible as the outcome of his sordid avarice; but it is difficult to understand how Leah could acquiesce in a proposal so as to wrong her sister by marrying one who neither sought nor loved her. She must herself have been attached to Jacob; and it is probable that Laban had explained to her his plan for bringing about a double wedding" (Pulpit Commentary, Vol. I, "Genesis," p. 360).

It was not until morning that Jacob discovered the deception, when daylight disclosed to him the fact that his companion was actually Leah (v.

25). We can only imagine the scene that took place in that home!

But we are told what Jacob said to his selfish uncle (v. 25). Did Jacob recall Esau's reactions when he discovered that his younger brother had double-crossed him and robbed him of his father's blessing? The old saying is still true: "Chickens *will* come home to roost." Whitelaw comments: "If Jacob's deception, even with the veiled bride, may still be difficult to understand, it is easy to perceive in Leah's substitution for Rachel a clear instance of Divine retribution for the imposition he had practised on his father" ("Genesis").

Laban's excuse was that it was the established custom in that country that the oldest daughter must always be given in marriage first (v. 26). There is evidence that this has been true in various eastern countries.

D. Getting the Wife He Loved: vv. 27-30

Laban then sought to assuage Jacob's anger by making this proposition: "Complete the bridal week of this one, and we will give you the other also for the service which you shall serve with me for another seven years" (NASB). The bridal week would be the seven days of festivities that usually accompany weddings in the culture of that day (cf. Judges 14:12), even now.

Laban was the epitome of greediness. He had gained seven years of free service out of Jacob, and now he maneuvers things so as to get another seven years the same way. "It takes a thief to catch a thief," but Jacob was beaten at the game.

Jacob was so in love with Rachel that he was glad to accept the new arrangement. At the end of the week of feasting he married Rachel and lived happily (?) ever after. No, he found that two wives, plus two concubines, created strife rather than peace. Yet out of this seeming mess God worked out His will for His chosen people Israel.

CONTEMPORARY APPLICATION

Esau sold his birthright for "a mess of pottage" and so forfeited the blessing. Today there are millions of people who are selling their souls and missing eternal blessing just to enjoy the pleasures of this life.

It's a shortsighted decision! Esau was willing to throw away his future in order to have a few minutes of physical satisfaction. And that is exactly what many people are doing right now. Just to "feel good" for a few moments they will sacrifice health, happiness, and life, besides eternal bliss.

FINDING SELF IN DIVINE ENCOUNTER

DEVOTIONAL READING	Galatians 1:10-17

ADULTS

Topic: *From Dream to Fulfillment*

Background Scripture: Genesis 28:10-22; 32:1–33:4

Scripture Lesson: Genesis 28:10-17; 32:24-29

Memory Verse: *Humble yourselves therefore under the mighty hand of God, that in due time he may exalt you.* I Peter 5:6

YOUTH

Topic: *From Dream to Fulfillment*

Background Scripture: Genesis 28:10-22; 32:1–33:4

Scripture Lesson: Genesis 28:10-17; 32:24-29

Memory Verse: *Humble yourselves therefore under the mighty hand of God, that in due time he may exalt you.* I Peter 5:6

CHILDREN

Topic: *God Is Always Near*

Background Scripture: Genesis 28:10-22; 32:1–33:4

Scripture Lesson: Genesis 28:10-22

Memory Verse: *The Lord is near to all who call upon him, to all who call upon him in truth.* Psalm 145:18

DAILY BIBLE READINGS

Mon., Oct. 27: The Mystery of God's Presence, Genesis 28:10-17
Tues., Oct. 28: Covenant with God, Genesis 28:18-22.
Wed., Oct. 29: Threatened by Past Sins, Genesis 32:1-7.
Thurs., Oct. 30: Nothing to Do but Pray, Genesis 32:8-12.
Fri., Oct. 31: Confronted by God, Genesis 32:22-32.
Sat., Nov. 1: The Power of Graciousness, Genesis 33:1-11.
Sun., Nov. 2: Trust, Joy, and Safety, Psalm 4.

LESSON AIM

To see how God can work out His will in spite of our faults and failings, and how we find our true selves in Him.

LESSON SETTING

Time: Around 1700 B.C.

Place: Chapter 28: Beersheba in southern Palestine, Bethel in central Palestine. Chapter 32: the Jabbok River, east of the Jordan.

Finding Self in Divine Encounter

LESSON OUTLINE

I. Jacob's Ladder Vision: Genesis 28:10-15
  A. Escaping from His Brother: v. 10
  B. A Hard Bed to Sleep On: v. 11
  C. A Ladder Reaching to Heaven: v. 12
  D. A Message from the Lord: vv. 13-15

II. Jacob at the House of God: Genesis 28:16-22
  A. God's Awesome Presence: vv. 16-17
  B. A Shrine at Bethel: vv. 18-19
  C. Jacob's Vow: vv. 20-22

III. Jacob's Fear of Esau: Genesis 32:1-23

IV. Jacob Wrestling at Peniel: Genesis 32:24-29
  A. Wrestling All Night: vv. 24-25
  B. Confessing His Identity: vv. 26-27
  C. Getting His Name Changed: vv. 28-29

SUGGESTED INTRODUCTION FOR ADULTS

Jacob is a study in contrasts. He evidently reciprocated his mother's special love for him and was submissive to his parents. He had keen spiritual sensitivity, which was his main redeeming virtue.

On the other hand he was crafty, deceitful, greedy, unscrupulous. And before God could bless him he had to confess his meanness and become a new person.

There were two main crises in Jacob's life that changed his character, and these two incidents comprise today's lesson. The first was at Bethel (house of God), where he seems to have had his first crucial encounter with God. It left him shaken, but vowing to be God's man. The second was at Peniel (face of God), where he wrestled all night and became a submissive servant to his sovereign Lord.

SUGGESTED INTRODUCTION FOR YOUTH

Every young person needs to meet God—sometime, somewhere. It is the divine encounter that makes the difference in our lives. Without it our lives are empty and meaningless. With it life takes on purpose and fulfillment.

Young people are searching for self-identity. This can only be found in a transforming encounter with God. That is where we find ourselves.

There is a third aspect in today's lesson: "From Dream to Fulfillment." Youth is a time of dreaming dreams. But if we want our best dreams to come true we must let God have His way completely in our lives.

CONCEPTS FOR CHILDREN

1. God is always near when we need Him.
2. We need to become more and more aware of His presence.
3. If we respond to Him, He will come nearer.
4. God wants us always to rejoice in the fact that He is with us.

THE LESSON COMMENTARY

I. JACOB'S LADDER VISION: Genesis 28:10-15

A. Escaping from His Brother: v. 10

To keep from being murdered by his angry brother Esau, Jacob had to leave home. He left his father's home at Beersheba, far south of Jerusalem, and went toward Haran. The journey would take him about a month on foot. It was a long, lonely experience for one who had always stayed close to home and had been the object of his mother's special love.

B. A Hard Bed to Sleep On: v. 11

As the sun set, he stopped for the night. He was alone—all, all alone, it seemed—with nothing but the stars twinkling overhead. If he could have thought of them as God's thousands of lanterns that He had hung in the sky to assure His children that He was watching over them during the hours of darkness, it would have helped. But probably no such thoughts crossed his troubled mind.

As if to add to his discomfort, he put a stone down for a pillow and stretched out to sleep. With a stone under his head it is no wonder that he dreamed!

C. A Ladder Reaching to Heaven: v. 12

In his dream he saw a ladder (or, "stairway," *Anchor Bible*) set up on earth, with its top reaching to heaven. On it the angels of God were ascending and descending. The order here is striking. The angels had been on earth, ministering to men. Now they were returning to heaven, while others were coming down to take their places. Probably the main intent of the vision was to show Jacob that he was not alone: God knew where he was and His angels were watching over the lonely young man.

Any alert adult Christian would probably identify this ladder with Jesus Christ, the only mediator between God and man (I Timothy 2:5) and the One through whom His angels minister to us. But this identification is made explicitly by Christ Himself. He said: "Hereafter ye shall see heaven open, and the angels of God ascending and descending upon the Son of man" (John 1:51). All the ministry we receive from God comes to us in Christ. He is the only One who bridges the tremendous gap between heaven and earth. Jacob experienced an Old Testament foregleam of this on that night when God and home and loved ones seemed so far away.

D. A Message from the Lord: vv. 13-15

The word "behold" occurs twice in verse 12 and once in verse 13. This highlights the wonder of the vision, the most meaningful vision that mortal man could have.

The word also introduces the three stages of the vision. First Jacob saw a ladder. Then he saw angels on the ladder, engaged in ministry for men. Finally, and climactically, he saw God standing at the top of the ladder—or, "beside him" (*Anchor Bible*; NASB, margin). God Himself was watching over him.

Better still, the Lord spoke to him. The message was a confirmation of the divine covenant made with his grandfather and father, and now extended to him. Jacob must have been much encouraged with the Lord's first words: "I am the Lord God of Abraham thy father, and the God of Isaac." Just as the Lord had led and blessed those two patriarchs, so He would care for Jacob.

But the message went further. Just as God had promised all that land to Abraham and then to Isaac, so now it was confirmed to Jacob and to his descendants, who would be as the dust of the earth (v. 14). They would spread in all four directions—as indeed they did. Then comes the beautiful promise, first given to Abraham (12:3): "And in thee and in thy seed shall all the families of the earth be blessed." This was fulfilled in Christ.

Very graciously the Lord came back to Jacob's personal, present condition. As we have noted, Jacob was doubtless lonely and somewhat afraid. Tenderly the Lord said to him: "And, behold, I am with thee" (v. 15). That was the message he needed most at the moment. The Lord assured him that He would guard him wherever he went and bring him back safely to the land of promise. This must have been a great consolation to a young man who was facing an uncertain path and an unknown future. God said in effect, "I will not leave you until I have carried out all my promises to you."

II. JACOB AT THE HOUSE OF GOD:
Genesis 28:16-22

A. God's Awesome Presence: vv. 16-17

When Jacob wakened, his first reaction was: "Surely the Lord is in this place; and I knew it not." Immediately he was afraid and blurted out: "How dreadful is this place! this is none other but the house of God, and this is the gate of heaven" (v. 17). The last phrase favors the idea that what Jacob saw in his vision was more in the nature of a stairway than a ladder. Gates have stairs leading to them, but not ladders.

B. A Shrine at Bethel: vv. 18-19

Getting up early the next morning, Jacob took the stone he had used for a pillow and set it up for a pillar. Then he poured oil on the top of it, to consecrate it as a sacred place. He called the place Bethel. As we noted previously, this is compounded of two Hebrew words: *beth*, "house," and *el*, "God." It was truly the house of God.

This place, twelve miles north of Jerusalem, had an illustrious history as a spiritual shrine. Abraham had stopped there when he entered Canaan (12:8; 13:3). Jacob revisited the place when he was returning home from Haran (35:1-7). The ark resided there for awhile (Judges 20:27, NASB). Samuel made it a point of worship (I Samuel 7:16; 10:3). But during the period of the divided kingdom it was used as a center for idolatrous worship (I Kings 12:26-30).

C. Jacob's Vow: vv. 20-22

This man was a trader by nature. So now he made a deal with the Lord. If God would be with him and keep him and give him food and clothing and bring him safely back to his father's house in peace—"then shall the Lord be my God" (vv. 20-21). The conditions were all met, and Jacob kept his vow. He also agreed to treat Bethel as a sacred shrine, as God's house. What really showed that he meant business was his promise to pay God his tithe. When we think of how greedy and grasping Jacob was, we realize that to let go of his tenth to the Lord was evidence of a change of heart.

III. JACOB'S FEAR OF ESAU:
Genesis 32:1-23

Laban's sons became jealous of Jacob, because he prospered so greatly (31:1). Then the Lord said to him: "Return unto the land of thy fathers, and to thy kindred; and I will be with thee" (31:3).

Jacob's first problem was getting away from Laban's family. He sneaked out with his many possessions (31:20-21). When Laban chased after him there were some unpleasant moments. But finally Laban gave his blessing (31:55), and Jacob was safely on his way.

But now a more serious problem confronted him. He sent a message to his offended brother, referring to himself as "thy servant Jacob" and addressing Esau as "my lord" (32:4-5). But he was badly shaken with fear when the messengers returned with the report that Esau was coming to meet him—accompanied by four hundred men! (v. 6). This was enough to strike terror to the bravest heart. Jacob had visions of himself and his whole family being destroyed, and his flocks and herds being captured.

Once more Jacob schemed and planned. He divided his many animals, with their attendants, into two companies with some distance between. His thinking was that if the first company was attacked the second one might escape.

Having done this, he resorted to prayer (vv. 9-12). Humbly he confessed his unworthiness and prayed for protection from the brother he had cheated and from whom he had fled.

After he had prayed, he again laid careful plans to protect those he loved most. First he assembled a bountiful gift to placate his brother. It consisted of nine groups, to be properly placed for extended effect (vv. 13-21). Jacob was taking no chances.

IV. JACOB WRESTLING AT PENIEL:
Genesis 32:24-29

A. Wrestling All Night: v. 24-25

This was the most significant night of Jacob's career. He had schemed and planned, plotted and connived all his

---

DISCUSSION QUESTIONS

1. What part did Jacob's spiritual heritage play in his life?
2. What lesson is there for us in the two epochal crises in Jacob's life?
3. What does the ladder-vision teach us?
4. What makes a place a "house of God"?
5. Why did Jacob have to wrestle all night?
6. What is the final secret of spiritual victory?

---

life. Now he must surrender fully to the sovereignty of God.

"Jacob was left alone." It is then that the greatest battles of our life are fought and the greatest victories won. With all the human props knocked away, we have to stand alone before God if we are going to know Him at the highest level as Lord of all in our lives.

"And there wrestled a man with him until the breaking of day." We may well conclude that this was a Christophany, the Eternal Logos bringing Jacob to a place of complete submission. Finally the Visitor touched the hollow of Jacob's thigh and put it out of joint.

B. Confessing His Identity: vv. 26-27

The divine wrestler said, "Let me go." But Jacob hung on: "I will not let thee go, except thou bless me" (v. 26). This implies that Jacob recognized his opponent as a divine being.

Before granting His blessing, the Visitor asked, "What is thy name?" (v. 27). The answer was just one word— "Jacob." But how much was wrapped up in it! In those days a person's name was considered to be a revelation of his nature. So when Jacob uttered his name he was confessing: "I'm a supplanter, a grabber, a cheater."

Before God can grant us His blessing we have to recognize and confess what we are. Do we want Him to make us patient? We must confess our impatience. Do we want Him to make us loving? We must confess our lack of love. "What is your name, your nature?" We must be open and honest before God.

C. Getting His Name Changed: vv. 28-29

When Jacob had confessed his bad name, the Lord gave him a good name—Israel. There is considerable debate as to the exact meaning of this name. The popular explanation has been "prince with God," based on this text. The New American Standard Bible gives in the margin: "I.e., He who strives with God, or, God strives." Another suggestion is, "May God persevere." At any rate, this man was no longer the cheater but the one who had prevailed with God. He was conquered by the Lord and now he could prevail with men, not in his own strength but in a new strength from God.

The main point seems to be that Jacob's character was changed when he was given a new name. He would no longer be the crafty schemer, but the obedient servant of the Lord.

Jacob called the name of the place where he wrestled Peniel—which unquestionably means "the face of God" —"for I have seen God face to face, and my life is preserved" (v. 30). It is clear that Jacob felt he had been wrestling with the Divine One in human form. "Penuel" (v. 31) is a variation of "Peniel."

Now Jacob was ready to meet Esau and he soon discovered that God had prepared the way before him. When he saw his brother approaching, and the four hundred men with him, he divided his family into four groups (33:1). He put the two handmaids and their children first, in the most exposed place, followed by Leah and her children and last of all Rachel and Joseph. Then he stepped ahead of them all, bowing to the ground seven times before he reached his brother.

But God had moved on Esau's heart. He ran to meet Jacob, embraced him, fell on his neck and kissed him. The two brothers then wept together. It was a beautiful scene of reconciliation, after the sad estrangement of many years.

Esau greeted Jacob's two wives and two concubines, with their children. He tried to get Jacob to take back the large gifts of herds and flocks he had sent on ahead as a peace offering. But Jacob insisted that Esau keep them. Actually, this was just making restitution for the way he had cheated his brother. He needed to do this in order to have a good conscience.

Then Esau offered to escort Jacob and his family back to Canaan, which by now was not far away (v. 12). But Jacob wisely demurred, explaining that he would have to move slowly with the young children and with the flocks and herds (vv. 13-14). So Esau headed back home to Mount Seir, southeast of the Dead Sea. It was safer for the two brothers to go their own separate ways, even after they were reconciled.

Jacob moved back into the Promised Land and settled at Shechem, where Abraham had first stopped. There he built an altar and called it El-elohe-Israel—"God, the God of Israel" (v. 20). He was now acknowledging God as the Lord of his life.

After some unfortunate and unhappy experiences at that place (chap. 34), God told him to move south to Bethel (35:1), where he had had his first divine encounter. There Jacob ordered all the members of his large household to put away the pagan idols they had brought from Haran (vv. 2-4). Then God appeared to him with fresh promises of blessing on him and his descendants (vv. 9-12). Jacob was now back in the place where God wanted him, with a new name, Israel. His descendants were known across the succeeding centuries as the Israelites.

CONTEMPORARY APPLICATION

One of the most important achievements in life is finding our self-identity. But we can only find ourselves truly as we lose ourselves in Christ and let Him make us a real person in Him. The real person is the Christed person.

STRUGGLING WITH PRIDE AND JEALOUSY

DEVOTIONAL READING	Matthew 20:20-28

ADULTS

Topic: *Struggling with Pride and Jealousy*

Background Scripture: Genesis 37

Scripture Lesson: Genesis 37:5-11, 17b-24

Memory Verse: *Love is patient and kind; love is not jealous or boastful; it is not arrogant or rude.* I Corinthians 13:4-5

YOUTH

Topic: *Struggling with Pride and Jealousy*

Background Scripture: Genesis 37

Scripture Lesson: Genesis 37:5-11, 17b-24

Memory Verse: *Love is patient and kind; love is not jealous or boastful; it is not arrogant or rude.* I Corinthians 13:4-5

CHILDREN

Topic: *When Jealousy Rules the Family*

Background Scripture: Genesis 37

Scripture Lesson: Genesis 37:5-11, 17b-24

Memory Verse: *Let each of you look not only to his own interests, but also the interests of others.* Philippians 2:4

DAILY BIBLE READINGS

Mon., Nov. 3: A Troubled Family, Genesis 37:1-4.
Tues., Nov. 4: True Visions and Proud Words, Genesis 37:5-11.
Wed., Nov. 5: The Jealous Long to Destroy, Genesis 37:12-18.
Thurs. Nov. 6: A Murder Is Thwarted, Genesis 37:19-24.
Fri., Nov. 7: Making Money Out of Hatred, Genesis 37:25-28.
Sat., Nov. 8: Deception and Sorrow, Genesis 37:29-36.
Sun., Nov. 9: God's Power over Wickedness, Psalm 37:1-11.

LESSON AIM

To see how God exonerates his own, in spite of all opposition.

LESSON SETTING

Time: About 1700 B.C.

Place: Hebron, 20 miles south of Jerusalem; Dothan, about 13 miles north of Shechem; Egypt

70

Struggling with Pride and Jealousy

SUGGESTED
INTRODUCTION
FOR ADULTS

The story of Joseph is one of the most interesting ones in the entire Bible. Its importance is shown by the fact that it comprises thirteen of the fifty chapters of Genesis (chaps. 37, 39—50)—one fourth of the whole book. Only Abraham is given as much space.

Joseph is of special interest for another reason. He is the most complete type of Christ of any character in the Old Testament. One can list at least thirty specific ways in which Joseph's career was like that of Jesus. It is a fascinating thing to work out.

There is a third way in which Joseph is unique, and that is that not one criticism is made of him in the Bible. This is not true of any other leading person in the Scriptures, except Christ Himself. Adam sinned; Noah got drunk; Abraham lied, as did Isaac; Jacob was a cheater; Moses lost his temper; David committed adultery and murder. But not one sin is recorded against Joseph. It is true that Joseph may have been unwise in what he said to his brothers. But the Bible does not anywhere condemn him.

SUGGESTED
INTRODUCTION
FOR YOUTH

What do we do when our close friends or relatives show jealousy and ill-will toward us? That is what Joseph had to put up with for years. But he came out triumphantly.

Why? Because he kept close to the Lord and sought to do the right. We have no record of his ever answering back or showing a bad spirit toward his brothers. He seems to have suffered in silence. There is not even any record of his complaining, though he did plead for mercy. Apparently he trusted God.

1. We should not try to be a favorite in the family.
2. This always provokes envy and a bad spirit.
3. Neither should we envy others who seem to get more attention than we do.
4. Love in our hearts will keep us from being jealous.

THE LESSON COMMENTARY

I. JOSEPH AND HIS BROTHERS: Genesis 37:1-4

As noted in the introduction, Joseph is the central figure in the last part of Genesis. The chapter that we study today tells about his younger days.

He was seventeen when the story begins (v. 2). His father Jacob had many flocks and herds, and his twelve sons had to take care of them. At this particular time Joseph was with the sons of the two concubines, Bilhah and Zilpah. Because these mothers were maidservants, their sons probably had a lower status in the family, which was unfortunate. To add to the problem, Joseph reported to his father their misbehavior.

We are told that Israel (Jacob) "loved Joseph more than all his children" (v. 3). This, too, was unfortunate. For parents to show favoritism always creates trouble in the family. Jacob was sowing the seeds of envy and jealousy that later came to full fruitage. We are told that Jacob loved Joseph "because he was the son of his old age." But it was also because Joseph was the son of Rachel, the wife whom he especially loved (29:30). Rachel, like Sarah and Rebekah, was barren for a long time. But she finally gave birth to Joseph (30:22-24), much to the delight of both parents. Rachel had been dead for sometime now (she had died at Benjamin's birth, 35:19), and so Jacob poured out his love on Joseph, her firstborn son.

Unfortunately (again!), Jacob made for Joseph "a coat of many colours," or "an ornamented tunic" (*Anchor Bible*). We are not sure what this looked like. Some think it was simply a tunic that reached to the ankles and had long sleeves—worn by wealthy people or nobility. Others think that it was actually composed of different colored pieces of expensive cloth sewed together. In any case it was a mark of special affection. But intended love turned out to be thoughtless cruelty, for seeing Joseph wearing this garment made his brothers hate him (v. 4). It must be admitted that Joseph may have shown an obnoxious pride in wearing it. But if so, the fact is not recorded. And in any case it was primarily his father who was to blame for the unhappy situation that developed.

II. JOSEPH'S FIRST DREAM: Genesis 37:5-8

A. Supreme over His Brothers: vv. 5-7

One night Joseph had a surprising dream. Perhaps unwisely, he told it to his brothers, "and they hated him yet the more" (v. 5).

In his dream he and his brothers were binding sheaves of grain in the field. Suddenly his sheaf stood upright, and the other sheaves bowed down to it.

B. The Reaction of His Brothers: v. 8

The interpretation and application of this dream were too obvious to miss. The answer of Joseph's brothers was to the point: "Are you actually going to reign over us? Or are you really going to rule over us?" (NASB). And so his brothers hated him still more.

III. JOSEPH'S SECOND DREAM:
Genesis 37:5-11

A. Supreme over His Parents and Brothers: v. 9

This dream was worse, as far as its effect on the family was concerned. Jacob saw the sun, moon, and eleven stars bow down to him. Clearly the sun and moon represented his father and mother, and the eleven stars his eleven brothers.

B. Reaction of His Father: v. 10

There is no evidence that the father was troubled by the first dream—if, indeed, he heard of it. But this was too much. His father rebuked him, asking: "What is this dream that thou hast dreamed? Shall I and thy mother and thy brethren indeed come to bow down ourselves to thee to the earth?" In that oriental culture, especially, this was utterly unthinkable. But it all finally happened.

C. Reaction of His Brothers: v. 11

His brothers "envied him ["were jealous of him" (NASB)]—but his father kept the saying in mind." The Anchor Bible gives a good translation: "But while his brothers were wrought up at him, his father pondered the matter." Perhaps Jacob began to sense that God had ordained a great future for his favorite son, and so he had better keep still. Fortunately, he lived to see the fulfillment of Joseph's dreams.

Understandably there has been considerable discussion, pro and con, about Joseph relating his dreams. His doing so has even been labeled "arrogance."

But we are not convinced that this characterization is fair. Joseph was probably naive. Showered with his mother's affection, and then his father's favoritism, he may well have been emotionally and socially immature. But there is no evidence that he was a "spoiled brat."

Something should probably be said in his favor. Whitelaw puts it this way: "Though Joseph did not certainly know that his dream was supernatural, he may have thought that it was, the more so as dreams were in those times commonly regarded as mediums of Divine communication; and in this case it was clearly his duty to impart it to the household, and all the more that the subject of it seemed to be for them a matter of peculiar importance. In the absence of information to the contrary, we are warranted in believing that there was nothing either sinful or offensive in Joseph's spirit or manner in making known his dreams. That which appears to have excited the hostility of his brethren was not the mode of their communication, but the character of their contents" (Pulpit Commentary, Vol. I, "Genesis," p. 428).

Alexander Maclaren takes much the same point of view. He suggests that Bilhah and Zilpah (v. 2) may well have resented Jacob's special love for Rachel and their own status as slave girls. We surely have evidence in this chapter that their sons were coarse, cruel men. Joseph, a devout young man, was doubtless greatly shocked when he saw the sinful ways of his older brothers, and so he reported the matter to his father (v. 2). Maclaren goes so far as to say: "Jacob had a right to know, and Joseph would have been wrong if he had not told him the truth about his brothers. Their hatred shows that his purity had made their doing wrong more difficult" (Expositions of Holy Scripture, Vol. I, I, "Genesis," p. 236). It would seem that since there is no hint of criticism of Joseph in Scripture, we should give him the benefit of the doubt.

IV. JOSEPH MISTREATED BY HIS BROTHERS:
Genesis 37:17-24

A. Conspiracy to Kill Him: vv. 17-20

It would appear that there may have been something of a drouth in Hebron, twenty miles south of Jerusalem, for Joseph's brothers were grazing the flocks far north in Shechem (v. 12). Jacob asked his son to go there and see how his brothers were getting along. Because of his "evil report" (v. 2) the brothers may very well have objected to his being with them.

When Joseph arrived in the vicinity of Shechem he hunted in vain for his brothers and their flocks. Finally he was told that they had moved on to Dothan, thirteen miles farther north. So Joseph followed them up and found them there (v. 17).

When they saw him coming across the fields, their resentment rose rapidly and "they conspired against him to slay him" (v. 18). Jealousy and hate easily lead to murder.

Contemptuously they said, "Behold, this dreamer cometh" (v. 19). They proposed to kill him and throw his dead body into a pit, where it would not be found. Then they would tell their father that some wild animal had devoured him. They added scornfully: "And we shall see what will become of his dreams" (v. 20). They obviously considered Joseph's dreams to be a reflection of his pride and self-ambition. The brothers gave frequent evidence of lacking spiritual insight. The possibility that God had initiated the dreams seems never to have crossed their minds.

B. Reuben's Counter Advice: vv. 21-22

Reuben was the oldest brother and felt a special responsibility toward the

---

DISCUSSION QUESTIONS

1. What major mistake did Jacob make?
2. What did this do to Joseph?
3. What did it do to Joseph's brothers?
4. Why did God permit these hardships to befall Joseph?
5. How can we make our God-given dreams come true?
6. What are the results of jealousy as seen in this chapter?

---

younger lad. So he "rescued him out of their hands" (NASB), pleading, "Let us not kill him. . . . Shed no blood, but cast him into this pit in the wilderness." We are told that his intention was to get Joseph out of their murderous hand and then secretly return the lad to his father. Reuben, who was the son of Leah, certainly showed here a commendable concern for both his father and his brother.

C. Cast into a Pit: vv. 23-24

The other brothers acquiesced in Reuben's proposal. When Joseph reached them, they grabbed him, stripped off his coat of many colors—notice the fullness of the language in verse 23, emphasizing this item—and threw him into a pit. Fortunately for Joseph the pit was empty, with no water in it.

We may well question Joseph's wisdom in wearing the coat of many colors. He must have known that his brothers hated it as a symbol of their father's unfortunate favoritism. But had Jacob ordered him to wear it? Perhaps so.

V. JOSEPH SOLD BY HIS BROTHERS: Genesis 37:25-28

The cruel callousness of these men is shown by the fact that they could treat their younger brother in such a diabolical way and then immediately sit down to eat (v. 25). While they were eating they saw a caravan of Ishmaelites who were coming from Gilead (east of the Jordan), "bearing spicery and balm and myrrh, going to carry it down to Egypt" (v. 25).

Judah had a bright idea. What profit would come from killing their brother? A smarter thing would be to sell him as a slave to these Ishmaelites and get some money out of the deal! Again we are amazed at the callous cruelty of these brothers.

So they drew Joseph up from the pit and sold him to the traders. In verse 28 they are called both Midianites and Ishmaelites. Both of these groups were descended from Abraham. There may well have been a mixture of the two in the caravan.

They sold Joseph for "twenty pieces of silver." This was later specified as the price for a boy between five and twenty years of age (Leviticus 27:5). This would fit Joseph very well (cf. v. 2). The average price of an adult slave was thirty silver shekels (Zech. 11:12). These merchantmen doubtless made a good profit on Joseph when they sold him into slavery in Egypt.

How did Joseph feel about the scurrilous treatment his brothers gave him? We are given a glimpse into this, when these mockers actually did bow down before Joseph (42:6). When Joseph accused them of being spies and let them "soak" in prison for three days (42:17), they declared to each other: "We are verily guilty concerning our brother, in that we saw the anguish of his soul, when he besought us, and we would not hear; therefore is this distress come upon us" (42:21). Evidently, as would be expected, he cried hard and pleaded with them not to throw him into the pit, and, even more, not to sell him into slavery. He had every reason to believe that he would never see his father again. "Anguish" is not too strong a term to describe his feelings. But the hardhearted brothers appear to have been unmoved by all this.

VI. JACOB'S SORROW:
Genesis 37:29-35

Reuben was absent, for some reason, when Joseph was sold to the passing traders. When he returned to the pit to pull his younger brother out and restore him to his father, he found to his consternation that Joseph was gone. He was so distressed that he tore his clothes to show his deep sorrow. Returning to his brothers, he expressed overwhelming concern by saying: "The child is not; and I, whither shall I go?" His plan had fallen through, and there was no help now for his father.

Again not caring how their father

would feel, the brothers took Joseph's coat and dipped it in the blood of a goat that they had killed for the purpose. Then they brought the bloodstained coat to their father with the words: "This have we found: know now whether it be thy son's coat or no" (v. 32).

Predictably, Jacob replied: "It is my son's coat; an evil beast hath devoured him; Joseph is without doubt rent in pieces" (v. 33). Then he "rent his clothes, and put sackcloth upon his loins, and mourned for his son many days" (v. 34). When his sons and daughters tried to console him, he refused to be comforted, but said, "I will go down into the grave unto my son mourning" (v. 35). It seemed to be the darkest hour in Jacob's life. And it was all because of the diabolical cruelty of his own sons.

Maclaren comments: "The cruel trick by which Jacob was deceived is perhaps the most heartless bit of the whole heartless crime. It came as near an insult as possible. It was maliciously meant. The snarl about the coat, the studied use of 'thy son,' as if the brothers disowned the brotherhood, the unfeeling harshness of choosing such a way of telling their lie—all were meant to give the maximum of pain" ("Genesis," p. 246).

We have already remarked that Joseph is a striking type of Christ in many ways. Pascal, in his *Pensees* (ii. 9.2) notes some of them: "In his father's love for him, his being sent to seek after the peace of his brethren, their conspiring against him, his being sold for twenty pieces of silver, his rising from his humiliation to be lord and saviour of those who had wronged him; and with them the saviour also of the world. As too, he was in prison with two malefactors, so was our Lord crucified between two thieves; and as one of these was saved and one led to his condemnation, so Joseph gave deliverance to the chief butler, but to the chief baker punishment" (cited in Ellicott's *Commentary on the Whole Bible*, I, 137).

CONTEMPORARY APPLICATION

The lesson today is a vivid warning against the sad results of parents showing favoritism among their children. It always breeds jealousy and may well produce hate, as in this case. Parents should try to treat all children alike and should teach their children to be kind to each other, without preference or prejudice.

November 16, 1975

FINDING STRENGTH IN SERVING GOD

DEVOTIONAL READING

II Corinthians 4:7-18

ADULTS

Topic: *Finding Strength in Serving God*

Background Scripture: Genesis 39

Scripture Lesson: Genesis 39:6b-12, 16-21

Memory Verse: *God is faithful, and he will not let you be tempted beyond your strength, but with the temptation will also provide the way of escape, that you may be able to endure it.* I Corinthians 10:13

YOUTH

Topic: *Finding Strength in Serving God*

Background Scripture: Genesis 39

Scripture Lesson: Genesis 39:6b-12, 16-21

Memory Verse: *God is faithful, and he will not let you be tempted beyond your strength, but with the temptation will also provide the way of escape, that you may be able to endure it.* I Corinthians 10:13

CHILDREN

Topic: *How a Man Served God*

Background Scripture: Genesis 41

Scripture Lesson: Genesis 41:25-36, 53-57

Memory Verse: *The Lord is good to all, and his compassion is over all that he has made.* Psalm 145:9

DAILY BIBLE READINGS

Mon., Nov. 10: The Slave Rises to Power, Genesis 39:1-6.
Tues., Nov. 11: A King's Strange Dream, Genesis 41:1-8.
Wed., Nov. 12: Joseph Interprets the Dream, Genesis 41:25-37.
Thurs., Nov. 13: The Man Worthy of Trust, Genesis 41:37-44.
Fri., Nov. 14: A Wise Governor, Genesis 41:53-57.
Sat., Nov. 15: Joseph's Hungry Brothers, Genesis 42:1-12.
Sun., Nov. 16: Man's Passions and God's Grace, James 4:1-6.

LESSON AIM

To show that God is able to keep His own under the most adverse circumstances.

LESSON SETTING

Time: After 1700 B.C.

Place: Egypt

77

Finding Strength in Serving God

  I. Joseph in Potiphar's House: Genesis 39:1-6a
     A. Purchased by Potiphar: v. 1
     B. Prospered by the Lord: v. 2
     C. Put in Charge of Potiphar's House: vv. 3-6a

 II. Joseph and Potiphar's Wife: Genesis 39:6b-12
     A. A Seductive Woman: v. 6b-7
     B. Joseph's Steadfastness: vv. 8-9
     C. A Desperate Attempt: vv. 10-12

III. Joseph and Potiphar's Wrath: Genesis 39:16-20
     A. A Scheming Woman: v. 16
     B. False Accusation: vv. 17-18
     C. Potiphar's Anger: vv. 19-20

 IV. Joseph in Prison: Genesis 39:21-23
     A. Presence and Favor of God: v. 21
     B. Put in Charge of the Prisoners: v. 22
     C. Prospering in Prison: v. 23

There is a tremendous contrast between chapters 38 and 39. In the former we have the story of Judah, who had just sold his own brother into slavery. He took up with a Canaanite woman, who bore him three sons. It is not said whether they were married. Then he had relations with a supposed prostitute, who turned out to be his daughter-in-law. When this woman was found pregnant, Judah in righteous indignation wanted to burn her (v. 24). Fortunately she had required a pledge from him in the form of his signet ring, his bracelets, and his shepherd's staff. When she produced these, he confessed.

What a contrast to this sordid mess is the story of Joseph in chapter 39. He was forcibly seduced by a wealthy woman, his master's wife. But he refused to compromise his integrity, even under terrific pressure.

It would be difficult to imagine a more severe test that could come to any young man than what confronted Joseph in Egypt. In the first place, Joseph was away from family and friends and among people of pagan religion and pagan morals. It seemed that he had everything to gain and nothing to lose by acceding to the urgent wishes of Potiphar's wife.

But Joseph stayed true, and so can you and I. If we trust and obey, as he did, we can overcome any temptation that confronts us. That is the lesson we learn from this chapter.

1. Joseph was a faithful servant, even though in a foreign land.
2. God used him to save a nation, as well as people of other nations.

3. Joseph made careful plans to meet the crisis of a food shortage.
4. God prospered him because Joseph obeyed.

THE LESSON COMMENTARY

I. JOSEPH IN POTIPHAR'S HOUSE: Genesis 39:1-6a

A. Purchased by Potiphar: v. 1

Chapter 37 ends with the statement: "And the Midianites sold him into Egypt unto Potiphar, an officer of Pharaoh's, and captain of the guard." The *Anchor Bible* translates this "a courtier of Pharaoh, his chief steward." The latter term in Hebrew means "chief of the slaughterers"—that is, executioners. In II Kings 25:8 the same title is given to Nebuzar-adan. It is commonly thought that this indicates "commander of the king's bodyguard" (cf. NASB, "the captain of the bodyguard"), whose business it was to execute condemned criminals. The same two terms are used here in the first verse of chapter 39, when the story of Joseph is picked up again where it left off at the end of chapter 37.

Martin Luther conjectured that on the way to Egypt Joseph may have been taken right through his home town of Hebron. If so, this would have been an excruciatingly painful experience for the young victim. It is possible, however, that the caravan went down to the coast from Shechem and followed the coastal road.

B. Prospered by the Lord: v. 2

The keynote of this chapter is: "the Lord was with Joseph" (vv. 2, 21, 23). This is what made all the difference. Rejected by his brothers and separated from his father, yet the Lord was with him.

When we realize that Joseph was probably still a teen-ager (cf. 37:2), we can imagine something of the tragic agony of this experience. Those last hours with his brothers were unbearably cruel. How did he feel as he lay in the pit, wondering if he would ever get out alive? What were his thoughts on that long journey of hundreds of miles to Egypt, as he walked beside the camels? How did it seem to be a slave in the house of "an Egyptian" (v. 1), at the mercy of his master?

His family had forsaken him. It would certainly seem that fate had turned against him. He had no friends in Egypt. He certainly must have felt at times that God had forsaken him; he had no friends anywhere. But, no, "the Lord was with him." This chapter and those that follow teach dramatically the lesson that ultimately there is only one thing that matters—God's presence with us. This is worth more than all other things combined. If we believe that God is All-Power, All-Wisdom, and All-Love, we know that this statement is not an exaggeration. And Joseph's life story proves it!

Because the Lord was with Joseph, "he was a prosperous man"—literally, "he was a man who succeeded." Instead of being put out to work in the field like a common slave, he was retained "in the house of his master the Egyptian."

C. Put in Charge of Potiphar's House: vv. 3-6a

Potiphar was a keen man, as shown by the important position he held. He soon observed that this new slave of his was a different sort of person. He sensed the fact that the Lord was with him and made everything he did prosper. It seemed that whatever Joseph was involved in worked out just right. This was doubtless the Lord making up to him for what he had suffered.

We cannot assume that this Egyptian official had any knowledge of the true God. But he was persuaded that his servant was under divine protection and blessing.

"So Joseph found favor in his sight" (v. 4, NASB). He appreciated having such a fine, faithful servant. The statement "and he served him" seems rather flat. A better translation is: "and became his personal servant" (NASB), or "attendant."

Not only did Potiphar make Joseph his personal attendant but he also made him the "overseer," or steward, of his household. Everything he had he put into his trusted servant's care. This was a great honor for Joseph. As we saw in the case of Abraham's Eliezer, the steward was often given great responsibility and treated almost like a member of the family.

From that time on, "the Lord blessed the Egyptian's house for Joseph's sake; and the blessing of the Lord was upon all that he had in the house, and in the field" (v. 5). Potiphar "left everything he owned in Joseph's charge; and with him around he did not concern himself with anything except the food which he ate" (v. 6, NASB). He was a fortunate man indeed to have such a capable and completely honest steward to take care of all the household concerns.

Joseph, also, was happy. Things had turned out for him far better than anything he could possibly have anticipated. It seemed that everything was going perfectly.

But that is exactly the time when life's greatest temptations often confront us. And so it proved to be with Joseph.

II. JOSEPH AND POTIPHAR'S WIFE: Genesis 39:6b-12

A. A Seductive Woman: v. 6b-7

The last part of verse 6 introduces us to the scenes that follow. We are told that "Joseph was a goodly person, and well favoured," or "handsome in form and appearance" (NASB). That made him the target of feminine attention.

Sure enough, about this time his master's wife "looked with desire at Joseph" (NASB) and asked him to lie with her (v. 7). This was about as great a temptation as could come to a young man far from friends and loved ones.

It seemed that his family had rejected him. Why shouldn't he accept this wealthy lady's offer? Wasn't everything to be gained and nothing to be lost by doing so? We can well imagine that the great Tempter was there to reason this way with him.

B. Joseph's Steadfastness: vv. 8-9

In such cases one's safety lies in promptly turning away from temptation. This is what Joseph did. Immediately "he refused." Then he reasoned with Potiphar's wife very logically and fittingly. His master had put all that he had in Joseph's hands—all but his wife. She belonged to her husband and only to him. Joseph concluded: "How then can I do this great wickedness, and sin against God?"

Those who would criticize Joseph as a spoiled child in his father's house need to face up to the implications of this incident. Only a young man of strong character and rugged integrity could have withstood the pressure of this woman's pleading. She may well have been unusually attractive, her beauty adding to the appeal. Joseph seemed caught in a trap, snared by his master's wife who could affect his financial future. The case was heavily weighted on her side. Not every young man living in a Christian home would have come off as victoriously as Joseph did. No wonder God blessed and used him so greatly. He had passed the big test and now could be fully trusted.

Lest any reader think that Joseph had an easier time living a pure life than young people today, we should point out that moral conditions in Egypt at that time were very low. Joseph was probably confronted with as much temptation in this area as would a young man be in America today.

C. A Desperate Attempt: vv. 10-12

There is nothing more dangerous to a healthy young man that a beautiful but unprincipled woman. Day after day Potiphar's wife sought to seduce Joseph, and every time he refused.

Time and effort did not wear down his determination to remain steadfast in his moral character.

Finally one day Joseph "went into the house to do his business; and there was none of the men of the house there within" (v. 11). Someone might raise the logical question: "If Joseph knew that Potiphar's wife was after him, why did he expose himself to her continued approaches by going through the house where she was?"

Fortunately, archaeology has provided us with the adequate answer. We now know that all the wealthy homes of that day had a common feature. The storeroom, where the food and other supplies were kept, was located at the rear of the family's quarters. It had no windows or outside door—just solid walls. This was for protection against thieves. A person would have to go through the family part of the house to get to this storeroom. As steward, Joseph had to go there daily to take care of his assigned tasks. He was in the line of duty when he met his most pressing temptation.

There is nothing so desperate as a desperate woman. This time Potiphar's wife grabbed hold of Joseph's coat, saying, "Lie with me!" If he was going to escape her forceful advances this time, there was only one thing he could do. And he did it! He left his coat in her hand and fled from the house as fast as he could.

Desperate situations demand desperate measures. There are some cases in which our only safety lies in immediate escape. To dally may be fatal. There are times when we must literally flee for our lives. This was one such. For spiritual death is a worse tragedy than physical death. And sin always brings spiritual death as its ultimate consequence.

III. JOSEPH AND POTIPHAR'S WRATH:
Genesis 39:16-20

A. A Scheming Woman: v. 16

A woman rejected can become a veritable demon, bent on destroying the one who has rejected her. This was the case with Potiphar's wife.

When she saw that Joseph had left his coat in her hand and fled outside, she called to the menservants: "Look, he had to bring us a Hebrew fellow to make love to us! He broke in on me to sleep with me, but I screamed as loud as I could! When he heard me screaming for help, he left his coat near me and fled outside" (vv. 14-15, *Anchor Bible*). What a bold lie! But Potiphar's wife conforms to the pattern of the society life of that day as revealed by archaeological research. Immorality was the accepted way of life.

With the menservants now secured as potential witnesses, Potiphar's wife proceeded to lay her plans to punish Joseph. If he would not fulfill her desires, he must be destroyed. So she kept his coat to show to his master when he came home.

B. False Accusation: vv. 17-18

When her husband returned she told him the same story that she had given to the menservants: "The Hebrew slave whom you brought to us only to make love to me broke in on me. But when he heard me screaming for help, he left his coat near me and fled outside" (vv. 17-18, *Anchor Bible*).

There is nothing so good as a good woman and nothing so bad as a bad woman. This one stooped so low as to accuse Joseph of trying to rape her when actually he refused her seductive advances. But lying seems like a little sin to such a depraved person as she was. Her infatuation turned to intense hatred.

C. Potiphar's Anger: vv. 19-20

One would think that this man would have been aware of what kind of a character his wife was. We do not know whether he did or not. It would have been unusual for that time and place if he was a man of purity himself. But probably we should not assume any guilt on his part. At any rate, when he heard his wife's words,

"This is what your slave did to me," he reacted strongly: "his anger burned" (NASB). So he put Joseph in the prison where the king's prisoners were confined.

IV. JOSEPH IN PRISON: Genesis 39:21-23

A. Presence and Favor of God: v. 21

Again we read, "But the Lord was with Joseph"—even in prison—"and shewed him mercy, and gave him favour in the sight of the keeper of the prison." Because Joseph kept true and showed a good spirit, he made good wherever he was. Honesty and a good spirit always pay off in the end.

B. Put in Charge of the Prisoners: v. 22

Sold into slavery in Potiphar's house, Joseph rose to the place where he was in charge of all his master's possessions. Now in prison he so conducted himself that the prison warden put all other prisoners in his care; "so that whatever was done there, he was responsible for it" (NASB).

One is reminded of the old adage, "You can't keep a good man down." But perhaps we should modify this a bit to read: "You can't keep God's man down." Joseph was God's man, and he acted like it. The result was that he always came to the top.

DISCUSSION QUESTIONS

1. What was the secret of Joseph's strength?
2. How did his home background help?
3. Why did the Lord keep him waiting until he was thirty years old?
4. What are some factors that demand time?
5. Why are attitudes important?
6. How is this illustrated in the case of Joseph?

C. Prospering in Prison: v. 23

What a paradox! It must have seemed to Joseph that he had hit bottom when he was put in prison. But, "the way up is down." Joseph's life is one of the greatest illustrations of this important truth. And it was all because "the Lord was with him."

Two notable king's prisoners were brought in while Joseph was in prison—the chief of the butlers and the chief of the bakers—and they were put in his care (40:1-4). Both of these men had dreams the same night, and Joseph interpreted them. The chief butler was to be restored to Pharaoh's service, while the chief baker was to be hanged.

Joseph made a special request of the chief butler: "But think on me when it shall be well with thee, and shew kindness, I pray thee, unto me, and make mention of me unto Pharaoh, and bring me out of this house [prison]" (v. 14). But when the butler was back at the palace he forgot all about Joseph (v. 23). So the poor fellow had to stay in prison two more years (41:1). He must have been tempted severely to feel that the Lord really had forsaken him by this time.

But the Lord was maturing him by all these trials to fill a large place. Fortunately, Joseph held steady and kept true, and so he was ready.

Finally Pharaoh had a dream. When no one could interpret it, the chief butler at last recalled the one who had interpreted his dream in prison, and he told Pharaoh about it (41:9-13).

Now, after all these endless years of waiting, things began to happen fast. Verse 14 catches the mood: "Then Pharaoh sent and called Joseph, and they brought him hastily out of the dungeon: and he shaved himself, and changed his raiment, and came in unto Pharaoh." A dozen years of waiting—and in a few moments he was ushered into the palace and became a part of its life. When God begins to work, He often works fast!

Joseph   interpreted   Pharaoh's

dream. As a reward he was made the second in the kingdom, with only Pharaoh above him (v. 40). The one who had been stripped of his coat of many colors thirteen years before, now at the age of thirty (v. 46) was given the highest honor possible. Pharaoh took off his own signet ring and put it on Joseph's finger, put royal robes on him and a gold chain around his neck (v. 42).

One is reminded of the words: "It will be worth it all, when we see Jesus." Probably Joseph felt that way when honored by Pharaoh.

CONTEMPORARY APPLICATION

Let's imagine a scene on the Judgment Day. A person brought up in a godly home and church pleads the excuse that he couldn't make it. The Lord calls Joseph as a witness.

"Who was your pastor down in Egypt?"

"I didn't have any pastor."

"Well, who was your Sunday school teacher?"

"I didn't have any."

"No? What church did you go to?"

"There weren't any churches down there."

"Well, how about godly friends?"

"There were none. Everybody around me was a pagan, worshiping idols."

"But you found comfort in reading the Bible?"

"No, the Bible hadn't been written."

"Yet you held true?"

"Yes."

November 23, 1975

PLACING OTHERS BEFORE SELF

DEVOTIONAL READING	John 10:7-18
ADULTS	Topic: *Placing Others Before Self* Background Scripture: Genesis 43–44 Scripture Lesson: Genesis 44:18-23, 30-34 Memory Verse: *Do nothing from selfishness or conceit, but in humility count others better than yourselves.* Philippians 2:3
YOUTH	Topic: *Placing Others Before Self* Background Scripture: Genesis 43–44 Scripture Lesson: Genesis 44:19-23, 30-34 Memory Verse: *Do nothing from selfishness or conceit, but in humility count others better than yourselves.* Philippians 2:3
CHILDREN	Topic: *Placing Others Before Self* Background Scripture: Genesis 44 Scripture Lesson: Genesis 44:18-23, 30-34 Memory Verse: *Love one another with brotherly affection; outdo one another in showing honor.* Romans 12:10
DAILY BIBLE READINGS	Mon., Nov. 17: Joseph Lays His Plans, Genesis 42:18-25. Tues., Nov. 18: The Family Crisis, Genesis 43:1-10. Wed., Nov. 19: Going to Egypt Again, Genesis 43:11-16. Thurs., Nov. 20: Joseph's Love for His Family, Genesis 43:11-16. Fri., Nov. 21: Disaster on the Road, Genesis 44:1-13. Sat., Nov. 22: Terror in Joseph's House, Genesis 44:14-23. Sun., Nov. 23: Judah's Care for His Father, Genesis 44:24-34.
LESSON AIM	To see what our attitude should be toward others and especially those of our family.
LESSON SETTING	Time: After 1700 B.C. Place: Egypt
LESSON OUTLINE	Placing Others Before Self I. Judah's Pledge: Genesis 43:1-14

84

II. **The Brother's Fear:** Genesis 43:15-25

III. **Joseph's House:** Genesis 43:26-34

IV. **A Shocking Experience:** Genesis 44:1-13

V. **Joseph's Accusation:** Genesis 44:14-17

VI. **Judah's Plea:** Genesis 44:18-34
   A. His Humble Submission: v. 18
   B. Joseph's Demand: vv. 19-23
   C. Jacob's Objection: vv. 24-29
   D. Judah's Concern: vv. 30-31
   E. Judah's Pledge: v. 32
   F. Judah's Offer: v. 33
   G. Judah's Compassion for His Father: v. 34

SUGGESTED INTRODUCTION FOR ADULTS

After interpreting Pharaoh's dream as meaning that there would be seven years of plenty followed by seven years of famine, Joseph was put in charge of storing wheat in preparation for the time of need.

Finally the famine came and people were coming from all countries to buy grain from Joseph (41:57). Jacob decided to send his sons down to Egypt to buy some wheat (KJV, "corn") for them. Benjamin, the youngest son, was kept at home.

When Joseph's brothers came before him they bowed low toward the ground (42:6). At last Joseph's first dream had been fulfilled!

He immediately recognized them, but they did not recognize him. So he spoke to them roughly and accused them of being spies (v. 9). To clear themselves, they described their family. Joseph then told them that they had to bring their youngest brother to him. (Benjamin was his full brother, for whom he felt a special love.) Then he put the ten men into prison for three days (v. 17). They needed to see what it felt like to be put in prison under false accusation, as had happened to him. He was deeply moved by their confession of guilt (vv. 21-24). Retaining Simeon, he sent the others home.

SUGGESTED INTRODUCTION FOR YOUTH

This lesson teaches us the importance of being thoughtful of our own family, and especially of our parents. Joseph's brothers treated him unmercifully. But they finally became mature enough to be concerned about their father's welfare. This is a lesson that all young people should learn.

CONCEPTS FOR CHILDREN

1. Even young children should love their parents and be kind to them.
2. Judah was finally more concerned for his father than for himself.
3. Real love helps us to put others before ourselves.
4. We should seek ways of showing our love.

THE LESSON COMMENTARY

I. JUDAH'S PLEDGE:
Genesis 43:1-14

Joseph's brothers had been envious, vicious, cruel, hateful, and even murderous toward him. Now he is cooperating with God in convicting them of their sin and bringing them to a place of repentance. We have already noted in the introduction how he spoke roughly to them, accused them of being spies, and put them in prison.

To add to their distress, he ordered that the money they had paid for the grain should be put back into their sacks (42:25). When they discovered this the first evening on their way home, "their hearts sank, and they turned trembling to one another, saying, 'What is this that God has done to us?'" (v. 28, NASB). The Hound of Heaven was on their trail and getting ever closer.

Arriving home, they told their father all that had happened, and particularly the demand that they had to bring their youngest brother when they went back to Egypt. His reaction was that of pessimistic sorrow: "You have bereaved me of my children; Joseph is no more, and Simeon is no more, and you would take Benjamin; all these things are against me" (v. 36, NASB). What a contrast to Paul's confident testimony in Romans 8:28! Yet Paul had suffered far more than Jacob. It isn't the circumstances that count; it's our attitude toward them.

When Reuben, the oldest son, offered to go bond for Benjamin, Jacob was adamant. His final assertion was: "My son shall not go down with you; for his brother is dead and he is left alone; if mischief befall him by the way in which ye go, then shall ye bring down my gray hairs with sorrow to the grave" (v. 38). So there was nothing more to be said.

But finally the situation got so desperate that they had to go back to Egypt for more food. Jacob told his sons to go (43:2). They said they couldn't without Benjamin. Jacob, who shows a sad lack of faith, whined, "Why did you tell him that you had a younger brother?" (v. 6).

Things had reached an impasse. But Judah spoke up and said, "I will be surety for him ... if I bring him not unto thee, and set him before thee, then let me bear the blame for ever" (v. 9). This was a far different attitude from what he had shown back there in the case of Joseph. God was working in the hearts of these cruel brothers and melting them down.

Jacob finally gave his consent, since there was nothing else he could do. But typically he ended on a negative note: "If I am bereaved of my children, I am bereaved" (v. 14).

II. THE BROTHER'S FEAR:
Genesis 43:15-25

The nine men took the present Jacob was sending (cf. v. 11), double money in their sacks, and Benjamin, and returned to Egypt (v. 15). When Joseph saw Benjamin, he ordered his steward to prepare a feast for these men at his house. So the steward brought the ten men to Joseph's home.

The brothers were filled with consternation. They thought they were going to be punished because of the money they found in their sacks (v. 18). So they went to the steward and explained to him about the money; they had not stolen it, but had brought it back again, together with money for more food (vv. 19-22). His answer is amazing: "Peace be to you, fear not: your God, and the God of your father, hath given you treasure in your sacks: I had your money"—or, "I got your payment" (v. 23). Then he brought Simeon out to them.

Courteously the steward gave them water for washing their feet, in keeping with the custom of that day. He also fed their animals. Then they waited for Joseph to come home at noontime from his task of dispensing wheat.

III. JOSEPH'S HOUSE:
Genesis 43:26-34

When Joseph came in, the brothers presented the gifts their father had sent. Again they bowed low before him (v. 26), fulfilling his dream of long ago. Joseph anxiously asked about their father's welfare: "Is he yet alive?" (v. 27). As they answered, they once more "bowed down their heads, and made obeisance" (v. 28). Certainly Joseph must have recalled his dream.

When Joseph saw his brother Benjamin, "his bowels did yearn upon his brother" (v. 30). Obviously this is not a helpful translation for today. How much better, and more accurate, is the Anchor Bible: "He was overcome with feeling"—or, "with compassion." He had to hurry from the room and find a place to weep in his own bedroom Finally he regained control of himself, washed his face and ordered the meal set on. When the food was served to the men in the order of their age, the brothers looked at each other in astonishment. Also they could not fail to note that Benjamin was given a special treat (v. 34).

IV. A SHOCKING EXPERIENCE:
Genesis 44:1-13

Joseph again instructed his steward to fill the men's sacks with food and put every man's money in his sack (cf. 42:25). But this time he added a very significant directive: "And put my cup, the silver cup, in the sack's mouth of the youngest" (v. 2).

Early the next morning the eleven brothers left on their long trek back to Hebron. Before they had gone far, Joseph told his steward to follow them up and confront them with this challenge: "Why have you repaid evil for good? Is not this the one from which my lord drinks, and which he indeed uses for divination? You have done wrong in doing this" (vv. 4-5, NASB).

When the steward conveyed this message to the brothers, they sincerely and earnestly protested. They would never think of stealing something out of the house of the governor of Egypt.

Then they made a proposition they soon regretted: "With whomsoever of thy servants it be found, both let him die, and we also will be my lord's bondmen" (v. 9). The steward quickly agreed, except that he made the conditions less severe. The one who had the cup would become his slave, while the others would go free (v. 10).

With great confidence the brothers opened their bags, positive that they would soon be proved innocent. The steward searched their sacks beginning at the oldest and finishing at the youngest. (He had observed Joseph's seating arrangement, 43:33, and remembered well.)

And then came the dramatic moment: the cup was found in Benjamin's sack! Filled with anguish, the brothers "rent their clothes" (v. 13), reloaded their donkeys and returned to the city. It was the most mournful hour they had ever spent. How could this have happened to them?

V. JOSEPH'S ACCUSATION:
Genesis 44:14-17

When they got back to Joseph's house he was still there. This time "they fell before him on the ground" (v. 14). They were prostrate with grief.

In keeping with his policy of bringing his brothers to a place of genuine repentance, Joseph again spoke roughly to them. "What is this deed that you have done?" (NASB) he asked.

Speaking for the group, Judah began with great courtesy, yet deep feeling. He pleaded: "What shall we say unto my lord? What shall we speak? or how shall we clear ourselves?" Then he added: "God hath found out the iniquity of thy servants: behold, we are my lord's servants, both we, and he also with whom the cup is found" (v. 16). At last there was open confession of sin, paving the way for forgiveness.

But Joseph replied: "God forbid that I should do so: but the man in whose hand the cup is found, he shall be my servant; as for you, get you up in peace unto your father" (v. 17). They were free to leave.

There were two things that Joseph

wanted to discover. The first was whether these brothers would be willing to abandon Benjamin, as they had long ago treated him. The second was whether they would go back and let their father suffer, and probably die with the shock of the loss of his beloved youngest son. Did these men really care about their father? Were they concerned at all about his health and happiness? Or were they still the same selfish brutes that they had been? It was a tense moment both for him and for his brothers.

VI. JUDAH'S PLEA:
Genesis 44:18-34

A. His Humble Submission: v. 18

"Then Judah came near unto him." He was so desperate that he was willing to do anything for his father now. With great humility and submissiveness he said: "Oh my lord, let thy servant, I pray thee, speak a word in my lord's ears, and let not thine anger burn against thy servant: for thou art even as Pharaoh" (v. 18). Was this the same Judah who had so callously and cruelly proposed that his own brother be sold into slavery to keep his dreams from coming true? No, it was not the same Judah; he was now a changed man. He was human. He cared. A miracle had happened and he was a different person. This was what Joseph had longed to see.

DISCUSSION QUESTIONS

1. How does Jacob show up in this lesson?
2. What excuses might be made for him?
3. Name at least three things that Joseph did to help his brothers repent.
4. What attitude does this show on his part?
5. How is the steward a type of the Holy Spirit?
6. Why do you think Judah changed his attitude so remarkably?

B. Joseph's Demand: vv. 19-23

Judah recounted what had happened on their first visit to Egypt. Joseph had asked the men, "Have ye a father, or a brother?" (v. 19). Naturally they had answered his question, informing him: "We have a father, an old man, and a child of his old age, a little one; and his brother is dead"— still perpetrating this lie—"and he alone is left of his mother, and his father loveth him" (v. 20).

A comparison of this with 42:13 is very revealing. There we find a bare statement of fact. But here Judah's words are filled with tenderness. It is obvious that he had mellowed a great deal in the brief interval. The whole situation got to him, and he now felt a deep compassion for his father and his youngest brother. God's grace was working in his heart.

Then Judah reminded Joseph that the latter had placed a demand on them. He had ordered them to bring their youngest brother down to Egypt, so that he could see him (v. 21). Understandably Joseph was very eager to set eyes on Benjamin, whom he hadn't seen for over twenty years.

The brothers had quickly pointed out the impossibility of doing this: "The lad cannot leave his father: for if he should leave his father, his father would die" (v. 22). This item is not recorded in the account of their first visit, in chapter 42. But they may well have said this.

Joseph had been adamant. He had said to them: "Except your youngest brother come down with you, ye shall see my face no more" (v. 23). And they knew he meant what he said. They were at his mercy.

C. Jacob's Objection: vv. 24-29

Judah went on to tell how they returned to their father and reported to him all that had happened. After some time passed, their father had urged them to go back to Egypt for more food. But they replied: "We cannot go down: if our youngest brother be with us, then we will go down: for we may not see the man's face, except our youngest brother be with us" (v. 26). There was no use wasting time and energy on a trip which they knew would be fruitless, and perhaps dangerous.

Judah went on to tell how his father had reminded them: "Ye know that my wife"—his favorite wife, Rachel—"bare me two sons"—Joseph and Benjamin—"and the one [Joseph] went out from me, and I said, Surely he is torn in pieces; and I saw him not since." Then Jacob had finished his protest by saying: "If ye take this also from me, and mischief befall him, ye shall bring down my gray hairs with sorrow to the grave" (cf. 42:38). It had been a moving moment, and it was still fresh in Judah's mind.

D. Judah's Concern: vv. 30-31

How it must have moved Joseph's heart with deep emotion and great thankfulness to hear the next words of Judah. The older brother felt that he could not go back to his father without Benjamin. He feared that the shock of this would kill his father, and he did not want this to happen. He felt that if it did, he and his brothers would be responsible.

This is a very different attitude from that shown when the brothers had sold Joseph into slavery and then carried his blood-stained coat to their father. At that time they had shown no pity or compassion whatever. Now they all seemed concerned and distressed about their father's condition under such circumstances. Joseph must have been thanking the Lord silently for answering prayer.

E. Judah's Pledge: v. 32

Judah went on to tell how he had gone surety for Benjamin (cf. 43:9). He had agreed to assume all the blame if he did not bring the lad back with him. But it is good to sense that now his primary concern was for his father, not for himself. That is the test of true character, and it is always the test of love.

F. Judah's Offer: v. 33

The final test of devotion is: Are you ready to put your own life on the line? Judah passed this test. He said to Joseph: "Now therefore, I pray thee, let thy servant abide instead of the lad a bondman to my lord; and let the lad go up with his brethren." This proved that Judah cared more for his father and for his youngest brother than he did for himself. At last he had become a genuinely mature, loving person. And a person is not mature until he loves unselfishly.

G. Judah's Compassion for His Father: v. 34

This is the most beautiful verse in the entire chapter. Judah felt that he simply could not face his father unless he had Benjamin with him. He had come to the place where this was the thing that mattered most. He was willing to spend the rest of his life in slavery rather than see his father suffer.

There is no substitute for compassionate love. This is what the world desperately needs today. It is the only redemptive way of life. God give us more of it!

CONTEMPORARY APPLICATION

"How shall I go up to my father, and the lad be not with me?" This is a crucial question for fathers and mothers, for pastors and teachers, for youth workers and all of us. A Christian father should ask himself, "How can I go up to my heavenly Father, if my lad is not with me?" And this question confronts everyone who has any concern about the salvation of our youth. We must do what we can to be sure that they are not missing in heaven.

BECOMING RECONCILED

DEVOTIONAL READING	Ephesians 2:11-22

ADULTS

Topic: *Becoming Reconciled*

Background Scripture: Genesis 45; 50:14-26

Scripture Lesson: Genesis 45:4-8, 15; 50:15-21

Memory Verse: *If you are offering your gift at the altar, and there remember that your brother has something against you . . . first be reconciled to your brother, and then come and offer your gift.* Matthew 5:23-24

YOUTH

Topic: *Becoming Reconciled*

Background Scripture: Genesis 45; 50:14-26

Scripture Lesson: Genesis 45:4-8, 15; 50:15-21

Memory Verse: *If you are offering your gift at the altar, and there remember that your brother has something against you . . . first be reconciled to your brother, and then come and offer your gift.* Matthew 5:23-24

CHILDREN

Topic: *Forgiving One Another*

Background Scripture: Genesis 45:1-28; 50:14-26

Scripture Lesson: Genesis 50:15-21

Memory Verse: *Be kind to one another, tenderhearted, forgiving one another, as God in Christ forgave you.* Ephesians 4:32

DAILY BIBLE READINGS

Mon., Nov. 24: The Moment of Truth, Genesis 45:1-8.
Tues., Nov. 25: Joyful Reconciliation, Genesis 45:9-15.
Wed., Nov. 26: God Reunites a Family, Genesis 45:24–46:7.
Thurs., Nov. 27: The Ways of God with His People, Psalm 105:16-24.
Fri., Nov. 28: Christian Life Together, Colossians 3:12-17.
Sat., Nov. 29: The Strong and the Weak, Romans 15:1-6.
Sun., Nov. 30: The Commandment of Love, I John 2:7-11.

LESSON AIM

To see the conditions of reconciliation and the importance of it.

LESSON SETTING

Time: After 1700 B.C.

Place: Egypt

Becoming Reconciled

LESSON OUTLINE

SUGGESTED INTRODUCTION FOR ADULTS

One of the greatest needs in the world today is for reconciliation. There is a special sense in which only fellow Christians are our brothers—our brothers in the Lord. But there is also a general sense in which I am a brother to every other human being. We are all descended from Adam, and according to the Biblical picture we are all descended from Noah.

An excellent example of this problem of reconciliation is the case of Arabs and Jews. Here the common ancestry comes closer—probably in Abraham. So in a very real sense Arabs and Jews are brothers. But the relationship in the past has too often been like the earlier one between Joseph and his brothers. What is needed is a full reconciliation that will make the relationship like that which existed at the end of Genesis. We should always help to bring about reconciliation.

SUGGESTED INTRODUCTION FOR YOUTH

Are there bad feelings between different groups at your school? This may be due to either cultural or racial distinctions.

If there are, you should seek to be a point of reconciliation. Become a good friend to those in both groups and then try to bring them closer together in understanding and good will.

The truth is that most prejudice is due to ignorance. We don't like people because we do not really know them. If we would try to understand them we would find ourselves appreciating them more.

Instead of erecting barriers between people, we should try to build bridges. This is one of the most important tasks we can be engaged in.

CONCEPTS FOR
CHILDREN

1. One of the greatest things we can do is to forgive people.
2. We need for others to forgive us our faults; so we should be quick to forgive them.
3. We should always remember that Jesus forgives us.
4. His forgiveness helps us to forgive others.

THE LESSON COMMENTARY

I. JOSEPH REVEALING HIMSELF TO HIS BROTHERS: Genesis 45:1-3

Judah's words of confession, compassion, and concern were more than Joseph could take. Overcome with emotion, he was not able to control his feelings any longer. So he cried out, "Cause every man to go out from me." With no Egyptian in the house, Joseph made himself known to his brothers. It was a moment of high drama. No outsider was there, "But his sobs were so loud that the Egyptians could hear, and so the news reached Pharaoh's palace" (v. 2, *Anchor Bible*).

As soon as he could contain himself so that he could speak, he said, "I am Joseph; doth my father yet live?" (v. 3). This was his first concern. But his brothers were unable to answer him, "for they were troubled [or, "terrified"] at his presence." It is evident that in all the hours they had been with him, including eating dinner in his home, they had never once even suspected his identity. He looked and talked like a real Egyptian.

II. JOSEPH COMFORTING HIS BROTHERS: Genesis 45:4-8, 15

A. The One They Had Sold: v. 4

Joseph asked his brothers, who were standing at a respectful distance, to come closer to him. Hesitatingly, probably half afraid, they obeyed. Then he said, "I am Joseph your brother, whom ye sold into Egypt."

What a flood of memories that brought to their minds! Doubtless they sensed the contrast. At that time they were in command, and he was their helpless victim. Now he was the governor of Egypt, the man most admired everywhere at the moment, and they were at his mercy. Did they recall his dream about their eleven sheaves bowing down to his? Now that dream had come true. But Joseph was not taking advantage of it.

B. God's Purpose in It All: v. 5

Seeing their troubled faces, Joseph said in effect, "Don't worry; don't get angry with yourselves because you sold me here"—"for God did send me before you to preserve life" (v. 5). The Lord knew that the famine would come at a certain time, and so He had His servant Joseph ready to be the savior of the world as far as food was concerned.

But the fact that God was working out His purpose in having Joseph go to Egypt does not absolve the brothers from blame for the way they treated him. The relationship between divine sovereignty and human freedom is too great a problem for the finite mind to understand. But we have to hold the two unmistakable facts in tension just as we see them both operating in life. The man who isn't willing to live with unsolved intellectual problems hasn't grown up yet. God is infinite and we are finite. It is therefore inevitable that we cannot comprehend Him fully. We can know Him, but we cannot compass His greatness. God makes use of men's faults, but they are still responsible for them. We can't blame God for our failures. That truth is emphasized over and over in the Bible.

C. Continued Famine: v. 6

The famine had been in effect for two years now. This shows that the sons of Jacob had come down to Egypt at the end of both the first and second years of the drouth, when the crops failed. Famine is a very real specter in that part of the world, where people are directly dependent on adequate rainfall.

Because of Pharaoh's dream, Joseph knew that there would be five more years without crops. So his role would become more, rather than less, important and significant.

D. Saving His Brother's Lives: v. 7

Joseph's brothers had wanted to kill him. Now he reminds them that they would be dying of starvation if it were not for what he did. The whole future of Israel, God's people, was tied to his role of providing food to keep the sons of Israel alive. He had saved their lives by a "great"—gadol, "extraordinary"—deliverance. Joseph was thus a type of the great Savior of the world who was to come.

E. A Father to Pharaoh: v. 8

Joseph saw the hand of God in his life. Rather than condemning his brothers for their atrocious act, he could say, "So now it was not you that sent me hither, but God." Actually it was both. But Joseph preferred to acknowledge the divine overruling—that God works all things together for good to those who love him, to those who are called according to His purpose (Romans 8:28). Jacob was pessimistic by nature, and too often failed to see the divine working behind the human. But Joseph was optimistic by nature. That was one thing that kept him going when the road was rough.

Faith breeds optimism, for we know what the final outcome will be.

Joseph reminded his brothers that God had made him "a father to Pharaoh, and lord of all his house, and a ruler throughout all the land of Egypt." This was a tremendous honor. But it all came because Joseph held steady and trusted God.

F. Brotherly Love: v. 15

Joseph "fell upon his brother Benjamin's neck, and wept; and Benjamin wept upon his neck" (v. 14). Then he kissed all his brothers, in typical oriental style, and wept on their shoulders. It is no wonder that we read, "and after that his brethren talked with him." In the time of weeping together and showing love for each other their hearts had been melted together in love. Now they were truly brothers again. A genuine reconciliation had been effected.

III. JOSEPH SENDING FOR HIS FATHER: Genesis 45:9-13, 16-28

A. Message to His Father: vv. 9-13

Joseph told his brothers to hurry back to their father and tell him the good news that his son was alive and "lord of all Egypt" (v. 9). Jacob was to come down without delay and live in "the land of Goshen" (v. 10). This was in the northeast section of the Delta and was the best and most fertile part of Egypt. There Jacob, with his children and grandchildren would be near Joseph, for the capital of Egypt at this time was in the Delta. It was an excellent section for grazing—almost all of Egypt is desert—and so would care for Jacob's large herds and flocks. Joseph promised to take good care of his father and all the family during the remaining five years of the famine (v. 11).

Then Joseph said in effect: "You recognize me now, don't you" (v. 12). He wanted them to tell their father "of all my glory in Egypt, and of all that ye have seen" (v. 13). He concluded: "But hurry and bring my father down here" (*Anchor Bible*). After all these years of separation, Joseph was getting very anxious to see his father.

B. Pharaoh's Kindness: vv. 16-20

When the news about Joseph's brothers reached Pharaoh's palace, he and all his courtiers were pleased. This shows that Joseph had won a large place in their hearts.

Pharaoh then told Joseph to have his brothers load their donkeys and go back to Canaan and get their father. They were to bring him and all their families down to Egypt. And tell them, he said, "I will give you the best of the land of Egypt" (v. 18, NASB). They were to take wagons back with them for the women and children to ride in, as also their aged father (v. 19). Then Pharaoh added this message for them: "Do not concern yourselves with your goods, for the best of the land of Egypt is yours" (v. 20, NASB). It was very generous of Pharaoh to offer them the best place in the land.

C. Joseph's Provision for His Father: vv. 21-24

In accordance with Pharaoh's directions, Joseph supplied his brothers with wagons, provided them with food for the long journey, and gave each of them a new set of clothes. He showed his special love for Benjamin by giving him five changes of clothes and three hundred pieces of silver. He also sent to his father an abundant supply—"ten donkeys loaded with the best things of Egypt, and ten female donkeys loaded with grain and bread and sustenance for his father on the journey" (v. 23, NASB).

Wisely Joseph gave his brothers a parting word of advice: "See that ye fall not out by the way" (v. 24). He knew that there might easily be some quarreling about who was most responsible for their harsh treatment of Joseph. But it was no time for recriminations.

D. Jacob's Joy: vv. 25-28

When the brothers reached home, they immediately reported to their father: "Joseph is yet alive, and he is governor over all the land of Egypt." It would be hard to over-use our imagination in reconstructing that scene. We can see the incredulous look on the aged father's face. Impossible! It can't be! The description here is brief: "And Jacob's heart fainted"—better, "But he was stunned" (v. 26). At first he couldn't believe them.

Then the brothers told their father all that Joseph had said to them. When he saw the wagons that Joseph had sent to carry him, Jacob's spirit revived (v. 27). Thankfully he said: "It is enough; my son Joseph is still alive. I will go and see him before I die" (v. 28, NASB). He had never dreamed that this hour would ever come, and he must have been overjoyed.

And so he set out from Hebron. On the way he stopped at the desert town of Beersheba, "and offered sacrifices unto the God of his father Isaac" (46:1), who had lived there long before.

That night God appeared to him and assured him that what he was doing was right. He said: "I am God, the God of thy father: fear not to go down into Egypt; for I will make of thee a great nation: I will go down with thee into Egypt" (46:3-4). These words must have been a great comfort to Jacob.

IV. JOSEPH FORGIVING HIS BROTHERS: Genesis 50:15-21

A. The Concern of the Brothers: v. 15

Jacob had died. At Joseph's order, his father's body was embalmed and he was accorded a royal period of mourning—seventy days (v. 3). Then his body was carried in a large funeral procession of horsemen and chariots (v. 9). All twelve of his sons accompanied the body back to Canaan and buried it in Hebron. Then they all returned to Egypt.

With their father gone, the brothers were worried as to what Joseph's attitude toward them might be. They expressed their fear in these words: "What if Joseph should bear a grudge against us and pay us back in full for all the wrong which we did to him!" (NASB).

It is the tendency of everyone to judge others by himself. The brothers knew how hateful they had been toward Joseph in those younger years. They felt that he would certainly be resentful toward them for it all. It was hard for them to imagine anything else.

B. Asking for Forgiveness: vv. 16-17

So they sent a messenger to Joseph—they were evidently afraid to go themselves at first—to tell him that their father had made a special request before his death. He had asked them to say to Joseph: "Please forgive, I beg you, the transgression of your brothers and their sin; for they did you wrong." The brothers added, "And now please forgive the transgression of the servants of the God of your father" (v. 17, NASB).

The brothers had acknowledged to each other their sin in mistreating Joseph. But what they needed now was to confess it to him and definitely ask his forgiveness. This is what they were now doing. When Joseph heard their confession, he broke into tears.

C. Willing Submission of the Brothers: v. 18

Having paved the way through the messenger they sent, the brothers now approached Joseph personally. Bowing low before him, they said, "Behold, we are your servants" (NASB). They were willing to place themselves in

slavery to their younger brother, whom they had once sold into slavery. He would have been justified in accepting their offer. It was what they deserved, and they knew it.

D. Joseph Reassuring His Brothers: vv. 19-21

The one who was now in command of the situation quickly set their minds at ease. Joseph said to them: "Fear not: for am I in the place of God?" The Bible gives us God's word on this: "Vengeance is mine; I will repay, saith the Lord." We are not to show revenge in any way, but leave that to the Lord. When we seek vengeance ourselves for wrong, we are usurping God's authority. No man, whatever his office or position on earth, has a right to do it.

And then Joseph reminded his brothers of what he had already told them (45:5). "And as for you, you meant evil against me, but God meant it for good in order to bring about this present result, to preserve many people alive" (v. 20, NASB). This is a wonderful illustration of the old saying, "Man proposes, but God disposes."

This is also a striking illustration of God's omniscience, and particularly

DISCUSSION QUESTIONS

1. Why did Joseph not reveal to his brothers his identity when they first came?
2. What traits of character does Joseph exhibit in today's lesson?
3. In what ways was Joseph "a father to Pharaoh"?
4. Why did God approve Jacob and his family going down to Egypt?
5. What lessons of filial and fraternal love come out of this lesson?
6. What are some ways in which we may have a ministry of reconciliation?

His foreknowledge. A dozen years before the long and severe famine came, God knew it would come. He spent those dozen years preparing his young servant to be, in a physical sense, the savior of the world.

Again Joseph said, "Don't be afraid" (v. 21). He continued: "I will provide for you and your little ones" (NASB). He comforted them, and spoke "kindly to them"—literally, "to their heart."

Once more we see Joseph as a type of Christ, who prayed for His persecutors, "Father, forgive them for they know not what they do."

So Joseph reassured his fearful brothers. They must have marveled at his wonderful spirit of forgiveness. They didn't deserve it, but then, not one of us deserves God's forgiveness and the grace He so freely pours out on us.

CONTEMPORARY APPLICATION

Jesus said, "Love your enemies." This is one of the greatest tests of our Christian profession. Such love is not natural; it is supernatural. We cannot have this kind of love in our hearts except as the Holy Spirit fills our hearts to generate such love within.

And one of the greatest proofs of love is forgiveness. To say that we love and then refuse to forgive is to give the lie to our testimony. If we love, we can and must forgive everyone who has wronged us, regardless of the circumstances.

SECOND QUARTER

THE GOSPEL OF MATTHEW

UNDERSTANDING MATTHEW'S GOSPEL

DEVOTIONAL READING	Psalm 9:1-8

ADULTS

Topic: *Understanding Matthew's Gospel*

Background Scripture: Matthew 1:1-17; 4:23-25; 9:9-13

Scripture Lesson: Matthew 9:9-13; 1:1, 17; 4:23-25

Memory Verse: *He went about all Galilee, teaching in their synagogues and preaching the gospel of the kingdom and healing every disease and every infirmity among the people.* Matthew 4:23

YOUTH

Topic: *Understanding Matthew's Gospel*

Background Scripture: Matthew 1:1-17; 4:23-25; 9:9-13

Scripture Lesson: Matthew 9:9-13; 1:1, 17; 4:23-25

Memory Verse: *He went about all Galilee, teaching in their synagogues and preaching the gospel of the kingdom and healing every disease and every infirmity among the people.* Matthew 4:23

CHILDREN

Topic: *Come and Follow*

Background Scripture: Matthew 4:23-25; 9:9-13

Scripture Lesson: Matthew 9:9-13

Memory Verse: *He said to him, "Follow me." And he rose and followed him.* Matthew 9:9

DAILY BIBLE READINGS

Mon., Dec. 1: Ancient Promises, Isaiah 40:1-5.
Tues., Dec. 2: Good Tidings, Isaiah 40:6-11.
Wed., Dec. 3: Jesus' Ministry Begins, Matthew 4:17-22.
Thurs., Dec. 4: A Time for Joy, Matthew 9:14-17.
Fri., Dec. 5: The Authority of Jesus, Matthew 8:5-13.
Sat., Dec. 6: Christ's Power over Us, Ephesians 2:1-10.
Sun., Dec. 7: New Life for All, Colossians 3:1-11.

LESSON AIM

To help us understand the nature and purpose of Matthew's Gospel.

LESSON SETTING

Time: The call of Matthew was probably in A.D. 28. His Gospel was written around A.D. 60 or 70.

Place: The call came in Capernaum, on the northern shore of the Lake of Galilee. The Gospel was probably written in Palestine.

Understanding Matthew's Gospel

SUGGESTED INTRODUCTION FOR ADULTS

Renan, the famous French critic, said that Matthew's Gospel was "the most important book of Christendom—the most important book that has ever been written." It was the most widely used Gospel in the early church, and today we especially treasure it for such passages as the Sermon on the Mount.

It is fitting, therefore, that twenty sessions should be devoted to a study of its twenty-eight chapters. Today's lesson deals with the nature and purpose of this Gospel. The next lesson notes the Messianic emphasis of Matthew. Then the major events and teachings of the Gospel are studied in succession.

The word *gospel* means "good news." It is used in the New Testament (77 times) for the good news of salvation through Jesus Christ. Later the church applied the term "Gospel" to each of the first four books of the New Testament. But always it is the "Gospel According to Matthew," " . . . According to Mark," etc. It is one gospel or good news, but described by four writers. (The custom today is to capitalize "Gospel" when it refers to one or more of these four books, but not to capitalize it when used for the good news of salvation.)

SUGGESTED INTRODUCTION FOR YOUTH

What can Jesus mean to you? The answer to this question can be found, at least in part, through a study of the Gospel According to Matthew. Here we see Jesus meeting people's needs everywhere He went, and we know that He can meet our needs today.

Jesus called Matthew to follow Him. And He is still calling young people. May we follow Him, as Matthew did!

CONCEPTS FOR CHILDREN

1. Matthew had a well-paying job as tax collector.
2. He was willing to leave his job and follow Jesus.

3. In his Gospel he shares with us his understanding of Jesus.
4. Jesus calls all of us to follow Him.

THE LESSON COMMENTARY

I. THE CALL OF MATTHEW: Matthew 9:9-13

A. The Call: v. 9

Matthew is spoken of as Levi in the other two Synoptic Gospels (Mark 2:14; Luke 5:27, 29) in connection with his call. But he is designated as Matthew in the four lists of the twelve apostles (Matthew 10:3; Mark 3:18; Luke 6:15; Acts 1:13). These are the only five times that the name Matthew is used in the New Testament.

Levi is a familiar name in the Old Testament. We think immediately of the tribe of Levi, from which the priests were taken. Matthew is a Greek term, derived from the Hebrew meaning "gift of Yahweh" (or Jehovah). We do not know whether Levi adopted this second name, as Jews often did in that day (for example, Saul-Paul, John-Mark) or whether it was given him when he became a Christian. In any case, he is always referred to in the early church as "Matthew."

He was a tax collector in Capernaum, the city that Jesus had selected as His headquarters (Mark 1:21). When Jesus passed by on the street, Matthew was sitting at the "receipt of custom." This is one word in Greek, *telonion.* The meaning of this term is uncertain. It could have been a sort of customs office, where fishermen paid a tax on the fish they caught in the Lake of Galilee. Or it might have been a "place of toll" (ASV), a tollhouse on the highway between Damascus and Egypt where caravans would have to pay a toll on their goods. Probably the best translation is "tax collector's booth" (NIV), an open stall facing on one of the main streets of Capernaum.

In any case, it was here that Matthew received his call—just two words:

"Follow me." But these two words changed the course of his whole life. Up to this time he had been concerned with making money and taking care of himself. From now on he would be a follower of the Master. He had a new Boss and a new vocation.

What was Matthew's response to this call? "And he arose, and followed him." The Greek is more forceful than the English. By the use of the aorist tense for both verbs it suggests immediate action: "He got right up and followed Jesus." There was no hesitation, no debate, no putting off the decision. It seems altogether likely that Matthew had been observing Jesus and perhaps listening to some of His teaching. Now he was ready to become His disciple.

B. The Banquet: v. 10

"Sat at meat" means "reclined at the table." In those days many Jewish homes had adopted the Roman custom of reclining on couches around the table while eating their main meals. This is clearly the setting in the upper room at the Last Supper, making it easy for Jesus to wash the disciples' feet.

"The house" would naturally mean "his house"—that is, Matthew's—which Mark specifically says (Mark 2:15). But Luke is even more explicit as to the place and also as to the nature of the meal. He says, "Then Levi held a great banquet for Jesus at his house" (5:29, NIV). It probably served a twofold purpose, serving as a "going away party," when Matthew left his old job and associates, and also honoring his new Master.

But there was something more, something extremely important. We read that "many publicans and sinners came and sat down ["reclined to-gether"] with him and his disciples." Matthew wanted his former colleagues to get acquainted with Jesus. As we would say it now, there was an evangelistic purpose in Matthew's expensive banquet.

A word should be said about the term *publicans* that occurs frequently in the Synoptic Gospels (22 times, and nowhere else in the New Testament). The Greek *telonai* should be translated "tax collectors." The Roman *publicani* were wealthy aristocrats who had the responsibility of securing the taxes of large areas of the empire. But the *telonai* of the Gospels were local Jews who did the actual collecting of taxes on animals, fruit trees, wells, and other property.

C. Complaint of the Pharisees: v. 11

The term *Pharisees* means "separated ones." They comprised a sect in Judaism that sprang up during the intertestamental period in revolt against the "worldliness" of the Sadducees, the priestly group. Like many separatists, these Pharisees had degenerated into harsh legalists, condemning others. They considered themselves to be the only "pure" people among the Jews.

The word *sinners* here does not necessarily mean those who lived in outbroken wickedness, but rather the common people who failed to keep all the meticulous regulations of the Law—both the Mosaic law in the five books of the Old Testament and the oral tradition that the Pharisees had added to it. These "sinners" were considered to be ceremonially unclean and not fit for godly people to associate with.

So the Pharisees asked the disciples, "Why does your teacher eat with tax collectors and 'sinners'?" (NIV). These religious legalists felt that they would be contaminated if they ate with "unclean" people. It is a significant fact that "common" and "un-clean" were synonymous terms in the thinking of the Pharisees.

D. The Reply of Jesus: vv. 12-13

Jesus answered His critics by quoting what may have been a popular proverb: "It is not the healthy who need a doctor, but the sick" (NIV). The Pharisees considered themselves to be in good spiritual health; so they rejected the Great Physician. But the common people recognized their own sickness, and so turned to Him. One of the greatest hindrances to evangelism has always been the fact that people are complacent about their condition in God's sight. Until they see themselves as sinners they will not seek His salvation.

The Master then reminded these teachers of the Law that the Old Testament supported His point of view. He quoted from Hosea 6:6: "I desire mercy, not sacrifice" (NIV). No amount of animals offered on the altar would compensate for the lack of compassionate mercy. It is still true today that ritualism is no substitute for righteousness, and legalism will not be accepted in place of love. It was the Pharisees who were actually the ungodly ones, because of their lack of Godlike love.

Then Jesus added: "For I have not come to call the righteous, but sinners" (NIV). The additional phrase "to repentance" (KJV) is not in the early Greek manuscripts but was supplied by a medieval scribe.

Self-righteousness is one of the greatest barriers to salvation. As long as people think they are all right they are not going to seek God. We should not infer from this text that Jesus considered the Pharisees as actually righteous; "the righteous" and "sinners" were the labels they used to distinguish themselves from other people.

Jesus was accused of being the friend of sinners. Actually that was the greatest compliment He could have been given. If we are His true followers, we must also be the sinner's friend—in holy, redeeming love.

II. THE GENEALOGY OF JESUS: Matthew 1:1-17

A. The Heading: v. 1

The Greek word translated "book" is *biblos*, from which we get "Bible." The Bible is "The Book," as Sir Walter Scott said on his deathbed.

The word translated "generation" is *genesis*, which we have taken over into English in the sense of "beginning." It could be translated "origin." Scholars are divided on the question as to whether verse 1 is to be taken as the title of the entire book or just as the heading for 1:2-17. Most favor the latter—"A record of the genealogy of Jesus Christ, son of David, son of Abraham" (NIV).

The dual name "Jesus Christ" is of special interest. "Jesus" is the Greek equivalent of the Hebrew *yehoshua* (Joshua), meaning "Yahweh will save." The Greek *christos* equals the Hebrew *mashia* (Messiah)—"anointed one." The Subject of this Gospel is identified as the Savior-Messiah.

Two other titles are given Him. The first, "son of David," was a common Messianic title (21:9). It showed that Jesus was the rightful heir to the throne of David and to the kingdom that God had promised to David's descendants forever (II Samuel 7:16).

The second, "son of Abraham," indicated that Jesus was a true Israelite. No Gentile would be acceptable to the Jews as their leader.

This leads us to note the first and most evident characteristic of Matthew: It was written by a Jew and for Jews, to present to them Jesus as their Messiah and King. This is why it begins with the genealogy of Jesus, tracing it to Abraham, whereas Luke's genealogy of Jesus goes back to Adam (Luke 3:23-38). After the Babylonian captivity the Jews gave a great deal of attention to genealogies, as evidenced by Ezra, Nehemiah, and the first nine chapters of I Chronicles. The first thing that Matthew must say to his Jewish readers about Jesus was that He was the son of Abraham and the son of David. Then he had to support this claim by tracing Jesus' descent from Abraham through David to His foster-father, Joseph. This gave Him the legal right to the throne.

B. The Names: vv. 2-16

Of special interest is the list of names between David and the end of the Kingdom of Judah in 586 B.C. (vv. 6-11). These were the kings of Judah whose reigns are described in Kings and Chronicles. So Jesus was the living heir to the throne of David.

A unique feature of the genealogy is the mention of four women. Two of them, Rahab and Ruth, were Gentiles. The other two, Tamar and Bathsheba ("the wife of Urias") were guilty of adultery or incest. This underscores Jesus' mission of salvation to all men, and outstandingly to sinners and Gentiles. It displays the "exceeding grace" of God.

We must not fail to note the significance of verse 16. Joseph did not physically beget Jesus. So the language changes from the repeated "begat" of verses 2-15 to "Joseph the husband of Mary, of whom [Mary] was born Jesus, who is called Christ." Thus the virgin birth, which is explicitly asserted in the opening chapters of Matthew and Luke, is carefully protected in the wording of this genealogical table.

C. The Divisions: v. 17

Why did Matthew divide the genealogy of Jesus into three sections of fourteen generations each? The answer seems to be that the numerical value of the Hebrew letters in *David* adds up to fourteen. So it is a play on the word "David." The first section gives us the period of the patriarchs and judges, the second that of the kings and the third that of Gentile domination.

This feature underscores another characteristic of Matthew's Gospel: systematic arrangement. Matthew, as a tax collector, was used to keeping books. His Gospel is more systematic than the others. He organizes it around five great discourses: the Sermon on the Mount (chaps. 5–7), Instructions to the Twelve (9:35–10:42), Parables of the Christian Community (chap. 13), the Christian Community (chap. 18), and the Olivet Discourse (chaps. 24–25). In between these are narrative sections. The idea of having five discourses is evidently patterned on the five Books of Moses (Genesis–Deuteronomy).

In connection with this we might note Matthew's fondness for numbers. We have already noticed two of them— three and five. In chapter 13 he has seven (perfect number) parables of the Kingdom. He adds seven and three to make ten miracles in chapters 8 and 9.

III. A MINISTRY TO THE MULTI-TUDES:
Matthew 4:23-25

A. A Threefold Ministry: v. 23

There were three aspects of Jesus' ministry to the large crowds that gathered around Him—teaching, preaching, and healing. The teaching was carried on at first mainly in the "synagogues." This word, which we have taken over from the Greek, literally means "a gathering together." So it referred primarily to an organized group that gathered for worship. But, as in the case of "church," it soon came to be used for the building in which the congregation met. These synagogues sprang up after the temple was destroyed—either during or right after the Babylonian captivity.

Jesus' preaching seems to have been mainly by the lakeside, or on mountain slopes. Wherever the crowds gathered, Christ was eager to preach to them "the gospel of the kingdom"— that in Him the kingdom of God had come.

Along with His teaching and preaching, Christ carried on a healing ministry to the multitude. This helped to swell the size of the crowds, so that more people heard the gospel.

B. A Healing Ministry: v. 24

This phase is enlarged on in this verse. "All Syria" would include Palestine, as well as what we now know as Syria and Lebanon. The fame of Christ spread through all this area.

The result was that people brought to Him their sick from all directions. "Divers" we now call "diverse." In the New Testament "devils" (KJV) should always be translated "demons." The Greek word is *daimonia*; there are many demons. But the word for "devil," *diabolos*, is always in the singular; there is only one devil. "Lunatick" should be translated "epileptics." The New International Version gives the correct translation of this verse: "News about him spread all over Syria, and people brought to him all who were ill with various diseases, those suffering severe pain, the demon-possessed, the epileptics and the paralytics, and he healed them." Jesus was adequate for every need, and He still is.

C. A Widespread Ministry: v. 25

Large crowds followed Jesus. They came from "Galilee," the northern part of Palestine. They came from the "Decapolis," which means "Ten Cities." This was the area dominated by ten cities with Greek culture, situated east of the Jordan River and the

---

DISCUSSION QUESTIONS

1. How does Christ call people today?
2. What does it mean to "follow" Jesus?
3. In what ways is the personality of Matthew reflected in his Gospel?
4. How was healing related to Jesus' ministry?
5. Should it have any place today in the church?
6. What is the relation of teaching and preaching?

Sea of Galilee. They also came from "Jerusalem," which was a hundred miles to the south—nearly a week's walk away. "Judea" refers to the southern part of Palestine, in which Jerusalem was situated. "Beyond Jordan" means the east side of the Jordan River, opposite Judea. In modern times this has been called Transjordan. In Jesus' day it was called Peraea, from the Greek preposition *peran*, "across." Jesus drew them all.

CONTEMPORARY APPLICATION

Matthew has set us an example of how we may win people to Christ. He put on a big banquet for his fellow tax collectors. The result is that we read in the Gospels of many of these following Jesus.

One of the best ways to win the unsaved is to invite them to your home for dinner on Sunday and ask if they would like to go to church with you before dinner. Most will accept. An alternative would be to invite them for dinner some evening and then present the claims of the gospel. A little unselfish effort and expense could mean the salvation of souls.

MATTHEW AND THE MESSIAH

DEVOTIONAL READING | Isaiah 42:1-9

ADULTS

Topic: *Matthew and the Messiah*

Background Scripture: Matthew 12:15-21; 13:34-35; 21:1-5

Scripture Lesson: Matthew 12:15-21; 13:34-35; 21:1-5

Memory Verse: *All this has taken place, that the scriptures of the prophets might be fulfilled.* Matthew 26:56

YOUTH

Topic: *Matthew and the Messiah*

Background Scripture: Matthew 12:15-21; 13:34-35; 21:1-5

Scripture Lesson: Matthew 12:15-21; 13:34-35; 21:1-5

Memory Verse: *All this has taken place that the scriptures of the prophets might be fulfilled.* Matthew 25:56

CHILDREN

Topic: *Who Is Jesus?*

Background Scripture: Genesis 12:2; I Kings 11:9-13; Isaiah 9:6-7; Matthew 9:27-31; 12:15-21; 13:34-35; 21:4-5; 26:56

Scripture Lesson: Matthew 9:27-31

Memory Verse: *For to us a child is born,*
 to us a son is given;
 and the government will be upon his shoulder,
 and his name will be called
 "Wonderful Counselor, Mighty God,
 Everlasting Father, Prince of Peace."
 Isaiah 9:6

DAILY BIBLE READINGS

Mon., Dec. 8: Assurance of God's Victory, Isaiah 52:7-15.
Tues., Dec. 9: The Coming of the Messiah, Isaiah 9:1-7.
Wed., Dec. 10: The Suffering Servant, Isaiah 53:1-6.
Thurs., Dec. 11: Peter's Witness to Christ, Acts 2:22-36.
Fri., Dec. 12: Jesus Exalted, Philippians 2:5-11.
Sat., Dec. 13: The Sign of the Messiah, Zechariah 9:9-14.
Sun., Dec. 14: A Song of Exultation, Psalm 118:19-26.

LESSON AIM | To understand Matthew's presentation of Jesus as the Messiah.

LESSON SETTING | Time: About A.D. 29-30.

Place: Galilee and Jerusalem

Matthew and the Messiah

LESSON OUTLINE

SUGGESTED INTRODUCTION FOR ADULTS

The main characteristic of Matthew's Gospel is that it presents Jesus to the Jews as their Messiah. That is why it comes first in the New Testament, even though Mark's Gospel was probably written earlier. Paul tells us that salvation was first offered to the Jews and then to the Gentiles (Romans 1:16). Also, this Gospel, with its opening genealogy and its many quotations from the older Scriptures, forms a logical transition from the Old Testament to the New. It is the connecting link between the two.

Matthew presents the Messiah as the divine King. There is more emphasis on "the kingdom" in his Gospel than in the others. In fact, that expression occurs over fifty times. Most of the parables in Matthew's Gospel are related to the kingdom. For instance, in the thirteenth chapter we find seven parables of the kingdom (see Lesson 10).

The Jews of Jesus' day were looking for the Messiah to come. This was especially evident among such groups as the Essenes at Qumran, as revealed in the Dead Sea Scrolls. But the last part of our lesson today shows that the Messiah was to come in meekness, not in a display of political power.

SUGGESTED INTRODUCTION FOR YOUTH

Who was Jesus? He was the Son of God who became the Son of Man. He was also the Messiah, for whom long generations had waited. And He became the Savior of the world.

But the important question is: What does Jesus mean to you? Is He your Savior and Lord? That is the question that each person must answer.

CONCEPTS FOR CHILDREN	1. When Jesus was on earth people turned to Him for help. 2. They sensed that He was the Son of David, the Messiah whom God had sent. 3. Jesus is present today in spiritual power. 4. He wants us to turn to Him for help.

THE LESSON COMMENTARY

I. THE SERVANT OF THE LORD: Matthew 12:15-21

A. The Messianic Secret: vv. 15-16

Jesus had just healed the man with the withered hand (vv. 9-13). This infuriated the Pharisees, because He had done it on the sabbath day, when such work as healing was not to be done. So they "went out, and held a council against him, how they might destroy him" (v. 14).

"Aware of this, Jesus withdrew from that place" (v. 15, NIV). His life was not safe in Capernaum at the moment. So He went out by the Lake of Galilee, where He would have the protection of large crowds surrounding Him (Mark 3:7). The religious leaders wanted to kill Jesus, but the common people loved Him and flocked to hear Him. The Pharisees would not dare to try to arrest Him when these sympathetic followers were with Him.

The compassionate Christ healed all who came to Him with their illnesses and diseases. But He was "warning them not to tell who he was" (v. 16, NIV). Why? The answer is given in Mark 1:45. When Jesus had healed a leper, He strictly charged the man not to tell anyone about it. But, "instead he went out and began to talk freely, spreading the news. As a result, Jesus could no longer enter a town openly but stayed outside in lonely places. Yet the people still came to him from everywhere" (NIV). The people were flocking to Jesus to be healed. This prevented Him from carrying on His teaching ministry, which was far more important. The people had to realize that their souls needed to be healed more than their bodies. This truth still needs to be sounded today.

But there was another reason for the enjoined silence. After Peter's confession at Caesarea Philippi that Jesus was the Messiah, Christ warned His disciples that they should "tell no one that he was Jesus the Christ"—the Messiah (Matthew 16:16-20). Why? Because the Jews of that day thought that the Messiah would come as a military and political leader, to free them from the foreign domination of Rome. The Zealots of Jesus' day were carrying on guerrilla uprisings against the Roman government and seeking to overthrow it. Jesus would have none of this. He did not want talk about His Messiahship to precipitate a Palestinean revolt against Rome (John 6:15). He had come to set up a spiritual kingdom in the hearts of men, not a political kingdom. So he sought to quash any publicity about His being the Messiah.

This is what is called the Messianic secret. Because the Jews had a distorted concept of the Messiah, it would not have been safe or wise for Him to be known publicly as such.

B. Fulfillment of Prophecy: v. 17

One of the key phrases of Matthew's Gospel is "that it might be fulfilled." In that or similar form it occurs no less than thirteen times in Matthew, but not at all in Mark or Luke. D. A. Hayes notes: "Altogether nineteen Old Testament books ... are used by Matthew in the composition of his Gospel. Fifteen Old Testament characters are mentioned by name, besides those whose names occur in the genealogy. The Gospel according to Matthew is a New Testament book, but it is built upon Old Testament foundations throughout" (*The Synoptic Gos-*

pels and the Book of Acts, p. 47).
Hayes comments: "The first Gospel is
almost a manual of Messianic prophecy" (ibid., p. 44).

"Esaias" is the Greek form of the
Hebrew "Isaiah." If one is reading the
King James Version of the New Testament in public and comes across a
name like this, he should always use
the form which is familiar to us from
the Old Testament.

C. God's Chosen Servant: v. 18

The quotation in verses 18-20 is
taken from Isaiah 42:1-3. It appears to
be a rather free translation of the Hebrew.

One of the striking features of the
latter part of Isaiah is the so-called
Servant Songs, where the coming Messiah is presented as the Servant of the
Lord. Isaiah 42:1-4 is the first of
these. The second is found in 49:1-13
and the third one in 50:4-11. The
fourth and greatest of them is Isaiah
52:13—53:12, which pictures the Suffering Servant of the Lord. The Jews
have generally referred these passages
to Israel, as the Lord's servant, suffering in exile but to be restored. The
New Testament, however, shows that
they are Messianic.

Jesus was God's "chosen" and "beloved" servant, as the Father's voice
from heaven indicated at the baptism
(3:17). The Greek word for "servant,"
pais, may also be translated "son."
Jesus was both the Son of God and the
Servant of the Lord, fulfilling the Old
Testament prophecies concerning the
latter.

"I will put my spirit upon him"
was fulfilled at the time of Jesus' baptism by John, when the Holy Spirit
descended on Him in the form of a
dove (3:16). "Judgment" is better
translated "justice." Jesus came to
bring justice and mercy not only to
the Jews, but to all nations.

D. The Gentleness of the Messiah: v. 19

The Messiah would not come as a
military despot or a domineering poli-

tician. Rather, He would be a gentle
leader of men. And Christ wants His
followers to be gentle, not self-assert-
ive and abusive.

The quotation from Isaiah is poetic
in form. This verse should read (NIV):
"He will not quarrel or cry out; no one
will hear his voice in the streets."
Christ was not a debater or a dema-
gogue. He simply declared divine truth
in love.

E. The Patience of the Messiah: v. 20

What is meant by the "bruised
reed" and "smoking flax" (wick)? William Hendriksen suggests that in the
context of the reference to justice
being proclaimed to the Gentiles (v.
18) and the Gentiles trusting in His
name (v. 21) these terms "must be
taken figuratively, as referring to those
from afar, to the weak and helpless,
those of little faith, etc." He adds:
"What a contrast between the cruelty
of the Pharisees and the kindness of
Jesus, between their vanity and his re-
serve, their love for display and his
meekness" (*New Testament Commentary:* "Matthew," pp. 521-22).

Commenting on verses 19 and 20
in the *Cambridge Greek Testament,*
Carr says: "These verses describe the
gentleness and forbearance of Christ.
He makes no resistance or loud proclamation like an earthly prince. The
bruised reed and the feebly burning
wick may be referred to the failing
lives which Jesus restores and the
spark of faith which He revives"
("Matthew," p. 179). Alford writes
that these metaphors represent "a proverbial expression for 'He will not
crush the contrite heart, nor extin-
guish the slightest spark of repentant
feeling in the sinner' " (*Greek Testament,* I, 127).

"Till he send forth judgment unto
victory" means "till he leads justice to
victory" (NIV). In a world that is po-
litically corrupt and morally wicked,
justice will finally triumph through
Christ. James Morison comments:
"The idea is that the Messiah shall

persevere in His own quiet, gentle, meek, unostentatious, unobstreperous way, healing heart after heart, and adjusting difference after difference, until He shall succeed in getting His gracious arbitrative action thrust in victoriously upon all the injustices and unrighteousnesses that alienate man from man, and men from God" (*A Practical Commentary on the Gospel According to St. Matthew*, p. 204).

F. Salvation for the Gentiles: v. 21

"Trust" should be translated "hope"—"In his name the nations will put their hope" (NIV). Christ is the only hope for the world today, for Jews and Gentiles alike.

II. JESUS' USE OF PARABLES: Matthew 13:34-35

A. His Regular Method of Teaching: v. 34

The word *parable* comes from the Greek *parabole*, which literally means "a throwing beside," that is, a comparison—a story is placed beside a truth to illustrate it. So Jesus' parables were somewhat like sermon illustrations today.

To capture the attention of the thousands of people who crowded around Him, Jesus spoke in parables. When talking to His disciples He used a more direct method of teaching.

The comparisons that Jesus used were taken mostly from life in the home or out in the fields. It is still true that homely illustrations are often most effective because most familiar.

It is generally agreed by scholars that there are no true parables in John's Gospel—though some dispute this. How many are there in the Synoptic Gospels? There is not complete agreement here. If one includes short, parabolic statements, a list of fifty or more can be compiled. But the number of parable-stories would be about thirty. Taking this figure—which we prefer—there are four parables in

Mark, fifteen in Matthew, and about eighteen in Luke.

B. Fulfillment of Prophecy: v. 35

Again we find the expression "that it might be fulfilled which was spoken." The quotation is attributed to "the prophet," but comes from Psalm 78:2. This simply underscores the fact that the psalmist was in a real sense a prophet. The word *prophet* comes from the Greek *prophetes*, which means "one who speaks for another." That is what all the Biblical writers do.

Psalm 78 is credited to Asaph. As a prophet he recounted God's dealings with Israel. In a sense these constituted a parable of what God intended to do with His people ahead. So the whole psalm could be thought of as a parabolic discourse, revealing truth that had been somewhat hidden.

III. THE PRESENTATION OF THE MESSIAH: Matthew 21:1-5

A. Jesus' Final Approach to Jerusalem: v. 1

It was Jesus' last fateful journey to Jerusalem. Here He had always encountered the sharpest opposition and here His life was in greatest danger.

The longest span of Christ's public ministry was centered in Galilee. But He had left there for the last time and was now headed for the Passover celebration in the Holy City.

Coming in from the east, Jesus arrived at Bethphage ("house of figs") on the slopes of the Mount of Olives. The Master sent two of His disciples into that village on an important errand.

B. Securing a Donkey: vv. 2-3

Jesus told the two men that they would find in the village a donkey tied in the street, with its colt by its side. They were to untie them and bring them to Him. The other Gospels mention only the colt. But anyone who has handled animals knows that it would be much easier to lead the colt away if its mother was allowed to accompany it.

If anyone protested to the disciples about their untying and taking the animals, they were to say, "The Lord needs them." In the first two Gospels Jesus is called "Lord" only here and in the parallel passage in Mark (11:3). Luke refers to Jesus as Lord sixteen times.

The explanation would satisfy the bystanders, and they would permit the animals to be taken. It is evident that Jesus here shows supernatural knowledge of unseen circumstances.

C. Fulfillment of Prophecy: v. 4

Characteristically, Matthew again quotes from the Old Testament. And once more we find the familiar formula: "that it might be fulfilled which was spoken by the prophet." Jesus' life and ministry were a fulfillment of Old Testament prophecy.

D. The Meekness of the Messiah: v. 5

The quotation is from Zechariah 9:9, a passage with Messianic overtones. When Jesus rode the donkey into Jerusalem on Sunday of Passion Week, He was deliberately presenting Himself to the nation as its Messiah. The religious leaders, who were very familiar with their Scriptures, could hardly fail to recognize this. The so-called Triumphal Entry was an enacted parable of His Messiahship. Jesus was unmistakably fulfilling a Messianic prophecy. The die was cast.

"The daughter of Sion" (Zion) was a poetic expression for "the people of Jerusalem." It was to them that Jesus presented Himself that day as their Messiah-King.

The poetic form of the quotation is brought out well in the New International Version:

"Say to the daughter of Zion,
   'See, your king comes to you,

gentle and riding on a donkey,
   on a colt, the foal of a donkey.' "

The parallelism of Hebrew poetry would suggest that only one animal is mentioned in Zechariah. "And a colt" could just as accurately be translated "even a colt."

But verse 7 indicates that two animals were actually brought to Jesus. The disciples took off their outer cloaks and put them on the animals, "and he sat on them" (literal rendering). On the two animals? This is preposterous! Jesus sat on the clothes that they had placed as a blanket on the colt.

Carping critics have had a field day asserting that Matthew pictures Jesus riding on two animals at once. The simplest answer to that is that a person stupid enough to portray that could never have written this masterly Gospel. R. V. G. Tasker says quite succinctly: "The authors of Scripture did not write nonsense, and Jesus did not ride on two animals at once" (*The Gospel According to St. Matthew*, p. 198).

The crowds that accompanied Jesus on His "Triumphal Entry" were composed of Passover pilgrims from Galilee. They had seen His matchless miracles, and now they acclaimed Him enthusiastically as the Messiah, "the son of David" and "he that cometh in the name of the Lord" (v. 9). "Hosanna" literally means "Save, we pray."

DISCUSSION QUESTIONS

1. What was the purpose of the Messianic secret?
2. What is the nature of Christ's kingdom?
3. By what methods should we seek to bring it in?
4. What does Jesus' use of parables suggest to us?
5. Why did the Jewish leaders reject Jesus?
6. What will happen at His second coming?

But here it was probably equivalent to the cry, "God save the king!"

Since these first two lessons of the quarter are intended to serve as introductory to Matthew, we should like to close with a striking resumé of that Gospel by Farrar. He writes: "From the cradle to the Resurrection the action never pauses. Side by side in overwhelming scenes the teaching advances in depth and clearness, the power in mercy and miracle. Side by side there is an increasing vehemence of hatred and an intensified adoration of love and trust. Louder and louder roll over the maddened Pharisees the terrible thunders of His rebuke; softer and more softly are breathed to His disciples the promises of His infinite consolation. . . . Then the pillars of the kingdom of heaven seem to be shattered to the lowest foundations, as its King descends, amid the derision of raging and triumphant enemies, through shame and anguish, to the Valley of Death. But, lo! when all seems lost . . . suddenly, as with a flash of lightning out of the blue sky, the cross becomes the throne, and the sepulchre the portal of immortality; and shattering the gates of brass, and smiting the bars of iron in sunder, He rises from death to life, from earth to heaven, and sends forth His twelve chosen ones, armed with the implement of a malefactor's torture, and with 'the irresistible might of meekness,' to shake, to conquer, to evangelize, to enlighten, to rule the world" (*Messages of the Books*, pp. 46-47).

CONTEMPORARY APPLICATION

As Christians we are to represent Christ. He did not present Himself as a high and mighty personality, with military or political power, but as the meek and lowly Messiah. We are to follow in His footsteps.

December 21, 1975

IN SEARCH OF THE KING

DEVOTIONAL READING	Psalm 72:1-11

ADULTS

Topic: *In Search of the King*

Background Scripture: Matthew 1:18—2:23

Scripture Lesson: Matthew 2:1-12

Memory Verse: *His name shall be called Emmanuel (which means, God with us).* Matthew 1:23

YOUTH

Topic: *In Search of the King*

Background Scripture: Matthew 1:18—2:23

Scripture Lesson: Matthew 2:1-12

Memory Verse: *His name shall be called Emmanuel (which means, God with us).* Matthew 1:23

CHILDREN

Topic: *In Search of the King*

Background Scripture: Matthew 1:18—2:23

Scripture Lesson: Matthew 2:1-12

Memory Verse: *Where is he who has been born King of the Jews? For we have seen his star in the east and have come to worship him.* Matthew 2:2

DAILY BIBLE READINGS

Mon., Dec. 15: The Word of the Angel, Matthew 1:18-25.
Tues., Dec. 16: The Wise Men Come, Matthew 2:1-6.
Wed., Dec. 17: The Wise Men Worship, Matthew 2:7-12.
Thurs., Dec. 18: The Anger of Herod, Matthew 2:13-18.
Fri., Dec. 19: From Egypt to Nazareth, Matthew 2:19-23.
Sat., Dec. 20: Isaiah's Vision of the Kingdom, Isaiah 32:1-8.
Sun., Dec. 21: The Heavenly Reign, Revelation 21:22—22:5.

LESSON AIM

To see the importance of seeking Jesus, no matter what the cost.

LESSON SETTING

Time: About 5 B.C.

Place: Jerusalem and Bethlehem, both in Judea

LESSON OUTLINE

In Search of the King

I. The Birth of Jesus: Matthew 1:18-25

113

A. A Devastating Discovery: vv. 18-19
B. A Divine Disclosure: vv. 20-21
C. A Fulfillment of Prophecy: vv. 22-23
D. A Devout Servant: vv. 24-25

II. The Visit of the Wise Men: Matthew 2:1-12
    A. The Magi from the East: v. 1
    B. The Search in Jerusalem: v. 2
    C. The Concern of the King: v. 3
    D. The King's Question: v. 4
    E. The Reply of the Scribes: vv. 5-6
    F. The Duplicity of the King: vv. 7-8
    G. The Guiding Star: vv. 9-10
    H. Royal Gifts for a King: v. 11
    I. The Divine Warning: v. 12

SUGGESTED INTRODUCTION FOR ADULTS

For long centuries the Jews had waited for their Messiah. There were many Scriptures that foretold His coming, that described His character and ministry.

But when He came, the religious leaders did not recognize or accept Him It was lowly shepherds near Bethlehem who first saw Him, not the priests in the temple or the scribes in the synagogues. It was not the teachers of the Law who first came to worship Him, but Gentile astrologers from afar.

And so it has always been. While those who are supposed to be the people of God too often give their main energies to selfish pursuits, Christ is being sought in unexpected places and by those who seemed far away. The greatest numbers are turning to God in Korea, not in America.

SUGGESTED INTRODUCTION FOR YOUTH

This is a great day for young people. In a tired, sick world youth can bring new life and hope. In many dead or dying churches it is the young people who have had a vision of what God can do, who have prayed and worked and witnessed.

We first need to find Christ for ourselves, and then we need to help others find Him. This is the most exciting work in which we can engage.

The world is wanting a great leader, one who can lead us out of our messes and into a new day. We know that Christ is the answer. Let's share Him!

CONCEPTS FOR CHILDREN

1. The most important thing we can do is to seek and find Christ.
2. It was a long, costly journey for the wise men, but it need not be so for us.
3. If we seek Him sincerely we can find Him now.
4. Are we ready to accept Him?

THE LESSON COMMENTARY

I. THE BIRTH OF JESUS:
Matthew 1:18-25

A. A Devastating Discovery: vv. 18-19

The first seventeen verses of this chapter give us the genealogy of Jesus. Verses 18-25 tell the story of His birth.

Mary, who became His mother, was "espoused" to Joseph. Some versions say "betrothed" or "engaged." But among the Jews of that day a betrothal was far more binding than is a modern engagement in American society. It was a legal contract and could only be broken by divorce action. For this reason the New International Version reads, "Mary was pledged to be married to Joseph." Alfred Edersheim says that the betrothal was so sacred that "any breach of it would be treated as adultery; nor could the bond be dissolved except, as after marriage, by regular divorce" (*The Life and Times of Jesus the Messiah*, I, 150).

But "before they came together"—or, "before they began to live together"—it became obviously apparent that Mary was pregnant. This was a shocking discovery for Joseph to make. He loved Mary and trusted her implicitly. What had happened?

It may seem strange that Joseph is here, at this stage, called Mary's "husband." M'Neile explains it this way: "After betrothal, therefore, but before marriage, the man was legally 'husband' (cf. Gen. xxix. 21; Dt. xxii. 23f.); hence an informal cancelling of betrothal was impossible: the man must give to the woman a writ, and pay a fine" (*Gospel According to St. Matthew*, p. 7).

Joseph was a "just," or "righteous," man. He could not condone sin. Nor could he begin married life with a woman who had obviously been guilty of immorality. Yet he loved Mary and was "not willing to make her a publick example"—better, "did not want to expose her to public disgrace" (NIV). So he "was minded to put her away privily"; "he had in mind to divorce her quietly" (NIV). It was a traumatic experience for Joseph. He was trying to make the best of a bad situation.

B. A Divine Disclosure: vv. 20-21

When Joseph had reflected on the matter, or pondered it, he finally went to sleep. During the night an angel of the Lord appeared to him in a "dream." The Greek word here, *onar*, is used in the New Testament only by Matthew (6 times). It occurs five times in the first two chapters (1:20; 2:12, 13, 19, 22). Then it is used for the dream that Pilate's wife had (27:19). This is a unique feature in Matthew's Gospel. It was the regular way that God spoke to Joseph and made His will known to him.

The angel addressed him as "Joseph, thou son of David"—a fact which we have already seen proved by the genealogy in the first chapter. As a descendant of David in the royal line (1:6-11), Joseph was heir to the throne. It was this that gave Jesus the legal right to the throne of David.

Joseph was assured by the angel that he need not fear to take Mary as his wife. The verb translated "take unto thee" is a compound word meaning "take to one's side." So the words of the angel may be rendered, "Do not be afraid to take Mary home as your wife" (NIV).

Why? Because "that which is conceived in her is of the Holy Ghost." This revelation is in exact accord with what Luke's Gospel tells us was revealed to Mary by the angel Gabriel. The fact of the virgin birth is clearly indicated in both Matthew and Luke. Jesus had a human mother. But He had no earthly father. The Holy Spirit took the place of a human father in bringing about conception (Luke 1:35).

"And she shall bring forth" [give birth to] a son, and thou shalt call his name Jesus." This was a Greek name commonly used in Jesus' day. It came from the Hebrew word Yehoshua, "Jehovah (Yahweh) will save," in its late form Yeshua. The meaning of this name is implied in the reason cited by the angel: "for he shall save his people from their sins"—not "in their sins" but "from their sins." The expression "his people" at first meant the Jews. But in the New Testament it takes in the Gentile believers in Christ.

C. A Fulfillment of Prophecy: vv. 22-23

We noted in a previous lesson that Matthew frequently uses the expression "that it might be fulfilled" (13 times) and cites altogether some sixty passages from the Old Testament. Here it is Isaiah 7:14, with its prediction of the virgin birth. The supernaturally born child would be called "Emmanuel," a Hebrew word meaning "God with us."

D. A Devout Servant: vv. 24-25

Obediently Joseph obeyed the angel's instructions, starting about the business promptly as soon as he wakened. He took Mary to his home as his wife. But he had no marriage relations—"know" is a euphemism for this in both the Old and New Testaments— with her until she gave birth to a son ("first-born" is not in the earliest Greek manuscripts). Following the angel's command, he named the child "Jesus."

The language of this verse clearly implies that Joseph did have marital relations with Mary after Jesus was born. This refutes the doctrine of the perpetual virginity of Mary, held by some. Christianity is not a religion of asceticism.

II. THE VISIT OF THE WISE MEN: Matthew 2:1-12

A. The Magi from the East: v. 1

Jesus, the Bread of Life (John 6:35), was born in Bethlehem, which means "house of bread." This small village, as it was then, was situated in Judea, about six miles south of Jerusalem. Because it was the birthplace of Christ it has become a thriving town in modern times.

Jesus was born "in the days of Herod the king." This was Herod the Great, who was appointed by the Roman government as king of all Palestine in 40 B.C. But it was a voyage of several months from Rome, and after Herod arrived it took him two years to gain control of the rebellious country. So he actually *ruled* the country from 37 B.C. until his death in 4 B.C. But he *reigned* 40-4 B.C.

Herod was an Idumean, that is, of Edomite descent. He had lived most of his life in Palestine and so was familiar with Jewish customs. But his character left much to be desired. He was wicked, cruel, and power-mad. He killed his favorite wife, Mariamne, probably the only person he ever loved—and that was mainly infatuation. He also had three of his sons put to death, causing a prominent Roman writer of the time to say (with a play on words in the Greek) that it was safer to be Herod's pig (*hus*) than to be his son (*huios*). It was jealousy for the throne that caused the death of the sons. So we can understand why Herod put to death the innocent little boys in Bethlehem (2:16-18), to make sure that one of them did not become king.

After Jesus had been born, "wise men" came from the east to Jerusalem. They were probably Persian astrologers from the Mesopotamian region. The Greek word for "wise men" is *magoi* from which we get our word "magic." It is used in this sense in Acts 13:6—"sorcerer," or "magician." But here it is used in a good sense for men who studied the stars. The term originally denoted the priestly caste of Persia and Babylonia.

How many wise men were there? The simple answer is that we do not know. The idea that there were three was possibly suggested by the three kinds of gifts they brought (v. 11). Furthermore, the modern reference to them as "three kings of Orient" is based on purely legendary tradition of a later time. As we have already noted, they were probably astrologers, possibly priests, but almost certainly not kings.

Why did they come to Jerusalem? Because it was the capitol city, and they naturally assumed that that was where the king of the Jews would be born.

B. The Search in Jerusalem: v. 2

Joseph Seiss, in his book *The Gospel in the Stars*, claims that the ancient astrologers identified the Jewish nation with the zodiacal sign Pisces, or Fishes. They also believed that a conjunction of Jupiter and Saturn signaled the birth of some notable person. Seiss says that shortly before the birth of Christ in 5 B.C. there were three conjunctions of Jupiter and Saturn, all of them in the sign Pisces. So the Eastern astrologers concluded that a great leader was born among the Jews and came to seek him.

The wise men did not speak of having had any vision or receiving any direct revelation. All they said was, "We have seen his star in the east, and are come to worship him." Some have thought that the star of Bethlehem was a spectacular comet. But it would seem more probable that a special star appeared in the sky and finally disappeared. At any rate, God used the starry heavens to bring the wise men to see the Christchild.

C. The Concern of the King: v. 3

When the king heard of the visit of these astrologers from the East and learned what question they had asked, he was "troubled." He could not stand the thought of any threat to his throne. The appearance of a possible rival could not be tolerated.

But we are told that "all Jerusalem" was troubled with him. Why so? Didn't the Jews want to get rid of Roman rule?

Yes, but the Jewish leaders were afraid that if word of a new king's birth should get to Rome, the rulers there would consider it to be a sign of rebellion and would move in to crush the revolt. They could not afford to risk such a contingency.

D. The King's Question: v. 4

Herod summoned "all the chief priests and scribes of the people." The priests were in charge of the temple and were Sadducees. The scribes were the Pharisees who taught the Law in the synagogues. These were the two main groups in the Great Sanhedrin at Jerusalem, the governing body of Jews. They were supposed to know the Scriptures.

The king asked them "where Christ should be born." The Greek says "the Christ," that is, "the Messiah." Herod had been brought up in Palestine and was familiar with the Jewish religion. He was evidently aware that "King of the Jews" (v. 2) must mean the Messiah. He may also have been well enough acquainted with Jewish teaching to believe that the coming Messiah would deliver His people from foreign rule.

E. The Reply of the Scribes: vv. 5-6

The chief priests and scribes had no difficulty in answering the king's question. The Messiah would be born in Bethlehem of Judea. How did they know? Because this had been definitely prophesied. They then proceeded (v. 6) to quote Micah 5:2. In the Greek "princes" and "governor" have basically the same meaning (they are from the same root). "Rule" is literally "shepherd." The Messiah would be the Great Shepherd of His sheep (cf. John 10:11). Bethlehem was a small town in a small country. But it has become one of the best-known names on the lips of millions of people around the world. Why? All because Jesus was born there!

F. The Duplicity of the King: vv. 7-8

Herod secretly summoned the wise men to his palace. There he "enquired of them diligently what time the star appeared." It is evident that he assumed, rightly or wrongly, that the star had first appeared at the time of the Messiah's birth.

Having fixed this time in his mind, the king sent the men to Bethlehem. When they found the child they were to report back to him—"that I may come and worship him also." These words reveal something of the depth of depravity in Herod's heart. His whole intention was to destroy Christ, not to worship Him. Herod was not only a cruel politician but also a consummate liar.

G. The Guiding Star: vv. 9-10

After listening to the king, the wise men started out again. As soon as they got away from Jerusalem, lo, there was

the star! It led them on until it came to a standstill over Bethlehem. They had at last arrived at their proper destination.

Verse 10 is very significant: "When they saw the star, they rejoiced with exceeding great joy." The guiding star was a symbol of the Holy Spirit, who wants to guide us through life. Jesus said, "When he, the Spirit of truth, is come, he will guide you into all truth" (John 16:13). We cannot always depend on human advice, but we can depend on Him.

H. Royal Gifts for a King: v. 11

Every Christmas the wise men are pictured worshiping at the manger and there presenting their gifts to the baby Jesus. But it was the shepherds who found the babe in a manger (Luke 2:16). Here we are distinctly told that the wise men found "the young child" in "the house"—not a baby in a manger in the stable. Furthermore it says that Herod slew all the male children in Bethlehem "from two years and under, according to the time which he had diligently enquired of the wise men" (v. 16). This implies that Jesus was at least several months old when the wise men came. It would have taken months for them to prepare a caravan and take the long trip across the desert from Mesopotamia to Palestine. Everything in the narrative combines to indicate that Jesus was perhaps as much as six months, or even a year, old by this time.

When the wise men saw Jesus they fell on their knees and worshiped Him. Then they presented their gifts: gold, frankincense, and myrrh. Barclay points out the symbolical significance of these three. Gold was the appropriate gift for a king, and so for the King of kings. Frankincense was the gift for a *priest*, since he offered incense in the temple, and so a fitting gift for the great High Priest. Myrrh was a gift for one who would die; it was used for embalming, and so was appropriate for the One who would

---

DISCUSSION QUESTIONS

1. Why are all events now dated A.D. or B.C.?
2. What does this say to us about the importance of Christ's birth?
3. Why did not the priests and scribes go to Bethlehem?
4. Why is Christ the Lord of history?
5. How can our lives be dated "B.C." and "A.D."?
6. What treasures should we bring to Christ?

die on the cross. As Barclay says, these three gifts "foretold that He was to be the true King, the perfect High Priest, and in the end the supreme Saviour of men" (*Gospel of Matthew*, I, 22-24).

I. The Divine Warning: v. 12

In a dream the wise men were warned not to return to Herod. Had they done so, the king would have sought to kill Jesus immediately. Instead Joseph took Jesus and His mother to Egypt for safety (vv. 13-15).

CONTEMPORARY APPLICATION

The wise men followed the star from the east to Palestine. They evidently assumed that the King of the Jews would be born at the palace, so when they arrived there they went directly to the capitol city, Jerusalem. As a result King Herod learned of their coming and massacred all the male infants in Bethlehem.

Would this tragedy have been averted if they had carefully followed the star instead of being guided by a wrong assumption? Verses 9 and 10 suggest this possibility. It is a warning to all of us to follow carefully the guidance of the Spirit and not depend on our own wisdom.

JESUS' DILEMMA AND DECISION

DEVOTIONAL READING	Psalm 18:1-6
ADULTS	Topic: *Wrestling with Temptation* Background Scripture: Matthew 3–4 Scripture Lesson: Matthew 4:1-11 Memory Verse: *Because he himself has suffered and been tempted, he is able to help those who are tempted.* Hebrews 2:18
YOUTH	Topic: *Dilemma and Decision* Background Scripture: Matthew 3–4 Scripture Lesson: Matthew 4:1-11 Memory Verse: *Because he himself has suffered and been tempted, he is able to help those who are tempted.* Hebrews 2:18
CHILDREN	Topic: *A New Kind of King* Background Scripture: Matthew 3:1–4:22 Scripture Lesson: Matthew 4:1-11 Memory Verse: *This is my beloved son, with whom I am well pleased.* Matthew 3:7
DAILY BIBLE READINGS	Mon., Dec. 22: John the Baptist, Matthew 3:1-10. Tues., Dec. 23: Jesus Is Baptized, Matthew 3:11-17. Wed., Dec. 24: Another Account of the Baptism, John 1:29-36. Thurs., Dec. 25: Luke's Christmas Story, Luke 2:8-20. Fri., Dec. 26: Through Christ We Are God's Children, Hebrews 2:10-18. Sat., Dec. 27: Finding the Grace of Christ, Hebrews 4:11-16. Sun., Dec. 28: Strong When Tempted, I Corinthians 10:1-13.
LESSON AIM	To see how Jesus successfully resisted temptation, and so how we may succeed.
LESSON SETTING	Time: Probably A.D. 27 Place: The Wilderness of Judea, between Jerusalem and the Jordan River

Jesus' Dilemma and Decision

LESSON OUTLINE

I. The Preparation: Matthew 3
    A. The Forerunner: vv. 1-6
    B. His Preaching: vv. 7-12
    C. The Baptism of Jesus: vv. 13-17

II. The Temptation of Jesus: Matthew 4:1-11
    A. The Setting: vv. 1-2
    B. The First Temptation: vv. 3-4
    C. The Second Temptation: vv. 5-7
    D. The Third Temptation: vv. 8-10
    E. The Culmination: v. 11

III. The Early Ministry of Jesus: Matthew 4:12-25
    A. The Beginning in Galilee: vv. 12-17
    B. The Call of the First Disciples: vv. 18-22

SUGGESTED INTRODUCTION FOR ADULTS

Christ was Son of God but He became Son of man. In His humanity He went through the same kinds of experiences that we have. There were crucial hours in His life, as there are in ours.

And so we can speak of "the crises of the Christ." Two of them we find in today's lesson: the baptism and the temptation. Others that came later were the transfiguration, the crucifixion, the resurrection, and the ascension. All of these were real experiences in the life of Jesus.

Jesus is our Example. By following His example we can meet temptation successfully, as He did, and come off "more than conquerors through him" (Romans 8:37).

SUGGESTED INTRODUCTION FOR YOUTH

It often seems that life is made up of crises. Many of them crop up at school. Later will come the choice of a companion and of one's vocation.

When these crises confront us, we need to remember that Jesus also had His crises. Probably a young Christian's most crucial hours are those when the pressure of temptation seems overwhelming. It is then that we look to Jesus. Realizing that He was bombarded by Satan but came off victoriously, we know that we can do the same.

Jesus had a physical body, with the same bodily appetites we have. He went through childhood and adolescence, just as we have to. If He came through victoriously, then with Him as our constant Companion and Helper we can make it, too.

CONCEPTS FOR CHILDREN

1. Jesus came as "the King of the Jews," but He took the path of lowly service.
2. His baptism was a sign that He was one of us.
3. Jesus was tempted just as we are tempted.
4. He remained true to His heavenly Father, and so can we.

THE LESSON COMMENTARY

I. THE PREPARATION:
Matthew 3

A. The Forerunner: vv. 1-6

John the Baptist appeared in the Wilderness of Judea about six months before Jesus began His ministry. He was six months older than Jesus (Luke 1:36), and they probably both began their ministry at the usual age of thirty (Luke 3:23; Numbers 4:3).

"The wilderness of Judaea" was a desolate region stretching from the high plateau, on which Jerusalem and Bethlehem were situated, down to the Jordan River and the Dead Sea. It has always been a desolate waste of hills and gullies, largely uninhabited.

John was "preaching" (v. 1). The Greek word means "proclaiming as a herald." John the Baptist had an important divine proclamation to make: "Repent ye: for the kingdom of heaven is at hand" (v. 2). He was the voice of one crying in the wilderness: "Prepare ye the way of the Lord, make his paths straight" (vv. 2-3). Repenting and straightening out their crooked lives was the necessary preparation for the coming of the King.

John the Baptist was a rugged man who had spent his youth in the wilderness (Luke 1:80). His clothing was made of rough camel's hair, a kind of sackcloth that would irritate the skin— a fitting symbol for his preaching of repentance. He wore a leather belt around his waist. His food was "locusts," which was clean food according to the Law (Leviticus 11:22), and wild honey, of which there was an abundance in the wild area where he lived. It has been suggested that John may have spent some time with the Essenes at Qumran, who produced the Dead Sea Scrolls. This is not at all impossible, since the Essenes were an ascetic group that looked for the coming of the Messiah.

John was a popular preacher. People flocked to the banks of the Jordan, even coming from Jerusalem (v. 5), twenty miles away. John was baptizing them in the Jordan River as they were "confessing out" their sins—so the Greek. This was the prerequisite for baptism.

B. His Preaching: vv. 7-12

John the Baptist was a rugged preacher of repentance, who did not mince his words. Among those who came to hear him were many "Pharisees." The name means "separated ones." They prided themselves on strict adherence to the Law and were careful to keep themselves ceremonially clean. The leading Pharisees were rabbis, who taught the Law in the synagogues. Another group that appeared was the "Sadducees." They were more worldly minded. The priests, who controlled the temple worship, were Sadducees. So these two groups comprised the religious leaders of the nation.

What did John say to them? "You brood of vipers! Who warned you to flee from the coming wrath?" (v. 7, NIV). Strong words, those. But this was the jolt that these self-righteous leaders needed. He told them to produce evidence ("fruits") of genuine repentance (v. 8). They could not depend on their physical descent from Abraham to give them acceptance with God (v. 9). The "axe" of divine judgment was about to strike them. Every tree that did not produce good fruit would be cut down and thrown into the fire (v. 10).

Then John made an important announcement: "I baptize you with water for repentance. But after me will come one who is more powerful than I. . . . He will baptize you with the Holy Spirit and with fire" (v. 11, NIV). Jesus referred to this shortly before His ascension (Acts 1:5). In the light of this, it is difficult to understand why the Christian church across the centuries has given great emphasis to water baptism but has been largely silent about the baptism with the Holy Spirit.

C. The Baptism of Jesus: vv. 13-17

Why was Jesus baptized by John? The Baptist himself protested: "I need to be baptized by you, and do you come to me?" (NIV).

Jesus' answer gives the clue. As the perfect Sacrifice for our sins it was necessary for Him to fulfill all the righteous requirements of the Law—which we could not do.

There is another important item in connection with the baptism. Here we find, for the first time in the Bible, a clear revelation of the Trinity. As Jesus, the Son of God, came up out of the water, the Holy Spirit descended on Him in the form of a dove and the Father's voice from heaven proclaimed: "This is my beloved Son, in whom I am well pleased" (vv. 16-17). It was a great moment in the life of Jesus and a great moment in the history of the human race.

We might note also that Jesus' baptism indicated His full identification with us. Though He had done no sin, He identified Himself with sinful humanity, so that He might become our Savior.

II. THE TEMPTATION OF JESUS: Matthew 4:1-11

A. The Setting: vv. 1-2

Right after His baptism (cf. Mark 1:12) Jesus was led by the Spirit out into the wilderness "to be tempted by the devil." Before He could begin His public ministry He must be tested and proved.

In the desolate Wilderness of Judea, Jesus fasted forty days and forty nights. It was a lonely vigil.

At the end of this period He was hungry. Not during the forty days? It seems to be generally true that a person feels the pangs of hunger during the early days of a prolonged fast and then loses all desire for food. Jesus was probably so wrapped up in spiritual contemplation that He did not think about eating. But at the end of the forty days He was terribly hungry.

B. The First Temptation: vv. 3-4

It was then that the devil hit Him, and hit Him hard. "If you are the Son of God," he said, "command these stones to become bread." Why go hungry, when He had the power to provide food?

There would have been nothing intrinsically wrong with Jesus' turning stones into bread. The sin would have been in obeying the voice of Satan. A true child of God must obey his Father's voice.

But the problem goes a little deeper. Jesus had identified Himself with our humanity. It would have been unfair for Him to make use of His divine powers for selfish reasons. G. Campbell Morgan puts it well: "The enemy asked Him to do a right thing in a wrong way, to satisfy a lawful appetite in an illegal fashion, to make use of the privileges of Sonship for violating its responsibilities" (*The Crises of the Christ*, p. 168).

Jesus replied, "It is written." This is in the perfect tense in Greek, which combines the ideas of completed action and continuing state. So the full force is, "It has been written and still stands written." The Word of God is eternal, unchangeable.

Christ quoted from Deuteronomy 8:3. Man is more than body; he is spirit. So he cannot live on bread alone. His soul must be fed with spiritual food. Jesus lived by the Word of God, not by the whims of His own appetite, and we must do the same.

C. The Second Temptation: vv. 5-7

The devil took Jesus to "the holy city"—a designation for Jerusalem that occurs in the New Testament only in Matthew and Revelation, but which is found four times in the Old Testament. There Satan put Him on "a pinnacle of the temple," the highest point in the holy city. Morgan comments: "The choosing of the place is first evidence of the subtlety of the foe" (*Crises of Christ*, p. 175).

"In just such a setting, hallowed by sacred associations, probably with a waiting crowd below, Satan made an entirely different approach. This time he appealed to Jesus' complete trust in God. Before, the temptation was on the physical level. This time it was on a high spiritual plane" (*Beacon Bible Commentary*, VI, 58).

In this lofty atmosphere, the devil made bold to quote Scripture himself. So he tried to quote Psalm 91:11-12. But he left out a significant phrase: "in all thy ways." Christ's ways were God's ways. It is only when we are in the way that God chooses for us that we can claim His care.

The Jews expected that their Messiah would make a sudden, spectacular appearance in the temple. If Jesus jumped from the pinnacle of the temple—about 150 feet high—and landed safely, He could expect the crowd to acclaim Him as Messiah. It would be a quick, easy way to achieve this recognition.

But Jesus, unlike some of His professed followers, rejected the temptation to do something sensational. Instead He took the path of humble obedience. The kingdom of God is advanced not by sensationalism but by submission.

Again Jesus dipped into the Old Testament for an answer. This time it was, "Thou shalt not tempt the Lord thy God" (Deuteronomy 6:16). Some people drive carelessly and say, "The Lord will take care of me." This is presumption, not faith. We have more than once heard people say, "A Christian is immortal here until his work is done." But we have seen the tragedy of great men cut off before their work was finished, simply because they paid no attention to doctor's warnings and continued to neglect their health. We have no right to tempt the Lord by ignoring the laws of life.

D. The Third Temptation: vv. 8-10

Satan chose still another setting for the third temptation. He took Jesus to a high mountain and in a vision showed Him all the kingdoms of the world. Then he made this proposition: "All these things will I give thee, if thou wilt fall down and worship me" (v. 9). To gain the whole world without going to the cross! It will be noted that Jesus did not dispute the devil's claim to these kingdoms. For Satan is called "the prince of this world."

But once more Jesus rejected the temptation. Again He quoted Scripture: "Thou shalt worship the Lord thy God, and him only shalt thou serve" (Deuteronomy 6:13).

Satan tempted Jesus on three levels: (1) the physical—food; (2) the intellectual—do something sensational; (3) the spiritual—"worship me." The devil still uses all three avenues of temptation.

Jesus had had enough. So He commanded sternly: "Away from me, Satan!" (v. 10, NIV). He did not care to talk further with the tempter, whom He had now defeated.

E. The Culmination: v. 11

The devil left Him, and angels came to minister to Him. They probably provided Him with food (cf. I Kings 19:5-7), as well as spiritual sustenance.

Several questions come to mind as one reads the accounts of Jesus' temptations. One of them concerns the form of the temptation. There are good scholars who feel that Satan appeared to Jesus in physical form. In *Paradise Regained* John Milton has the devil coming in the form of an old man.

But there are some difficulties with this view. Did Satan take Jesus bodily to the pinnacle of the temple? Perhaps so. But with regard to the third temptation we know that there is no mountain on earth from which one could see with physical eyes all the kingdoms of the world.

Hebrews 4:15 says that we have "one who has been tempted in every way, just as we are—yet was without sin" (NIV). Most of our temptations come to us as mental suggestions, although sometimes people's spoken words do become the vehicle of temptation.

A more important question is, "Why did Christ suffer?" The Epistle to the Hebrews deals with this more fully than any other book in the New Testament. In 2:18 we read: "Because he himself suffered when he was tempted, he is able to help those who are being tempted" (NIV). He is "a merciful and faithful high priest" (2:17)—"merciful" because He has shared our human frailties, and "faithful" to help us because He knows how much we need His help.

In Hebrews the humanity of Jesus is portrayed vividly. We read that "he learned obedience from what he suffered" (5:8, NIV). In His humanity Jesus had to learn, and He learned by suffering.

Another question that is sometimes raised is this: Could Jesus have failed? That is really an academic question. It is our feeling that the Father would not have let Him fail. But we also feel strongly that *in His own human consciousness* Jesus felt as though He might fail. Otherwise the temptations would have been unreal. If you know you *cannot* do wrong, you are not tempted.

What we must insist on is that these temptations were no play-acting; they were the real thing! For Jesus the temptations were agonizingly real. We have just noted that in Hebrews it says He "suffered when he was tempted."

He went through all this in order to be the perfect sacrifice for our sins. And He also went through it so that He could truly sympathize with— literally, "suffer with"—us in our times of temptation. The Son of God became the Son of man not only so that He might die on the cross but so that He might live our lives with us.

III. THE EARLY MINISTRY OF JESUS: Matthew 4:12-25

A. The Beginning in Galilee: vv. 12-17

"When Jesus heard that John had been put in prison, he returned to Galilee" (v. 12, NIV)—from Judea, where He had been tempted. But He did not settle down again in His hometown. Instead we read: "Leaving Nazareth, he went and lived in Capernaum, which was by the lake in the area of Zebulun and Naphtali" (v. 13, NIV). "Upon the sea coast" (KJV) is obviously misleading, for the ordinary reader would take this as meaning the Mediterranean coast, whereas it actually refers to the shores of the Lake of Galilee, which is only about twelve miles long and seven miles wide. From numerous hillsides one can see the whole extent of the lake, but the Mediterranean Sea fades into the distant horizon.

Capernaum was a sizable city on the north shore of the lake, about twenty miles from the obscure village of Nazareth. It was a much more suitable place as the headquarters of Jesus' ministry.

Again (vv. 15-16) Matthew quotes from Isaiah (9:1-2). This is one of fifteen quotations that Matthew takes from this "prince of prophets."

The northern part of Palestine is referred to as "Galilee of the Gentiles"

DISCUSSION QUESTIONS

1. Why is temptation essential to the Christian?
2. What are some values of temptation?
3. What temptations beset the spiritually mature?
4. What are some specific temptations of modern society?
5. What is our best protection in times of temptation?
6. How may we help those who are being tempted?

because it bordered on Gentile territory. Later it became the first part of
the country to go into captivity.

The text that Jesus chose (v. 17)
was the same one that John the Baptist had used (3:2). Jesus was picking
up where John left off.

A word should be said about the
phrase "the kingdom of heaven." In
the New Testament it is found only in
Matthew's Gospel, where it occurs
thirty-two times. (Luke has "kingdom
of God" thirty-three times.) The Jews
preferred not to use the name of God
very often, substituting such euphe-
misms as "heaven," "power," or "the
Blessed One." Out of deference to
their feelings, Matthew, who was
writing to Jews, adopted "kingdom of
heaven." Only five times does he say
"kingdom of God."

B. The Call of the First Disciples: vv. 18-22

All three Synoptic Gospels tell of
the call of the first four disciples. They
were two sets of brothers in partner-
ship (Luke 5:10) in the fishing business. From making money catching
fish, Jesus called them to be fishers of
men (v. 19).

The men did not hesitate: "At
once they left their nets and followed
him" (v. 20, NIV). James and John
were helping their father Zebedee
mend the nets and prepare them for
the next day. Mark says that Zebedee
had hired servants in the boat (Mark
1:20). So the man was not left desti-
tute when his sons got up and followed Jesus.

All four of these men made a great
contribution to the Kingdom. The
most important thing that Andrew did
was to introduce his brother to Jesus
at an earlier time (John 1:40-42). Now
he and Peter (Simon) were ready to
follow Jesus in full-time service. Peter,
of course, became the leading spokesman of the apostles. Perhaps his greatest hour was when he preached on the
Day of Pentecost and three thousand
people were saved (Acts 2).

James the son of Zebedee became
the first apostolic martyr (Acts 12:2).
John, according to early church tradition, lived the longest of the Twelve
and wrote the five books that bear his
name—the Gospel, three Epistles, and
Revelation. Jesus chose well.

CONTEMPORARY APPLICATION

Martin Luther was once asked,
"What is the most important preparation for the ministry?" Surprisingly,
he answered, "Temptation." The second most important? Again the same
answer, "Temptation." And when
asked for the third he gave the same
reply.

This is obviously an over-simplifi-
cation. But it suggests an important

truth: Only those who have been
tested can be trusted.

What is the difference between pig
iron, that is sold by the ton, and watch
springs, for instance, that are expensive by the ounce? The obvious answer
is that metal has to be tested in the
fiery furnace before it is tempered
steel. And so it is with every Christian
worker.

JESUS AND THE LAW

DEVOTIONAL READING	Romans 8:1-8

ADULTS

Topic: *Living by a Higher Law*

Background Scripture: Matthew 5:1–6:18

Scripture Lesson: Matthew 5:38-48

Memory Verse: *Think not that I have come to abolish the law and the prophets; I have come not to abolish them but to fulfil them.* Matthew 5:17

YOUTH

Topic: *Maximums, Not Minimums*

Background Scripture: Matthew 5:1–6:18

Scripture Lesson: Matthew 5:38-48

Memory Verse: *Think not that I have come to abolish the law and the prophets; I have come not to abolish them but to fulfil them.* Matthew 5:17

CHILDREN

Topic: *A New Kind of Kingdom*

Background Scripture: Matthew 4:23–6:18

Scripture Lesson: Matthew 5:1-11

Memory Verse: *Let your light so shine before men, that they may see your good works and give glory to your Father who is in heaven.* Matthew 5:16

DAILY BIBLE READINGS

Mon., Dec. 29: The Beatitudes, Matthew 5:1-12.
Tues., Dec. 30: The Christian Influence, Matthew 5:13-16.
Wed., Dec. 31: Jesus Interprets the Law, Matthew 5:17-26.
Thurs., Jan. 1: Further Interpretations, Matthew 5:27-37.
Fri., Jan. 2: Practicing Your Piety, Matthew 6:1-4, 16-18.
Sat., Jan. 3: And When You Pray, Matthew 6:5-15.
Sun., Jan. 4: Our Relation to the Law, Romans 7:1-6.

LESSON AIM

To see how Jesus reinterpreted the law of Moses and how that affects us.

LESSON SETTING

Time: About A.D. 28

Place: On a hillside on the northwest shore of the Lake of Galilee

Jesus and the Law

LESSON OUTLINE

I. The Beatitudes: Matthew 5:1-12

II. Salt and Light: Matthew 5:13-16

III. True Righteousness Demanded: Matthew 5:17-20

IV. True Righteousness Illustrated: Matthew 5:21-48
   A. Peaceableness: vv. 21-26
   B. Purity: vv. 27-30
   C. Harmony: vv. 31-32
   D. Honesty: vv. 33-37
   E. Kindness: vv. 38-42
   F. Love: vv. 43-48

V. Righteous Acts: Matthew 6:1-18
   A. Introduction: v. 1
   B. Almsgiving: vv. 2-4
   C. Praying: vv. 5-15
   D. Fasting: vv. 16-18

SUGGESTED INTRODUCTION FOR ADULTS

There are many great sermons in print, written by great preachers. But probably most people would agree that the most important of them all is the so-called Sermon on the Mount. Certainly Jesus was the greatest preacher who ever lived, and here we have the heart of His preaching. Even Mahatma Gandhi, who remained a Hindu to the end, said that he wanted to live by the Sermon on the Mount; it was the finest guide to life. It is certainly worthy of our closest study.

For the Jews the Mosaic law was the final authority. Jesus was born and brought up in Judaism. He did not renounce His heritage. But the Pharisaical religion of Jesus' day had to a sad extent degenerated into legalism without love. In the Sermon on the Mount Jesus reinterprets the law of Moses, giving it a more spiritual tone and application. The ancient moral principles still stand. But their application needs to be spelled out in terms of compassionate love.

SUGGESTED INTRODUCTION FOR YOUTH

To the sincere Christian the most important question for him to ask is, "What would Jesus do—if He were in my shoes right now?" To answer that we must begin with the prior question, "What *did* Jesus do—while He was here on earth?"

The four Gospels give us a lot of information on that point. But they tell us not only what He did. They also record many of His teachings on how we should live.

No one can live the Sermon on the Mount without the help of the Holy Spirit in his heart. For Jesus put the primary emphasis on inner attitudes rather than outward actions. It is His *Spirit* that we need, to make and keep our spirit as it should be.

CONCEPTS FOR
CHILDREN

1. We cannot let our light shine until we have the Light of the World in our hearts.
2. If we want God to bless us, we must live as Jesus taught us.
3. Jesus told us to watch our attitudes.
4. The most important attitude is love.

THE LESSON COMMENTARY

I. THE BEATITUDES:
Matthew 5:1-12

When Jesus saw the large crowds, He "went up into a mountain," or a high hill. This was probably the hillside now called "the Mount of Beatitudes," at the northwest corner of the Lake of Galilee.

Verse 1 would seem to suggest that Jesus left the crowds of people and retired to a quiet place to give the Sermon on the Mount to His disciples alone. But at the end of the sermon we read: "And it came to pass when Jesus had ended these sayings, the people were astonished at his doctrine" (7:28). So it would appear that many people followed Him up the hill.

"When he was set" is literally "when He had sat down." Preachers today follow the Greek and Roman custom of standing to speak. But the Jewish rabbis always sat down to teach, and Jesus followed this custom.

The Greek word for "disciples" means "learners." That is what all true disciples of Christ must be.

Someone has called the Beatitudes "a sort of title page to the teachings of Jesus." Verses 11 and 12 are usually thought of as an elaboration of verse 10. So that would give us eight beatitudes.

The first beatitude points out the doorway into the Christian life: "Blessed are the poor in spirit, for theirs is the kingdom of heaven" (v. 3). The first step we have to take is the confession of our spiritual poverty— the fact that we are utterly bankrupt of any spiritual assets that would make us acceptable to God.

The oldest Christian church in the world is the Church of the Nativity in Bethlehem, built over the manger where Christ is supposed to have been born. Erected in the fourth century by Queen Helena, the mother of Constantine the first Christian emperor, it still stands.

It is an impressive stone church, with a four-bell tower above. One would expect a large entrance. Instead, the main doorway is about four feet high and two or three feet wide. One can see that the once massive doorway has been blocked in with building stones. This was done centuries ago to keep the Turks from riding in on horseback and killing the worshipers. Now one has to stoop low to enter.

They call it "The Door of Humiliation." To me it seems a parable of entrance into the kingdom of God. Most of us came in literally on our knees, confessing our sins and asking God's forgiveness.

"Blessed are they that mourn: for they shall be comforted" (v. 4). The first application of this is that those who sense their complete spiritual bankruptcy mourn over this lost condition and are comforted with forgiveness. But the beatitude has also a wider, general application. God, who is pure love, wishes to comfort all who mourn, whatever their need. And there is a sense in which this mourning continues all our lives, as we become increasingly aware of how far we fall short of perfect Christlikeness. Only shallow Christians are complacent.

"Blessed are the meek: for they shall inherit the earth" (v. 5). Again we note the application to the beginnings of the Christian life. Those who have acknowledged their spiritual poverty, confessed their sins and found forgiveness realize that they have nothing to be proud of. They are humbled by the fact that all is of Christ, nothing of themselves but acceptance of His grace. This makes them truly "meek."

But again there is a general application. It is the meek, not the proud, who inherit the earth. Military tyrants try to conquer the earth. Wealthy men try to buy it. But both die without inheriting it and take nothing with them.

Meanwhile the meek inherit the earth. They enjoy its beauties and blessings, which too often the wealthy cannot and the despots will not. It doesn't cost a penny to revel in a glorious sunset or become enraptured with a garden of roses. It is those who are in touch with God who are able to be in tune with the universe. As Christians we can enjoy billions of dollars' worth of "unassessed real estate," for which we don't have to pay any taxes.

Meekness is not weakness. It is not a self-effacing, negative, false humility. William Fitch says: "Meekness is yieldedness to God, submissiveness to His will, preparedness to accept whatever He may give, and readiness to take the lowest place" (*The Beatitudes of Jesus*, p. 49).

"Blessed are they which do hunger and thirst after righteousness: for they shall be filled" (v. 6). The last word may well be translated "satisfied." It is the picture of cattle or sheep eating "grass"—that is the root of the Greek word—until they are completely satisfied, and then lying down to rest. We cannot be fully at rest until our souls are satisfied with God's abundant grace. But only those who "hunger and thirst" with deep longing for all of God's righteousness, for His holiness, can be filled with His Spirit's presence.

"Blessed are the merciful: for they shall obtain mercy" (v. 7). When we realize how merciful God has been to us in forgiving our sins, we should certainly be merciful to others. And as we extend mercy to all men, we continue to be the recipients of God's mercy. We also have a right to expect mercy from our fellowmen. The unmerciful often here, and always ultimately, get back the unkindness they give.

"Blessed are the pure in heart: for they shall see God" (v. 8). Kierkegaard put it succinctly when he said that purity of heart is to will one intention. It is to have only one purpose: to please God by doing His will.

We instinctively realize that we must have pure hearts if we are to live eternally in the presence of the holy God. But it is not only needed for seeing Him then. "Blessed are the pure in heart, for they shall see God"—now and always. Sin is like dust in the eyes; it keeps us from seeing clearly. It is only as our hearts are cleansed from sin and selfishness that we can see God.

"Blessed are the peacemakers: for they shall be called the children of God" (v. 9). This could have a twofold application. The first is that God will only acknowledge us as His children if we are peacemakers. The second is that if we are creating peace rather than strife people will say that we are God's children because we act like our Father. And peacemaking must begin in our homes and then reach out to others.

"Blessed are they which are persecuted for righteousness' sake: for theirs is the kingdom of heaven" (v. 10). The sad thing is that today many who claim to be persecuted for righteousness' sake are actually being punished for their own foolishness. We need to avoid the martyr complex, which is a denial of true Christianity.

II. SALT AND LIGHT: Matthew 5:13-16

Jesus did not say: "You are the sugar of the earth." Christianity is more than sentimental sweetness.

What does salt do? Two things. First, it gives flavor to food. Oatmeal or gravy without salt is disgustingly tasteless. Christianity gives tang and tone to life. It makes life worth living.

But salt is also a preservative. In

Jesus' day people caught fish in the Lake of Galilee and carried them a hundred miles on the backs of donkeys to Jerusalem—a journey that would take most of the week between Sabbaths. They had no refrigeration. But salt kept the fish from spoiling. Just so, Christians are the moral and spiritual preservative of society.

Salt typifies the unseen influence of Christianity, whereas "light" (v. 14) symbolizes the visible witness of Christians. Jesus said, "I am the light of the world" (John 8:12). What an honor and what a responsibility that He says to us: "You are the light of the world"! It is only Christ in us that can make us this.

"Candle" and "candlestick" (v. 15) should be "lamp" and "lampstand." They had no candles in Jesus' day, but used little clay lamps that burned olive oil.

We are to let our light shine before men (v. 16). This should be done tactfully, and in love and humility. An old Puritan preacher commented that Jesus did not say, "Smash your lamp in your neighbor's face." We cannot force people into the kingdom of God.

III. TRUE RIGHTEOUSNESS DEMANDED:
Matthew 5:17-20

Jesus declared that He did not come to destroy "the law, or the prophets"—the Old Testament—but to "fulfill" it. The verb can equally well be translated "fill full." Christ came to fulfill all the righteous demands of the Law for us. But He also filled the Law full of new spiritual meaning and reality.

Jesus went on to say that "one jot or one tittle" would not pass from the Law until all was fulfilled (v. 18). The Greek for "jot" is *iota*—the smallest letter of the Greek alphabet—which we have taken over into English to represent a very little thing. "Tittle" was the tiny "horn" on some Hebrew consonants that distinguish them from others. The modern equivalent for this

expression would probably be—"one dotting of an *i* or crossing of a *t*." Till heaven and earth pass away, not the least thing will perish from the Law.

"Least in the kingdom of heaven" (v. 19) means "least in relation to the kingdom of heaven." Obviously the one who breaks God's commandments and teaches men to do so is not actually "in" the Kingdom.

Verse 20 is often spoken of as the key verse of the Sermon on the Mount. Only those whose righteousness exceeds that of the scribes and Pharisees can enter the kingdom of heaven. Jesus demanded a higher righteousness than that of the religious leaders of Israel. What did He mean? The righteousness of the Pharisees was outward, formal, ceremonial, legalistic. The righteousness that Christ requires is inward, spiritual, moral, loving.

In the rest of this chapter (vv. 21-48) we find six paragraphs giving six illustrations of what Jesus meant by this higher, true righteousness. We might say that they describe six "characteristics of the Christian life." They are enumerated below.

IV. TRUE RIGHTEOUSNESS ILLUSTRATED:
Matthew 5:21-48

A. Peaceableness: vv. 21-26

Each one of these six paragraphs begins with the formula: "Ye have heard that it was said" (vv. 21, 27, 33, 38, 43; abbreviated in v. 31). "By them of old time" can equally well be translated "to them of old time." In each case Jesus quoted something from the Old Testament—except the second part in verse 43.

Every time he came back with the assertion, "But I say unto you" (vv. 22, 28, 32, 34, 39, 44). The Greek is even more emphatic than the English. *Ego de lego hymin* means "But *I* say to you." When Jesus spoke this way He was either the world's worst egotist or He was what He claimed to be—the eternal Son of God, who spoke with divine authority. Vincent Taylor makes this excellent observation: "Jesus will always remain a challenge to be met rather than a problem to be solved." The centuries have validated Jesus' claim to speak with authority.

The sixth of the Ten Commandments said, "Thou shalt not kill." Jesus in effect declared, "If you hate your brother, you are a murderer." This gives us the cue to the nature of the higher righteousness of the New Testament: It is a matter of inner attitude, not just of outward action. If a man *wants* to kill his brother he has already committed murder in his heart. And it is recorded as murder in the books of heaven.

B. Purity: vv. 27-30

This time Jesus quoted the seventh commandment: "Thou shalt not commit adultery." Then He declared, "Whosoever looketh on a woman to lust after her hath committed adultery with her already in his heart." Again it is a matter of inward attitude, not just outward act. Desire can be sinful, as well as deed. The law can only deal with the latter, but God deals with the former.

In verses 29 and 30 Jesus is speaking metaphorically, not literally. If something as precious to us as our right eye is causing us to stumble, we should get rid of it at once. If a friend who seems as close to us as our right hand is seeking to lead us astray, we must break off the friendship immediately and completely. Nothing is more important than our getting to heaven.

It will be noted that Jesus talks here very definitely about "hell" (vv. 29-30). The Greek word is Gehenna, which first referred to the Valley of Hinnom (II Kings 23:10). This had been a place of horrible idolatry and then was turned into the city dump—a place of perpetual burning and destruction. Jesus followed the Jewish custom of using this term for the place of final punishment.

C. Harmony: vv. 31-32

The Mosaic law permitted divorce but required a divorce certificate to be given (Deuteronomy 24:1). Jesus came out strongly against divorce, saying that it could only be allowed in the case of "fornication" (the word includes adultery). Divorce is one of the national scandals in the United States today, when about one marriage out of three ends in divorce. But God is still unalterably opposed to it.

There is another tragedy, however, and that is homes where divorce is shunned but where life is a hell on earth. Bickering, quarreling, fussing go on day after day. Christ wants to bring harmony into our homes as well as into our hearts.

D. Honesty: vv. 33-37

Jesus cited another Old Testament passage (perhaps Leviticus 19:2): "Do not break your oath, but keep the oaths you have made to the Lord" (v. 33, NIV). The Master's higher righteousness affirmed, "Swear not at all." He concluded: "Simply let your 'Yes' be 'Yes' and your 'No,' 'No'; anything beyond this comes from the evil one" (v. 37, NIV). We are to tell the truth always, and not back it up by swearing that it is true. We have had people say to us: "Honestly, I'm telling you the truth this time." We have felt like replying: "What do you tell the rest of the time?" Honesty comes close to being the supreme virtue in life.

E. Kindness: vv. 38-42

Once more Jesus quoted an old adage: "An eye for an eye, and a tooth for a tooth." This concept is found several times in the Old Testament (Exodus 21:24; Leviticus 24:20; Deuteronomy 19:21). The purpose of this was not to encourage personal revenge but rather to forbid the extravagant and unjust vengeance that was often carried out. It was now limited to sheer justice: an eye for an eye.

But again Jesus gave a higher rule: "Resist not evil." Christ, the great Peacemaker, was advocating kindness and nonretaliation. What He was saying was: "Never strike back!" He applied this principle in five specific ways: turn the other cheek (v. 39), let him take your coat (v. 40), go the second mile (v. 41), give to the one who asks, and lend to the would-be borrower (v. 42).

A person once said: "I believe in turning the other cheek. Then when the fellow hits that one, I can hit him back all I want to." But that is legalism, not love. It completely misses Jesus' emphasis on the spirit a man shows, not just his outward action.

In verse 40 "coat" is the undergarment, or tunic. "Cloke" is the outer robe. The modern application would be: If a person takes your shirt, let him have your coat, too.

Verse 41 reflects the custom of that day. A military officer or political official could require a passerby to carry his luggage for him the distance of one mile. Jesus said, "Go with him two miles." On the second mile, undertaken voluntarily, one could witness for the Lord. The other man's heart would be open to receive the witness because of the unexpected kindness shown. It is when we go the second mile that we show our Christianity.

This is a good place to point out the fact that giving a completely literal interpretation to everything in the Bible can be a senseless thing to do, with sad consequences. We have already noted how verses 29 and 30 must be taken metaphorically. We do not gain spiritually by mutilating our bodies.

So here. Should we literally give to everyone who asks? Suppose parents gave their children everything they asked for. Suppose a man asks you for money; you give it to him; he uses it to get drunk and then beats up and perhaps kills his wife or children. Have you done a kindness to him or his family? No! You have done a very unkind thing—thoughtlessly.

God gave us brains, and He expects us to use them. All principles should be applied with sanctified common sense.

F. Love: vv. 43-48

The Old Testament command was: "Thou shalt love thy neighbour" (Leviticus 19:18). But the second part was what later teachers had added as a supposedly logical corrollary.

Jesus' rejoinder was, "Love your enemies." This is the real test of love, and the best way we can demonstrate divine love in our hearts and lives. Do we bless those who curse us? Do we do good to those who hate us? Do we pray for those who persecute us? This is not natural; it is supernatural—only by the grace of God.

When we do these things we are actually the children of our heavenly Father and we prove it by our lives (v. 45). He sends his lifegiving sun and rain on both the just and the unjust. We should follow the divine example by showing love and kindness to all people.

Then Jesus threw out an incisive challenge: "If you love those who love you, what reward will you get? Are not even the tax collectors doing that? And if you greet only your brothers, what are you doing more than others? Do not even the pagans do that?" (vv. 46-47, NIV). How do our lives, particularly our attitudes, differ from those of the unsaved around us? Do some of these people show more kind-

---

DISCUSSION QUESTIONS

1. What is our relation to the Mosaic law today?
2. Does love rule out all law?
3. What is the relation between law and love in the home?
4. What does Paul say was the function of the Law?
5. How did Jesus fulfill the Law?
6. How do we benefit by this?

ness to minority groups than we do? Are they more thoughtful of those in need? These are disquieting questions that we ought to face.

The last verse (48) sums it all up: "Be ye therefore perfect, even as your Father which is in heaven is perfect." In terms of the immediate context (vv. 43-47), this means perfection in love. But the larger context is the whole chapter, and this verse challenges us to Christlikeness of character and conduct.

V. RIGHTEOUS ACTS:
Matthew 6:1-18

A. Introduction: v. 1

The oldest Greek manuscripts have "righteousness" rather than "alms" in this verse, which should therefore read: "Be careful not to do your 'acts of righteousness' before men, to be seen by them. If you do, you will have no reward from your Father in heaven" (NIV). In other words, "Don't parade your piety."

So this verse is not a part of the discussion of almsgiving. Rather, it is a cover-verse or introduction to three acts of righteousness: almsgiving, praying, and fasting.

B. Almsgiving: vv. 2-4

"So when you give to the needy, do not announce it with trumpets, as the hypocrites do in the synagogues and on the streets, to be honored by men. I tell you the truth, they have received their reward in full" (NIV). We are to give unostentatiously, seeking only God's approval and blessing.

C. Praying: vv. 5-15

It is not the words we say in prayer but the attitudes we show that count with God. Verse 6 does not rule out public prayer, for Jesus engaged in this (John 17). The whole emphasis in connection with all three topics is that we are not to perform our religious acts *in order to be seen by men*. It is the motive that God is concerned about.

The so-called Lord's Prayer—more accurately called "the disciples' prayer"—is addressed to "Our Father in heaven." It is then composed of six petitions, three (vv. 9-10) for others, followed by three for ourselves (vv. 11-13). The closing doxology—"For thine is the kingdom, and the power, and the glory, forever. Amen"—is not in the earliest Greek manuscripts. It was added at a later time to give a liturgical ending to the prayer when it was recited in public.

D. Fasting: vv. 16-18

Jesus was not an ascetic, and He did not advocate fasting for its own sake. As in the case of the other two religious acts, He warned against doing it to make an impression on others and gain a reputation for piety. When we do these things to get men's approval, we have received our reward here on earth and will have no reward for it in heaven.

CONTEMPORARY APPLICATION

Deshazer was one of Doolittle's "Raiders" that bombed the city of Tokyo. The Japanese people were infuriated at this affront to their deified emperor.

When Deshazer was shot down, the enemy understandably wreaked vengeance on him. He was confined to a solitary cell and tortured. He learned to hate his captors bitterly.

But in the few belongings he had was a Bible that his godly mother had given him when he left. It had gone untouched. But now in desperate boredom he read it. The message of God's love got through to him. He was beautifully born again. His intense hate was turned to love. On his return at the close of the war he took theological studies and then went back to Japan not to bomb but to preach the gospel. That is loving one's enemies.

THE WAY OF THE KINGDOM

DEVOTIONAL READING	Romans 12:9-21

ADULTS

Topic: *First Things First*

Background Scripture: Matthew 6:19—7:29

Scripture Lesson: Matthew 6:19-21, 24-33

Memory Verse: *Seek first his kingdom and his righteousness, and all these things shall be yours as well.* Matthew 6:33

YOUTH

Topic: *First Things First*

Background Scripture: Matthew 6:19—7:29

Scripture Lesson: Matthew 6:19-21, 24-33

Memory Verse: *Seek first his kingdom and his righteousness, and all these things shall be yours as well.* Matthew 6:33

CHILDREN

Topic: *First Things First*

Background Scripture: Matthew 6:19—7:29

Scripture Lesson: Matthew 6:19-21, 25-28, 33

Memory Verse: *Seek first his kingdom and his righteousness, and all these things will be yours as well.* Matthew 6:33

DAILY BIBLE READINGS

Mon., Jan. 5: Caution Against Judging, Matthew 7:1-5.
Tues., Jan. 6: The Golden Rule, Matthew 7:7-12.
Wed., Jan. 7: Known by Their Fruits, Matthew 7:13-20.
Thurs., Jan. 8: The Wise and the Foolish, Matthew 7:21-29.
Fri., Jan. 9: Value in God's Eyes, Luke 12:1-7.
Sat., Jan. 10: Be Not Anxious, Luke 12:22-31.
Sun., Jan. 11: The Narrow Door, Luke 13:22-30.

LESSON AIM

To help us understand our role in relation to the kingdom of God.

LESSON SETTING

Time: About A.D. 28 or 29

Place: Northwest of the Lake of Galilee

LESSON OUTLINE

The Way of the Kingdom

    I. Singleness of Purpose: Matthew 6:19-24

A. A Single Treasure: v. 19-21
B. A Single Eye: vv. 22-23
C. A Single Master: v. 24

II. Simplicity of Trust: Matthew 6:25-34
A. Trusting for Food: vv. 25-27
B. Trusting for Clothes: vv. 28-30
C. Trusting for All Necessities: vv. 31-32
D. Trusting Based on Obedience: v. 33
E. Trusting for the Future: v. 34

III. Giving and Receiving: Matthew 7:1-12

IV. The Two Ways: Matthew 7:13-29

SUGGESTED INTRODUCTION FOR ADULTS

We might preface our study of "The Way of the Kingdom" by noting one verse near the close of last week's lesson: "But if ye forgive not men their trespasses, neither will your Father forgive your trespasses" (6:15). The way of the Kingdom is first of all the way of forgiveness: God forgiving us and we forgiving others. Jesus declared categorically: If you forgive others, God will forgive you (v. 14); if you do not forgive others, God will not forgive you (v. 16).

This is a very solemn truth. Someone has said: "God can forgive the unforgiven; He cannot forgive the unforgiving." George Buttrick writes: "An unforgiving spirit in us shuts the door in God's face, even though his compassions still surround the house. He is ready to forgive, but we are not ready to be forgiven" (*Interpreter's Bible*, VII, 314).

And our forgiveness must be spontaneous and complete. Henry Ward Beecher is credited with having said: " 'I can forgive, but I cannot forget' is only another way of saying, 'I will not forgive.' Forgiveness ought to be like a canceled note—torn in two and burned up, so that it can never be shown against the man."

SUGGESTED INTRODUCTION FOR YOUTH

Anxiety is a common experience of young people, as well as older folk. What vocation will I choose? Will I be a failure, or will I succeed? How can I win the approval of others? These and other questions often haunt the minds of youth.

This lesson teaches us that we should trust God, regardless of what our future may hold. We cannot trust and worry at the same time. John Wesley said that worry is a sin. "Don't worry" should be more than a flippant escapism; it should be a basic philosophy of life.

CONCEPTS FOR CHILDREN

1. Success in life requires putting first things first.
2. If our first concern is God's kingdom, He will guide our lives and supply our needs.
3. We are not to be careless, but free from anxiety.
4. Righteousness is the foundation of life.

THE LESSON COMMENTARY

I. SINGLENESS OF PURPOSE: Matthew 6:19-24

A. A Single Treasure: vv. 19-21

The Greek literally says, "Do not treasure up treasures on the earth." Why not? Because all earthly treasures are insecure. Many people found that out in 1929 and 1930. Men went to bed millionaires and woke up paupers—and some of them committed suicide. Whole fortunes of stocks and bonds were wiped out overnight. Banks have usually been considered the safest place to put one's money. But in the Great Depression banks closed by the hundreds, and people found that their life's savings were gone. This could happen again!

In Jesus' day people's wealth was often measured in terms of the expensive linens they possessed. But moths could destroy the most costly clothes. "Rust" is literally "eating" and may refer also to moth-worms that eat clothes. But it could also include the rusting of metals. Material things are not eternal; they waste away.

"Break through" is literally "dig through." The homes in that day were commonly made of mud or sun-dried brick. It was comparatively easy for persistent thieves to dig through these walls and steal the treasures in the house. There were no modern banks in those days to provide for safe deposits of money.

So Jesus was giving wise advice when He said, "But treasure up for yourselves treasures in heaven. There they are safe forever."

If people really believed this there would be an abundance of money for the Lord's work. Everybody knows that a man cannot take his money with him when he dies. He leaves it all—every penny. Lawyers often gobble a slice of it. The government takes another slice. And too often relatives quarrel over what is left or squander what was God's money in their ungodly living. How much better it

would have been if the man of means had given his money to the Lord's work. He would have reaped two benefits. First, he would have had the great joy of seeing the good that his money accomplished in furthering the Kingdom and winning souls to Christ. And second, he would be receiving dividends eternally from his investment. Jim Elliott expressed this thought well when he declared, "He is no fool who gives up what he cannot keep to gain what he cannot lose."

Do we really believe that? Does our giving reflect that fact? The man who is truly sensible will order his life in keeping with what Jesus taught here.

Perhaps a word of comment should be made at this point. What we have said does not rule out the need for getting life insurance. Dedicated Christians are killed in accidents on the highways or skyways or drop dead of a heart attack. Every husband and father has a responsiblity to protect his wife and family. But this is different from selfishly laying up treasures.

Then Jesus enunciated an important principle: "For where your treasure is, there will your heart be also." This is a strong argument for encouraging unsaved people to invest their money in the church. A businessman who has never attended church but who gives to the building fund is apt to want to see what his money has helped to provide. And so his giving may lead to his going, and ultimately to his being saved. So we do a man a favor when we encourage him to give to the work of the Kingdom.

B. A Single Eye: vv. 22-23

Jesus declared that the eye is the lamp of the body. It is through the eye that the light enters, so that by means of our eyes we can see what is in the light around us.

The Master went on to say that if one's eye is single, his whole body is full of light. He was now speaking metaphorically. If we have a single purpose in life—to please God—our eye sees things clearly, without distortion.

The opposite is also true. If one's eye is "evil"—*poneros*, a strong term—then the whole body (personality) is full of darkness. And how great is the darkness of the man with evil purpose!

Among the Jews "a good eye" meant a bountiful heart and "an evil eye" meant a covetous heart. This gives us the connection with what precedes. The person who lays up treasure in heaven by giving to the Lord's work has a bountiful heart, and this is always a happy heart. The one who lays up treasure for himself has an evil eye, a covetous heart. Because of this he dwells in darkness here, and will forever.

C. A Single Master: v. 24

The Greek literally says, "No one can be a slave to two masters." One may work for two bosses, but he cannot belong to both as slave. One cannot, said Jesus, be a slave to God and money ("mammon"). He cannot serve God and gold. Ultimately the choice must be made. The one who lives to make money forfeits eternal life.

Carr thinks that the term "mammon" literally means "that in which one trusts." He adds: "It stands here for all that mostly estranges men from God" (*The Gospel According to Matthew*, p. 134). A. B. Bruce says of the last sentence of this verse: "The meaning is not, 'ye cannot serve God and have riches,' but 'ye cannot be faithful to God and make an idol of wealth' " (*Expositor's Greek Testament*, I, 124).

II. SIMPLICITY OF TRUST: Matthew 6:25-34

A. Trusting for Food: vv. 25-27

"Take no thought" obviously needs to be interpreted. If one took this wording literally he would soon die! The correct translation in terms of today's language is "Do not be anxious," or "Do not worry." Worry is a sin, but thoughtfulness is one of the finest virtues.

What Jesus was saying is this: "Do not worry about your life, what you will eat or drink; or about your body, what you will wear. Is not life more important than food, and the body more important than clothes?" (v. 25, NIV). ("Meat" is the term used in the King James Version for all "food.") Carr observes: "The argument in the verse is: such anxiety is unnecessary; God gave the life and the body; will He not give the smaller gifts of food and clothing?" (*Matthew*, p. 134).

Jesus then took up specifically the matter of food. He said, "Look at the birds of the air." ("Fowls" today means domestic hens and roosters, and so is incorrect here.) The Master called attention to the fact that birds do not sow seed or harvest crops, yet God feeds them. Are not we, as human beings, much more valuable than they? Surely God will feed us too.

Then Jesus showed the folly and uselessness of being anxious. He said, "Which of you by taking thought ["being anxious"] can add one cubit unto his stature?" (v. 27).

The last word here, "stature," has caused considerable discussion. The Greek is *helikia*, which occurs eight times in the New Testament. In John 9:21, 23 it clearly means "age." The parents of the blind man whom Jesus had healed said to the critics, "He is of age; ask him." But in Luke 19:3 it just as clearly means height—Zacchaeus was "short of stature." But which does it mean here and in the parallel passage (Luke 12:25)? It would perhaps seem more logical to talk of adding a cubit (18 inches) to one's height than to his age. Abbott-Smith says of *helikia:* "But the prevailing usage in the Septuagint and papyri favours the former meaning (age) in these doubtful passages" (*Lexicon*, p. 199). The context here seems also to favor "length of life." The irony is that anxiety shortens one's life, rather than adding to it. The best translation, therefore, seems to be: "Who of you by worrying

can add a single hour to his life?"
(NIV).

B. Trusting for Clothes: vv. 28-30

"And why do you worry about
clothes? See how the lilies of the field
grow. They do not labor or spin"
(NIV). They neither have to raise
plants nor spin the fibers into cloth.
Yet they are clothed with greater
beauty than was Solomon in all his
magnificent splendor.

The lilies are a part of "the grass of
the field," which appears today and
perishes tomorrow. "Oven" refers to
an open fire. In those days grass was
often used for fuel, due to the scarcity
of trees.

Then Jesus threw out a challenge
to greater faith: "Shall he [God] not
much more clothe you, O ye of little
faith?" It is unanswerable logic. "O ye
of little faith" is all one word in
Greek, the adjective *oligopistoi*
—"little-faithed."

C. Trusting for All Necessities: vv. 31-32

Again we have the recurring warning against anxiety: "Therefore take
no thought." A better translation is:
"So do not worry, saying, 'What shall
we eat?' or 'What shall we drink?' or
'What shall we wear?'" (NIV). The
pagans, who have no trust in the heavenly Father, are constantly seeking, or
running after, material things. But we
should remember that God is actually
our heavenly Father, and as such He
cares for us and our needs.

D. Trusting Based on Obedience: v. 33

Unquestionably this is one of the
greatest verses in the Sermon on the
Mount. Faith is based on obedience. If
we seek first God's kingdom and righteousness, all the necessary things of
life will be supplied to us.

It is a matter of getting our priorities straight. If we put material things
above the spiritual, we ultimately lose

both. If we give first place to spiritual
matters, rather than material, we gain
both. Why don't we live in the light of
this truth?

Verse 33 presents the positive side
of the duty that has been exhibited
negatively in verses 25-32. If we give
highest priority to the spiritual, God
will take care of our material needs.
Both Clement of Alexandria (second
century) and Origen (third century)
quote a traditional saying of Christ:
"Ask great things, and little things
shall be added; ask heavenly things,
and earthly things shall be added."

E. Trusting for the Future: v. 34

"Therefore do not worry about
tomorrow, for tomorrow will worry
about itself. Each day has enough
trouble of its own" (NIV). We are to
live one day at a time. Actually, that is
all that we can live. If we try to live in
tomorrow, we destroy today. We only
need to trust God a day at a time, and
leave tomorrow to His faithfulness.

III. GIVING AND RECEIVING: Matthew 7:1-12

Jesus said, "Don't condemn others,
or you will be condemned yourself."
Perhaps we would say it this way today: "Don't be critical, or you will be
criticized." George Buttrick puts it
succinctly: "Critical censure is a
boomerang" (*Interpreter's Bible*, VII,
325).

The second verse can be summar-
ized in a brief epigram: "You get what
you give." Usually if we give a smile,
we get a smile; if we give a growl, we
get a growl. Life is like that.

The Master proceeded to show the
unreasonableness of a censorious spirit. He said to His hearers: "Why do
you look at the speck of sawdust in
your brother's eye and pay no attention to the plank in your own eye?
How can you say to your brother, 'Let
me take the speck out of your eye,'
when all the time there is a plank in
your own eye? You hypocrite, first

take the plank out of your own eye, and then you will see clearly to remove the speck from your brother's eye" (vv. 3-5, NIV).

This, of course, is ludicrous hyperbole. But that is precisely the method that Jesus used to enforce important truth, as when He talked about a camel going through the eye of a needle, or a man straining a little gnat out of his drinking water and at the same time swallowing a camel. An important principle of pedagogy is that people remember the ridiculous. Every good teacher uses this effective device.

Verse 5 is sound advice, especially for legalists. Get rid of that harsh, critical spirit, that is like a saw log in your eye. Pray for a compassionate, understanding spirit of love. Then you may be able to help your brother remove the little fault that shows up in his eye (his outlook on life).

Verse 6 has often been misapplied. Some Christians in quoting this text have inadvertently given the implication that they thought their unsaved relatives or friends were "dogs" or "pigs." That sort of attitude could cause problems!

E. Stanley Jones suggests another, quite different, interpretation, one that fits in much better with the context and with the spirit of Christ. He offers this application: "That we are not to take the holy thing of personality that is being perfected and give it to the dogs of desire, nor take the pearl of our spiritual life and cast it

before the swine of our lower appetites, lest they trample that holy thing in the mire and rend the most precious thing we have, namely, our spiritual life" (*The Christ of the Mount*, p. 250).

In the English, though not in the Greek, verse 7 furnishes an acrostic:

Ask
Seek
Knock

The first suggests sincere praying, the second earnest praying, the third desperate praying. Sometimes we get the answer by simply asking. At other times we need to keep seeking. And sometimes we must resort to desperate knocking.

Jesus uses a beautiful illustration in verses 9-11. If earthly parents give good gifts to their children, "how much more will your Father which is in heaven give good things to them that ask him?"

Verse 12 contains what is usually called "The Golden Rule." It might be summed up in this way: "Give what you would like to get." Previous philosophers and religious leaders had stated the Golden Rule in *negative* form, as in Judaism: "Don't do to others what you don't want them to do to you." But Jesus' demand is far higher. We are not only to avoid wronging others; we must offer the help and kindness that we would like to receive from them. This rule applies to every area of life!

IV. THE TWO WAYS:
Matthew 7:13-29

The theme of two ways in life is an ancient one. It finds graphic portrayal in the First Psalm, which is a sort of introduction to the entire Psalter.

Jesus took over this thought and pinpointed it very precisely: "Enter through the narrow gate. For wide is the gate and broad is the road that leads to destruction, and many enter

DISCUSSION QUESTIONS

1. Why is it unreasonable to spend our lives amassing wealth?
2. What is meant by a "single" eye?
3. How do men today try to serve two masters?
4. How may we demonstrate our trust in God?
5. Why is worry sinful?
6. Why can we trust the future to God?

through it. But small is the gate and narrow the road that leads to life, and only a few find it" (vv. 13-14, NIV). The Greek word for "broad" is a strong compound, suggesting the wide-open country. The truth is that any path outside the will of God for our lives is the Broadway to perdition.

We are not to judge others (v. 1), but we can recognize people's character by the fruit in their lives (vv. 15-20). Jesus draws a contrast between the good tree and the bad tree.

Then He distinguishes between two kinds of people: those who profess but do not obey, and those who do the will of God (vv. 21-23). The sermon closes with an illustration of this difference (vv. 24-27). Those who hear His words and obey them are like a wise man who built his house on solid rock, so that it withstood the storms. Those who hear but do not obey are like a foolish man who built his house on the sand, only to have it swept away.

CONTEMPORARY APPLICATION

One of the main emphases of this lesson was on "Simplicity of Trust." We have a kind heavenly Father and we should trust Him for our necessities.

I once heard a preacher tell of an experience in his early ministry. He and his wife had come to the end of their financial resources. They had no money to buy food for the family's next meal. The situation was desperate.

After breakfast the wife shook the tablecloth out the back door. The happy sparrows came twittering to eat up the crumbs, chirping their praises to God as they flew away.

It was exactly the lesson they both needed. If the heavenly Father feeds the birds, how much more you! That day a generous check came unexpectedly in the mail. God cares for His own.

January 18, 1976

JESUS' HEALING POWER

DEVOTIONAL READING	Psalm 61

ADULTS

Topic: *Giver of Life and Health*

Background Scripture: Matthew 8:1–9:34

Scripture Lesson: Matthew 9:18-31

Memory Verse: *He took our infirmities and bore our diseases.* Matthew 8:17

YOUTH

Topic: *Giver of Life and Health*

Background Scripture: Matthew 8:1–9:35

Scripture Lesson: Matthew 9:18-31

Memory Verse: *He took our infirmities and bore our diseases.* Matthew 8:17.

CHILDREN

Topic: *Jesus Helps the Sick*

Background Scripture: Matthew 8:1–9:37

Scripture Lesson: Matthew 8:5-13; 9:35-38

Memory Verse: *And Jesus went about all the cities and villages teaching in their synagogues and preaching the gospel of the kingdom, and healing every disease and infirmity.* Matthew 9:35

DAILY BIBLE READINGS

Mon., Jan. 12: If You Will, You Can, Matthew 8:1-13.
Tues., Jan. 13: The Authority of Jesus, Matthew 8:14-27.
Wed., Jan. 14: What Have You to Do with Us? Matthew 8:28-34.
Thurs., Jan. 15: Power to Meet Human Need, Matthew 9:1-8.
Fri., Jan. 16: Healing a Paralyzed Man, John 5:1-9.
Sat., Jan. 17: Healing a Blind Man, John 9:1-11.
Sun., Jan. 18: Evidence of Christ's Power, Matthew 11:1-6.

LESSON AIM

To note the healing power that Jesus exercised while on earth and to study its implications for us today.

LESSON SETTING

Time: About A.D. 28

Place: Capernaum and the surrounding region of Galilee; the east side of the Lake of Galilee

142

Jesus' Healing Power

LESSON OUTLINE

I. Three Healing Miracles: Matthew 8:1-17
   A. A Leper: vv. 2-4
   B. A Centurion's Servant: vv. 5-13
   C. Peter's Mother-in-Law: vv. 14-17

II. Three More Miracles: Matthew 8:23—9:8
    A. Stilling the Storm: vv. 23-27
    B. Casting Out Demons: vv. 28-34
    C. Healing a Paralytic: 9:1-8

III. Third Group of Miracles: Matthew 9:18-34
     A. Woman with Hemorrhage: vv. 20-22
     B. Daughter of Jairus: vv. 18-19, 23-26
     C. Two Blind Men: vv. 27-31
     D. Dumb Demoniac: vv. 32-34

SUGGESTED
INTRODUCTION
FOR ADULTS

In our first lesson on Matthew we noted that one of its main features is systematic arrangement. The whole Gospel is built around five great discourses, with narrative sections between.

We have just devoted two sessions to a study of the first discourse, the Sermon on the Mount (chaps. 5—7). Today we look at ten miracles of Jesus that are grouped together in chapters 8—9. Nine of them are healing miracles. The other, the stilling of the storm, is a nature miracle. As the lesson outline indicates, these miracles are gathered together into three groups.

After three chapters of teaching we now have two chapters of miracles. Jesus' *words* are followed by His *works*.

C. S. Lewis defined a miracle as "an interference with Nature by supernatural power" (*Miracles*, p. 15). He also made this excellent observation: "The central miracle asserted by Christians is the Incarnation. . . . Every other miracle prepares for this, or exhibits this, or results from this" (p. 131).

SUGGESTED
INTRODUCTION
FOR YOUTH

Can we, in this scientific age, still believe in miracles? Or are the miracle-stories just legends, reflecting the superstitions of ancient times? These are crucial questions for young people.

Probably the best answer we can provide is this: Given the miracle of the incarnation—that the eternal Son of God came in human flesh—supernatural works naturally follow. He himself was a miracle; it is no wonder that He wrought miracles! If we believe that He was the Creator of the universe, we know that He could do mighty works while on earth.

CONCEPTS FOR
CHILDREN

1. Jesus had compassion on those who needed His help.
2. He was able to meet every need.

3. Jesus is concerned about our bodies as well as our souls.
4. We should come to Him with our physical needs.

THE LESSON COMMENTARY

I. THREE HEALING MIRACLES: Matthew 8:1-17

A. A Leper: vv. 2-4

This incident is recorded in all three Synoptic Gospels. Matthew says that the leper "worshipped" Jesus. Mark 1:40 has him falling on his knees, and Luke 5:12 falling on his face. The primary idea of the Greek word here in Matthew is that of doing obeisance, and it may be translated "knelt before him" (NIV). The man had a great need, and he came with great humility and earnestness.

As he knelt before Jesus he said, "Lord, if you are willing, you can make me clean" (NIV). He did not doubt the Master's power—he had probably seen it demonstrated a number of times—but he was not quite sure about His willingness.

What was the response? "Jesus reached out his hand and touched the man. 'I am willing,' he said. 'Be clean!' " (v. 3, NIV).

In that day lepers were considered "unclean." When Jesus touched the man He was made ceremonially unclean, according to the law of Moses. But actually His touch made the leper clean; he was healed from his leprosy. It is not God's will that we should be contaminated by our contact with sinners. Rather, the presence of the Holy Spirit should be so powerful in our lives that we touch people redemptively. Instead of being victimized we should be victorious. Since leprosy in the body is a striking symbol of sin in the soul, it is fitting to speak of a leper being cleansed.

The cure was instant and complete. Jesus ordered the man not to tell anyone about his healing, "but go thy way, shew thyself to the priest, and offer the gift that Moses commanded, for a testimony unto them" (v. 4; cf. Leviticus 14). The Revised Standard Version says, "for a proof to the people." But since Jesus had warned him not to tell any man, it would seem that "them" refers to the priests. They were the ones who opposed Jesus and they needed to be challenged to believe in Him.

Why was the man instructed not to tell anyone? The account in Mark gives us the answer: "Instead he went out and began to talk freely, spreading the news. As a result, Jesus could no longer enter a town openly but stayed outside in lonely places. Yet the people still came to him from everywhere" (1:45, NIV). The healed man intended it as a kindness to Jesus, but actually it was a great hindrance to His most important work, that of preaching and teaching. The large crowds that flocked to Him to be healed prevented His spiritual ministry. What Christ wants of all of us is not just good intentions but strict obedience. He knows what is best.

B. A Centurion's Servant: vv. 5-13

Again Jesus went into Capernaum, which He had made His headquarters. "A centurion [officer in charge of one hundred Roman soldiers] came to him, asking for help. 'Lord,' he said, 'my servant lies at home paralyzed and in terrible suffering' " (vv. 5-6, NIV). Promptly Jesus replied, "I will come and heal him" (v. 7).

The answer of this military officer is amazing: "Lord, I do not deserve to have you come under my roof. But just say the word, and my servant will be healed" (v. 8, NIV). He went on to say that he gave orders that were obeyed, and he knew that Jesus could do the same. Carr suggests that the reasoning of the centurion (v. 9) was like this: "If I who am under authority command others, how much more hast thou power to command who art under no authority? If I can send my soldiers or my slaves to execute my orders, how much more canst thou send thy ministering spirits to do thy bidding" (*Matthew*, p. 146).

When Jesus heard the centurion's words, He marveled at them and told His followers: "I tell you the truth, I have not found anyone in Israel with such great faith" (v. 10, NIV). Only one other time are we told that Jesus marveled, and that was at the unbelief of His own townspeople in Nazareth (Mark 6:6). Here it was at the amazing faith of a foreigner. Some have thought that the centurion may have been a Jewish officer in the army of Herod Antipas. But verses 10-12 seem to indicate definitely that he was a Gentile. "Children of the kingdom" (v. 12) refers to the Jews, who were under God's covenant with Abraham, Isaac, and Jacob.

So Jesus sent the centurion on his way with the assurance that his remarkable faith was rewarded. Sure enough, "his servant was healed in the selfsame hour" (v. 13). The Master could heal at a distance just as easily and effectively as by a direct touch.

C. Peter's Mother-in-Law: vv. 14-17

Jesus evidently stayed at Peter's house when He was at Capernaum. One day when they arrived for dinner at noon (cf. Mark 1:29) Peter's mother-in-law was in bed with a sudden fever. Jesus "touched her hand, and the fever left her" (v. 15). Such was the compassionate love and incomparable power of His touch. And His touch still brings healing to bodies and souls.

It was the sabbath day when this happened (cf. Mark). People heard about it. So when the sabbath ended at sunset (Saturday evening) and it was lawful to carry loads, the people began bringing their sick folk to the Healer. They brought many that were demon-possessed, "and he cast out the spirits with his word, and healed all that were sick" (v. 16). Again Matthew quotes a fulfilled prophecy from Isaiah: "Himself took our infirmities, and bare our sicknesses" (v. 17; Isaiah 53:4).

II. THREE MORE MIRACLES: Matthew 8:23–9:8

A. Stilling the Storm: vv. 23-27

Jesus had been extremely busy (v. 18). So He got into a boat with His disciples and headed across the Lake of Galilee to the eastern shore, where things were quiet.

"Without warning, a furious storm came up on the lake, so that the waves swept over the boat. But Jesus was sleeping" (v. 24, NIV). Terrified, the disciples wakened Him with the cry, "Lord, save us! We're going to drown!" (v. 25, NIV). Reproving them for their lack of faith, He "rebuked the winds and the sea; and there was a great calm" (v. 26). Now it was the disciples' turn to marvel at His power (v. 27).

Someone may ask, "Do you believe that Jesus was able to calm the storm on the Lake of Galilee?" My answer is, "Yes!" He quieted the storm in my own heart, and there is no doubt that He could control the elements He had made.

B. Casting Out Demons: vv. 28-34

When they arrived safely on the eastern shore of the lake, two demon-possessed men met Him. Mark (5:1-20) and Luke (8:26-30) both mention only one Gadarene demoniac. But there is no contradiction here. There were two demoniacs, but Mark and Luke mention only the more prominent one. We find this feature several times in Matthew's Gospel, although we do not know the exact reason for his fondness for calling attention to two individuals.

These men were so fierce that people were afraid to come near them. They greeted Jesus with the cry:

"What have we to do with thee, Jesus, thou Son of God? art thou come hither to torment us before the time?" (v. 29). We are told in James 2:19 that even the demons believe and tremble. They knew who He was, the Son of God, and they were afraid of Him.

Fearing that they would be sent back to the abyss, the demons asked for permission to go into a herd of hogs nearby. When the Master said "Go," they entered the hogs and caused them to stampede down a steep place into the lake, where they were all drowned. Thereupon the people of the nearby city urged Him to leave their area. They preferred their hogs to the Savior of mankind. And people are still making that choice.

C. Healing a Paralytic: 9:1-8

Jesus entered a boat and returned to the west side of the lake, which was heavily populated. He "came into his own city" (v. 1). This was Capernaum, where He made His headquarters.

A paralytic was brought to Him. When Jesus saw "their faith"—that of the men who carried the helpless paralytic—He said: "Son, be of good cheer; thy sins be forgiven thee" (v. 2)—rather, "Your sins are forgiven." It was not a wish but a declaration.

Some scribes were present and in their minds they accused Jesus of blasphemy (v. 3). In reply to their critical thoughts He asked a question: "Which is easier: to say 'Your sins are forgiven,' or to say, 'Get up and walk'?" (v. 5, NIV). The answer is that it would be easier to *say* the former, for no one could know whether or not it happened. But to say to the paralytic, "Get up," would put Jesus on the spot. Nevertheless He did just that, as proof that He had forgiven the man's sins. The Pharisees believed that a man could not be healed until his sins were forgiven. On the basis of their own logic, they had no right to deny that Jesus had forgiven the man's sins, for he was now healed.

III. THIRD GROUP OF MIRACLES: Matthew 9:18-34

A. Woman with Hemorrhage: vv. 20-22

Jesus was on His way to Jairus's house when "a woman who had been subject to bleeding for twelve years came up behind him and touched the edge of his cloak" (v. 20, NIV). Her physical condition would have been very embarrassing to her—pale face and emaciated body. So, to avoid being noticed, she slipped up behind Him unobtrusively and quickly touched the edge of His robe. She had remarkable faith: "If I may but touch his garment, I shall be whole" (v. 21). The last clause is all one word in Greek, *sothesomai*. The verb *sozo* is used in the Gospels and the first part of Acts for physical healing. But in the latter part of Acts and throughout the Epistles it is used for spiritual salvation. This emphasizes the fact that salvation means spiritual health or wholeness.

Jesus turned around, saw her and said to her: "Daughter, be of good comfort; thy faith hath made thee whole" (v. 22). It was not the act of touching Jesus' garment that healed her, as if by some magic, but her faith in the Master. However, it should be noted that her faith demonstrated itself in action, as all true faith does.

B. Daughter of Jairus: vv. 18-19, 23-26

While Jesus was talking to a group one day, a "ruler" came to Him. Mark (5:22) gives his name, Jairus, and both he and Luke (8:41) identify him further as a "ruler of the synagogue"—one who had charge of the services in the synagogue.

The synagogue ruler said to Jesus, "My daughter is even now dead." On the surface this seems in conflict with the statement as quoted in Mark 5:23—"My little daughter lieth at the point of death"—literally, "is at her last gasp." Mark and Luke both say that while Jesus was on the way to the house, someone reported that the girl had died. The statement in Matthew has been translated, "My daughter is at the point of death" (NIV). The stronger assertion in this Gospel may well be explained as due to Matthew's repeated habit of telescoping the separate events of a narrative into a brief summary. It should be noted that Matthew does not mention the messenger who came later with the word of the girl's death.

The ruler of the synagogue showed great faith when he said, "But come and lay thy hand upon her, and she shall live" (v. 18). Desperation had driven him to turn to the Master, though he must have felt that he might lose his position by doing so. But it was worth the risk.

After healing the woman with the hemorrhage, Jesus went on to the ruler's house. There he saw the "minstrels" (flute-players) and the mourners already gathered and making a big "noise"—literally, "tumult." The regulations required that a person must be buried the day he died, and it was the custom to hire mourners. The louder they wailed, the better they were paid. Jesus said to them: "Go away. The girl is not dead but asleep" (v. 24, NIV). This only provoked cynical laughter on their part.

Putting out the unbelievers—who would have hindered His miracle-working power—Jesus entered the room, took the girl by the hand and she got up. Mark and Luke state that the Master took with Him into the room only the parents and His three closest disciples—Peter, James, and John. He needed an atmosphere of faith, not mockery.

The story of the raising of Jairus's daughter caused a great deal of excitement. The news spread all over that region (v. 26), causing more people to come to Jesus.

C. Two Blind Men: vv. 27-31

This miracle is recorded only by Matthew, though each of the other Gospels tells of Jesus giving sight to the blind. Again we find here Matthew's fondness for doublets. This may have been due in part to his habit of keeping exact records as a tax collector.

The two blind men followed Jesus, crying out, "Son of David, have mercy on us" (v. 27). As we have already noted, "Son of David" was a Messianic title. These blind men showed great faith in recognizing Jesus in this way.

The blind men went so far as to follow the Master right into the house, pressing their plea (v. 28). Jesus challenged them with a question: "Do you believe that I am able to do this?" (NIV). Their single answer was, "Yes, Lord." Then Jesus touched their eyes and said to them, "According to your faith be it unto you" (v. 29).

Suppose they had not followed Jesus into the house: All their seeking up to that time would have been in vain. This should be a lesson to us not to stop too soon in our praying for what we really need. We must ask, seek, and even knock!

As soon as they received their sight, Jesus sternly warned them, "See that no one knows about this" (v. 30, NIV). But, as did the leper, these men went out and "spread the news about him all over that region" (v. 31, NIV). Again, their intentions were good, but they should have obeyed Christ's command.

DISCUSSION QUESTIONS

1. Should the church give more attention to healing today?
2. How should a healing ministry be carried on?
3. What does James (chap. 5) say about the healing of the sick?
4. Is it God's will to heal everybody? (II Corinthians 12:7-10).
5. What should be our attitude if not healed?
6. What is the relative importance of physical and spiritual healing?

D. Dumb Demoniac: vv. 32-34

As the two healed blind men left, people brought to Jesus "a man who was demon-possessed and could not talk" (v. 32, NIV). This was a pitiful case.

As we have noted before, the Greek always distinguishes between "devil" (*diabolos*) and "demon" (*daimonion*). The distinction should be carried over into English, though the King James Version fails to do so. The correct translation here is: "When the demon was driven out, the man who had been dumb spoke" (v. 33, NIV).

There were two reactions to this. First, the crowd was amazed and said, "Nothing like this has ever been seen in Israel." But the Pharisees had something quite different to say: "It is by the prince of demons that he drives out demons" (v. 34, NIV). This was moral perversion, deliberately labeling divine power as demon power.

These last two healings—of the two blind men and the dumb demoniac—are found only in Matthew's Gospel. While he concentrates on the teachings of Jesus—contrary to Mark—yet he does here list together ten miracles of Jesus.

What was the purpose of the miracles? Probably it was twofold. As all the Gospels seem to indicate, Jesus' miracles were a demonstration of His deity. But they were also an outpouring of His compassionate love. Jesus did not, and does not, want people to suffer. In His love He still seeks to minister to those in need.

CONTEMPORARY APPLICATION

Should we expect healing miracles to occur today? There are several factors that affect the answer.

The first is that in this day of scientific medicine there is much less need for direct divine healing than there was in Jesus' day. At that time the "physicians" were mostly what we would now call "quacks." The remedies they prescribed were often ridiculous, much like those used by the "medicine man" in the jungles of Africa today. Most prescriptions had no medical value whatever. Now we have the "miracle drugs," and good doctors are healing thousands of people. And a second factor is that government now provides medicare.

But there is still a place for "divine healing." God can and does heal cases too hard for physicians and surgeons.

THE MISSION OF THE TWELVE

DEVOTIONAL READING	Isaiah 52:7-10

ADULTS

Topic: *The Call to Mission*

Background Scripture: Matthew 9:35—10:42

Scripture Lesson: Matthew 9:35—10:1, 16-20, 40-41

Memory Verse: *He who receives you receives me, and he who receives me receives him who sent me.* Matthew 10:40

YOUTH

Topic: *The Call to Mission*

Background Scripture: Matthew 9:35—10:42

Scripture Lesson: Matthew 9:35—10:1, 16-20, 40-41

Memory Verse: *He who receives you receives me, and he who receives me receives him who sent me.* Matthew 10:40

CHILDREN

Topic: *Guidance for Disciples*

Background Scripture: Matthew 9:35—10-42

Scripture Lesson: Matthew 10:5-14

Memory Verse: *And whoever gives to one of these little ones even a cup of cold water because he is a disciple, I say to you, he shall not lose his reward.* Matthew 10:42

DAILY BIBLE READINGS

Mon., Jan. 19: The Twelve Sent Forth, Matthew 10:1-7.
Tues., Jan. 20: Rules of the Road, Matthew 10:8-15.
Wed., Jan. 21: Instruction for Mission, Matthew 10:16-23.
Thurs., Jan. 22: The Role of the Disciple, Matthew 10: 24-33.
Fri., Jan. 23: Conditions of Discipleship, Matthew 10:34-39.
Sat., Jan. 24: Need for Additional Workers, Luke 10:1-12.
Sun., Jan. 25: The Return of the Disciples, Luke 10:17-24.

LESSON AIM

To see how Christ uses His disciples to carry out His mission.

LESSON SETTING

Time: About A.D. 28

Place: Galilee

The Mission of the Twelve

I. **The Need for Workers:** Matthew 9:35-38
   A. Jesus' Tour of Galilee: v. 35
   B. His Compassion for the Crowds: v. 36
   C. His Call to Prayer: vv. 37-38

II. **Appointment of the Twelve:** Matthew 10:1-8
   A. Authority for Their Ministry: v. 1
   B. Names of the Twelve: vv. 2-4
   C. Their Commission: vv. 5-8

LESSON OUTLINE
III. **Instructions for the Journey:** Matthew 10:9-15
   A. Equipment: vv. 9-10
   B. Lodging: vv. 11-13
   C. Rejection: vv. 14-15

IV. **Warnings of Persecution:** Matthew 10:16-23
   A. Religious and Civil Persecution: vv. 16-18
   B. Assurance of Guidance: vv. 19-20
   C. Intensity of the Persecution: vv. 21-23

V. **Discipleship under Christ:** Matthew 10:24-42
   A. Identity with the Master: vv. 24-33
   B. The Price of Discipleship: vv. 34-39
   C. The Privilege of Discipleship: vv. 40-42

SUGGESTED INTRODUCTION FOR ADULTS

We have noted several times that one of the main features of Matthew's Gospel is systematic arrangement. This is illustrated in today's lesson. Matthew devotes the whole of this tenth chapter to the appointment of the twelve apostles, their mission and warnings of persecution. These three items are found in scattered places in Mark and Luke. The names of the Twelve are given in Mark 3:13-19 and Luke 6:12-16, their mission in Mark 6:7-13 and Luke 9:1-6 and the warnings of persecution in Mark 13:9-13 and Luke 21:12-17. It is typical of Matthew that he likes to group things together in topical arrangements. The differences in pattern between the four Gospels is a fascinating study. God speaks the same message in different ways through different people.

Christ chose those that He wanted to carry on His mission. And He is still choosing today. It is a great privilege to be commissioned by Him to special service. But every Christian has a mission to perform in winning souls to Christ.

SUGGESTED INTRODUCTION FOR YOUTH

Christ is still calling and commissioning workers to carry out His mission on earth. Young people should be alert to hear His call. We should keep our hearts and minds open to hear His voice and obey His will.

It is a great honor to be called by Christ as one of His ambassadors, one of His representatives on earth. It is a special privilege to spend one's life in full-time service for the Master.

But there is also a price to pay. In this lesson we see something of the cost of discipleship. But it is worth the price! There is no greater thrill than knowing that one is carrying out Christ's commission.

CONCEPTS FOR
CHILDREN

1. Children can have a part in Christ's mission.
2. They can invite other children to their church.
3. They can also show Christ's spirit in their lives.
4. We can tell other children how Jesus has saved us.

THE LESSON COMMENTARY

I. THE NEED FOR WORKERS:
Matthew 9:35-38

A. Jesus' Tour of Galilee: v. 35

"And Jesus went about all the cities and villages." This was in Galilee, which was heavily populated. We find a close parallel to this verse in 4:23—typical summary statements such as Matthew likes to make. The opening clause there is: "And Jesus went about all Galilee." After these similar introductory clauses, the two verses are identical. (The phrase translated "every sickness and every disease" is exactly the same in the Greek as the one translated "all manner of sickness and all manner of disease" that we find in 4:23. Obviously they should be translated the same way.)

In both these verses attention is called to the threefold ministry of Jesus: teaching, preaching, and healing. The teaching was carried on "in their synagogues," after the reading of the Law and the Prophets in the Sabbath services (cf. Luke 4:16-21). This gave Jesus the golden opportunity of speaking to thousands of Jews who had gathered for worship. The situation was made to order! The custom of that day was that visiting teachers were invited to expound the Scriptures in these services (cf. Acts 13:15). Jesus and Paul especially availed themselves of this providential opportunity.

The "preaching"—literally, "heralding" or "proclaiming"—was carried

on largely on the shores of the Lake of Galilee or on some sloping hillside. The "healing" went on everywhere, both in the country and inside the cities. It was often connected with large crowds, but there are several cases of Jesus healing individuals privately.

B. His Compassion for the Crowds: v. 36

"When he saw the crowds, he had compassion on them because they were harassed and helpless, like sheep without a shepherd" (NIV). Jesus saw more than a mass, a large crowd—He saw people. And that is what we must see: individuals with needs.

"He was moved with compassion" is one word in Greek—*esplangchnisthe.* "The verb occurs five times in Matthew, four in Mark and three in Luke. It comes from *splangchnon*, which means 'inward parts.' It is used once literally in the New Testament (Acts 1:18), and ten times metaphorically, meaning 'the heart, affections.' Here the thought is that Jesus' heart was stirred with compassion—which literally means 'suffering with.' Since the verb is in the aorist passive, it is better to translate it: 'He was *gripped* with compassion.' That was Christ's immediate reaction to human need" (Earle, "Matthew," *Beacon Bible Commentary*, VI, 104).

Jesus saw the people as sheep without a shepherd—scattered and confused. He had come as the Good Shepherd (John 10:11) and He was eager to draw them into His flock.

C. His Call to Prayer: vv. 37-38

When Jesus looked at the people, it "suggested two pictures to His mind: a neglected flock of sheep, and a harvest going to waste for lack of reapers. Both imply, not only a pitiful plight of the people, but a blameworthy neglect of duty on the part of their religious guides—the shepherds by profession without the shepherd heart, the spiritual husbandmen without an eye for the whitening fields and skill to handle the sickle" (*Expositor's Greek Testament*, I, 156-57).

The harvest is still "plenteous" and the workers are still "few." While the workers are more numerous, the unharvested fields are still bigger than ever before because of the mammoth increase in population during the last hundred years. After nineteen centuries of Christian history there are yet unnumbered millions who have never heard the gospel. The call to prayer (v. 38) is more pertinent than ever before. ("Send forth" is literally "thrust out.")

But we have no right to pray unless we are ready to go or give as "the Lord of the harvest" may direct. Every Christian must be a worker in the harvest field, functioning wherever the Lord places him.

II. APPOINTMENT OF THE TWELVE: Matthew 10:1-8

A. Authority for Their Ministry: v. 1

At once the Lord of the harvest proceeded to thrust out His own workers into the harvest field. He summoned His twelve apostles and conferred His authority on them, so that they could cast out "unclean spirits"— Mark's favorite expression for demons (10 times)—and heal every sickness

and disease (same expression as in 4:23 and 9:35).

"Power" should be translated "authority." The proper Greek word for "power" is *dynamis*, from which we get the English terms "dynamic, dynamite, dynamo." But the word here is *exousia*, "authority."

B. Names of the Twelve: vv. 2-4

There are four lists of the twelve apostles (Matthew 10:2-4; Mark 3:16-19; Luke 6:14-16; Acts 1:13). Several interesting comparisons could be made. All the lists begin with Peter and end with Judas Iscariot. The four fishermen are always named first, though in differing order. Matthew and Luke present them as pairs of brothers. In Mark we find Peter, James, and John named first—the three composing the inner circle. In the best Greek text of Acts 1:13 Peter and John come first, because we find them working closely in the opening chapters of Acts. "Thaddaeus" (Matthew and Mark) is listed by Luke as "Judas the brother [or, son] of James" (Luke 6:16; Acts 1:13). It may be that this man chose the name Thaddaeus because of the stigma attached to Judas Iscariot. "Canaanite" should be translated "Cananaean." This is perhaps the Aramaic equivalent of "the zealot," which Luke calls him. "Iscariot" is probably Ish-Kerioth, "man of Kerioth"—a village in Judea. If this is correct, Judas Iscariot was evidently the only one of the Twelve who was not from Galilee. This may have given him a false sense of superiority, since we know that the Judeans looked down on the Galileans. "Who also betrayed him" is the epithet regularly attached to his name. Judas's name never escaped the tarnish of his traitorous deed.

C. Their Commission: vv. 5-8

Jesus sent out these twelve men with the command: "Do not go among the Gentiles or enter any town of the Samaritans. Go rather to the lost sheep of Israel" (vv. 5-6, NIV). Theirs was to be a mission entirely to the Jews. The evangelization of the Gentiles would have to wait until Jesus had died for the sins of the whole world.

As they went they were to "preach" (or "proclaim") this message: The kingdom of heaven is at hand. This was the message of John the Baptist (3:2) and Jesus (4:17). In the person of Christ the Kingdom had come, and it was being presented to Israel.

The disciples were also told to do four things along with their main task of preaching—"Heal the sick, raise the dead, cleanse the lepers, cast out demons" (v. 8, so the Greek). There is no record in the Gospels of the disciples raising dead people, but later Peter raised Dorcas from death (Acts 9:40).

Jesus closed the commission by saying, "Freely ye have received, freely give." This applies even more strikingly to us than to them. We have a heritage of nineteen centuries of Christian history, beginning with the outpouring of the Holy Spirit at Pentecost. We are under deep obligation to give freely of our time, money, and loving compassion.

III. INSTRUCTIONS FOR THE JOURNEY:
Matthew 10:9-15

A. Equipment: vv. 9-10

Provide means "procure for oneself" or "acquire" (NASB). They were to take along only what they already had, what was readily available. This resolves what seems on the surface to be a contradiction with Mark 6:8, where the disciples are told to take only one staff.

They were not to provide themselves with gold, silver, or brass—the three levels of coinage. As is the case today, gold was scarce. But Roman silver and copper coins were used constantly. "Purses" is literally "belts"—that is, money belts, the safest place to carry money.

They were not to take any "scrip" for their journey. Today "scrip" means something written. The Greek word here was used for a traveler's leather bag or pouch. Deissmann thinks that it referred to a "beggar's collecting-bag" (*Light from the Ancient East*, p. 109). They were neither to provide themselves with money nor to beg for it. Instead they were to accept the hospitality that was offered to them.

The disciples were not to take two "coats." The Greek word indicates the undergarment, or "tunic." The modern equivalent for a man would be "shirts" (Moffatt). "Shoes" should be "sandals." The word "staves" is singular in the best Greek text—"nor a staff."

To apply these instructions of Jesus to an evangelist or missionary today would be unreasonable. The disciples were going on a brief, hasty mission in a warm climate and among people whose regular custom it was to provide free board and room for any stranger that appeared at their door.

B. Lodging: vv. 11-13

Whenever they entered a city or town they were to search for some worthy person and stay at his house until they left the community. To move around from house to house could create many problems.

When they entered a house, they were to "salute it" (v. 12)—"give it your greeting" (NIV). The common greeting among the Jews was "Shalom," the Hebrew word for "Peace." If the "house" (family) was worthy, "Let your peace rest on it" (v. 13, NIV). If not, peace would return to the disciples, but the home would be left without divine blessing.

C. Rejection: vv. 14-15

When rejected, the disciples were to shake the dust off their feet as they left the house or city. This is what Paul and Barnabas did when they were driven out of Pisidian Antioch (Acts

13:51). Jesus said that in the day of judgment it would be more tolerable for Sodom and Gomorrah than for that city.

IV. WARNINGS OF PERSECUTION: Matthew 10:16-23

A. Religious and Civil Persecution: vv. 16-18

Jesus warned His disciples that they would be like sheep among wolves. This was not a very inviting prospect for these pioneer preachers! The Book of Acts documents Jesus' statement. These messengers of Jesus were to be "wise as serpents and harmless as doves." This can be translated "as shrewd as snakes and as innocent as doves" (NIV). Quite a combination! But that is what a Christian worker has to be.

The Jews had an ancient proverb: "God says: 'With me the Israelites are simple as the dove, but against the heathen cunning as the serpent' " (*Expositor's Greek Testament*, I, 162).

We often see the sign, "Beware of the dog." But Jesus said, "Beware of men!" (v. 17). As Paul discovered, and others since have found, men can be as dangerous as vicious dogs.

The Master warned that some men would hand the disciples over to "councils" (*synedria*). These would be the local councils that were connected with the synagogues, where minor cases would be tried. But these local synagogue courts had the right to administer severe beatings to those whom they judged to be guilty. Jesus said they would "scourge" or "flog" them "in their synagogues."

In verse 17 Christ was warning His disciples of severe persecution from their fellow Jews, and the first part of Acts furnishes many examples of this. But in verse 18 He warns them of persecution by "governors and kings"—"the Gentiles." These were the Roman rulers. Paul was brought before two governors, Felix and Festus (Acts 24 and 25) as well as King Agrippa

(Acts 26). So Jesus' words were literally fulfilled. "For a testimony against them" is better translated, "for a witness to them." Paul had an excellent opportunity to witness for Christ before these Roman rulers, and he made the most of it.

B. Assurance of Guidance: vv. 19-20

These two verses have often been quoted as an alibi for not making careful sermon preparation. Such a distortion of Scripture is criminal. Jesus was talking about emergency situations when His messengers would be hailed into court. It has nothing whatever to do with regular preaching assignments.

It should also be noted that "take no thought" is not a correct translation, as we noted in chapter 6. It is the same verb here and means "Do not be anxious." The correct translation is: "But when they arrest you, do not worry about what to say or how to say it" (NIV). In such times the Holy Spirit would give the disciples the right words to say, speaking through them with more than human wisdom.

C. Intensity of the Persecution: vv. 21-23

The conditions described in verse 21 are almost incredible. But history furnishes many examples. Jesus said: "Brother will betray brother to death, and a father his child; children will rebel against their parents and have them put to death" (NIV). This is still happening, especially in Communist countries and to Muslims who have been converted to Christianity.

To be hated by all men is a sad prospect, but it has been the lot of many Christians in certain areas. By way of both challenge and promise, Jesus added: "But he that endureth to the end shall be saved" (v. 22).

There is a sense in which we were saved when we accepted Jesus as our Savior. There is an equally valid sense in which we are being saved as we walk in the light and obey God. But there is also a final sense in which we will be saved eternally if we keep true to the end. These are the three tenses of salvation—past, present, and future. All are essential.

Jesus told His disciples that when they were persecuted in one city they should flee to another; and then He added this: "Ye shall not have gone over the cities of Israel, till the Son of man be come" (v. 23). What did He mean? R. V. G. Tasker makes this suggestion: "This very difficult verse, found only in Matthew, is best understood with reference to the coming of the Son of man in triumph immediately after His resurrection, when He appeared to the apostles and commissioned them to make disciples of all nations" (*The Gospel According to St. Matthew*, p. 108). But it is possible that what He meant was: "You will not have had time to evangelize all the towns of Galilee until I will be catching up with you on my tour."

V. DISCIPLESHIP UNDER CHRIST: Matthew 10:24-42

A. Identity with the Master: vv. 24-33

The Greek word for "disciple" means "learner," the word for "master" means "teacher," and the word for "lord" is used for masters of slaves. So the better translation of verse 24 is: "A student is not above his teacher, nor a servant above his master" (NIV). It is certainly enough if they are equal (v. 25). So if the critics (the Pharisees) have called the head of the house (literally, "house-master") Beelzebub, how much more is it to be expected that they will use such insulting names for the members of His household. Beelzebub—the Greek is *Beelzeboul*—is supposed at first to have meant "lord of flies," but perhaps at this time signified "lord of the dwelling"—that is, the dwelling of the demons. The scribes said about Jesus: "He hath Beelzebub, and by the prince of the devils casteth he out devils" (Mark 3:22). But this verse would seem to indicate that they actually called Him Beelzebub.

Jesus told the disciples not to be afraid of their persecutors, who could only kill the body, "but rather fear him who is able to destroy both soul and body in hell" (v. 28). Many have thought that the reference is to Satan, but most commentators are agreed that it means God.

To encourage faith, Jesus spoke of the sparrows. Two of them were sold for a "farthing"—"a penny" (NIV). Yet not one sparrow, worth half a penny, could fall to the ground without God noting it. To make it a bit more personal, Jesus added: "But the very hairs of your head are all numbered" (v. 30). The logic of all this was obvious: "So don't be afraid; you are worth more than many sparrows" (v. 31, NIV).

Christ went on to say that anyone who acknowledged Him before men would be acknowledged by Him before His Father in heaven; but whoever disowned Him would be disowned (vv. 32-33). Silence is one way of disowning Him.

B. The Price of Discipleship: vv. 34-39

At first sight, verse 34 seems a bit shocking. The Prince of Peace did not come to bring peace, but a sword? It is

---

DISCUSSION QUESTIONS

1. What is the difference between compassion and pity?
2. How are we helped by praying for missions?
3. Why did Jesus choose twelve apostles?
4. How may we apply some of His instructions to ourselves?
5. What kinds of persecution do we suffer today?
6. What is the price of discipleship?

obvious that what Jesus is saying is this: "My coming to earth will result many times in strife, rather than peace, because those who reject Me will persecute My followers." He is not talking about the purpose of His coming, but of its inevitable consequences. The immediate context indicates this clearly.

Verse 39 is a very significant statement of Jesus, recorded in all four Gospels (cf. Mark 8:35; Luke 9:24; 17:33; John 12:25). Floyd Filson says of the first part: "Self-seeking is self-defeating" (*Matthew*, p. 134). On the second part J. N. Davies writes: "Self-denial and self-sacrifice are the only ways to self-discovery" (*Abingdon Bible Commentary*, p. 972).

C. The Privilege of Discipleship: vv. 40-42

Jesus so identifies Himself with His followers that He says whoever receives them receives Him (v. 40). He also identifies Himself closely with the Father (cf. John 17:21-33).

In the next two verses He extends the matter further: Whoever receives a "prophet" (preacher) or a righteous man will receive the appropriate reward. ("In the name of" is a Hebraism, meaning "for the sake of" or "out of regard to.") Even a cup of cold water given to "one of these least little ones" (a new convert) will be rewarded. God takes note of the times when we try to refresh those who need help.

CONTEMPORARY APPLICATION

Many people say that the day of "missionaries" is over with. But with multiplied millions who have never heard the gospel, the need for missionaries is as great as ever. The truth is that the non-Christian population has been growing faster than the Christian population.

But we must not forget that a whitened harvest field lies right at the door of all of us and stretches around the world. We need to be workers in this wherever the Lord leads.

February 1, 1976

JESUS INVOLVED IN CONFLICT

DEVOTIONAL READING | II Corinthians 4:1-6

ADULTS

Topic: *Involved in Conflict*

Background Scripture: Matthew 11–12

Scripture Lesson: Matthew 12:1-14

Memory Verse: *Blessed is he who takes no offense at me.* Matthew 11:6

YOUTH

Topic: *Concern and Conflict*

Background Scripture: Matthew 11–12

Scripture Lesson: Matthew 12:1-14

Memory Verse: *Blessed is he who takes no offense at me.* Matthew 11:6

CHILDREN

Topic: *Jesus and the Sabbath*

Background Scripture: Matthew 11–12

Scripture Lesson: Matthew 12:9-14

Memory Verse: *Of how much more value is a man than a sheep! So it is lawful to do good on the Sabbath.* Matthew 12:12

DAILY BIBLE READINGS

Mon., Jan. 26: In Tribute to John, Matthew 11:7-15.
Tues., Jan. 27: Judgment to Come, Matthew 11:16-24.
Wed., Jan. 28: Taking Christ's Yoke, Matthew 11:25-30.
Thurs., Jan. 29: God's Chosen Servant, Matthew 12:15-21.
Fri., Jan. 30: The Unforgivable Sin, Matthew 12:22-37.
Sat., Jan. 31: Seeking for a Sign, Matthew 12:38-45.
Sun., Feb. 1: The Sabbath Controversy, Mark 2:23–3:6.

LESSON AIM | To seek to understand what, in the eyes of Christ, are the highest values of life.

LESSON SETTING

Time: About A.D. 28

Place: Galilee

LESSON OUTLINE

Jesus Involved in Conflict

I. Working on the Sabbath: Matthew 12:1-8
  A. Disciples Plucking Heads of Wheat: v. 1

157

B. Accusation of the Pharisees: v. 2
C. Example of David: vv. 3-4
D. Work of the Priests: vv. 5-6
E. Lord of the Sabbath: vv. 7-8

II. Healing on the Sabbath: Matthew 12:9-14
A. Question of the Pharisees: vv. 9-10
B. Answer of Jesus: vv. 11-12
C. Healing of Withered Hand: v. 13
D. Conspiracy Against Jesus: v. 14

III. The Beelzebub Controversy: Matthew 12:22-30
A. Healing of Blind, Dumb Demoniac: v. 22
B. Amazement of the People: v. 23
C. Accusation of the Pharisees: v. 24
D. Answer of Jesus: vv. 25-30

IV. The Unpardonable Sin: Matthew 12:31-37

V. Request for a Miraculous Sign: Matthew 12:38-45

VI. The Family of God: Matthew 12:46-50

SUGGESTED
INTRODUCTION
FOR ADULTS

Last week we studied the second discourse of Jesus, His instructions to the Twelve (chap. 10). Today we take up the next narrative section (chaps. 11–12). The highlight here is the controversy between Jesus and the Pharisees in chapter 12.

In the eleventh chapter we find first the question of John the Baptist and the answer of Jesus. John had heralded the coming of the Messiah and had doubtless expected Jesus to deliver the nation from foreign oppression and set up His Messianic kingdom. But nothing like this was happening; John was languishing in prison, disappointed. So he sent two of his disciples with the question: "Are you the one who was to come, or should we expect someone else?" (v. 3, NIV).

Instead of giving a categorical answer, Jesus told the questioners to report to John what they saw and heard—not only the miracles that Jesus was performing, but the fact that "the poor have the gospel preached to them" (v. 5). These were His credentials, the evidence that He was the Messiah.

Then Jesus pronounced judgment on a nation that had rejected both John and Him (vv. 16-19). He especially singled out the cities where He had worked and taught the most (vv. 20-24). The chapter ends with the matchless words of verses 28-30.

SUGGESTED
INTRODUCTION
FOR YOUTH

The question of keeping the sabbath—or the Lord's Day (Sunday)—is an old one. The Puritans enforced sabbath observance with perhaps too much of the zealous legalism of the ancient Pharisees.

Nevertheless, it does make a difference what we do on

the Lord's Day. We want to discover in this lesson what Jesus had to say about keeping the sabbath, and how we may apply this today.

CONCEPTS FOR CHILDREN	1. Jesus said that it was all right to do what is good on the sabbath. 2. We should try to do on Sunday what we believe Jesus would do. 3. We need to go to church and Sunday school in order to keep our hearts in spiritual health. 4. We should try on Sunday to be especially kind to others.

THE LESSON COMMENTARY

I. WORKING ON THE SABBATH
Matthew 12:1-8

A. Disciples Plucking Heads of Wheat: v. 1

One sabbath day Jesus was walking through "the corn." This term is the British name for "grain," and specifically for wheat. In fact, wheat is still referred to as "corn" in the British Isles. But in the United States "corn" means Indian corn, which is something quite different—something discovered in the New World.

Furthermore, the King James Version says that the disciples "were an hungred"—we would say "were hungry"—and began to pluck "the ears of corn"—a quite misleading description for Americans. The grains grown in Palestine were wheat, eaten by the better classes, and barley, eaten by the poor people. Luke says that the disciples were rubbing the heads of grain "in their hands" (6:1), which would indicate that the grain was wheat. The correct translation of this verse is: "At that time Jesus went through the grainfields on the Sabbath. His disciples were hungry and began to pick some heads of grain and eat them" (NIV).

B. Accusation of the Pharisees: v. 2

When the Pharisees saw what was going on, they immediately protested: "Look! Your disciples are doing what is unlawful on the Sabbath" (NIV). In the minds of these narrow-minded legalists, the disciples were guilty of harvesting grain on the sabbath day, which of course was forbidden labor. Probably these critics contended that when the disciples rubbed the heads of wheat they were threshing, and when they blew the husks away from the kernels they were winnowing. This is what we call making mountains out of molehills—a favorite occupation of legalists.

The trouble with the Pharisees was that they were more interested in principles than in persons. They cared more about protecting their law than they did about guarding human rights. In fact, they repeatedly said that their multitude of minute regulations was intended to "build a fence around the law." God is not interested in protecting law but in producing godly persons.

C. Example of David: vv. 3-4

In answering the accusation, Jesus first cited the case of David. He and his companions went into the house of God and ate the consecrated bread (KJV, "shewbread") which was not lawful for them to eat; only the priests were permitted to do so. What Jesus was saying is that human need is a higher law than religious rules and regulations. Love requires that human need must be met, even if some legal technicalities have to be laid aside in the process. Love and common sense form the combination that makes for real Christian living. Actually, legalism is a human denial of divine love. The Sermon on the Mount clearly indicates that Jesus valued human personality as the most sacred thing in life. He enunciated this truth when He declared: "The sabbath was made for man, and not man for the sabbath" (Mark 2:27). So the correct criterion is always, "What is best for man, who was made in the image of God?" That is what Christ gave His life for.

D. Work of the Priests: vv. 5-6

Jesus proceeded to cite another example to show how technicalities must sometimes be set aside for the higher good of humanity. This was the case of the priests who labored in the temple on the sabbath day, so that sacrifices would be offered for the people. In this imperfect world of ours it is often true that one law cancels out another; and the highest law is always love.

Then Jesus drove home the point that the Pharisees were missing: "In this place is one greater than the temple" (v. 6). The True Temple, the meeting place of God and man, was Christ the God-man. Though the temple at Jerusalem was God's house, Jesus was God's Son. This was something far "greater."

E. Lord of the Sabbath: vv. 7-8

The Pharisees were constantly studying their Scriptures (our Old Testament) and teaching it to the people. But they were too often missing its true meaning. Love gives spiritual insight, but legalism distorts the understanding.

So Jesus quoted a passage from Hosea 6:6—"I will have mercy, and not sacrifice." True religion is a matter of right attitude rather than ritual acts. The great prophets of the eighth century B.C. hammered away at this point. And whenever Christianity finds its main focus in liturgy rather than life it is retrogressing, not progressing.

Jesus declared that if the Pharisees had understood the meaning of Hosea 6:6 they would not have condemned "the guiltless" (plural in the Greek, referring to the disciples, whom they had falsely accused).

Then the Master asserted a great truth: "For the Son of man is Lord even of the sabbath day" (v. 8). This is the heart of the whole matter. Since Christ is Lord of the sabbath, He alone has the ultimate authority to say what is right or wrong to do on that day. If He is also Lord of our lives, then our responsibility is to ask Him, as our Lord, what He wants us to do. And what He directs us to do is right, regardless of what others may think.

II. HEALING ON THE SABBATH: Matthew 12:9-14

A. Question of the Pharisees: vv. 9-10

The first controversy between Jesus and the Pharisees took place in the country. Now He is in the synagogue. Both controversies had to do with sabbath observance which was one of the main emphases of the Jews in Jesus' day and is still a very important phase of Orthodox Judaism.

In the synagogue that sabbath (Saturday) morning there was a man whose hand was all dried up. The Pharisees asked Jesus, "Is it lawful to heal on the sabbath days?" Their purpose was not to learn something, but "that they might accuse him." They were intent on getting Him arrested and, if possible, put to death.

B. Answer of Jesus: vv. 11-12

Jesus answered these cruel critics very logically. If they had a sheep that fell into a deep hole, they would pull it out on the sabbath day, out of pity. Then Jesus clinched the point: "How much then is a man better than a sheep?" In God's sight human personality is the most important value in the world.

Then the Master added this general principle: "Wherefore it is lawful to do well on the sabbath days." The Pharisees held that it would be wrong to heal on the sabbath. They spelled this out in great detail in their minute rules and regulations. A person in severe pain might be given some medicine. But one could not lay a poultice on a boil on the sabbath day because the poultice would draw the pus, and that would be work! If it appeared that a person might die on the sabbath, this was an emergency situation that permitted healing. Otherwise, no! He must suffer it out until the sabbath was ended, and then he could be healed. Jesus revolted strongly against this legalistic system that lacked concern for human need.

C. Healing of Withered Hand: v. 13

Jesus knew full well what the attitude of the Pharisees was. But Christ was Love Incarnate, and so He ministered to the man's need. He said to him, "Stretch out your hand" (NIV). The poor victim might well have answered, "I can't! You can see that it is paralyzed."

But he didn't. Instead he exerted his will in obedience to Christ's command, and as he did so, new life came into his arm and he was able to stretch it out. Because he demonstrated his faith by obedience, his hand "was restored whole, like as the other."

The lesson is clear: Our place is not to argue, but to obey. Instead of saying, "I can't," we should say, "I will." And as we exert our will obediently Christ does the rest. The healing is God's work. Our work is faith and obedience. These give God a chance to do His part.

D. Conspiracy Against Jesus: v. 14

It was wrong for Jesus to heal a man on the sabbath day, but the Pharisees could go out on the sabbath and plot His death! This whole thing is a good illustration of Christ's saying in the Sermon on the Mount about a person with a plank in his own eye wanting to pull a speck of sawdust out of his brother's eye. The picayunish attitude of the Pharisees of Jesus' day is a sad commentary on the state of Judaism.

This incident has a lot to say to us. It is always right, always pleasing to God, for us to do kind deeds to others on the sabbath day. We can remember when legalistic Christians said that they would never ride a street car (like a bus) on Sunday. But we have felt led by the Spirit to do just that, resulting in the salvation of the old lady we visited that Sunday afternoon.

III. THE BEELZEBUB CONTROVERSY: Matthew 12:22-30

A. Healing of Blind, Dumb Demoniac: v. 22

"Then they brought him a demon-possessed man who was blind and mute, and Jesus healed him so that he could both talk and see" (NIV). The man's condition was a serious combination: He could neither see nor talk. Being blind, he couldn't even write. It must have been very frustrating to have no way of communicating with those around him. But Jesus took pity on him and healed him completely. The man found himself in a new world.

B. Amazement of the People: v. 23

Astonished at what had happened, the people said, "Is not this the son of David?" But the Greek clearly indicates that a negative answer is expected: "This is not the son of David, is it?" The first edition of the King James Version (1611) correctly translated it, "Is this the son of David?" So did four following editions. Then "not" was wrongly inserted and became standard in 1769. So the meaning was distorted. Perhaps there was some hope mixed with the people's incredulity, so that they were thinking, "Can this possibly be the son of David?"

C. Accusation of the Pharisees: v. 24

The Pharisees had a very different reaction. Cynically they sneered: "It is only by Beelzebub, the prince of demons, that this fellow drives out demons" (NIV). This was the most cruel accusation they could have brought against the holy Son of God, who in compassionate love was healing people by divine power. They were without excuse in offering this insult.

D. Answer of Jesus: vv. 25-30

Reading their thoughts, Christ challenged their logic. A kingdom, city, or house that is divided against itself will come to ruin. If Satan (Beelzebub) was driving out Satan, how could his kingdom stand? It just didn't make any sense!

Then Christ scored another bull's-eye by asking: "And if I by Beelzebub cast out devils [demons], by whom do your children cast them out? therefore they shall be your judges" (v. 27). Exorcism was practiced by a number of Jews in that day (Acts 19:13-16). Were these people under the authority of Beelzebub? While they were thinking that one over, Jesus went on to give the true explanation: "But if I cast out devils [demons] by the Spirit of God, then the kingdom of God is come unto you" (v. 28). In His person the kingdom of God had come, and the healing miracles (works of love) were evidence of this.

Jesus suggested a further point: No one can plunder the household goods of a strong man unless he first ties the man up. The Master concluded this part of His discourse by saying: "He that is not with me is against me; and he that gathereth not with me scattereth abroad" (v. 30). We cannot be neutral with regard to Jesus Christ. We are either for Him, loyal to Him, or we are disloyally against Him.

IV. THE UNPARDONABLE SIN: Matthew 12:31-37

Now Jesus throws out a warning to the Pharisees: Blasphemy against the Holy Spirit will never be forgiven. One may insult Christ and be forgiven, but not if he insults the Holy Spirit. The context suggests that the unpardonable sin is willfully attributing to Satan the work of the Holy Spirit. This is the way John Wesley put it: "It is neither more nor less than the ascribing of those miracles to the power of the devil which Christ wrought by the power of the Holy Ghost" (*Explanatory Notes on the New Testament*, p. 64). It is when men deliberately reject what they know to be true and persist in stubborn hatred of the truth that they finally become impenitent beyond help or hope.

John the Baptist had called the Pharisees "a generation of vipers" (3:7). Now Jesus applies the same epithet to them (v. 34). Their hearts were wicked, and so their mouths poured out evil words. Then comes the warning that in the day of judgment we shall give account for every "idle" (worthless) word we speak.

V. REQUEST FOR A MIRACULOUS SIGN: Matthew 12:38-45

The "scribes" (teachers of the Law) and the Pharisees were still on Jesus' trail, trying to get Him into trouble. This time they said to Him, "Teacher, we want to see a miraculous sign from you" (v. 38, NIV). What about His healing miracles they had just witnessed? What more could they ask for? The question was insulting.

DISCUSSION QUESTIONS

1. What causes legalism?
2. How is legalism a denial of love?
3. What is the remedy for legalism?
4. What is proper to do on Sunday?
5. How may it best be observed as a day of rest and worship?
6. What works of mercy might we do on the sabbath?

No wonder the Master replied: "A wicked and adulterous generation asks for a miraculous sign! But none will be given it except the sign of the prophet Jonah" (v. 39, NIV). He went on to explain what He meant. Just as Jonah was three days and nights in the belly of a huge fish, so the Son of Man would be three days and nights in the heart of the earth (v. 40). Christ's resurrection on "the third day" (16:21) would be the adequate proof that He was the Messiah.

Jesus went on to say that both the men of Nineveh and the queen of "the south" (Sheba) would rise up in the judgment and condemn His generation. They responded in their day, and yet this generation would not recognize the presence of One who was far greater than Jonah or Solomon (vv. 41-42).

Then Jesus gave a graphic illustration of the condition of the Pharisees' hearts. He pictured an unclean spirit leaving a man but returning later to find the man's life "empty, swept, and garnished" (v. 44). So he takes along seven spirits worse than himself and they enter the man's heart; "and the last state of that man is worse than the first" (v. 45). It is a picture of reformation without regeneration. Christ added: "Even so shall it be also unto this wicked generation." The Jews of His day prided themselves on their righteous living and ceremonial cleanness. But they were possessed by the spirit of Satan, not the Spirit of God. Their determination to kill their best Friend and Benefactor showed that.

VI. THE FAMILY OF GOD: Matthew 12:46-50

While Jesus was carrying on this conversation with the Pharisees in a house, His mother and His brothers were standing outside, wanting to talk to Him. Finally someone told Him about it (v. 47).

Christ's reply was first in the form of a challenging question: "Who is my mother? and who are my brothers?" (v. 48, NIV). Pointing to His disciples He said, "Behold my mother and my brothers!" (v. 49, NIV).

Who belongs to the family of God? Jesus puts it clearly: "For whosoever shall do the will of my Father which is in heaven, the same is my brother, and sister, and mother" (v. 50). We must note that He did not add "and father." Jesus had only one father, "my Father who is in heaven." But He had an earthly mother, as well as earthly brothers and sisters. Above and beyond that, all who obey the heavenly Father are in Christ's family. We enter the family of God through the New Birth. And we maintain our relationship in the family by obedience.

CONTEMPORARY APPLICATION

One of the great tragedies of history illustrates a false concept of values. In the last century there was a great famine in Russia; people were dying by the thousands without food. At the same time, the interiors of the great Orthodox churches were plated with millions of dollars' worth of gold.

Finally a delegation waited on the czar, who was the titular head of the church. "Why can't some of the gold be stripped off and used to buy wheat from other countries, to save the people from starvation?"

Anyone can guess the answer: "No, the gold is consecrated gold; it is too sacred to be used for that purpose." Is it any wonder that the people of Russia turned against the church and adopted atheistic Communism?

PARABLES OF THE KINGDOM

DEVOTIONAL READING	Psalm 78:1-8
ADULTS	Topic: *The Challenge of the Kingdom* Background Scripture: Matthew 13 Scripture Lesson: Matthew 13:31-33, 44-52 Memory Verse: *Blessed are your eyes, for they see, and your ears, for they hear.* Matthew 13:16
YOUTH	Topic: *Is It Worth My Life?* Background Scripture: Matthew 13 Scripture Lesson: Matthew 13:31-33, 44-52 Memory Verse: *Blessed are your eyes, for they see, and your ears, for they hear.* Matthew 13:16
CHILDREN	Topic: *Responding to the Good News* Background Scripture: Matthew 13 Scripture Lesson: Matthew 13:18-23 Memory Verse: *The unfolding of thy words gives light; it imparts understanding to the simple.* Psalm 119:130
DAILY BIBLE READINGS	Mon., Feb. 2: The Parable of the Sower, Matthew 13:1-9. Tues., Feb. 3: The Secrets of the Kingdom, Matthew 13:10-17. Wed., Feb. 4: Understanding the Parable, Matthew 13:18-23. Thurs., Feb. 5: The Wheat and the Weeds, Matthew 13:24-30. Fri., Feb. 6: The Parable Explained, Matthew 13:34-43. Sat., Feb. 7: Parables in Seeds, Mark 4:26-34. Sun., Feb. 8: The Wisdom of Jesus, Matthew 13:53-58.
LESSON AIM	To discover the true nature of the kingdom of heaven and its challenge for us.
LESSON SETTING	Time: About A.D. 29 Place: Galilee
LESSON OUTLINE	Parables of the Kingdom I. The Sower: Matthew 13:3-9, 18-23

164

A. The Four Kinds of Soil: vv. 3-9
B. The Meaning of the Parable: vv. 18-23

II. The Tares: Matthew 13:24-30, 36-43
A. The Parable: vv. 24-30
B. The Explanation: vv. 36-43

III. The Mustard Seed: Matthew 13:31-32

IV. The Leaven: Matthew 13:33

V. The Hidden Treasure: Matthew 13:44

VI. The Pearl of Great Price: Matthew 13:45-46

VII. The Dragnet: Matthew 13:47-50
A. The Parable: vv. 47-48
B. The Explanation: vv. 49-50

Conclusion: Matthew 13:51-52

SUGGESTED INTRODUCTION FOR ADULTS

We have studied two of the five discourses of Jesus in Matthew's Gospel—the Sermon on the Mount (chaps. 5–7) and the Instructions to the Twelve (9:35–10:42). Now we take up the third one, the Parables of the Kingdom (chap. 13).

In keeping with his systematic arrangement of material, Matthew has gathered into one place seven parables of the Kingdom. These, with the explanation of three of them, comprise most of chapter 13.

The main topic in the Gospel of Matthew is the kingdom of heaven. All but the Parable of the Sower here begin with the phrase: "The kingdom of heaven is like." Furthermore, these six parables are clearly in three pairs— the tares and the dragnet, the mustard seed and the leaven, the hidden treasure and the pearl of great price. The two in each pair teach essentially the same truth.

SUGGESTED INTRODUCTION FOR YOUTH

Is it worth my life? The answer is, "Yes!" It is worth your life to invest your all in the kingdom of God. For this investment pays eternal dividends. And even in this life there is a tremendous satisfaction and sense of fulfillment that one gets from serving Christ as Lord and Master.

Jesus said to His disciples: "Blessed are your eyes, for they see: and your ears, for they hear" (v. 16). Across the long centuries many people had waited for the coming Messiah. It is our great privilege to live this side of Bethlehem's manger, in the light of Christ's having come. We should be joyful and thankful for this.

CONCEPTS FOR CHILDREN

1. The parables were stories told to illustrate truth.
2. Each parable has one special point.

3. Jesus used parables to make His message clearer.
4. We should try to help people understand His good news.

THE LESSON COMMENTARY

I. THE SOWER:
Matthew 13:3-9, 18-23

A. The Four Kinds of Soil: vv. 3-9

The setting of this parable is described in the first two verses of the chapter. Jesus left Peter's house in Capernaum and went out beside the lake where He sat down. Such a great crowd gathered that He had to get into a boat—not a "ship" (KJV)!—and sat down to teach the people. The crowd that stood on the shore could hear Him well, since the lake's surface acted as a sounding board. And because the ground slopes down to the shore, they could all see Him.

His first words were: "Behold, a sower went forth to sow." It is possible that at that moment a farmer was striding across a nearby field in plain sight of the crowd, reaching into a bag slung over his shoulder and scattering the seed with wide sweeps of his hand. One can still see this going on in Palestine today—at least we saw it at Christmas of 1950. (Israel is fast introducing modern agricultural methods.)

As the man sowed, the seed fell on different types of ground. The real point of the parable is the four kinds of soil, so that it is sometimes referred to as "The Parable of the Soils."

The first ground was "by the way side," or "along the path" (NIV). Here the ground was hard, beaten down by the many feet that had passed that way. Since the seed lay exposed on the surface, the birds of the air came and ate it up.

Some seed fell on "stony places"—better, "rocky places." This does not refer to ground covered with small stones, but to thin soil on top of a ledge of solid rock. Because the dirt was warm and moist, the seed quickly sprouted and the plants appeared above ground. But when the hot sun

scorched them, they withered away because they had no strong roots.

Other seed fell among thorns. The latter grew faster than the wheat and soon choked it to death.

Fortunately, part—probably the greater part—of the seed "fell into good ground." This "produced a crop, a hundred, sixty or thirty times what was sown" (NIV). Then Jesus added this admonition, which we find in other places: "He who has ears, let him hear" (v. 9, NIV).

B. The Meaning of the Parable: vv. 18-23

The hardened path typifies the person who hears the gospel message but does not understand it. It doesn't sink in. Satan, "the wicked one," comes quickly and snatches away the seed that was sown. Too many people's hearts are beaten down by the heavy traffic of modern living and hardened by callous indifference, so that the truth of the gospel doesn't penetrate.

The thin soil on top of a rocky ledge (v. 20) symbolizes those who have shallow hearts. Such people may receive the message with joyful enthusiasm. But emotionalism is no substitute for a moral decision. Such a person only lasts for a short time in the Christian life. As soon as the way gets hard, he quits—"When trouble or persecution comes because of the word, he quickly falls away" (v. 21, NIV). (The Greek word translated "by and by" in the King James Version means "immediately," and "he is offended" is weaker than the original verb.) Shallow Christians don't last long!

But it is the third kind of soil that poses the biggest warning for all of us as Christians. The hard soil suggests those who are never really born again. The thin soil symbolizes those who have an emotional experience without moral depth. But the thorny ground describes the alarming proportion of Christians who allow their spiritual life to be choked out by the things that crowd in on them—"the worries of this life and the deceitfulness of wealth" (v. 22, NIV). We live in an age of anxiety—the Greek literally says "the anxieties of this age"—that has aptly been described as "the Aspirin Age." Nervous tension is wrecking too many people spiritually. The daily grind can wear a person down if he doesn't keep his heart fresh and tender with divine love. And in this day of high wages too many are succumbing to "the deceitfulness of riches." We need to keep our priorities straight.

There is one feature in this parable that is often overlooked: Even the good soil produces in varying measure. We should not be satisfied with producing thirtyfold, when it ought to be sixty or a hundred.

We sometimes blame the preacher for the lack of evangelistic results. But here the farmer sows good seed and scatters it widely. The disappointing results are due to the lack of receptivity and steadfast purpose on the part of the hearers.

II. THE TARES:
Matthew 13:24-30, 36-43

A. The Parable: vv. 24-30

Jesus told about another man who "sowed good seed in his field." But at night, while everybody was sleeping, an enemy came and sowed "tares" ("weeds," NIV) among the wheat. No one knew about this until the wheat began to grow, when the weeds also put in their appearance. It is generally held that the "tares" were darnel, which can hardly be distinguished from wheat until the heads of grain are formed. "When the wheat sprouted and formed heads" (NIV) is obviously more accurate today than "when the blade was sprung up, and brought forth fruit." We don't speak of grain as "fruit."

The servants of the landowner came to him wondering where the weeds had come from. When he suggested that an enemy was responsible, they offered to go and pull out these obnoxious weeds. But the owner answered: "No, because while you are pulling the weeds, you may root up the wheat with them" (v. 29, NIV). Anyone who has done any gardening can appreciate this necessary warning.

B. The Explanation: vv. 36-43

When Jesus had dismissed the crowd and gone back into the house, His disciples said to Him, "Explain to us the parable of the weeds in the field" (v. 36, NIV). The Master was glad to oblige.

In recent years many writers on the parables have insisted that we should look for only one point in each parable; we should be careful to avoid all allegorizing. While this was doubtless a needed corrective to some wild speculations, it should be noted that in this chapter Jesus gives the meaning of three of the seven parables—Sower, Tares, and Dragnet—and that in each case He offers an allegorical interpretation! That is, He explained the typology of each item.

So here, He says that the sower is the Son of Man, the field is the world, the good seed are the children of the Kingdom, the tares are the children of Satan, the enemy that sowed them is the devil, the harvest is the end of the age, and the reapers are the angels. The separation between the good and the bad will be made at the end of the age. The wicked will be cast into "a furnace of fire: there shall be wailing and gnashing of teeth" (v. 42). But the righteous will "shine forth as the sun in the kingdom of their Father" (v. 43). It should be noted that the most solemn warnings in the New Testament against the final punishment of the wicked are to be found in the so-called simple teachings of the gentle Jesus.

The Parable of the Tares teaches an important lesson: It is not our prerogative to make the separation between the righteous and the wicked. Judgment is God's work, not ours. If we start pulling up the weeds, we may uproot some new converts and young Christians while we are doing so. At the end of the age God will take care of the separation.

III. THE MUSTARD SEED:
Matthew 13:31-32

Jesus declared that the kingdom of heaven is like a mustard seed that a man planted in his field. Botanists have protested against the statement that this is "the least of all seeds" (v. 32). They point out the indisputable fact that there are other seeds smaller than the mustard seed. But this was a proverbial saying of that time. When anyone wished to emphasize how tiny a thing was, he would say that it was as small as a mustard seed. This was evidently the smallest seed then in common use. So probably the best translation is: "Though it is the smallest of all your seeds, yet when it grows it is the largest of garden plants and becomes a tree" (v. 32, NIV).

The idea of "mustard seed faith" (17:20; Luke 17:6) growing into a large, fruitful tree of blessing has been beautifully demonstrated in missionary work. "Little is much, if God is in it."

IV. THE LEAVEN:
Matthew 13:33

Jesus used the familiar picture of a woman who mixed yeast into "three measures" (about a bushel) of flour "until it worked all through the dough" (NIV). The yeast pervaded the whole mass and expanded its size.

As we noted above, these last two parables form a pair, teaching essentially the same lesson. But what is that lesson?

From the second to the nineteenth centuries the standard interpretation of these parables was that they both portray the growth of the church under God's blessing. The former symbolizes the outer growth—numerically and geographically. The latter emphasizes the inner growth in spirituality and unseen influence. But for the past hundred years some have insisted that leaven is always a type of sin in the Bible and that these parables signify the wicked growth of the church in political influence and in large, worldly institutions.

Which is right? Possibly both. But we should not lightly reject the concensus of the centuries.

V. THE HIDDEN TREASURE:
Matthew 13:44

In those days there were no banks as we know them now. Someone had dug a hole in the ground and hidden a sum of money (cf. 25:18). By accident another man found it. He buried it again, went and sold all his possessions and purchased the field. It is obvious that the treasure had been hidden for a long time, or the owner would not have sold the field without removing the treasure. This probably takes care of the criticism that the buyer acted unethically. It would seem that the treasure did not belong to the present owner of the field; so it was more like finding pirate's gold.

VI. THE PEARL OF GREAT PRICE:
Matthew 13:45-46

Here is the picture of a merchant looking for fine pearls. When he found a very valuable one, he sold everything he had and bought it. The obvious connection of the two parables is that in both cases the man involved was willing to give all he had in order to gain the precious treasure.

Again we have two very different interpretations. Some think that these parables refer to Christ's giving His all at Calvary to purchase the church. But most scholars interpret them as meaning that one should be willing to give up all he has to gain salvation. It is true that salvation, as such, cannot be bought. But it is also true that one has to give his all to get it. This is the paradox of Christianity. The kingdom of God is the hidden treasure and also the pearl of great price.

The former parable typifies those who suddenly and unexpectedly find Christ, with no forethought. The latter parable symbolizes those who search a long time for reality, for something that will really satisfy. When they discover that Christ and His salvation are the precious pearl that they have sought so long, they give their all to gain Him. Both types of conversion happen frequently.

VII. THE DRAGNET:
Matthew 13:47-50

A. The Parable: vv. 47-48

"Once again, the kingdom of heaven is like a net that was let down into the lake and caught all kinds of fish" (v. 47, NIV). When it became full, the fishermen dragged it to shore, as they can still be seen doing in that area. Then they sorted out the fish, putting the good fish into baskets and throwing the bad away.

B. The Explanation: vv. 49-50

Jesus went on to say: "This is how it will be at the end of the age. The angels will come and separate the wicked from the righteous and throw them into the fiery furnace, where there will be weeping and grinding of teeth" (NIV).

It is obvious that this parable teaches the same lesson as that of the Tares: that God will make the final separation of the righteous and the wicked at the end of the age. Probably the Parable of the Tares is placed earlier because, like the Parable of the Sower, it has to do with sowing grain. But in interpretation it belongs with the Parable of the Dragnet.

Perhaps we should think of the lesson of these parables as twofold. It is first of all a warning to us as individuals that we make sure to be among the good wheat or fish in the Kingdom,

not the bad. Also it teaches that human leaders should not usurp God's prerogative of judgment. This is His task.

Of the seven parables in this chapter, that of the Sower is the longest and the most important. That would probably be assumed from the fact that it is in all three Synoptic Gospels, as is also the Parable of the Mustard Seed. The Parable of the Leaven is found in Matthew and Luke. The other four—Tares, Hidden Treasure, Pearl of Great Price, and the Dragnet—are found only in Matthew. They are distinctly "parables of the Kingdom."

CONCLUSION:
Matthew 13:51-52

The New International Version prints this last part in keeping with correct literary style today:

'Have you understood all these things?" Jesus asked.

"Yes," they replied.

He said to them, "Therefore every teacher of the law who has been instructed about the kingdom of heaven is like the owner of a house who brings out of his storeroom new treasures as well as old."

The "new treasures" may well refer to the teachings of Christianity, while the "old" would have reference to the Old Testament. Every good preacher and Bible teacher finds treasures in both Testaments.

DISCUSSION QUESTIONS

1. What are some applications of the Parable of the Sower?
2. How would you apply the Parable of the Tares?
3. How can "mustard seed faith" grow?
4. How has Christianity leavened society?
5. What is the greatest treasure on earth?
6. What false pearls do people spend their money for?

James Morison describes the force of the reference to "new treasures" in these words: "A man who is really *understanding* things makes steady progress and ascends, reaching higher and still higher standpoints, and thence getting wider and still grander views. There is hence a *new* element that is ever mingling with the *old* in his ideas. He sees things in *new* relations, and yet they are the *old* things still. His ideas never become obsolete and stale; they never stagnate. His mind is not a mere cistern in which the collected water may grow stagnant and unwholesome. It is a perennial wellspring, whose waters are ever living and fresh" (*A Practical Commentary on the Gospel According to St. Matthew*, p. 242).

Jesus, of course, was the perfect example of this. His teaching was based on the Old Testament. But He was always bringing to these ancient Scriptures fresh insight into spiritual reality.

CONTEMPORARY APPLICATION

Perhaps the most significant lesson for us in this thirteenth chapter of Matthew is found in the Parable of the Sower. Here we are warned of the danger of having our hearts choked by two things: "the anxieties of the age" and "the deceitfulness of riches."

Regarding the first we may say this: "The cluttering cares of our daily doings can strangle the spiritual life. This is the greatest threat to every Christian. Too busy to pray, too busy to take time to be holy. Choked, starved, dead!"

Concerning the second we need only explode the idea that money spells happiness. Riches are deceitful; they sell us short. Only spiritual things last.

CONTRASTING RESPONSES OF FAITH

DEVOTIONAL READING	Hebrews 11:1-6

ADULTS

Topic: *When Faith Takes Hold*

Background Scripture: Matthew 14—15

Scripture Lesson: Matthew 14:25-33; 15:21-28

Memory Verse: *Whatever you ask in prayer, you will receive, if you have faith.* Matthew 21:22

YOUTH

Topic: *Faith in Action*

Background Scripture: Matthew 14—15

Scripture Lesson: Matthew 14:25-33; 15:21-28

Memory Verse: *Whatever you ask in prayer, you will receive, if you have faith.* Matthew 21:22

CHILDREN

Topic: *Jesus Shows Compassion*

Background Scripture: Matthew 14—15

Scripture Lesson: Matthew 15:29-38

Memory Verse: *Give us this day our daily bread.* Matthew 6:11

DAILY BIBLE READINGS

Mon., Feb. 9: The Death of John the Baptist, Matthew 14:1-12.
Tues., Feb. 10: The Feeding of the Five Thousand, Matthew 14:13-21.
Wed., Feb. 11: Conflict with the Pharisees, Matthew 15:1-9.
Thurs., Feb. 12: Defilement from Within, Matthew 15:10-20.
Fri., Feb. 13: The Compassion of Christ, Matthew 15:29-39.
Sat., Feb. 14: Healing the Handicapped, Mark 7:31-37.
Sun., Feb. 15: The Nature of Faith, Hebrews 11:1-6.

LESSON AIM

To show the unlimited power of faith and the great consequences that can come from it.

LESSON SETTING

Time: About A.D. 29

Place: The Lake of Galilee and the area of Tyre and Sidon, north of Palestine

171

Contrasting Responses of Faith

LESSON OUTLINE

SUGGESTED INTRODUCTION FOR ADULTS

During the time of Jesus' public ministry Galilee was ruled by Herod the tetrarch. This was Herod Antipas, son of Herod the Great. Herod had ruled over all Palestine. But at his death in 4 B.C., probably a year after Christ's birth, his kingdom was divided and allotted to several of his sons.

When Herod Antipas heard about the miraculous ministry of Jesus, he said, "This is John the Baptist . . . risen from the dead" (v. 2). Then Matthew tells the sordid story of the death of that prophet.

Herod Antipas had gone to Rome, stayed with his brother there, and then rewarded Philip's hospitality by stealing his wife! When he got back to Galilee, the rugged, righteous preacher from the wilderness faced him with his crime: "It is not lawful for you to have her" (v. 4). Afraid to put John to death, Herod locked him up in prison.

But Herodias was determined to get John's head. So she arranged a big birthday party for Herod, and disgraced her own princess daughter publicly by having her dance like a common geisha girl before Herod and his drunken cronies. It worked! John's bloody head was delivered on a platter, and hate was satiated with revenge.

SUGGESTED INTRODUCTION FOR YOUTH

"Faith in Action"—that's what we read about in this lesson. Peter displayed a very bold faith in walking on the surface of the Lake of Galilee. The Syro-Phoenician woman showed boundless faith in believing that Jesus could heal her demon-possessed daughter at a distance.

Both of these two believers had their faith tested. In both cases faith was richly rewarded, as it always is. But we have to be willing to prove our faith by putting it into action.

CONCEPTS FOR
CHILDREN

1. Jesus had compassion on people in need.
2. His followers should show the same compassion today.
3. God multiplies what we give to help the needy.
4. We should be concerned about all kinds of human need.

THE LESSON COMMENTARY

I. FEEDING THE FIVE THOUSAND:
Matthew 14:13-21

A. The Needy Crowd: vv. 13-14

When Jesus heard about John the Baptist's death, He left the west side of the Lake of Galilee and went across to the quiet eastern shore. The tragedy must have struck Him a heavy blow. John was his close relative (Luke 1:36), as well as His forerunner. He Himself would experience human hate, as John had.

The crowds near Capernaum saw Jesus leaving by boat and hurried on foot around the north end of the lake. The slowness of travel by boat in those days is shown by the fact that the people could walk some eight or ten miles on land while the boat went about six or seven miles on the water. For when Jesus and His disciples disembarked, the crowd was waiting.

Instead of being annoyed at this intrusion on a much needed vacation, Jesus was "moved with compassion." He healed their sick, demonstrating divine love and power.

B. The Worried Disciples: vv. 15-17

As evening came on, the disciples became concerned about the crowd. They came to Jesus and urged Him to send the people to the surrounding villages to buy food. We can imagine their amazement when He replied: "They need not depart; give ye them to eat" (v. 16). How could they!

The disciples informed the Master that they had only five loaves and two fish. We learn from John's Gospel that these were the barley loaves and small fish that comprised a boy's lunch (John 6:9). The "loaves" of that day were about the size of a small pancake or a flat biscuit. What good would this do for a large crowd?

C. The Adequate Master: vv. 18-21

Christ's reply was brief: "Bring them here to me." After having the crowd sit down in orderly fashion on the grassy hillside, He took the little lunch, blessed it, and broke it into small pieces. Then He passed the food to His disciples, and they distributed it to the people. Everybody ate until he was full, and then the disciples filled their twelve lunch baskets with the broken pieces that were left over. This was their tip!

What lesson can we learn from this? It is very clear and simple. When Christ commands us to do something, our duty is not to argue but to obey. We are to give Him our little—all of it—and then let Him multiply it to meet the need.

Jesus told His disciples to feed the crowd. This was impossible! All they had was one boy's small lunch. But those disciples did feed that crowd! The lesson is that when we obey, turning our tiny assets over to Christ, He enables us to carry out His commands fully.

It is not our business to ask

"Why?" or "How?" Instead we should say, "Yes, Lord," and then let Him show us how we can do it with His supernatural help.

II. FACING THE STORM:
Matthew 14:22-24

Jesus "constrained" His disciples to get into their fishing boat (probably Peter's) and precede Him to the west side again, while He sent the crowd away. John's Gospel tells us why: The people wanted to take Jesus forcibly and make Him king (John 6:15). He would deliver them from Roman oppression. And with a man like this as ruler, they would never have any economic problems!

When Jesus had dismissed the crowd, He went up the hill alone to pray. Meanwhile the disciples were having a hard time getting across the lake. They were facing a strong northwest wind that impeded their progress. The boat was being "tossed"—literally, "tortured"—by the waves (v. 24). Mark says that the disciples were "toiling in their rowing" (6:48). The language is strong and is perhaps best translated "straining at the oars." It was a dark, difficult hour.

III. WALKING ON THE WATER:
Matthew 14:25-33

A. The Troubled Disciples: vv. 25-26

"In the fourth watch of the night [3:00–6:00 A.M.], Jesus went unto them, walking on the sea"—rather, "the lake." It is always true that in the darkest hour Christ comes to His own.

But when the disciples saw Him approaching on the lake, they were "troubled"—better, "terrified"—and cried out in fear, "It's a ghost" (v. 26, NIV). Probably Jesus, as usual, was wearing a long white robe, so that in the darkness He seemed like a ghost. And of course only a ghost could walk on top of the water!

B. The Comforting Master: v. 27

Jesus lost no time in calming the fears of His distraught disciples. Quickly He said, "Be of good cheer; it is I; be not afraid." And how often He comes to us in the darkness, when we are afraid, and speaks peace to our inner spirit. When we know that it is He, we are no longer afraid.

C. A Believing Disciple: vv. 28-29

Some people would challenge this heading. They say that Peter acted on a sudden impulse, not on faith. But we submit that it must have taken some faith for a man to step out of a boat on to the surface of deep water. Peter was no fool. He had fished the waters of the Lake of Galilee for many years and was well aware of the dangers of drowning. Yet when Jesus said, "Come," this rugged fisherman stepped right out on the water and started to meet the Master. After all, Peter actually "walked on the water" in his bare feet, and that is more than any of us have ever done!

D. A Doubting Disciple: vv. 30-31

As long as Peter kept his eyes on Jesus he was perfectly safe. But when he looked down, and saw the boisterous winds and beating waves, he became afraid. Beginning to sink, he cried out, "Lord, save me."

Immediately Jesus reached out His hand and caught hold of Peter. Too often the implication of this is missed. If Peter was near enough to Jesus to be caught by an outstretched hand, he must have walked some distance on the water. This, we say again, must have taken faith.

The Master did reprove His doubting disciple (v. 31). "O thou of little faith" is all one word in Greek, *oligopiste*—literally, "little-faithed." Gently Jesus chided him, "Why did you doubt?"

On the whole, Peter has had a bad press. People talk about his failure here, forgetting that he was the only one of the Twelve who had the courage and faith to step out on the water and walk toward Jesus. They condemn him for thrice denying his Lord, ignoring the fact that the rest of the disciples forsook Jesus and fled. Peter followed "afar off," but at least he followed! And it was impulsive Peter, filled with the Holy Spirit, who preached on the day of Pentecost, resulting in three thousand souls being saved. Who of us has ever matched that?

E. Worshiping Disciples: vv. 32-33

As soon as "they"—Jesus and Peter—got into the boat, the wind died down. What a thrilling moment that must have been for the courageous apostle!

The other eleven disciples in the boat came and "worshipped him"—fell on their knees before Jesus. They were probably motivated by three factors: the appearance of Jesus just when they needed Him, His miraculous walking on the water, and His stopping the wind from blowing. Spontaneously they cried out, "Truly you are the Son of God" (v. 33, NIV). He had demonstrated His deity abundantly.

We should note that they did not worship Peter because he walked on the water. They recognized the source of his ability in Jesus. And we must not worship men who are empowered by God.

IV. CONTENDING WITH THE CRITICS:
Matthew 15:1-20

"Scribes" (teachers of the Law) and Pharisees came all the way from Jerusalem to check on Jesus. This involved a distance of a hundred miles, which would take the week between sabbaths (walking fifteen to twenty miles per day). They were determined to subject to close scrutiny this new prophet from Nazareth.

We have already noted some of the controversies between Jesus and the Pharisees (see Lesson 9). This time it was something new, but still related to the ceremonial law. These critics asked Jesus: "Why do your disciples break the tradition of the elders? They don't wash their hands before they eat!" (v. 2, NIV).

Jesus answered by asking them a pertinent question in return: "And why do you break the command of God for the sake of your tradition?" (v. 3, NIV). Then He quoted the fifth commandment, "Honour thy father and mother" (Exodus 20:12). But the rabbis had ruled that a son whose parents needed help could say, "Whatever help you might otherwise have received from me is a gift devoted to God" (v. 5, NIV). Then, according to the rabbis, he was free from obligation to his parents. Bluntly Jesus declared, "Thus you nullify the word of God for the sake of your tradition" (v. 6, NIV).

Calling the crowd to Him, Jesus pointed out the difference between a materialistic religion of ritual and ceremonial regulations on the one hand, and the true religion of the spirit on the other. The Pharisees made a major issue of clean and unclean foods. But Christ pointed out the fact that it is not the food a man eats that makes him unclean but the evil words he speaks and the evil thoughts he harbors in his heart. In other words, defilement is not a matter of material, ceremonial factors. It is in the moral and spiritual realm that things are clean or unclean. He concluded: "eating with unwashed hands does not defile a man."

V. REWARDING A WOMAN'S FAITH:
Matthew 15:21-28

A. A Desperate Need: vv. 21-22

Once more Jesus left Galilee to have a quiet time instructing His disciples and perhaps to escape His critics. This time He went far north to the region of Tyre and Sidon. These were two coastal cities in ancient Phoenicia (modern Lebanon).

There "a Canaanite woman [described in Mark 7:26 as "a Greek, born in Syrian Phoenicia"] from that vicinity came to him, crying out, 'Lord, Son of David, have mercy on me! My daughter is suffering terribly from demon-possession' " (v. 22, NIV).

The expression "Son of David" was a Messianic title (cf. 1:1). How did this Gentile woman living in pagan territory recognize Jesus as the Jewish Messiah? The answer is that she may have been among those who came from around Tyre and Sidon to hear Jesus in Galilee (Mark 3:8).

B. The Disciples' Complaint: v. 23

Jesus gave the woman no answer. This seems strange, a bit out of character for the compassionate Christ. But He knew what He was doing. He wanted to teach His disciples a needed lesson in love.

Finally the disciples begged Jesus to tell the woman to go away. They were doubtless embarrassed and greatly annoyed to have the woman following them and "yelling after us." Disgusted, they wanted to get rid of her.

DISCUSSION QUESTIONS

1. How could the disciples have been so slow in expecting Jesus to feed the second big crowd?
2. Do we today forget great answers to prayer and seem surprised at new situations?
3. What are some lessons of faith we can learn from these two incidents?
4. Can we trust Christ never to let us down?
5. How was the Greek woman an example of faith?
6. What is the value of having our faith tested?

C. The Test of Faith: vv. 24-27

On the surface, the reply of Jesus seems very strange: "I am not sent but unto the lost sheep of the house of Israel" (v. 24). He seems to be saying that His mission did not include the Gentiles. But actually the Master was testing the faith of the woman, for her good.

And it worked. Undaunted by what He had said, she came and knelt before Him. Simply and humbly she begged, "Lord, help me" (v. 25).

The next reply of Jesus seems even more strange. He said to her, "It is not meet to take the children's bread, and cast it to dogs" (v. 26). The fiery furnace was getting hotter! Would the woman stand the test, or quit and leave in disgust at this bigoted Jew?

But there is an important point here in the Greek that usually does not appear in English translations. Jesus did not use the common word for "dog," the despised scavenger of the villages. Instead He said kynariois, "little dogs"—the pet dogs in the home. This thought is brought out in the New International Version: "It is not right to take the children's bread and toss it to their dogs"—the dogs the children loved.

The woman's quick wit and strong faith caught the word. With amazing courage—a Gentile woman talking in public to a Jewish man—she replied: "Truth, Lord: yet the dogs [little pet dogs] eat of the crumbs which fall from their masters' table" (v. 27).

There is another very important principle involved here. When we read the written report of someone's words, we miss the look of eye and tone of voice with which the words were said. Leslie Weatherhead suggests that the expression on Jesus' face and the tone of His voice may have conveyed to the woman that He was not saying something unkind to her but rather was reproving His disciples, by indirection, for their narrow, nationalistic attitude (It Happened in Palestine, pp. 198-202).

D. The Fruits of Faith: v. 28

No wonder Jesus exclaimed: "Woman, you have great faith! Your request is granted" (NIV). She had come through the test with flying colors. G. Campbell Morgan puts it this way: "Against prejudice she came, against silence she persevered, against exclusion she proceeded, against rebuff she won" (*Matthew*, p. 202). Her daughter was healed.

VI. FEEDING THE FOUR THOUSAND:
Matthew 15:29-39

Coming back down from the vicinity of Tyre and Sidon, Jesus went to the east side of the Lake of Galilee, the region called "the Decapolis" (Mark 7:31)—that is, "the Ten Cities." There again the crowds gathered around Him as He sat on a hillside, bringing their sick to be healed (v. 30). Seeing the dumb speak, the crippled made well, the lame walk, and the blind see, the people were amazed— "and they glorified the God of Israel" (v. 31).

Jesus called His disciples and told them that He had compassion on the many people who had been with Him for three days and had nothing to eat. He was afraid they might collapse on the way home (v. 32).

Again the disciples protested that it was impossible in that "wilderness" to find food for such a crowd (v. 33). When Jesus asked how many "loaves" they had, they answered, "Seven, and a few little fishes."

Then came a repeat performance. Jesus had the people sit down on the ground. He took the few little biscuits and fish, gave thanks for them, broke them, and gave the pieces to the disciples and the latter served the people. Again everyone had all he could eat. This time the disciples took up seven basketfuls of broken pieces that were left over. But these were larger baskets. The Greek word for "basket" used here is different from the one used in connection with the feeding of the five thousand. The word here is used in Acts 9:25 for the basket in which Paul was let down from the wall in Damascus. So it must have been a large basket, much larger than the lunch baskets of the twelve disciples.

Matthew says that there were four thousand men who ate, "beside women and children" (v. 38). He uses the same expression in 14:21, in connection with the five thousand. Matthew was writing his Gospel for Jews, among whom the men always ate separately from the women and children.

CONTEMPORARY APPLICATION

Is the Lord asking us to undertake something that seems far beyond our abilities and assets? Is the church being challenged to launch out in an impossible task? If so, the illustrations in this lesson ought to help us.

"Where God guides, God provides." It is still true today. Without Him we will fail even in doing what seems possible and reasonable. But "with God nothing is impossible."

The Kingdom belongs to God. And divine work is done by divine power. Faith brings God into every situation, no matter how difficult.

THE CHURCH'S MEANING AND MISSION

DEVOTIONAL READING	Micah 4:1-7

ADULTS

Topic: *Why the Church?*

Background Scripture: Matthew 16–17

Scripture Lesson: Matthew 16:13-26

Memory Verse: *If any man would come after me, let him deny himself and take up his cross and follow me.* Matthew 16:24

YOUTH

Topic: *Why the Church?*

Background Scripture: Matthew 16–17

Scripture Lesson: Matthew 16:13-26

Memory Verse: *If any man would come after me, let him deny himself and take up his cross and follow me.* Matthew 16:24

CHILDREN

Topic: *Jesus Is the Christ!*

Background Scripture: Matthew 16–17

Scripture Lesson: Matthew 16:13-18

Memory Verse: *Simon Peter replied, "You are the Christ, the Son of the living God."* Matthew 16:16

DAILY BIBLE READINGS

Mon., Feb. 16: Warning Against False Doctrine, Matthew 16:6-12.
Tues., Feb. 17: Taking Up the Cross, Matthew 16:24-28.
Wed., Feb. 18: The Transfigured Christ, Matthew 17:1-8.
Thurs., Feb. 19: Elijah Has Come, Matthew 17:9-13.
Fri., Feb. 20: Faith Works Wonders, Matthew 17:14-21.
Sat., Feb. 21: Give No Offense, Matthew 17:22-27.
Sun., Feb. 22: A Vision of Peace, Micah 4:1-7.

LESSON AIM

To seek to understand the meaning and mission of the church.

LESSON SETTING

Time: A.D. 29

Place: Caesarea Philippi, in northern Galilee

LESSON OUTLINE

The Church's Meaning and Mission

    I. The Great Confession: Matthew 16:13-17

A. What Do Men Say? v. 13
B. Various Opinions: v. 14
C. What Do You Say? v. 15
D. Peter's Affirmation: v. 16
E. A Divine Revelation: v. 17

II. The Church of Christ: Matthew 16:18-20
   A. Its Rock Foundation: v. 18
   B. Apostolic Authority: v. 19
   C. Injunction to Silence: v. 20

III. The First Prediction of the Passion: Matthew 16:21-23
   A. Suffering, Death, and Resurrection: v. 21
   B. Peter's Protest: v. 22
   C. Jesus' Rebuke: v. 23

IV. The Cost of Discipleship: Matthew 16:24-26
   A. Self-denial and Self-crucifixion: v. 24
   B. Losing to Save: v. 25
   C. The Value of the Soul: v. 26

SUGGESTED INTRODUCTION FOR ADULTS

The sixteenth and seventeenth chapters of Matthew contain two of the outstanding "crises of the Christ." They mark a turning point in Jesus' ministry. Before this He had given Himself largely to a ministry to the crowds. He had been busy teaching, preaching, and healing. From this time on He devoted most of His attention to His twelve disciples, seeking to prepare them to carry on His ministry after He left.

The first thing He had to do was to be sure that they recognized Him as the Messiah. This came in Peter's confession at Caesarea Philippi. Then Jesus told them that as the Messiah He would suffer and die at Jerusalem. To confirm Peter's confession, Jesus was transfigured on the mount. But lest the disciples think that He was now coming in glory to set up an outward kingdom, He again told of His coming death. He was going to Jerusalem not for a crown, but for a cross.

SUGGESTED INTRODUCTION FOR YOUTH

Many people today say that we don't need the church. Some even suggest that we would be better off without it.

We realize that salvation is through Christ, not through the church. Yet the church has played the major role in saving people. The question could well be asked: Where would Christianity be without the church?

So, in spite of all its faults, let's be thankful for the church. It deserves our appreciation and loyalty. Christ was concerned to build His church, and we should share that concern.

CONCEPTS FOR CHILDREN

1. Jesus was the Messiah, expected by the Jews.
2. He was also the Son of God, eternally with the Father (John 1:1).

3. The church is composed of those who believe in Jesus as Son of God and Savior.
4. The church should provide a fellowship for believers.

THE LESSON COMMENTARY

I. THE GREAT CONFESSION: Matthew 16:13-17

A. What Do Men Say? v. 13

Jesus had spent many months with His disciples. They had watched Him healing the sick, teaching the crowds, preaching the gospel to the poor. Now it was time for them to recognize and acknowledge Him as their Messiah.

The setting was the region of Caesarea Philippi. ("Coasts" in King James Version obviously does not signify what that word means for us today, for Caesarea Philippi is a long way from any seacoast.) That city was built by Philip, one of the sons of Herod the Great. He called it "Caesarea" after the emperor Tiberius at Rome. The further designation "Philippi" was added to distinguish it from the Caesarea on the coast of the Mediterranean that Herod the Great had built as the Roman capitol of Palestine.

Today the place is called Banias. This is a modification of its ancient name, Paneas—after the Greek God "Pan," which means "All." So it was a fitting place to confess that Jesus was the Son of the one true God, who alone is "All in all."

As noted in the Introduction, this was a crucial time in Christ's ministry. M'Neile puts it this way: "The public ministry in Galilee was at an end, the journey towards the Cross was soon to begin; and He wished to draw the disciples into closer sympathy with Himself than ever before" (*Gospel According to St. Matthew*, p. 238). The next few months would be a time of severe testing for both Him and His disciples. They needed to be firm in their faith.

It was in this setting of time and place that Jesus turned to His disciples and asked, "Who do people say the Son of Man is?" (NIV). He was not looking for information, or wanting to have His own faith bolstered, as some liberal critics have contended. He only wanted to clarify the disciples' thinking.

B. Various Opinions: v. 14

The disciples replied: "Some say John the Baptist; others say Elijah; and still others, Jeremiah or one of the prophets" (NIV). The King James Version gives the Greek form of the Old Testament prophets' names. But we should always use the familiar Hebrew form found in the Old Testament, so that readers and listeners today can know whom we are talking about. Many a modern reader of the King James Version has asked, "Who is this 'Elias'?" We owe it to the people to give them the Bible in a language that they can understand easily and accurately.

It is only natural that some people would think that Jesus was John the Baptist come back to life (cf. Mark 6:14). He echoed John's call to repentance and preaching about the Kingdom (see Matthew 3:2; 4:17). He was also like Elijah in His stern denunciation of sin and His demand for righteousness. And His warnings of impending doom sounded like those of Jeremiah. All in all, He seemed to be "one of the prophets."

C. What Do You Say? v. 15

It is interesting to know what others have thought about Jesus. But the crucial question is: Whom do *we* believe Him to be?

The question that Jesus put to His disciples is much more emphatic in the original Greek than it is in the King James Version. Literally it reads: "But you, who do you say me to be?" The New International Version brings out the force of this very well: " 'But what about you?' he asked. 'Who do you say I am?' "

The most important theological question that confronts every man today is, "Who is Jesus?" Unless we believe that He is the Son of God, He cannot be our Savior and Lord.

D. Peter's Affirmation: v. 16

Too often Peter said the wrong thing at the wrong time. But now he said the right thing at the right time. Rising magnificently to the occasion, he declared, "Thou art the Christ, the Son of the living God." As we noted in the second lesson of this quarter, "the Christ" means (in Greek) "the Anointed One," the same as the Hebrew "Messiah." Peter affirmed that Jesus was not only the long-awaited Messiah of the Jews but also the Son of God. It was a great declaration. Carr observes: "This confession not only sees in Jesus the promised Messiah, but in the Messiah recognizes the divine nature" (*Gospel According to St. Matthew*, p. 210).

The religious leaders of the Jewish nation rejected Jesus' claims to deity, and so would not accept Him as their Messiah. Instead they condemned Him to death on the charge of blasphemy (26:64-65).

E. A Divine Revelation: v. 17

The reply of Jesus is most significant. He affirmed the divine source and authority of what Peter said. "*Flesh and blood* was a rabbinical expression for humanity in contrast with Deity. Only a divine revelation from the Holy Spirit can make us really *know* that Jesus is the Son of God. Such a revelation gives an inner certainty that cannot be shaken" (*Beacon Bible Commentary*, VI, 155).

We can know many things about Jesus from hearsay. But we can only know Jesus Himself as the Holy Spirit reveals Him to us. We have two solid foundations for our faith in Jesus as the divine Savior. One is the Word of God, written by inspiration of the Spirit. The other is the inner witness of the Holy Spirit to our own souls.

II. THE CHURCH OF CHRIST: Matthew 16:18-20

A. Its Rock Foundation: v. 18

Peter's Jewish name was "Simon Bar-jona," that is, "Simon, son of Jonah." But Jesus had given him the name "Peter" (Greek *petros*, "a stone"). Now He reminds Peter of this, and then adds: "upon this rock [Greek, *petra*] I will build my church." Abbott-Smith says that *petra* means "a mass of live rock as distinct from *petros*, a detached stone or boulder" (*A Manual Greek Lexicon of the New Testament*, p. 359). "Many scholars object that there is only one word in Aramaic for both of these, *Kepha*, and that since Jesus spoke in Aramaic no distinction between the Greek words applies here. But in this Gentile, Greek-speaking area it is altogether possible that Jesus spoke in Greek and changed words intentionally" (*Beacon*, VI, 155).

It is common knowledge that the largest church in Christendom quotes this verse to prove that Christ's church is built on Peter as its rock foundation. But we are convinced that it is not Peter, but his confession of Jesus' deity, on which the church is founded. M'Neile comments: "The reference is probably to the truth which the apostle had proclaimed; the fact of the Lord's Messiahship was to be the immovable bed-rock on which His 'ecclesia' would stand secure" (*Matthew*, p. 241). If the church had been built on the human Peter, it would have collapsed a long time ago. Only the divine Christ can be the solid foundation of the church.

"Hell" (KJV) is the translation of the Greek *hades*, which means "the place of departed spirits." It should simply be transliterated as "Hades." The expression "the gates of Hades" probably means "the power of the unseen world," or "the power of death."

The Greek word for "church" is

ecclesia. It is found here and twice in 18:17, but nowhere else in the four Gospels. However, it is used 24 times in Paul's Epistles (115 times in the entire New Testament).

The word literally means "called out." It was used for the "assembly" of free, voting citizens in a Greek city (Acts 19:32, 39, 41). Perhaps more significantly, it is the term used in the Septuagint (Greek translation of the Old Testament) for the "congregation" of Israel. Today the church is the congregation of called-out ones, the true people of God. We are called out of the world, out of the mass of humanity, to be God's own chosen people, the church of Jesus Christ.

B. Apostolic Authority: v. 19

This verse has also been misapplied. It has sometimes been assumed that Jesus gave to Peter the keys of heaven, so that this human apostle can decide whether to let us in there! But Jesus did not say "the keys of heaven," but "the keys of the kingdom of heaven."

What did He mean? The Book of Acts gives the best answer. Peter used these keys at Pentecost, when he opened the door of the Kingdom to the Jews and proselytes, and three thousand entered that day. Later he used the keys to unlock the door to the Gentiles in the house of Cornelius. A. T. Robertson comments: "Every preacher uses the keys of the kingdom when he proclaims the terms of salvation in Christ" (*Word Pictures in the New Testament*, I, 135). Whenever we witness to people about Jesus as Savior we are unlocking the door of the Kingdom.

The second part of this verse is a bit more difficult to interpret. What is meant by "bind" and "loose"? In rabbinical language *bind* meant to declare a thing as forbidden, and *loose* meant to say that it was permitted. We should note that Jesus later gave this same authority to all the apostles (18:18).

John Wesley writes: "Under the terms of *binding* and *loosing* are contained all those acts of discipline which Peter and his brethren performed as apostles; and undoubtedly, what they performed on earth, God confirmed in heaven" (*Explanatory Notes upon the New Testament*, p. 82).

C. Injunction to Silence: v. 20

The word translated "charged" means "strictly charged" or "warned" (NIV). Why this injunction? The reason is obvious. If Jesus' Messiahship had been openly proclaimed at this time, it would have precipitated a political revolution against Rome. Jesus did not want this.

III. THE FIRST PREDICTION OF THE PASSION: Matthew 16:21-23

A. Suffering, Death, and Resurrection: v. 21

The word "began" marks a new departure in Jesus' teaching. Hitherto He had been talking mainly in parables, telling the large crowds about the coming of the Kingdom. Now He begins to explain to His disciples that this would involve His suffering and death. He was going to Jerusalem, not to set up a kingdom but to suffer and die, in order to bring the spiritual kingdom to the hearts of the redeemed.

The prediction was threefold: (1) suffer, (2) be killed, (3) be raised again. "The elders and chief priests and scribes" comprised the Sanhedrin, the Supreme Court of the nation. The "chief priests" were Sadducees and were in charge of the temple worship. The "scribes" were Pharisees who taught the law of Moses in the synagogues. The "elders" would be the other members of the Sanhedrin, which was composed entirely of older men. It was the Sanhedrin that condemned Jesus to death and handed Him over to Pilate to be executed—since the Roman government had taken away its right to administer capital punishment.

It was not until the disciples had recognized Him as Messiah that Jesus could tell them about His coming death at Jerusalem. Now that the confession had been made by Peter at Caesarea Philippi, Christ had to correct their wrong concepts of what the Messiah would do. They needed to realize that He must first be the suffering Servant of the Lord (Isaiah 53) before He could be the King on the throne.

B. Peter's Protest: v. 22

When Peter heard Jesus' prediction of His passion (suffering), he "took him." Probably "took him aside" (NIV) is a more adequate translation for the compound verb in Greek. Perhaps he grabbed hold of Him.

Then Peter said to Jesus, "Be it far from thee, Lord." This is only three words in Greek and may be translated "Pity yourself, Lord!" Peter had a big heart of affection for his Master, and he could not bear to think of Jesus going through this ordeal. "This shall not be unto thee" has the double negative in Greek for emphasis: "This shall never happen to you!" (NIV).

C. Jesus' Rebuke: v. 23

Peter's motive in saying this was right; he was moved by love for his Lord. But, as too often, he said the wrong thing.

"Get thee behind me, Satan" seems like very strong language. But Jesus was not calling Peter a devil. The word "Satan" (Hebrew and Greek, taken over into English) means "adversary." In opposing Jesus' going to the cross, Peter was being an adversary to God's will. The word "offence" (Greek, scandalon) is literally a "trap" or "snare." Peter was unknowingly setting a trap for Jesus, trying to keep Him from carrying out His main mission on earth—giving His life as ransom for many (20:28). Peter was thinking man's thoughts, not God's thoughts.

("Savourest" simply means "think" or "have in mind.")

IV. THE COST OF DISCIPLESHIP: Matthew 16:24-26

A. Self-denial and Self-Crucifixion: v. 24

This verse contains one of the most significant sayings of Jesus recorded in the Gospels. Discipleship is costly.

"Come after me" is rabbinical language for "be my disciple." Jesus said, "If you want to be my disciple, you must first deny yourself." We must realize that self-denial is the password into the Kingdom. To enter the kingdom of God we have to humble ourselves and renounce our sins.

"Take up his cross" means being crucified with Christ (Galatians 2:20), death to the carnal self, a full surrender of our will to God's will. In his book *The Cost of Discipleship*, Bonhoeffer says: "Discipleship means adherence to the person of Jesus, and therefore submission to the law of Christ which is the law of the cross" (p. 77).

"Let him deny" and "take up" are both in the aorist tense, suggesting the crises of conversion and complete consecration. But "follow" is in the present tense of continuous action. Following Christ is a lifelong assignment.

B. Losing to Save: v. 25

Jesus declared that the only way to save one's life is to lose it. The one

---

DISCUSSION QUESTIONS

1. What are some contemporary opinions about Christ?
2. Why is it essential to believe in His deity?
3. How can we be absolutely certain that He is God?
4. What is the church?
5. What are some of its proper functions?
6. What does discipleship involve?

who loses his life for Jesus' sake will find it. The songwriter put it well: "Let me lose myself and find it, Lord, in thee." Every consecrated Christian has demonstrated this truth. When we lose our lives in loving service to others, we find the highest and happiest life—the life in Christ.

C. The Value of the Soul: v. 26

If one could gain the whole world of wealth and material possession and yet lost his own soul eternally, what would it profit him? The obvious answer is, "Nothing!" The human soul is worth more than all the material universe.

CONTEMPORARY APPLICATION

We have a friend who left a lucrative business career to follow God's call to the ministry. A wealthy lady asked him to become manager of her oil wells. She would give him her Cadillac, her mansion, and a far larger salary than he would get as pastor. He declined, saying he must preach. She said, "Just give me three days a week, and I'll give you all that, plus a private plane." But this capable young man said No to it all. Today he is the president of a large Bible college.

THE WAY OF FORGIVENESS

DEVOTIONAL READING	Psalm 51:1-10

ADULTS

Topic: *Demands of Forgiveness*

Background Scripture: Matthew 18

Scripture Lesson: Matthew 18:21-35

Memory Verse: *For if you forgive men their trespasses, your heavenly Father also will forgive you.* Matthew 6:14

YOUTH

Topic: *The Way of Forgiveness*

Background Scripture: Matthew 18

Scripture Lesson: Matthew 18:21-35

Memory Verse: *For if you forgive men their trespasses, your heavenly Father also will forgive you.* Matthew 6:14

CHILDREN

Topic: *How Shall I Forgive?*

Background Scripture: Matthew 18

Scripture Lesson: Matthew 18:21-33

Memory Verse: *For if you forgive men their trespasses, your heavenly Father also will forgive you, but if you do not forgive men their trespasses, neither will your Father forgive you your trespasses.* Matthew 6:14

DAILY BIBLE READINGS

Mon., Feb. 23: The Greatest in the Kingdom, Matthew 18:1-6.
Tues., Feb. 24: The Lost Sheep, Matthew 18:10-14.
Wed., Feb. 25: The Presence of Christ, Matthew 18:15-20.
Thurs., Feb. 26: God Answers Prayer, Psalm 86:1-7.
Fri., Feb. 27: God Forgives Our Sins, Psalm 103:1-12.
Sat., Feb. 28: Forgiveness from the Cross, Luke 23:32-43.
Sun., Feb. 29: A Prayer for Forgiveness, Psalm 51:1-10.

LESSON AIM

To help us understand that because God has forgiven us freely for all our sins, so we should freely forgive others for all their wrongs against us.

LESSON SETTING

Time: A.D. 29 or 30

Place: Galilee

LESSON OUTLINE

The Way of Forgiveness

    I. Parable of the Lost Sheep: Matthew 18:12-14

II. **Discipline in the Church:** Matthew 18:15-20

III. **Unlimited Forgiveness:** Matthew 18:21-22
    A. Peter's Question: v. 21
    B. Jesus' Answer: v. 22

IV. **Parable of the Unmerciful Servant:** Matthew 18:23-35
    A. Day of Reckoning: v. 23
    B. Colossal Debt: v. 24
    C. Severe Punishment: v. 25
    D. Plea for Mercy: v. 26
    E. Complete Forgiveness: v. 27
    F. Total Lack of Mercy: vv. 28-30
    G. Deserved Punishment: vv. 31-34
    H. Application to Us: v. 35

SUGGESTED INTRODUCTION FOR ADULTS

In the latter part of Jesus' ministry the disciples became increasingly concerned about which of them was going to have the leading place in the coming kingdom. Jesus began His ministry by preaching: "Repent: for the kingdom of heaven is at hand" (4:17). So now the disciples asked Him, "Who is the greatest in the kingdom of heaven?" (18:1). They were thinking in terms of an earthly, political kingdom, which they hoped would soon be set up in Jerusalem with Jesus as the reigning Messiah-King.

The Master's reply was a bit shocking. He told them that unless they changed their attitude and became like little children they would not even enter the kingdom of heaven (v. 3). Then He gave a direct answer to their question: "Whosoever therefore shall humble himself as this little child, the same is greatest in the kingdom of heaven" (v. 4). True greatness consists of humility and a sense of dependence on God. This is a lesson we all need to learn.

SUGGESTED INTRODUCTION FOR YOUTH

Do you find it hard to forgive those who hurt you? Many people do. But this is an un-Christlike attitude. When we recall how horribly our Lord was treated in those last hours of His life, we are amazed and challenged by His prayer on the cross: "Father, forgive them; for they know not what they do" (Luke 23:34).

Forgiveness is not natural; it is supernatural. God's grace can help us to forgive everyone, no matter how great the wrong.

CONCEPTS FOR CHILDREN

1. All of us need to be forgiven, and God in His love is ready to forgive.
2. Because God has forgiven us, we should be quick to forgive others.
3. We should forgive and forget.
4. When we hold grudges we hurt ourselves.

THE LESSON COMMENTARY

I. PARABLE OF THE LOST SHEEP:
Matthew 18:12-14

This brief parable is found here and in Luke 15:3-7. It will be noticed that Luke's narrative is about twice as long as Matthew's, probably due to Matthew's habit of telescoping the material.

The picture was a very familiar one to the people of Palestine. A man had a hundred sheep. When the flock returned to the fold for the night, the shepherd discovered to his dismay that one sheep was missing. During the day it had wandered away from its companions, perhaps lured by some greener looking grass.

It would have been easier and simpler for the shepherd to forget the one lost sheep and rest for the night with the other ninety-nine. But love for his sheep would not let him do it. So he went out into the darkness and loneliness of the night to find it. When he did discover it—perhaps caught by its long wool in some bramble bush—he carried it safely to the fold. Jesus said that the shepherd rejoiced more over the return of the one lost sheep than he did over the ninety-nine that did not wander away. Then He made the application: "Even so it is not the will of your Father which is in heaven, that one of these little ones should perish" (v. 14).

This parable has two lessons for us. The first is that Jesus is the Good Shepherd who gave His life for the sheep and so does not want one single one to perish (John 10). The other is that we, as undershepherds of the flock, should be concerned for each individual lost sheep.

This is the heart of evangelism. It is not numbers that count, but souls. If Christ died for all, we should seek to win all to Him. Love for individuals is redemptive. We need to pray for more of this love.

II. DISCIPLINE IN THE CHURCH:
Matthew 18:15-20

"Up to this point in the chapter Jesus had been warning against the danger of causing someone to stumble, of sinning against another. Now, in the second part, He deals with the other side of the picture. What are you to do if your 'brother' (fellow church member) should 'trespass'—the Greek says 'sin' (hamartese)—against you?" (Beacon Bible Commentary, VI, 171).

The instruction that Jesus gives is very specific: "Go and tell him his fault between thee and him alone" (v. 15). "Tell . . . his fault" is one word in Greek, meaning "convict" or "rebuke." This same verb is found in the Septuagint of Leviticus 19:17—"Thou shalt not hate thy brother in thine heart: thou shalt in any wise rebuke thy neighbour, and not suffer sin upon him." We are to be honest and open in our dealings with each other.

Jesus added: "If he listens to you, you have won your brother over" (NIV). How much better that is than telling everybody else and antagonizing the erring brother. The procedure Jesus outlined could well result in his being saved rather than lost eternally.

Suppose the faulty brother will not listen—as will happen in some cases. Jesus' next prescription was: "Take one or two others along, so that 'every matter may be established by the testimony of two or three witnesses'" (v. 16, NIV). The quotation at the end of this verse is taken from Deuteronomy 19:15.

The presence of two or three witnesses could be very important. The erring brother might become enraged and later accuse the wronged person unjustly, or he might deny having said some cutting words. The two witnesses could verify what was said. They were a good protection.

Suppose the erring one was still stubborn and refused to listen to the added pleas of the accompanying friends. The third step was: "Tell it to the church." What then? "And if he refuses to listen even to the church, treat him as you would a pagan or a tax collector" (v. 17, NIV). In other words, by his actions he has shown that he is not a genuine Christian, and so must be considered an outsider.

It goes without saying that Jesus' clear instructions here have too seldom been followed by church members. How many have talked alone with the one who wronged them? The usual procedure is to tell everybody else about the wrong, instead of talking in strict privacy with the offender. Because we disobey Christ's command, His church is rent by schisms instead of being held together by love.

As noted in Lesson 12, the word "church" occurs in the four Gospels only here (v. 17) and in 16:18. In chapter 16 it refers to the entire church, the true church of Jesus Christ. But here it refers to a local congregation. These are the main two meanings of *ecclesia* in the New Testament.

Verse 19 forms a striking contrast to the two men arguing about some difference between them. Here we read: "If two of you shall agree on earth as touching any thing that they shall ask, it shall be done for them of my Father which is in heaven." This is the ideal situation in a church. When people are agreed in prayer, unity and love predominate.

The thing that differentiates the church from every other organization or club is the Divine Presence. Jesus said, "For where two or three are gathered together in my name, there am I in the midst of them" (v. 20). What a comfort this has been to small groups gathered in prayer and worship!

III. UNLIMITED FORGIVENESS: Matthew 18:21-22

A. Peter's Question: v. 21

Evidently Peter was still thinking about Jesus' words in verse 15. So he asked how often he should forgive his brother who wronged him—"till seven times?" The rabbinical rule was that no offender should ask for forgiveness more than three times. So Peter thought he was being very generous in offering to do it seven times. But he had completely missed the spirit of Christ. The true Christian does not keep a reckoning of such matters; he forgives freely and forgets.

B. Jesus' Answer: v. 22

The Master replied: "No, not seven times, but seventy times seven." The last expression may also be translated "seventy-seven times" (NIV). In either case it means an infinite number of times. Peter was putting the whole thing on a legalistic basis. What Jesus was saying is that love forgives without limit. This is one test of true love.

IV. PARABLE OF THE UNMERCIFUL SERVANT: Matthew 18:23-35

A. Day of Reckoning: v. 23

We have already noted that most of Jesus' parables in Matthew are parables of the Kingdom. This one is no exception.

Jesus said that there was a king "who wanted to settle accounts with his servants" (NIV). Though the Greek word for "servants" means bondservants or slaves, it is evident these men were not like the slaves on southern plantations. Instead, they handled large sums of money.

B. Colossal Debt: v. 24

As the reckoning of debts began, one servant was brought in who owed the king "ten thousand talents." By the very least figuring, this amounted to at least ten million dollars in our money. How could a servant possibly accumulate such an astronomical debt?

Two suggestions may be made. The first is that these Eastern monarchs handled vast sums of money. We have had striking examples of that in modern times. Some years ago the richest man in the world was reputed to be the ruler of Hyderabad, in poverty-stricken India. It was reported that he had a bathtub full of gold. Of course he couldn't eat it, nor could it buy him health and happiness!

It is possible, then, that this servant was a trusted agent of his master and that he handled business deals that involved the exchange of large sums. We are told that Solomon "made silver to be in Jerusalem as stones" (I Kings 10:27). In those days all the wealth was in the possession of a few people.

But it may be that Jesus, as He often did, was speaking in hyperbole, purposely using an utterly fantastic figure. What He meant, then, was that this man owed a debt that no one could possibly pay. As Carr observes, "The vast amount implies the hopeless character of sin" (*Matthew*, p. 224).

C. Severe Punishment: v. 25

Because the servant was unable to repay the debt, his master ordered that he and all his family should be sold and the proceeds applied to the debt. Of course this would bring in only a tiny fraction of the needed amount.

This seems very harsh. But it was all perfectly legal in those days. Not only was the slave the property of the master, but his wife and children were as well. He had no recourse to law, for he was simply a possession, like the man's sheep or cattle.

There have been few human institutions that were more fully ungodly than slavery. For any man to buy another human being is to dehumanize him, treating him like an animal. This is a diabolical murder of human personality. We should treat every person as one made in the image of God.

D. Plea for Mercy: v. 26

"The servant fell on his knees before him. 'Be patient with me,' he begged, 'and I will pay back everything' " (NIV). The servant had no way of paying the colossal debt. His only hope was to ask for mercy.

And that is all we can do. Every person has sinned and owes God a debt that it is completely impossible to pay. Our only hope is to throw ourselves on the mercy of God. No matter how long we live a righteous life or how hard we work for the Lord, the debt cannot even be diminished, to say nothing of being wiped out.

E. Complete Forgiveness: v. 27

"The servant's master took pity on him, canceled the debt and let him go" (NIV). Here was unlimited forgiveness, of the kind Jesus called for in verse 22. It all sounds incredible. But Eastern monarchs could be fantastically generous or fearfully cruel.

F. Total Lack of Mercy: vv. 28-30

The rest of the story is still more difficult to believe. Freely and fully forgiven, the servant must have left the king's presence almost in a daze. It would seem that his heart would be so overflowing with gratitude that he would feel kindly and generous toward the whole world.

Such was not the case: "But when that servant went out, he found one of his fellow servants who owed him a hundred denarii. He grabbed him and began to choke him. 'Pay back what you owe me!' he demanded" (v. 28, NIV).

This language seems utterly in-

DISCUSSION QUESTIONS

1. Why is it so hard to forgive?
2. How can we get rid of an unforgiving spirit?
3. How can we prove that we have forgiven?
4. How are we helped by asking forgiveness?
5. As Christians, do we ever need to be forgiven?
6. What happens to those who refuse to forgive?

credible from the lips of one who had just been forgiven for a debt five hundred thousand times as large! For the hundred denarii represented less than twenty dollars. (The denarius was a Roman silver coin worth about fifteen to twenty cents in our money.)

The fellow servant did exactly as the first servant had done (v. 29). One would think that the superior servant, when he heard the same words he had used to the king, would have been touched in his heart. Certainly he could forgive this trifling debt when he had been forgiven such an enormous, impossible sum. After all, he didn't need even the twenty dollars now to apply on the ten million dollar debt, for it was all canceled.

But no: "And he would not: but went and cast him into prison, till he should pay the debt" (v. 30). This custom of throwing debtors into prison was carried on in England even in modern times. The folly of it is obvious. How could a man earn money to repay a debt when he was confined in prison and unable to work? This was both cruel and stupid.

We find ourselves filled with righteous indignation at the very thought of this unmerciful servant. But how about us? When we have been forgiven for the debt of our sins that we could never, ever, possibly repay, do we refuse to forgive a fellow Christian for some trifling wrong—or even a supposed injury. Perhaps it was a careless or hasty word uttered thoughtlessly. Yet we hold a grudge against that person for years.

This is exactly what many professing Christians do, as most of us have observed. We have even had a seemingly fervent Christian say to us, "I can't forgive her for what she did to me." And too many times this is the attitude shown, even when those words are not bluntly said. What does God think of us?

G. Deserved Punishment: vv. 31-34

Perhaps these verses give a clue to the answer to our last question. We are told that when the other servants saw what had happened, they were greatly distressed and went and told the king all about it.

We can imagine the reaction the king had. It was incredible that the first servant could have acted in this way. Quickly the king summoned the diabolically cruel monster and castigated him with a reminder of the generous forgiveness extended to him, and his obligation to his fellow servant (vv. 32-33).

Justifiably enraged, the king "delivered him to the tormentors, till he should pay all that was due unto him" (v. 34). The cancelation of his enormous debt was now revoked; he was again liable for the whole amount. This is a sharp warning to us that if we refuse to forgive our fellow Christians, then God's forgiveness will be revoked.

H. Application to Us: v. 35

"So likewise shall my heavenly Father do also unto you, if ye from your hearts forgive not every one his brother their trespasses." Solemn words, these!

This parable is the most eloquent commentary that could ever be written on the words of Jesus: "But if ye forgive not men their trespasses, neither will your Father forgive your trespasses" (6:15). We need to be reminded again that God can forgive the unforgiven, but He cannot forgive the unforgiving.

An unforgiving spirit is perhaps the greatest single hindrance to revival. God cannot bless a congregation whose members carry grudges in their hearts. The absolute demand of every Christian is that he must forgive others as God has forgiven him.

CONTEMPORARY APPLICATION

We once knew a lady who professed that her heart was filled with

love for God. But one Sunday morning at the close of the service another lady made a remark to her that offended her. It happened in the center aisle, and we overheard the words—they really didn't sound that bad!

But the first woman refused to forgive the second, even though the latter asked for forgiveness. Instead she held a grudge in her heart for over twenty-five years. The result was that the congregation suffered untold damage. The church never again reached its former strength—all because of one person's unforgiving spirit.

THE GOSPEL OF MATTHEW (Continued)
A CHRISTIAN APPROACH TO FAMILY ISSUES

JESUS DEMONSTRATES TOTAL COMMITMENT

DEVOTIONAL READING	Matthew 19:23-30

ADULTS

Topic: *The Total Commitment of Jesus*

Background Scripture: Matthew 19—21:5

Scripture Lesson: Matthew 19:1-2; 20:17-28

Memory Verse: *The Son of man came not to be served but to serve, and to give his life as a ransom for many.* Matthew 20:28

YOUTH

Topic: *The Total Commitment of Jesus*

Background Scripture: Matthew 19—21:5

Scripture Lesson: Matthew 19:1-2; 20:17-28

Memory Verse: *The Son of man came not to be served but to serve, and to give his life as a ransom for many.* Matthew 20:28

CHILDREN

Topic: *Called to Serve*

Background Scripture: Matthew 19—21:5

Scripture Lesson: Matthew 19:1-2; 20:17-28

Memory Verse: *The Son of man came not to be served but to serve.* Matthew 20:28

DAILY BIBLE READINGS

Mon., Mar. 1: Faithfulness in Marriage, Matthew 19:3-12.
Tues., Mar. 2: Jesus and the Children, Matthew 19:13-15.
Wed., Mar. 3: The Burden of Riches, Matthew 19:16-22.
Thurs., Mar. 4: God's Possibilities, Matthew 19:23-30.
Fri., Mar. 5: God's Generosity, Matthew 20:1-16.
Sat., Mar. 6: Jesus Heals, Matthew 20:29-34.
Sun., Mar. 7: The Triumphal Entry, Matthew 21:1-11.

LESSON AIM

To see how we may follow Christ's example of total commitment to God's will.

LESSON SETTING

Time: Early in A.D. 30

Place: Perea (east of the Jordan); Jericho (west of Jordan)

LESSON OUTLINE

Jesus Demonstrates Total Commitment

I. Leaving Galilee for Perea: Matthew 19:1-2

II. The Divorce Question: Matthew 19:3-12

III. Blessing Little Children: Matthew 19:13-15

IV. The Danger of Riches: Matthew 19:16-30

V. The Sin of Greed: Matthew 20:1-16

VI. Third Prediction of the Passion: Matthew 20:17-19

VII. The Sin of Selfish Ambition: Matthew 20:20-23
   A. A Selfish Request: vv. 20-21
   B. A Challenging Reply: v. 22
   C. A Costly Discipleship: v. 23

VIII. The Secret of True Greatness: Matthew 20:24-28
   A. Indignation of the Others: v. 24
   B. Attitude of Pagan Rulers: v. 25
   C. Humility and Service: vv. 26-27
   D. Example of Jesus: v. 28

SUGGESTED INTRODUCTION FOR ADULTS

Jesus was coming toward the end of His period of public ministry. As the time approached for Him to leave this world, He realized that He must devote most of His time to instructing His own disciples to carry on after He was gone.

As we have already noted, this private ministry to the disciples began at Caesarea Philippi, after Peter had confessed Him as Messiah. It continued with the Transfiguration, when His divine glory was revealed to the three chosen disciples. Now, in the last few months before the crucifixion, it was intensified.

To be successful, a leader must develop strong followers. This is what Jesus sought to do. These followers must in turn be strong leaders, if the mission of Christ was to go on. This is what we find Jesus doing in today's lesson. And in the closing part we find Christ leading the way in setting an example to His followers.

SUGGESTED INTRODUCTION FOR YOUTH

What does it mean to be a follower of Jesus? It means that we take the same path that He took while on earth, and that He still wants to take through us. We cannot make Him come over to the path that we might selfishly choose. Rather we have to follow where He goes.

But the glorious thing is that He leads the way. So all we have to do is to follow Him. And with Him in the lead, we are not afraid to follow. That is why we can make a total commitment to Him.

CONCEPTS FOR CHILDREN

1. The disciples were selfish and self-ambitious.
2. It takes humility to follow Jesus.
3. True greatness consists in being willing to serve others.
4. Jesus is our example in serving others.

THE LESSON COMMENTARY

I. LEAVING GALILEE FOR PE-REA:
Matthew 19:1-2

"And it came to pass, that when Jesus had finished these sayings." This is the statement that is found, in similar form, at the end of each of the five great discourses of Matthew's Gospel (7:28; 11:1; 13:53; 19:1; 26:1). The eighteenth chapter comprises the discourse on the Christian community.

Now we are told that having ended these sayings He "departed from Galilee." The great Galilean ministry had lasted for perhaps a year and a half. Jesus was now leaving His home territory for the last time. Luke elaborates the point a bit by saying: "And it came to pass, when the time was come that he should be received up, he stedfastly set his face to go to Jerusalem" (Luke 9:51). His ministry of service was to climax in a ministry of sacrifice. That was His main purpose in coming to earth.

We read that He "came into the coasts (borders) of Judea beyond Jordan." The Greek word for "beyond" is *peran*—literally, "across"; that is, on the east side. So the official name for that area in Jesus' day was Perea. It is now the Jordan Kingdom, with its capital at Amman (called Philadelphia in Roman times).

The expression "Judaea beyond Jordan" seems a bit odd. Perea was ruled by Herod Antipas, tetrarch of Galilee—the one called "Herod" in the Gospels during the time of Jesus' ministry. Judea was on the west side of the Jordan River, between it and the Mediterranean Sea. It seems obvious that "Judaea" is here used in its widest sense as the land of the Jews, taking in all of Palestine.

As in Galilee, "great multitudes followed him: and he healed them there" (v. 2). Mark says in his parallel passage (10:1) that Jesus "taught." From what follows here in Matthew we know that He did both.

It seems clear that on His last journey to Jerusalem Christ and His disciples crossed the Jordan River south of the Lake of Galilee and went down the east side of the valley through Perea. This was the way the Galilean pilgrims usually went down to the annual feasts, since Samaria, the shortest route, was considered "unclean."

What were the people of Perea like? Samuel Andrews says: "The population was not purely Jewish, but rather a mixed one; not so largely heathen as in the Decapolis, and not likely to be so easily stirred up against the Lord as the inhabitants of Judaea, or even of Galilee" (*The Life of Our Lord*, p. 388).

It is sad to think of Jesus being treated worse in His own homeland than in partly pagan territory. Perhaps He was safer here for the moment.

II. THE DIVORCE QUESTION:
Matthew 19:3-12

Divorce is one of the oldest and most continuous problems in human society. Now the Pharisees came to Jesus, "tempting him"—or, "testing him"—by asking, "Is it lawful for a man to put away his wife for every cause?" (v. 3). Matthew, writing to the Jews, is the only Gospel writer who includes the last phrase, which reflects the controversy in the previous century between rabbis Hillel and Shammai.

The debate involved the interpretation of "uncleanness" in Deuteronomy 24:1. Shammai insisted on the strict meaning, as indicating immorality. Hillel was much more liberal, emphasizing the previous clause—"she find no favour in his eyes." He would permit a man to divorce his wife if she did anything that displeased him, such as burning his food.

How did Jesus answer the question? By referring to Scripture, as we should do. He cited Genesis 1:27—at the beginning God made them male and female. Then He quoted Genesis 2:24, which is also cited by Paul (I Corinthians 6:16; Ephesians 5:31).

When the Pharisees asked why Moses permitted divorce, Jesus replied that it was because of the hardness of the people's hearts. He then went on to repeat what He had already said in the Sermon on the Mount (5:32) that the only allowable cause for divorce is marital unfaithfulness. ("Fornication" here means "adultery.")

III. BLESSING LITTLE CHILDREN: Matthew 19:13-15

One of the beautiful revelations of Jesus' loving character comes in this incident recorded in all three Synoptic Gospels (cf. Mark 10:13-16; Luke 18: 15-17). The hard-hearted disciples rebuked the fond parents who brought their children to Jesus to have Him lay His hands on them and pray for them. Jesus in turn rebuked His disciples. Verse 14 should never be forgotten by Christian workers. The last clause could either mean that "of such" the kingdom of heaven is composed, or that the Kingdom belongs to them.

IV. THE DANGER OF RICHES: Matthew 19:16-30

The story of the Rich Young Ruler (vv. 16-22) is also related in all three Synoptic Gospels (cf. Mark 10:17-31; Luke 18:18-30). Addressing Jesus as "Teacher"—so the Greek—the man asked, "What good thing shall I do, that I may have eternal life?" (v. 16). Christ told him to "keep the commandments" and quoted several of the Ten Commandments.

The reply of this young man is poignant. Declaring that he had kept these commandments (duties toward man), he inquired, "What lack I yet?" (v. 20).

Jesus' reply was devastating: "If thou wilt be perfect, go and sell that thou hast, and give to the poor, and thou shalt have treasure in heaven: and come and follow me" (v. 21).

The sequel is sad: "But when the young man heard that saying, he went away sorrowful: for he had great possessions" (v. 22). He failed the test. He wanted eternal life, but he was unwilling to pay the price of total commitment to God.

Does verse 21 spell out a rule that all Christians must obey? Some have answered Yes to this question. But it seems apparent that after Peter left his fishing to follow the Master, he retained possession of his boat and put it at Jesus' disposal (Luke 5:3). He also kept his home and made that available as Christ's headquarters for His Galilean ministry (Luke 4:38). This indicates the ideal for stewardship: private ownership, but everything kept at God's disposal.

Why then did Jesus require that this man sell everything and give the proceeds to the poor? The answer is that he had made money his god. Jesus knew that the young man would never follow Him with all his heart until he got rid of his wealth—tore this false god from his affections. We have to give up whatever hinders us from following Christ.

V. THE SIN OF GREED: Matthew 20:1-16

This passage is generally referred to as the Parable of the Laborers in the Vineyard. Jesus said that the kingdom of heaven was like a landowner who needed men to work in his vineyard. Early in the morning he hired workmen, promising to pay them a day's wage of a "penny"—the Roman silver denarius, worth about twenty cents. At nine in the morning he hired more help. This was repeated at noon and at three in the afternoon.

Finally about "the eleventh hour" (5 P.M.) he went out and found others standing idle. When he asked them why, they said, "Because no man hath hired us" (v. 7). In other words, they would have worked if they had had the opportunity.

At the end of the day the owner instructed his foreman to pay the men, beginning with those who started last. To everybody's surprise, they each received a denarius—a full day's wage.

When those who had worked all day reached the foreman, they naturally expected more. Instead, they each received a denarius. Not surprisingly, they complained (vv. 11-12). But the owner defended his action (vv. 13-15).

There is no question but that he acted legally: he kept his agreement. But was he morally fair?

Here is one suggestion: The men who had worked only one hour would have worked all day if they could. Furthermore, they needed a denarius to buy enough food for their families for that day, just as much as the earlier workmen. It may well be that they worked harder and faster than the others, because their time was short.

The key to understanding this parable is found in 19:27. Peter said in effect: "We have left everything to follow you! What are we going to get for this?"

It was against this mercenary, greedy spirit that Jesus spoke out vividly in the parable. The connection is proved by the repetition of 19:30 in 20:16. This statement ties the two together. We must serve out of love, not for gain.

VI. THIRD PREDICTION OF THE PASSION:
Matthew 20:17-19

Jesus was "going up to Jerusalem" (v. 17). This might give the impression that He was on His way up the steep Jericho road from the Jordan Valley. But that this was not the case is shown by verse 29, where we find Him at Jericho.

The facts are that the Jews always spoke of "going up to Jerusalem," no matter where they were coming from— north, south, east, or west. When they left the Holy City they always "went down," even if they were going north or to a higher elevation.

Jesus "took the twelve disciples

apart in the way." This was to be a private conversation; the information was only for them.

We have already found two previous predictions of the passion. The first was right after Peter's confession at Caesarea Philippi (16:21). It simply predicted His suffering, death, and resurrection. The second, after His transfiguration, added the note of His betrayal (17:22-23). This one specifically says that He would be betrayed to the Sanhedrin (chief priests and scribes) and condemned to death by that body. Then the Sanhedrin would "deliver him to the Gentiles to mock, and to scourge, and to crucify him" (v. 19). As would be expected, the successive predictions became more precise. And every item was fulfilled as predicted.

VII. THE SIN OF SELFISH AMBITION:
Matthew 20:20-23

A. A Selfish Request: vv. 20-21

This incident is recorded elsewhere only in Mark 10:35-45. There we are told that James and John made the request. Here it says that their mother came with them and voiced the request herself. But there is no contradiction; the petition came from all three of them. They were all overly ambitious.

So earnest was this mother that she bowed down before Jesus—that is what "worshipping him" means. It says that she was "desiring a certain thing of him." She probably said something like this: "Would you please do a favor for me?"

Courteously Jesus answered, "What is it that you want?" (NIV). Her reply was a request that her two sons might sit beside Him in His kingdom, one on His right (the place of greatest honor) and the other on His left (the next highest place).

After the second prediction of the passion, the disciples had asked, "Who is the greatest in the kingdom of heaven?" (18:1). Jesus answered by setting a child in front of them and saying: "Whosoever therefore shall humble himself as this little child, the same is greatest in the kingdom of heaven." (18:4). Evidently that truth had not made much of an impression on them!

The trouble was that they were looking for Christ to set up an earthly, political kingdom. But the carnal attitude of their hearts is shown in their desire to get ahead of their colleagues and have first place in that kingdom.

B. A Challenging Reply: v. 22

"You don't know what you are asking," Jesus said. Then He asked them, "Can you drink the cup I am going to drink?" (NIV). The added words about "baptism" and being "baptized," here and in verse 23, are not in any of the earliest Greek manuscripts. Some copyist introduced them here from Mark 10:38-39, where they are genuine.

The disciples thoughtlessly replied, "We are able." But subsequent events showed that they certainly were not. They forsook their Master in Gethsemane and fled for their lives. Even though Peter followed "far off" to the high priest's house, he there thrice denied his Lord. It was only after these disciples had been filled with the Holy Spirit at Pentecost that they were able to share in Jesus' sufferings, to drink the cup of sorrow that He drank.

DISCUSSION QUESTIONS

1. What should be our attitude toward children?
2. What are some of the dangers in being rich?
3. Why are people greedy?
4. What part does ambition play properly in the Christian life?
5. What is the secret of true greatness?
6. What does total commitment mean?

C. Costly Discipleship: v. 23

Jesus assured these two political aspirants that they would indeed drink from His cup of suffering. Then He added: "But to sit on my right hand, and on my left, is not mine to give, but it shall be given to them for whom it is prepared of my Father." Probably the Greek here means: "It is not Mine to give except to those for whom God has planned it." Places of honor in the Messianic kingdom will be granted on the basis of fitness, not favoritism. We should be at our best, and then let God choose our place.

VIII. THE   SECRET   OF   TRUE GREATNESS: Matthew 20:24-28

A.   Indignation of the Others: v. 24

When the other ten disciples heard about the secret request of two of their colleagues, "they were moved with indignation." This is a strong verb. They were "aroused" and "angry" at the two brothers for trying to "steal a march" on them. But one is tempted to wonder if they were not "peeved" because they had not thought to ask first! This sounds very much like the "righteous indignation" of one crooked politician against another.

B.   Attitude of the Pagan Rulers: v. 25

Jesus called the whole group of the Twelve together. Solemnly He said to them: "You know that the rulers of the Gentiles lord it over them [that is exactly what the Greek says] and their high officials exercise authority over them" (NIV). Unfortunately, "power corrupts." There are many sad examples of this in national and international politics.

C.   Humility and Service: vv. 26-27

The Master warned His disciples: "This is not the way it is to be among you folk." And then He laid it right on the line: "Whoever wants to be great among you must be your servant, and whoever wants to be first must be your slave" (NIV). That is exactly what the Greek says. (The King James Version misses the force of the original with its "minister . . . servant.") The higher you want to go, the lower you must stoop in humble service.

D. Example of Jesus: v. 28

This is one of the great theological passages of the Gospels. Jesus declared: "The Son of Man did not come to be served, but to serve, and to give his life a ransom for many" (NIV). The Greek word for "ransom" is *lytron*. Its regular use in the first century was for the ransom price paid to release a slave. Jesus paid the ransom price to free us from the slavery of sin.

The Greek preposition translated "for" is *anti*, which in the papyri of that period most frequently meant "instead of." Its use here suggests the idea of substitutionary atonement: Christ died in our place. He "gave himself a ransom for all" (I Timothy 2:6, NIV). But only the "many" who believe in Him are saved.

CONTEMPORARY APPLICATION

There is no place in the true church of Jesus Christ for selfish ambition. It was only because Jesus "humbled himself, and became obedient unto death, even the death of the cross" (Philippians 2:8) that He could become our Redeemer. If we are to live redemptively, we must have the same total commitment to the will of God.

PARABLES OF REPENTANCE AND OBEDIENCE

DEVOTIONAL READING

Isaiah 55:6-13

ADULTS

Topic: *The Need for Repentance*

Background Scripture: Matthew 21:6–22:14

Scripture Lesson: Matthew 21:28-32, 42-46

Memory Verse: *Repent, for the kingdom of heaven is at hand.* Matthew 3:2

YOUTH

Topic: *A New Direction in Life*

Background Scripture: Matthew 21:6–22:14

Scripture Lesson: Matthew 21:38-41

Memory Verse: *Repent, for the kingdom of heaven is at hand.* Matthew 3:2

CHILDREN

Topic: *A New Direction*

Background Scripture: Matthew 21:6–22:14

Scripture Lesson: Matthew 21:28-32

Memory Verse: *Seek the Lord while he may be found, call upon him while he is near.* Isaiah 55:6

DAILY BIBLE READINGS

Mon., Mar. 8: Jesus Cleanses the Temple, Matthew 21:12-13.
Tues., Mar. 9: For and Against Jesus, Matthew 21:14-17.
Wed., Mar. 10: Jesus and the Priest, Matthew 21:23-27.
Thurs., Mar. 11: Parable of the Vineyard, Matthew 21:33-41.
Fri., Mar. 12: The Cornerstone, Psalm 118:21-25.
Sat., Mar. 13: The Source of Salvation, Acts 4:5-12.
Sun., Mar. 14: The Marriage Feast, Matthew 22:1-10.

LESSON AIM

To help us see the importance of repentance and obedience as necessary to salvation.

LESSON SETTING

Time: A.D. 30

Place: Jerusalem

LESSON OUTLINE

Parables of Repentance and Obedience

I. The Two Sons: Matthew 21:28-32

202

A. The One Who Refused and Repented: vv. 28-29
B. The One Who Promised and Procrastinated: v. 30
C. The Application: vv. 31-32

II. The Wicked Husbandmen: Matthew 21:33-41
    A. Preparation of the Vineyard: v. 33
    B. Persecution of the Servants: vv. 34-36
    C. Murder of the Son: vv. 37-39
    D. Punishment of the Tenants: vv. 40-41

III. The Rejected Stone: Matthew 21:42-46
    A. Stone Rejected and Honored: v. 42
    B. Nation Rejected: v. 43
    C. Nation Destroyed: v. 44
    D. Wicked Leaders: vv. 45-46

IV. The Wedding Feast: Matthew 22:1-14
    A. The Guests Who Refused: vv. 1-7
    B. The Guests Who Came: vv. 8-10
    C. The Guest Who Was Unprepared: vv. 11-14

SUGGESTED INTRODUCTION FOR ADULTS

The twenty-first chapter of Matthew narrates five events before the beginning of our printed lesson today. The first was the so-called Triumphal Entry (vv. 1-11). Jesus rode into Jerusalem on a donkey in fulfillment of Zechariah 9:9 (quoted in verse 9). In doing so He was performing a Messianic act, publicly presenting Himself to the Jews as their Messiah. But the leaders of the nation turned Him down.

The second event was the Cleansing of the Temple (vv. 12-13). Jesus cleared out the commercial "racket" that was going on in the court of the Gentiles.

The third event was the Complaint of the Chief Priests and Scribes (vv. 14-17). They objected to having the children praising the Lord out loud in the temple.

The fourth event was the Cursing of the Fig Tree (vv. 18-22), which then withered away. This symbolized the destruction of the Jewish nation for its false profession of piety.

The fifth event was the Challenge of the Jewish Leaders (vv. 23-27). They demanded that Jesus tell them who gave Him the authority to cleanse the temple. He countered by asking where John the Baptist got his authority. Then He told them the Parable of the Two Sons, with which our printed lesson begins.

SUGGESTED INTRODUCTION FOR YOUTH

Salvation means a new direction in life. It begins with repentance, which means turning "about face" and heading in the opposite direction.

Which of the two sons in the parable are you? You may have turned away from God, but you can repent and be saved. On the other hand, if you promise to obey Christ and then disobey, you forfeit eternal life.

CONCEPTS FOR CHILDREN	1. Jesus told about two brothers who were different.
	2. It is not what we say but what we do that counts.
	3. If at first we disobey, we can repent.
	4. Repentance means changing our lives.

THE LESSON COMMENTARY

I. THE TWO SONS:
Matthew 21:28-32

A. The One Who Refused and Repented: vv. 28-29

Jesus told a parable about two sons. The father came to the first and said, "Son, go work to day in my vineyard." Rebelliously this son answered, "I will not." But afterward he "repented" and went.

Verse 29 illustrates very helpfully the correct meaning of repentance. This young man evidently regretted his first decision and probably felt sorry that he had answered his father this way. He thereupon changed his mind and went. The literal meaning of the Greek verb here, *metamelomai* (6 times in NT), is to "regret." It is not as strong as the more usual verb in the New Testament, *metanoeo* (34 times), which literally means to "change one's mind." But the words are used somewhat interchangeably, and the context here indicates that the son did change his mind and carried out his father's orders.

B. The One Who Promised and Procrastinated: v. 30

When the second son received the same command, he responded, "I go, sir," but he "went not." Probably he intended to. But he just didn't get around to doing it. He was like a lot of people today who have good intentions but fail to carry them out. We have even heard a person say, "Oh, I'm going to get saved sometime, but not now." The sad thing is that most people who talk that way never do surrender to Christ, and so are lost eternally.

C. The Application: vv. 31-32

Jesus was not telling the Parable of the Two Sons just to be relating an interesting story. He was addressing Himself meaningfully to the needs of His hearers.

So here He asked, "Which of the two did the will of his father?" The religious leaders (cf. v. 23) answered, "The first."

Then Jesus made a devastating application: "I tell you the truth, the tax collectors and the prostitutes are entering the kingdom of God ahead of you" (NIV). Why? Because they "believed" the message of John the Baptist. They accepted his "baptism of repentance for the remission of sins" (Mark 1:4). But the chief priests and Pharisees did not "believe." Even when they saw these sinners changed in their lives, they "repented not" (same verb in the Greek) so that they might "believe."

Verse 32 illustrates well the meaning of "believe." It is more than mental assent; it is moral consent. This parable emphasizes the fact that one cannot separate believing and obeying. When one is not obeying God, he is not believing in God. And no unbeliever can get into heaven.

What is the lesson of this parable? It might be thought of as referring to the Gentiles (first son) and the Jews (second son). But the words of Jesus clearly indicate that the primary application was to two classes of Jews. The second son typified the religious leaders (chief priests and scribes) who said that they would obey God's law but failed to do it. The first son typified the despised tax collectors and prostitutes. These at first rebelled against God's will, but afterward they repented and obeyed. The whole point is that lip service is not enough; there must be real obedience to God's will for us.

The application to our day is clear. Too many church members are like the second son: They say, "I go," but they do not live in daily obedience to the will of God. Meanwhile, sinners repent and do God's will zealously.

II. THE WICKED HUSBANDMEN: Matthew 21:33-41

A. Preparation of the Vineyard: v. 33

Jesus told of a "householder"—*oikodespotes*, "house-manager"—who planted a vineyard. One of the most common sights in Palestine today is the vineyards near each town or village. He "hedged it round about," probably with a stone wall. Palestine is a very stony country. One can see fields covered almost solidly with stones, so that one wonders how a goat could find a blade of grass between them. There is an ancient legend that when God created the world He dispatched an angel with a bag of stones to distribute over the earth's surface. But when the angel was over the Holy Land, the bag broke and all the stones fell there! At any rate, there are stone walls everywhere, just to get the stones off the ground. Even very small yards are often surrounded with high stone walls.

Then the owner dug a "winepress." This would be a shallow pit lined with stone or mortar. The ripe grapes were thrown into this, to be trampled on with bare feet so as to squeeze out the juice. One can still see these winepresses in Palestine.

Lastly the owner built a "tower." This was a raised wooden platform, which the rabbis specified should be fifteen feet high and six feet square. When the grapes were ripe someone would sit on this tower to see that no thieves came to steal the fruit.

Having done all this, the owner rented the vineyard to some "husbandmen"—"vine-dressers" or "farmers"—and went off to a distant country. Perhaps as a wealthy man he traveled to Rome.

B. Persecution of the Servants: vv. 34-36

"When the harvest time approached"—September of the fifth year after planting (Leviticus 19:23-25)—"he sent his servants to the tenants to collect his fruit" (NIV). Obviously he had made a sharecropping arrangement with the tenants. They were to take care of the vineyard and harvest the grapes. He, as owner, would receive a certain percentage of the crop.

Instead of fulfilling the contract, the wicked tenants "took his servants, and beat one, and killed another, and stoned another" (v. 35). When the owner sent more servants, "the tenants treated them the same way" (v. 36, NIV). They were obviously intent on keeping the whole crop.

C. Murder of the Son: vv. 37-39

In desperation the owner finally sent his own son, saying to himself, "They will respect my son" (v. 37, NIV). But when the tenants saw the son approaching, they said: "This is the heir; come, let us kill him, and let us seize on his inheritance" (v. 38). So they caught him, threw him out of the vineyard and killed him.

This, of course, was very foolish reasoning and acting. They could not help knowing that the owner would come and kill them. But the point that Jesus was making is that all sin is stupid. The sinner always has to pay for his wrongdoing, and "the wages of sin is death" (Romans 6:23).

D. Punishment of the Tenants: vv. 40-41

With keen insight Jesus now asked His opponents: "Therefore, when the owner of the vineyard comes, what will he do to those tenants?" (NIV). Quickly the chief priests and scribes answered: "He will miserably destroy those wicked men, and will let out his vineyard unto other husbandmen, which shall render him the fruits in their seasons." Jesus let His enemies pass judgment on themselves and state the sentence for their own sins!

The meaning of the parable is crystal clear. The "vineyard" was the Jewish nation (Isaiah 5:1-7). The "husbandmen" were the religious leaders of the nation, the scribes and chief priests. The "servants" were the prophets of the Old Testament, many of whom were persecuted and even killed. The "son" was Jesus Himself, whom the leaders of the nation would soon condemn to death. The judgment pronounced in verse 41 was carried out in A.D. 70, when Jerusalem and the temple were destroyed, with thousands of Jews killed. The vineyard was then given to "other husbandmen"—the Gentile church of Jesus Christ that became the true people of God. It was a solemn warning to the Pharisees and Sadducees, but they refused to heed it.

This parable sounds a serious warning to the church of our day in America and Europe. If we persecute the true prophets of God and reject the lordship of Christ—as many "Christians" are doing—the vineyard will be given to new converts of Asia, Africa, and the streets of America.

III. THE REJECTED STONE:
Matthew 21:42-46

A. Stone Rejected and Honored: v. 42

To His opponents, who prided themselves on their knowledge of their sacred writings, Jesus said: "Did ye never read in the scriptures, The stone which the builders rejected, the same is become the head of the corner?" —either the cornerstone of the building or the keystone of an arch (cf. NIV, "capstone").

The Greek word translated "rejected" means "thrown aside after careful examination." The scribes and Pharisees in the synagogues of Galilee, and the chief priests in charge of the temple at Jerusalem, had carefully scrutinized Jesus' life and teachings. At the end of this examination they deliberately rejected Him, refused to accept Him into the religious structure of Judaism and cast Him aside. But the rejected Christ became the foundation stone and capstone of Christianity, which has circled the globe with salvation. No wonder the inspired psalmist wrote: "This is the Lord's doing, and it is marvellous in our eyes" (see Psalm 118:22-23, which the Jews sang together at every Passover).

B. Nation Rejected: v. 43

Lest His hearers should possibly miss the point of the Parable of the Wicked Husbandmen, Jesus now stated it with absolute precision: "Therefore say I unto you, The kingdom of God shall be taken from you, and given to a nation bringing forth the fruits thereof." The Jewish nation, as such, disappeared from history for nearly nineteen hundred years (A.D. 70-1948). The kingdom of God was taken from the Jewish religious leaders, who had been its main exponents and proponents, and was given to the Gentiles who would produce the fruits of righteousness. Jesus was sounding a final warning.

C. Nation Destroyed: v. 44

Again Jesus dipped back into the Old Testament. The first half of this verse reflects Isaiah 8:14-15. The second half reflects Daniel 2:34, 44-45.

The Jewish leaders had rejected Jesus, God's chosen cornerstone and capstone. They had thrown Him aside as useless. But now they would stumble over this stone that they had thrown away and would be "broken." The rare Greek word here means "crushed," as a pottery jar would be shattered when falling on a rock. In the same way, anyone who pushes Christ aside will ultimately stumble over Him and be crushed.

The second half of the verse gives an even more severe picture of judgment. If we reject Christ as our Savior, we shall sometime have to stand before Him as our Judge. Instead of His being our foundation, He will be our destruction.

D. Wicked Leaders: vv. 45-46

Jesus' words were so pointed and transparently clear that His enemies could not fail to grasp their meaning. "When the chief priests and the Pharisees heard Jesus' parables, they knew he was talking about them" (v. 45, NIV).

Did this cause them to repent, to change their attitude toward Him? Unfortunately not. Instead, "they looked for a way to arrest him" (v. 46, NIV). But they were afraid of what the crowd might do. The common people honored Jesus as a prophet. Actually, the leaders were afraid that the people might stone them (Luke 20:6). So they bided their time.

It was a tragic decision that the chief priests and scribes made. They had listened to Jesus' teaching and had felt His spirit of love. But they rejected it all, bringing divine judgment on them and their nation.

IV. THE WEDDING FEAST: Matthew 22:1-14

A. The Guests Who Refused: vv. 1-7

Jesus compared the kingdom of heaven to a king who made a wedding banquet for his son. When the time came for the banquet, the king sent his servants to notify those who had already been invited. But they refused to come (v. 3). So he sent a second detachment of servants with a more urgent request: "Everything is now ready. Please come" (v. 4).

"But they paid no attention and went off—one to his field, another to his business. The rest seized his servants, mistreated them and killed them" (vv. 5-6, NIV). Enraged, the king sent his armies, which destroyed those murderers and burned their cities (v. 7).

Again the identification is clear. These invited guests were the Jewish leaders, like the wicked husbandmen of the previous parable. They were punished and their city of Jerusalem was burned by the Romans in A.D. 70.

B. The Guests Who Came: vv. 8-10

The banquet was ready, but there were no guests. So the king told his servants to go out on the "highways" and bring in as many as they could find (v. 9). Obediently the servants went out and "gathered together all as many as they found, both bad and good: and the wedding was furnished with guests" (v. 10).

In the Greek the terms for "highway" in verses 9 and 10 are different. In the New International Version the first is translated "street corners" and the second "streets."

The meaning of this section is also clear. It could have a twofold application, as in the previous parable. One would be that because the Jews refused to come to the gospel banquet, the Gentiles would be invited. But, as there, the more precise application is to the leaders of the nation rejecting the invitation and the common people, including tax collectors and prostitutes, accepting it.

DISCUSSION QUESTIONS

1. What is the meaning of repentance?
2. What is the relation of repentance and obedience?
3. What is the relation of faith and obedience?
4. What dangers confront the church today?
5. How can pride of position be a danger?
6. How can we avoid the mistake the Pharisees made?

C. The Guest Who Was Unprepared: vv. 11-14

This paragraph is unique. It describes a guest whom the king discovered as not wearing a "wedding garment" (v. 11). When the king questioned him the man remained "speechless" (v. 12). Then the king gave the order: "Bind him hand and foot, and take him away, and cast him into outer darkness; there shall be weeping and gnashing of teeth" (v. 13). It is a terrible picture of eternal punishment, and one that should make every sinner reconsider and repent.

Verse 14 is a repetition of 20:16b, which comes at the end of the Parable of the Laborers in the Vineyard. It is a solemn truth: "Many are called, but few are chosen."

The Parable of the Wedding Feast teaches two lessons. The first is: Not all who are called will be saved. The second is: Those who prefer their own righteousness to Christ's righteousness will be lost.

CONTEMPORARY APPLICATION

It seems apparent that the king furnished a wedding garment for each guest. But one man preferred to wear his own clothes to the banquet. He is a type of those who think their own righteousness is good enough and therefore they refuse to accept Christ's righteousness. The fate of all such is outer darkness forever.

In Revelation 19:7-9 we read that the redeemed are clothed in "fine linen, clean and white: for the fine linen is the righteousness of the saints." But we are told in Isaiah 64:6 that "all our righteousnesses are as filthy rags." It is only Christ's righteousness, made our own righteousness by faith, that will be acceptable at the Marriage Supper of the Lamb.

THE CONSEQUENCES OF HYPOCRISY

DEVOTIONAL READING | Matthew 22:34-40

ADULTS

Topic: *An Indictment of Hypocrisy*

Background Scripture: Matthew 22:15–23:39

Scripture Lesson: Matthew 23:27-39

Memory Verse: *Woe to you, scribes and Pharisees, hypocrites! for you tithe mint and dill and cummin, and have neglected the weightier matters of the law, justice and mercy and faith; these you ought to have done, without neglecting the others.* Matthew 23:23

YOUTH

Topic: *The Importance of Being a Real Person*

Background Scripture: Matthew 22:15–23:39

Scripture Lesson: Matthew 23:27-39

Memory Verse: *Woe to you, scribes and Pharisees, hypocrites! for you tithe mint and dill and cummin, and have neglected the weightier matters of the law, justice and mercy and faith; these you ought to have done, without neglecting the others.* Matthew 23:23

CHILDREN

Topic: *The Danger of Being Unreal*

Background Scripture: Matthew 22:15–23:39

Scripture Lesson: Matthew 23:27-39

Memory Verse: *You . . . have neglected the weightier matters of the law, justice and mercy and faith; these you ought to have done without neglecting the others.* Matthew 23:23

DAILY BIBLE READINGS

Mon., Mar. 15: Caesar and God, Matthew 22:15-22.
Tues., Mar. 16: Questions by the Sadducees, Matthew 22:23-33.
Wed., Mar. 17: Questions by the Pharisees, Matthew 22:34-40.
Thurs., Mar. 18: Questions by Jesus, Matthew 22:41-45.
Fri., Mar. 19: Religion and Humility, Matthew 23:1-12.
Sat., Mar. 20: True Holiness, Matthew 23:16-22.
Sun., Mar. 21: Complete Holiness, Matthew 23:23-24.

LESSON AIM | To see how important it is to be a real person.

LESSON SETTING | Time: A.D. 30

Place: Jerusalem

The Consequences of Hypocrisy

LESSON OUTLINE

SUGGESTED INTRODUCTION FOR ADULTS

The last week of Jesus' ministry was the most trying one. It began with the so-called Triumphal Entry on Sunday, when Christ rode into Jerusalem on a donkey. He was enacting the prophecy of Zechariah 9:9. The Galilean pilgrims acclaimed Him as Messiah, "the Son of David." But the leaders of the nation turned Him down.

This was followed by His cleansing the temple, which brought Him into sharp conflict with the chief priests and the Sanhedrin. They challenged His authority. Then, as we found in last week's lesson, Jesus challenged them to repentance, warning them of the fatal consequences of refusing to repent.

In today's lesson the controversy goes on. In Jerusalem Jesus was questioned by three different groups in an effort to discredit Him before the crowds. But He met their questions successfully and then embarrassed them by asking them a question that they could not answer. It was a week filled with conflict.

SUGGESTED
INTRODUCTION
FOR YOUTH

"Are you for real?" That was a question that suddenly confronted a girl in her senior year in high school. For a moment she was startled and looked at her questioner in surprise.

Then she began to think seriously about it. Was she? Fortunately she was a sincere, dedicated Christian. As she searched her heart and studied her life she felt the assurance that she was a real person.

In some ways this is the most important thing in life. The highest virtue is sincerity. We cannot all be brilliant or have great successes in the world. But we can all be sincere.

When we are unreal we soon find that we cannot live with ourselves, to say nothing of living with others. If we are really to live, we must be real persons.

CONCEPTS FOR
CHILDREN

1. It is natural for children to play at being somebody or something else.
2. But we must be careful that this play-acting does not become a part of our personality.
3. We need to ask Jesus to make us real persons.
4. When we are fully given to Him we are real.

THE LESSON COMMENTARY

I. QUESTION OF THE PHARISEES AND HERODIANS:

Matthew 22:15-22

A. The Question: vv. 15-17

The motives of Jesus' opponents are vividly described in verse 15: "Then went the Pharisees and took counsel how they might entangle him in his talk." They were hoping to trap Him into saying something that would get Him into trouble.

So they sent some of their disciples with the Herodians to ask Him a question. Josephus, the Jewish historian of the first century, does not mention the Herodians. But their name indicates that they were supporters of Herod Antipas, who ruled Galilee for the Romans.

These men approached Jesus with the crassest kind of flattery: "Teacher, we know you are a man of integrity and that you teach the way of God in accordance with the truth. You aren't swayed by men, because you pay no attention to who they are" (v. 16,

NIV). They hoped that this would disarm Him, so that He would make some careless statement that would get Him into trouble.

Then they "popped" the question: "Tell us then, what is your opinion? Is it right to pay taxes to Caesar or not?" (v. 17, NIV). The Greek word for "tribute" (KJV) is $kensos$ (Latin, $census$), which was the poll tax paid annually. This was especially offensive to the Jews because it was a constant reminder to them that they were under Roman rule.

Now we see why it was that these two groups came together to question Jesus. Ordinarily the Pharisees, who opposed Roman rule, were at swords' points with the Herodians, who supported it. But they were willing to unite their forces in a common hatred for Jesus.

Each of them would have a part to play. If Jesus answered, "Yes," the Pharisees would say to the people: "You see, He is not a loyal Jew. He is taking the side of the Romans. He's not patriotic." This would have turned the common people against Him. But if He said, "No," the Herodians would have immediately reported Him to the government as fomenting rebellion against the Roman rule of Palestine.

B. The Answer: vv. 18-21

They thought they had Him on the horns of dilemma; there was no way for Him to escape. But He was more than a match for His critics. Knowing their evil intent, He chided them with the question: "You hypocrites, why are you trying to trap me?" (v. 18, NIV).

Then He made a request: "Show me the coin used for paying the tax" (v. 19, NIV). They brought Him a "penny." This was the Roman denarius, a silver coin worth about twenty cents.

Turning it around in His fingers, He asked: "Whose portrait is this? And whose inscription?" (v. 20, NIV). They answered with one word, "Caesar's" (v. 21). Then He made a very simple but very profound comment: "Render therefore unto Caesar the things which are Caesar's; and unto God the things that are God's." The denarius had on it the name and portrait of Tiberius Caesar, the reigning emperor at Rome. So it evidently belonged to him and should be given to him. Just so the human soul bears the image of God and so belongs to Him and should be given to Him.

C. The Effect: v. 22

Jesus disposed of these critics very quickly. The account says: "When they heard these words, they marvelled, and left him, and went their way." They were no match for the Master.

II. QUESTION OF THE SADDUCEES:
Matthew 22:23-33

A. The Question: vv. 23-28

That same day the Sadducees thought that they would take their turn in trying to get Jesus into trouble. Their purpose was to hold Him up to ridicule before the crowd. (We are informed that they did not believe in a resurrection.)

So they came with a ridiculous question. To appear pious, they began by quoting Moses' instructions that if a man died childless his brother was to marry the widow and have children for the deceased man (Deuteronomy 25:5). This was called levirate marriage (from Latin *levir*, "brother-in-law").

The Sadducees posed a hypothetical situation in which seven brothers were successive husbands to the same woman—which probably never happened! Finally the woman died. The question was this: "Therefore in the resurrection whose wife shall she be of the seven? for they all had her" (v. 28). The Sadducees were silly enough to think that this would throw Jesus into confusion.

B. The Answer: vv. 29-32

First, Jesus reproved the Sadducees: "Ye do err, not knowing the scriptures, nor the power of God" (v. 29). The only way that we can be saved from error is by knowing these two things. It is not enough to know the Scriptures alone, nor even the power of God. It must be both.

Then Jesus set the record straight be declaring that "in the resurrection they neither marry, nor are given in marriage, but are as the angels of God in heaven." That is, there will be no sex in the next life. So the question of the Sadducees was irrelevant. Reproduction will not be needed where there is no more death.

Not content with answering their question, Christ gave a supporting argument for the resurrection. God did not say that He *was* the God of Abraham, Isaac, and Jacob, but that He *is* their God. Jesus added the clincher: "God is not the God of the dead, but of the living" (v. 32). The patriarchs are still alive.

C. The Effect: v. 33

When the crowds heard Jesus' answer, they were astonished at His teaching (not "doctrine"). The Greek for "astonished" is literally "struck out." They were struck with astonishment at how quickly and fully the Master had silenced His foes. They had probably observed on other occasions the embarrassment of the Pharisees, who did believe in the resurrection, in trying to handle such questions from the Sadducees. But Jesus was more than a match for all His opponents, whether Pharisees or Sadducees.

III. QUESTION OF THE PHARISEES:
Matthew 22:34-40

A. The Question: vv. 34-36

Probably the Pharisees were delighted to hear that Jesus had silenced their theological opponents, the Sadducees, who had often plagued them in public with difficult questions. So they gathered together (v. 34). (The Greek for "put . . . to silence" is literally "muzzled" or "gagged.")

One of the Pharisees was a "lawyer." This does not mean "an attorney," as now, but an expert in teaching the Mosiac law.

To test Jesus out, he asked the familiar question as to what was the greatest commandment in the Law. "Which" literally means "what kind." Plummer comments on this: "The Rabbis divided the 613 precepts of the Law (248 commands and 365 prohibitions) into 'weighty' and 'light,' but the sorting of them caused much debate" (*Gospel According to Mark*, p. 283). Possibly the Pharisee was wondering whether the moral or ceremonial laws were most important.

B. The Answer: vv. 37-40

Jesus indicated that the heart of God's law is love. The greatest commandment is found in Deuteronomy 6:5, which every devout Jew is supposed to recite twice a day. We are to love God with all our heart, soul, and mind—that is, with all our being. Nothing less than this will satisfy God, and nothing else can make us the true persons that we ought to be.

This love is redemptive. When we love God with all our being, we become more and more like Him. This, not escape from hell, is the true goal of salvation.

Jesus declared that this was "the first and great commandment" (v. 38). Then He added another for good measure: "Thou shalt love thy neighbour as thyself" (v. 39). The first commandment is vertical; this is horizontal. Both relationships—to God and to our fellowmen—are essential to the Christian life. Christ declared that the Law and the Prophets—the entire Old Testament—hung on these two commandments. The first sums up the first four of the Ten Commandments, which have to do with duties to God. The second sums up the other six, which deal with duties to man. Both are essential. But the first is primary. We are not true to the Bible, nor to the words of Jesus, when we reverse the order of these two commandments, as the social gospel tries to do. Actually, we cannot love our neighbor as ourself until we love God with all our being.

The verb for "love" in these two commandments is not *phileo* which expresses friendship or affection. Rather, it is *agapao*, which takes in the mind and will. It is the love of full loyalty to God and the love that seeks the best good of our fellowmen.

IV. QUESTION OF JESUS:
Matthew 22:41-46

A. The Question: vv. 41-45

Since the Pharisees had tried to trap Him with a question, He decided to ask them one. He asked them what they thought about the Messiah— "Whose son is he?" They answered, "David's." We have already noted that "son of David" was a Messianic title.

Then Jesus posed a problem: How is it that David "in spirit" (v. 43)—

better, "by the Spirit" (NIV), that is, by inspiration—calls Him Lord? The passage Jesus quoted (v. 44) is Psalm 110:1, which says: "Yahweh said to my Adonai"—in this case, the Father said to the Son. Then He asked, "If David then calls him Lord, how is he his son?"

B. No Answer: v. 46

No one was able to answer Jesus' question. But the answer is clear to us: David's Lord became David's son in the incarnation. There is no answer to this question unless we accept the deity of Jesus.

V. POSITION AND PRIDE OF THE PHARISEES:
Matthew 23:1-12

A. Position: vv. 1-4

Jesus was now speaking to both the crowd and His disciples (v. 1). He said, "The scribes and the Pharisees sit in Moses' seat" (v. 2). That is, they were the authoritative interpreters of Moses' law, found in the first five books of the Bible.

Jesus continued: "So you must obey them and do everything they tell you. But do not do what they do, for they do not practice what they preach" (v. 3, NIV). This is a sad commentary indeed on the religious leaders of the nation. They were hypocrites, many of them. They laid on the people heavy burdens of multitudinous rules and regulations, but they gave the people no spiritual help in fulfilling the Law (v. 4).

B. Pride: vv. 5-12

In the Sermon on the Mount Jesus had warned His followers not to perform their righteous deeds "to be seen of men" (6:1). Now He charges the Pharisees with being guilty of this very thing (v. 5). Specifically, He said, "They make their phylacteries wide and the tassels of their prayer shawls long; they love the place of honor at banquets and the most important seats in the synagogues" (vv. 5-6, NIV). The phylacteries were small boxes containing Scripture verses, which were worn on the forehead and arms. One can still see many of these being worn by Jews praying at the West Wall—formerly called the Wailing Wall—in Jerusalem.

Verse 9 is a good example of the need for interpreting Scripture intelligently, rather than just literally. Did Jesus mean that a person cannot address his own father as "father"? Of course not. He was speaking against giving to human leaders the reverence that is due only to God.

Verse 12 is a vivid statement of one of the great principles of life: The way up is down! "Abased" and "humble" are the same verb in Greek. It means to have a humble mind. Humility is honest self-appraisal.

VI. DENUNCIATION OF THE PHARISEES:
Matthew 23:13-16

A. Woe upon Woe: vv. 13-26

In verses 13-33 we find seven woes that Jesus pronounced on the Pharisees. (Verse 14 is not in the earliest Greek manuscripts.) He scored these religious leaders for their perversity (v. 13), proselytizing (v. 15), false swearing (v. 16), neglecting essential things (v. 23), and emphasizing only outward ceremonial cleansing (v. 25).

Verse 24 needs a word of explanation. "Strain at a gnat" suggests the picture of a person trying to grab a little gnat out of the air. But the Greek clearly says, "strain out a gnat." Jesus was talking about the strict Pharisees' habit of pouring their drinking water through a thin cloth to strain out any possible gnat—the smallest unclean animal. But while they were doing that they swallowed the biggest unclean animal, a camel! They gave big attention to little things and little attention to big things. That is what all legalists do.

B. Whited Sepulchers: vv. 27-28

The "scribes" were the teachers of the Law (Old Testament) in the synagogues, and so were the main religious leaders of the people. The "Pharisees" were the "separated ones," who separated themselves from the common people in order to keep ceremonially clean. But while they were obsessed with the need of outer cleanliness, Jesus said that they were like whitewashed sepulchers. Outwardly they looked fine, but inwardly they were "full of dead men's bones and all uncleanness."

C. Worshiping the Past: vv. 29-33

We have noted before that "hypocrites" is an exact transliteration of the Greek word for "actor." In those days actors wore masks that contained small megaphones, so that their voices could be heard in the large amphitheaters. So a hypocrite is one who wears a false face.

Jesus denounced the Pharisees for caring more about the bones of their ancestors than the souls of their contemporaries. They honored the prophets of the past, some of whom were put to death for their preaching. But now they themselves were plotting to kill the greatest Prophet of all, the sinless Son of God, who had come to be the Savior of the world. It is only in the light of this fact that we can understand the strong language of verse 33.

D. Final Judgment: vv. 34-36

The Book of Acts is the best commentary on verse 34. The religious leaders of the nation stoned Stephen, a true prophet of God (Acts 7). They tried to bring about the death of Paul, the greatest Christian missionary and theologian of the first century (Acts 24–25). He was persecuted "from city to city" across Asia Minor (Acts 13–14) and Macedonia and Greece (Acts 16–18). Many of the early Jewish Christians were scourged in the synagogues, after being condemned by the local synagogue court. What Jesus predicted came to pass very literally.

Jesus declared that all the guilt of previous generations would find its final focus on that generation. "Abel" is mentioned as being the first martyr for his faith, killed by his wicked brother Cain (Genesis 4:8). The case of Zechariah the son of Berechiah is recorded in II Chronicles 24:20-22. Why is this man named as the last murder? Because Chronicles is the last book in the Hebrew Bible, even today. So it was like our saying "from Genesis to Revelation."

Verse 35 underscores the principle of community guilt. The generation that Jesus was addressing committed the climactic sin of rejecting Jesus Christ. So in a sense the accumulated guilt of previous generations fell on it.

VII. LAMENT OVER JERUSALEM: Matthew 23:37-39

These verses are full of pathos. Jesus had offered Himself to the nation as its King and Messiah, but the leaders had rejected Him and would soon turn Him over to Pilate for execution. It was in Jerusalem, where previous prophets had been stoned or killed, that the final rejection was taking place. No wonder Jesus wept over the city (Luke 19:41)!

The tenderness of His love is shown by the picture He paints. He had often wanted to draw the people of Jerusalem to Himself, as a mother hen gathers her chicks under her wings. "And ye would not" is one of the saddest epitaphs of the ages. "Be-

---

DISCUSSION QUESTIONS

1. What is a hypocrite?
2. What are some ways in which church members can be hypocritical?
3. Could playing a role be unconscious hypocrisy?
4. In what ways were the Pharisees hypocrites?
5. Do we ever stress the outward more than the inward?
6. What are the consequences of hypocrisy?

hold your house is left unto you desolate" had poignant reference to the destruction of Jerusalem and its temple in A.D. 70, just forty years later.

"Blessed is he that cometh in the name of the Lord" (v. 39) was what the Galilean pilgrims had cried at the Triumphal Entry (21:9). The people of Jerusalem will not see Him until they welcome Him with these words.

CONTEMPORARY APPLICATION

"And ye would not" reminds us of the words we saw on a tombstone in Texas: "Could love have saved, thou hadst not died." Draped over the top of the large stone was a weeping angel.

It was the grave of the son of godly parents. He had rebelled against his home and church, taken the bit between his teeth, and plunged into deep sin. At a. young age he died in a drunken brawl in Monterrey, Mexico.

PRAPARATION FOR THE LORD'S RETURN

DEVOTIONAL READING	Matthew 24:1-8

ADULTS

Topic: *Preparation for the Lord's Return*

Background Scripture: Matthew 24

Scripture Lesson: Matthew 24:36-51

Memory Verse: *Watch therefore, for you do not know what day your Lord is coming.* Matthew 24:42

YOUTH

Topic: *Are You Ready?*

Background Scripture: Matthew 24

Scripture Lesson: Matthew 24:36-51

Memory Verse: *Watch therefore, for you do not know on what day your Lord is coming.* Matthew 24:42

CHILDREN

Topic: *Be Prepared*

Background Scripture: Matthew 24; 25:1-13

Scripture Lesson: Matthew 25:14-30

Memory Verse: *A wise man is mightier than a strong man, and a man of knowledge than he who has strength.* Proverbs 24:5

DAILY BIBLE READINGS

Mon. Mar. 22: False Messiahs, Matthew 24:1-6.
Tues., Mar. 23: The Coming of the Son, Matthew 24:23-28.
Wed., Mar. 24: The Permanence of the Word, Matthew 24:32-35.
Thurs., Mar. 25: Words for Disciples, Acts 1:1-8.
Fri., Mar. 26: The Wages of Sin, Genesis 6:11-22.
Sat., Mar. 27: Safe in the Lord, Genesis 7:11-24.
Sun., Mar. 28: Salvation by God, Genesis 8:1-5.

LESSON AIM — To alert us to the need of being ready for Christ's return.

LESSON SETTING

Time: April, A.D. 30

Place: Jerusalem and the Mount of Olives

LESSON OUTLINE

Preparation for the Lord's Return

I. Question of the Disciples: Matthew 24:1-3
 A. The Buildings of the Temple: v. 1

217

B. The Prediction of Their Destruction: v. 2
C. The Disciples' Threefold Question: v. 3

II. **Signs of the End:** Matthew 24:4-14
A. False Messiahs: vv. 4-5
B. Wars, Famines, Earthquakes: vv. 6-8
C. Persecution, Deceit, Loss of Love: vv. 9-13
D. Evangelization of the Whole World: v. 14

III. **The Abomination of Desolation:** Matthew 24:15-22

IV. **The Coming of the Son of Man:** Matthew 24:23-28

V. **The Sign of the Son of Man:** Matthew 24:29-31

VI. **Parable of the Fig Tree:** Matthew 24:32-35

VII. **Suddenness of the Second Coming:** Matthew 24:36-44
A. Time Unknown: v. 36
B. As in the Days of Noah: vv. 37-39
C. One Taken, the Other Left: vv. 40-41
D. Watch and Be Ready: vv. 42-44

VIII. **Necessity for Faithfulness:** Matthew 24:45-51
A. Faithful Servant: vv. 45-47
B. Unfaithful Servant: vv. 48-51

SUGGESTED INTRODUCTION FOR ADULTS

The Olivet Discourse is the only long discourse of Jesus found in all three Synoptic Gospels (cf. Mark 13:1-37; Luke 21:5-36). It is significant that its theme is the Second Coming. Instead of this, John's Gospel has the last discourse of Jesus in the upper room. Its subject was the Holy Spirit, who prepares us to meet Christ.

There has been considerable disagreement as to how this twenty-fourth chapter should be interpreted. Some think it all refers to the destruction of Jerusalem in A.D. 70. Others apply it all to the end of this age. Both views are wrong.

Chrysostom and some other Fathers of the early church held that everything through verse 22 relates to the fall of Jerusalem, and the rest to the Second Coming. But it is difficult to draw such a sharp line of distinction, for some prophecies appear to refer to both.

In any case, we should not ignore the significance of the fact that before His death Jesus spent some time talking about His return. It is a subject we cannot ignore.

SUGGESTED INTRODUCTION FOR YOUTH

"Jesus is coming!" This is the cry that is being echoed by tens of thousands of youth across our land and around the world. Every young Christian should be excited about the prospect of our Lord's early return.

"Are you ready?" That is the question that should concern every Christian. We are warned not to speculate as to the exact date of the Second Coming. Jesus said that no one knows the day or the hour. Rather, we should be ready at all times for this most important event in all human history.

Today there is a great deal of disillusionment and pessimism about world affairs. But the Christian has "the blessed hope" that soon Christ will come back to set up His kingdom of righteousness and peace.

CONCEPTS FOR
CHILDREN

1. The ten bridesmaids all had lighted lamps.
2. Five of them neglected to take extra oil.
3. When the important moment came, their lamps were going out.
4. We must have the light of Jesus in our hearts when He comes again.

THE LESSON COMMENTARY

I. QUESTIONS OF THE DISCIPLES:
Matthew 24:1-3

A. The Buildings of the Temple: v. 1

Jesus "departed from the temple," for the last time that is recorded in the Gospels. He had told the religious leaders that their house would be left desolate (24:38).

As He was walking away His disciples came to Him to show Him the buildings of the temple, of which they were very proud. And well they might be! About 20 B.C. Herod the Great began to rebuild the temple, and He made it one of the most beautiful edifices of that day. Josephus says that the sanctuary itself was 150 feet long and 150 feet high (*Antiquities of the Jews*, xv. 11, 3).

B. The Prediction of Their Destruction: v. 2

The disciples must have been deeply shocked when Jesus replied: "See ye not all these things? verily I say unto you, There shall not be left here one stone upon another, that shall not be thrown down." This was literally fulfilled in A.D. 70. Josephus, who was an eyewitness of the event, says that Jerusalem was "laid even

with the ground" (*Jewish War*, vii. 1. 1).

C. The Disciples' Threefold Question: v. 3

A little later Jesus was sitting on the slopes of the Mount of Olives, which overlooks the temple area and the whole city of Jerusalem. The disciples came to Him privately. "Tell us," they said, "when will this happen, and what will be the sign of your coming and of the end of the age?" (NIV). It is this threefold question that Jesus proceeded to answer in the Olivet Discourse (so-called because of where it was delivered).

II. SIGNS OF THE END:
Matthew 24:4-14

A. False Messiahs: vv. 4-5

Jesus began this great message by saying to His disciples: "Watch out that no one deceives you" (v. 4, NIV). He declared that many would come saying, " 'I am the Christ' [that is, "the Messiah"] and will deceive many" (v. 5, NIV). We know of no false messiahs before A.D. 70. But in A.D. 132-135 there was a great revolt against Rome by Bar Cochba, who claimed to be the Messiah. In the twentieth centuries there have been several false messiahs.

B. Wars, Famines, Earthquakes: vv. 6-8

These have occurred in every generation and century since Christ made this prediction. But it seems to us that the evidence is clear that they are increasing in intensity and frequency as the return of Christ draws near. ("Pestilences" is genuine in Luke 21:10, but not here.)

Verse 8 says, "All these are the beginnings of sorrows." The Greek word for "sorrows" literally means "birth pains." The Jewish rabbis talked about the "birth pangs" of the Messianic age. The Millennium will be preceded by the Great Tribulation, with increasingly severe troubles leading up to it.

C. Persecution, Deceit, Loss of Love: vv. 9-13

Again we would say that all these phenomena have occurred in every century of the Christian era. The "false prophets" who "deceive many" (v. 11) remind us of the multiplicity of false cults in the twentieth century. Then Jesus warned: "And because iniquity [lawlessness] shall abound, the love of many [literally, "the many"] shall wax cold" (v. 12). Only those who stand firm to the end will be saved (v. 13).

D. Evangelization of the Whole World: v. 14

This is one of the most specific signs of the Second Coming. Has the gospel been given to "all nations"? If we use the word *nation* in its broadest sense, probably so. Of course not every tribe has been evangelized; there are many millions who have never heard the gospel. But it has been presented in a measure to every nation. However, the challenge still confronts us to evangelize all the *people* of the world.

Can we "evangelize the world in our generation," as leaders have challenged us to do? The answer is, "Yes."

Today there are hundreds of villages in Asia or Africa where no missionary has ever gone, but where the people gather around a transistor radio to hear the gospel in their own language. These radios are pre-tuned to a Christian station. Trans World Radio is blanketing much of the earth with gospel broadcasts. We can and must evangelize the world *now*.

III. THE ABOMINATION OF DESOLATION: Matthew 24:15-22

This expression (taken from Daniel 9:27; 11:31; 12:11) literally means "the abomination that causes desolation." Arndt and Gingrich define it as the detestable thing causing the desolation of the holy place" (*Lexicon*, p. 137). The expression referred first to the desecration of the temple by Antiochus Epiphanes in 168 B.C., when he offered a pig on the altar of sacrifice there. But here it refers to both A.D. 70 and the end of the age. Josephus suggests that the temple was destroyed in A.D. 70 because the Zealots massacred their fellow Jews in the temple and so desecrated it. The final application will be to the setting up of the image of the Antichrist in Jerusalem at the end of this age (Revelation 13:14).

Before the Roman siege finally tightened around Jerusalem so that no one could escape, the Jewish Christians there remembered Jesus' command (v. 16). They fled down the Jericho road, across the Jordan River and up the east side to Pella in the north. So after A.D. 70 the center of Jewish Christianity was no longer at Jerusalem but at Pella.

Mark 13:18 says that Jesus warned His disciples: "Pray ye that your flight be not in the winter." In his parallel passage Matthew adds "neither on the sabbath day" (v. 20). This is one of the many touches that show that Matthew's Gospel was written for the Jews. A strict Jew would not travel more than half a mile on the sabbath, and so would easily be caught by the enemy.

Verse 21 contains a very strong statement. But Josephus says of the Roman siege of Jerusalem: "It appears to me that the misfortunes of all men, from the beginning of the world, if they be compared to those of the Jews, are not so considerable as they were" (*War*, Preface, 4). The final reference, again, is to the Great Tribulation at the end of this age. That will be the worst ever to occur.

Verse 22 also has the double reference. The first would be to the shortening of the siege of Jerusalem in A.D. 70. Surprisingly it lasted only five months (April to September). The second would be to the brevity of the Great Tribulation.

IV. THE COMING OF THE SON OF MAN:
Matthew 24:23-28

Jesus said that false messiahs and false prophets would appear, showing great signs and wonders so that they try to "deceive the very elect" (v. 24). These impostors must be ignored.

The return of Christ will be sudden. Jesus said: "For as the lightning cometh out of the east, and shineth to the west; so shall also the coming of the Son of man be" (v. 27).

Verse 28 is obviously difficult to interpret. Both early church Fathers and some Reformers held that the "carcase" referred to Christ, to whom the saints (like eagles) would gather together. But "eagles" probably means "vultures." So the reference would seem to be to the many dead bodies in A.D. 70 and at the end of this age.

V. THE SIGN OF THE SON OF MAN:
Matthew 24:29-31

The disciples had asked, "What shall be the sign of thy coming?" (v. 3). Now Jesus says that "the sign of the Son of man" will appear in heaven (v. 30). What does this mean?

The simplest and most honest answer is, "We don't know." It could refer to some visible sign in the sky. But it could mean, "the sign, which is the Son of Man." Daniel 7:13 says, "Behold there was coming with the clouds of heaven one like unto a son of man." The middle part of verse 30—"and then shall all the tribes of the earth mourn"—is reminiscent of Zechariah 12:12. We find these Daniel and Zechariah passages combined again in Revelation 1:7.

Christ will come "with a great sound of a trumpet" (cf. I Corinthians 15:52; I Thessalonians 4:16). The angels will gather all the elect together from "the four winds"—the four points of the compass.

VI. PARABLE OF THE FIG TREE:
Matthew 24:32-35

The fig tree is a symbol of Israel. The restoration of the Jews to their own land and the setting up of the new nation of Israel in 1948 may well be a fulfillment of verse 32. "It is near" (v. 33) can just as accurately be translated "He is near." But the parallel in Luke 22:31 suggests that "it" is preferable.

What does verse 34 mean? There are three possible answers. If we restrict the reference as being to A.D. 70, it would be the destruction of Jerusalem. Jesus predicted it in A.D. 30 (v. 2) and it happened in A.D. 70, within that generation.

But the disciples not only asked, "When will this happen?" (v. 3), but went on to the further twofold question, "And what will be the sign of your coming and of the end of the age?" Jesus is answering this question also.

A second interpretation, then, takes the term "generation" used here to mean "race"—a proper meaning of the Greek *genea*. So they suggest that Jesus meant that the Jewish race would not disappear before His return.

A third possibility may be this: The generation that sees the rapid multiplication of the final signs will live to see the Second Coming and the end of the age.

VII. SUDDENNESS OF THE SECOND COMING: Matthew 24:36-44

A. Time Unknown: v. 36

Jesus declared that no one knew the day or hour of His coming. Mark 13:32 adds "neither the Son." That addition is also found here in Matthew in the oldest Greek manuscripts. In His incarnation Christ had limited Himself somewhat in His conscious knowledge, so that not even He knew the time of His return.

If He did not know, how dare we set dates? All those who have set exact dates for the Second Coming have made fools of themselves and brought reproach on the cause of Christ. The teaching here is so clear on this point that there is no excuse for anyone indulging in this pastime.

B. As in the Days of Noah: vv. 37-39

The time of Christ's return will be like those of Noah. All the things mentioned in verse 38 are legitimate in themselves. There is nothing wrong with "eating and drinking, marrying and giving in marriage." The sin lay in

---

DISCUSSION QUESTIONS

1. What are the most significant signs of the Second Coming?
2. What is the importance of the modern missionary movement?
3. What false messiahs have appeared in our day?
4. How is the revival of Israel related to Christ's return?
5. Why are we warned against setting dates?
6. What is the most important emphasis in regard to the Second Coming?

---

the fact that the people of that day were ignoring God. And the greatest peril that confronts the church today is not false doctrine or criminal activity but secularism. People are forgetting God. And that will bring judgment.

The antedeluvians were so engrossed in their pleasure-seeking and the round of daily existence without God that they "knew not until the flood came, and took them all away." Again Jesus declared, "So shall also the coming of the Son of man be" (v. 39; cf. vv. 27, 37).

C. One Taken, the Other Left: vv. 40-41

At the time of Christ's return there will be just two main groups of people in the world—those who are ready, and those who are not. To make this point more vivid Jesus became a bit more specific. He said that two (either men or women) would be in the field; "the one shall be taken, and the other left." Two women would be "grinding at the mill." This does not refer to a factory, called a "mill" in modern times, but to the little handmill that can still be seen occasionally in Palestine (and we have seen it in Korea). One can see two women sitting on the ground with this little mill between them, composed of two stones about as big around as dinner plates. Both women have one hand on a wooden peg in the upper millstone, and they turn it around rapidly to grind the grain between the two millstones. This is done each day to make a fresh batch of flour. Yet two women so close together will suddenly be separated—one caught up to meet the Lord and the other left to face the terrible judgment that will come on the world.

Luke (17:34) adds a still more poignant item: Two will be in one bed; the one will be taken and the other left. There are thousands of Christian women with unsaved husbands. The separation that will take place at the Second Coming is sad to contemplate.

And the question that confronts each one of us is this: Will I be the one taken to be with Christ, or the one left behind?

D. Watch and Be Ready: vv. 42-44

This is the central emphasis of Jesus' teaching on the Second Coming. It should be the main emphasis today as well when this subject is preached on. Not speculation, but evangelization!

"Watch" (v. 42) is literally, "Keep awake!" We are to be constantly on the alert. Once more we are reminded: "for ye know not what hour your Lord doth come." So we have to be ready all the time.

"Goodman of the house" (v. 43) is the same word, *oikodespotes*, that is translated "householder" in 20:1. In 20:11 it is rendered the same as here. It literally means "house-master."

If the owner of the home had known in what watch of the night the burglar was coming, he would have been on his guard and would not have permitted his house to be ransacked. The only remedy is to be on the watch all the time.

And so it is with the Second Coming. Christ will come unexpectedly, "as a thief in the night" (I Thessalonians 5:2). "Therefore be ye also ready: for in such an hour as ye think not the Son of man cometh" (v. 44). This is a solemn warning to all Christians.

The motto is still relevant:

Do nothing that you would not like to be doing when Jesus comes.
Say nothing that you would not like to be saying when Jesus comes.
Go to no place you would not like to be found when Jesus comes.

VIII. NECESSITY FOR FAITHFULNESS:
Matthew 24:45-51

A. Faithful Servant: vv. 45-47

This is a brief parable of final warning. Jesus told of a faithful and wise servant "whom the master has put in charge of the servants in his household to give them their food at the proper time" (v. 45, NIV). If the master, when He returns, finds the servant faithfully discharging his duties, "he will put him in charge of all his possessions."

In those days wealthy men had stewards—literally, "house-managers"—who took care of running all the business of the house for them. A faithful, trustworthy steward was one of the greatest assets a man could have. And any reasonable master would generously reward a faithful, honest steward. If we are faithful to our Christian responsibilities, we will not miss the reward.

B. Unfaithful Servant: vv. 48-51

Unfortunately, not all trusted servants are trustworthy. Jesus said: "But suppose that servant is wicked and says to himself, 'My master is staying away a long time,' and he then begins to beat his fellow servants and to eat and drink with drunkards" (vv. 48-49, NIV)—then the master of that servant will put in his appearance at a day and hour when the servant is not expecting him.

Verse 51 pictures the fate of the unfaithful. They will be "cut in sunder"—literally, "cut in two"—for trying to be two things at once. The place of the hypocrites will be eternal punishment, where "there shall be weeping and gnashing of teeth." Everyone of us should pray that we may not merit such a final end.

CONTEMPORARY APPLICATION

"The modern world missionary movement began with William Carey, in 1792. At about that time (1800) parts of the Bible had been printed in only 71 languages and dialects—50 in Europe, 13 in Asia, four in Africa, three in America, and one in Oceania. But in the next 30 years 86 more languages received at least some of the Scriptures—more than in all the previous 1,800 years put together. In 1938 the number passed the 1,000 mark. Of these, 173 were in Europe, 212 in Asia, 345 in Africa, 89 in the Americas, and 189 in Oceania. The total figure has gone well over 1,200 languages" (Earle, *What the Bible Says About the Second Coming*, p. 20).

THE BASIS OF JUDGMENT

DEVOTIONAL READING	Matthew 25:19-30

ADULTS

Topic: *Man Under Judgment*

Background Scripture: Matthew 25

Scripture Lesson: Matthew 25:31-46

Memory Verse: *Truly, I say to you, as you did it to one of the least of these my brethren, you did it to me.* Matthew 25:40

YOUTH

Topic: *Man on Trial*

Background Scripture: Matthew 25

Scripture Lesson: Matthew 25:31-46

Memory Verse: *Truly, I say to you, as you did it to one of the least of these my brethren, you did it to me.* Matthew 25:40

CHILDREN

Topic: *Using What We Have*

Background Scripture: Matthew 25

Scripture Lesson: Matthew 25:31-40

Memory Verse: *His master said to him, "Well done, good and faithful servant; you have been faithful over a little, I will set you over much; enter into the joy of your master."* Matthew 25:23

DAILY BIBLE READINGS

Mon., Mar. 29: Be Prepared, Matthew 25:1-13.
Tues., Mar. 30: The Way God Measures, Matthew 7:21-23.
Wed., Mar. 31: Parable of the Talents, Matthew 25:14-30.
Thurs., Apr. 1: The Heart with God, Luke 12:32-34.
Fri., Apr. 2: Those Who Love Jesus, John 21:15-19.
Sat., Apr. 3: Deeds to Match Words, James 2:14-17.
Sun., Apr. 4: True Faith Produces Works, James 2:18-26.

LESSON AIM

To see how we may be prepared for Christ's return and what is the basis of judgment.

LESSON SETTING

Time: A.D. 30

Place: Jerusalem

LESSON OUTLINE

The Basis of Judgment

    I. Parable of the Ten Virgins: Matthew 25:1-13

225

A. Waiting for the Bridegroom: vv. 1-5
B. Coming of the Bridegroom: vv. 6-9
C. Enjoying the Wedding: v. 10
D. Kept Outside: vv. 11-12
E. Warning to Watch: v. 13

II. **Parable of the Talents:** Matthew 25:14-30
A. Distribution of Talents: vv. 14-15
B. Treatment of Talents: vv. 16-18
C. Reward for Faithfulness: vv. 19-23
D. Punishment for Unfaithfulness: vv. 24-30

III. **The Sheep and the Goats:** Matthew 25:31-46
A. The Judgment Scene: vv. 31-33
B. Commendation of the Righteous: vv. 34-36
C. Question of the Righteous: vv. 37-39
D. Answer of the King: v. 40
E. Condemnation of the Wicked: vv. 41-43
F. Question of the Wicked: v. 44
G. Answer of the King: v. 45
H. Destinations of the Righteous and the Wicked: v. 46

**SUGGESTED
INTRODUCTION
FOR ADULTS**

One of the things that should most concern every Christian is the matter of being ready for the coming of Christ. This may be at His return to earth or it may be in the hour of death. In either case we need to be ready.

The twenty-fifth chapter of Matthew underscores three ways in which we need to be prepared for the Second Coming. The Parable of the Ten Virgins emphasizes the necessity of keeping up-to-date in our *spiritual experience*. The Parable of the Talents shows us that we must be busy in *service*. The story of the Sheep and the Goats indicates that we need to be concerned about our *social relationships*, in our caring for the needy.

Some Christians think only about their inner spiritual life and neglect the work of the Lord. They worship, but they do not serve. Some go to the opposite extreme. They give themselves unstintingly to the work of the church, but they do not take time to maintain the spiritual glow in their hearts. Then there are those who do both of these but are neglectful of their responsibility to needy people around them. We need to give careful attention to all three areas.

**SUGGESTED
INTRODUCTION
FOR YOUTH**

Some day we shall all stand before the judgment seat of Christ. One criterion of judgment will be our treatment of other people. Have we been concerned about their needs, or have we passed them by? In that day this will be an important question. To be ready for that time of reckoning we need to give attention to these matters now.

**CONCEPTS FOR
CHILDREN**

1. God gives all of us at least one talent.
2. We are responsible for what we do with the talents He gives us.

3. We should seek to identify our God-given talents and use them to the best advantage.
4. As we use them they multiply.

THE LESSON COMMENTARY

I. PARABLE OF THE TEN VIRGINS:
Matthew 25:1-13

A. Waiting for the Bridegroom: vv. 1-5

Jesus was a master at telling interesting stories to illustrate important truths. Here He uses the much-loved theme of a wedding to point out vividly the need of being ready for His coming as the heavenly bridegroom for His church, the bride.

As is sometimes the case in parables, the comparisons are not perfect. Here it is the ten virgins, or bridesmaids, that wait for the bridegroom. At the Second Coming it will be the true church, the bride, that will meet Him. But the poignant necessity of being ready comes through clearly.

These ten virgins took their "lamps" (Greek, *lampas*) and went out to meet the bridegroom. Even this small group was divided into two kinds of people. We read: "Five of them were foolish and five were wise" (v. 2, NIV). (This is the order of the best Greek text, which is reversed in the King James Version.) The word for "foolish" is *morai*, from which we get "moron." The word for "wise" is *phronimoi*, which means "sensible" or "prudent."

The first five were foolish because they did not prepare for any contingencies. They just assumed that everything would operate on schedule. So they "took their lamps, but did not take any oil with them" (v. 3, NIV). But things do not always go as planned!

The other five were wise. They "took oil in jars along with their lamps" (v. 4, NIV). They were sensible enough to prepare for emergencies. For emergencies do happen in life—frequently—and the sensible person prepares for them. That is why we buy insurance. To put it bluntly: Anyone who does not prepare for emergencies is foolish.

For some reason, "the bridegroom was late" (v. 5, NIV). Why a man would be late for his own wedding is difficult to figure out. Yet such a thing has happened. The definitive biography of the great missionary to China, J. Hudson Taylor, tells how his grandfather became so busy on his wedding day that he forgot about it and didn't show up for his own wedding! Fortunately for him, his bride-to-be forgave him and set another date. The second time he made it!

While the bridegroom tarried, "they all slumbered and slept." The first verb means "to nod" and is in the aorist tense. That is, they began to nod and doze. The second verb is in the imperfect tense of continuous action—"and kept on sleeping." The bridegroom was evidently coming from a distance and was slow in arriving.

B. Coming of the Bridegroom: vv. 6-9

At midnight the cry rang out: "Here's the bridegroom!" The added "cometh" (KJV) is not in the oldest manuscripts.

The bridegroom and his attendants were finally approaching. Evidently a city watchman saw their little lights flickering in the darkness. Or it may have been a member of the party sent ahead to alert the bride's attendants. At any rate, the shout was heard: "Here's the bridegroom! Come out to meet him!"

Rubbing the sleep out of their eyes, the ten virgins all got up quickly and "trimmed" their lamps (v. 7). They clipped the charred ends of the wicks, as we used to do half a century ago. We now know what these lamps looked like, as many of them from that period have been dug up. They were shallow clay lamps, with no chimneys, holding perhaps a quarter of a cup of oil. At one end was a hole for the wick. In the center was a larger hole for putting in the olive oil that they burned in those days. (I am holding in my left hand as I write one bought in Jerusalem.)

The foolish virgins said to the wise, "Give us of your oil; for our lamps are gone out" (v. 8). But the Greek clearly says, "Our lamps are going out." This is a very significant difference. It implies that at the coming of Christ there may be many who have not completely backslidden; their lamp of spiritual life has not "gone out" but is "going out." But, as the sequel here shows, they will not be ready when He comes. It is a solemn note of warning.

The wise answered, "Not so, lest there be not enough for us and you: but go ye rather to them that sell, and buy for yourselves" (v. 9). On the surface, this might seem a bit harsh. But it underscores the important truth that a spiritual experience cannot be transferred from one to another. Each individual has to have his own personal relationship to God.

C. Enjoying the Wedding: v. 10

While the foolish, thoughtless virgins hurried off to buy some oil, the bridegroom came. Then comes the crux of the whole parable: "They that were ready went in with him to the marriage: and the door was shut." When Christ comes, those who are ready will be caught up to meet Him "in the air: and so shall we ever be with the Lord" (I Thessalonians 4:17). We shall be enjoying the Marriage Supper of the Lamb. But when the door is shut, no one else can enter. Everyone's eternal destiny is finally sealed and settled.

"The door was shut." These are haunting words. Today mercy's door is open. All who will may enter. But once the door is shut, it is too late.

D. Kept Outside: vv. 11-12

Finally the five foolish virgins arrived at the house of the bride, where the wedding festivities were now in full swing. It is doubtful if they had been able to secure any oil at that late hour of the night. But they hurried back, anyhow, to join the wedding guests.

When they came to the bride's house, they called out, "Lord, Lord, open to us" (v. 11). But a voice from inside answered, "I tell you the truth, I don't know you" (v. 12, NIV). It was now well past midnight, and it would not be safe to open the door. There was always the danger of some villains crashing the party and robbing the guests.

E. Warning to Watch: v. 13

The picture is a very pathetic one. Inside were the guests, celebrating with the bride and groom. All was light and gladness. Outside in the dark—no streetlights in those days— were the five foolish virgins, who had been unprepared. They could hear the noise of music and singing, but they were lonely in the dark. No wonder Jesus said, "Watch, therefore, for ye know neither the day nor the hour" (v. 13). (The rest of the verse is not in the oldest manuscripts.)

II. PARABLE OF THE TALENTS: Matthew 25:14-30

A. Distribution of Talents: vv. 14-15

We need to be ready for the return of Christ not only in terms of inner spiritual experience but also of outer service. We all need to be something of a mixture of Martha and Mary.

So Jesus told the Parable of the Talents. A man was going on a long journey. This was a hint of the fact that He would soon be leaving His disciples and going back to heaven. The man called in his servants and handed over to them his money to take care of while he was gone.

He gave one servant five talents, another two, and still another one— "to every man according to his several ability" (v. 15). The "talent" was worth about a thousand dollars. The servants were charged with heavy responsibilities.

B. Treatment of Talents: vv. 16-18

The servant who had received five talents "went at once and put his money to work and gained five more" (v. 16, NIV). He made wise investments and turned a profit of 100 percent. The man who had been given two talents did the same (v. 17).

But the man who had received the one talent went away, dug a hole in the ground, and hid his master's money (v. 18). He was too lazy to put it to work and earn a profit for the owner.

C. Reward for Faithfulness: vv. 19-23

"After a long time" (v. 19) takes on added significance in the light of the fact that nineteen centuries have passed since Jesus went away. But He will, without any uncertainty, finally come back, just as the man in this parable did.

The master "reckoneth with them." The Greek literally says, "He takes up an account together with them"; that is, he "settled accounts" with the servants. We find the same expression in 18:23, where it is translated "take account." This business phrase, which probably reflects Matthew's background of keeping books in his tax office, is found only in this Gospel.

"The man who had received the five talents brought the other five. 'Master,' he said, 'you entrusted me with five talents. See, I have gained five more'" (v. 20, NIV). Delighted, the master replied, "Well done," or "Excellent!" He addressed him as "good and faithful servant" (v. 21). This is very significant. He did not say

"clever and capable servant." Fortunately, we will not be rewarded on the basis of ability or brilliance, but only on the basis of character and service. We cannot all do big things in public. But every servant of the Lord can, and must, be "good and faithful."

Because this servant had been "faithful over a few things," he would now be put in charge of many things. This hints at areas of service and responsibility in the next life. He was also to enter into "the joy of thy lord." We who are faithful will share the joy of our faithful Christ, who did His task well.

The second servant came and reported that he had likewise doubled the money given him. His additional two talents represented just as much work as the additional five talents of the first servant. So he received identically the same commendation and reward. It isn't how much we have to begin with that counts; it's what we do with it.

D. Punishment for Unfaithfulness: vv. 24-30

The man who had received the one talent came with a far different report. He said to his master: "I knew that you are a hard man, harvesting where you have not sown and gathering where you have not scattered seed. So I was afraid and went out and hid your talent in the ground. See, here is what belongs to you" (vv. 24-25, NIV). The spirit of this man shows through clearly in his words. He was blaming someone else for his own failure. People still do that today, even in the church.

Verse 26 should end with a question mark, showing the ridiculous reasoning of the servant's words in the previous verses. The New International Version puts it well: "His master replied, 'You wicked, lazy servant! So you knew that I harvest where I have not sown and gather where I have not scattered seed?'" If he knew this, as he claimed, he should have been all the more careful to invest his master's money to the best advantage. By his own words the man had effectively condemned himself. He should have deposited the money with the bankers ("exchangers") and then it would have earned interest ("usury"). The master then ordered the talent taken from this lazy wretch and given to the servant who had ten talents (v. 28).

Verse 29 is a striking statement of the principle "Use or lose." The word *talent* has been taken over from this parable and is now used in the sense of ability or mental gift. If we use our talents, we gain more. If we do not use them, we lose them. This is true of all learning, particularly of languages.

III. THE SHEEP AND THE GOATS: Matthew 25:31-46

A. The Judgment Scene: vv. 31-33

Verse 31 describes Christ's return in glory, accompanied by "all the holy angels." The first time He came in humility, to die on the cross. The second time He will come in power, to sit on the throne.

The language of verses 32-33 reminds one of Ezekiel 34:17—"And as for you, O my flock, thus saith the Lord God; Behold, I judge between cattle and cattle, between the rams and the he goats."

Before Christ will be gathered all "nations" (neuter in Greek): and he will separate "them" (masculine). This shows that the judgment is of people,

not nations as such. It is individuals that will be separated from each other, not nations. Those who are like sheep will be placed on the right side, and those who are goatlike will be put on the left.

B. Commendation of the Righteous: vv. 34-36

To those on his right, the King will say, "Come, you who are blessed by my Father" (NIV). These sheeplike people will be invited to inherit the Kingdom that was prepared for them since the creation of the world.

Why? Because "you gave me something to eat ... something to drink ... and you invited me in" (v. 35, NIV). That is, "When you saw me in need, you ministered to me."

C. Question of the Righteous: vv. 37-39

"The righteous," as they are now called, will ask in surprise, "When did we see you in need and help you?" They had never seen Him in person! What was He talking about? (It should be noted that "naked" in verses 36 and 38 means "needing clothes." People in that day, and some people now in Asia and Africa, are actually unable to buy clothes to wear.)

D. Answer of the King: v. 40

The King's reply will be, "Inasmuch as ye have done it unto one of the least of these my brethren, ye have done it unto me." There has been considerable discussion as to the meaning of the term "brethren." Some have insisted that it refers to the Jews, and that the scene here describes the judgment of the Gentile nations on the basis of their treatment of the Jew. But we have already noted that the Greek clearly indicates it is people, not nations, that are being judged. So the word "brethren" probably refers to the suffering people of earth, for whom Christ died in compassionate love.

DISCUSSION QUESTIONS

1. Of what is "oil" a type in the Bible?
2. How may we keep up our spiritual life?
3. What responsibility do talented people have?
4. What is the danger of being a one-talented person?
5. How did Jesus identify Himself with humanity?
6. How can we meet the challenge of the Sheep and the Goats?

E. Condemnation of the Wicked: vv. 41-43

To the righteous the Judge will say, "Come" (v. 34). But to the wicked He will say, "Depart" (v. 41). They are "cursed" by their own sins. And so they have to go into "everlasting fire, prepared for the devil and his angels." Again we note that it is Jesus Himself who uses the strongest language in the New Testament on eternal punishment. The charge against the goatlike people is that they did nothing for Him when they saw Him in need (vv. 42-43).

F. Question of the Wicked: v. 44

These people will likewise be surprised at the King's words. They will say, "Lord, when did we see you hungry or thirsty or a stranger or needing clothes or sick or in prison, and did not help you?" (NIV). They, too, had never seen Him before!

G. Answer of the King: v. 45

"Inasmuch as ye did it not" is a solemn warning to all of us. Negligence sometimes is treated as a trifling matter. But it can be a sin, and it is in fact treated as a crime under certain conditions ("criminal negligence").

H. Destination of the Righteous and the Wicked: v. 46

"And these [the wicked] shall go away into everlasting punishment: but the righteous into life eternal." The Greek has the same word for "everlasting" and "eternal." If there is eternal life in heaven there is also eternal punishment in hell.

CONTEMPORARY APPLICATION

This chapter emphasizes the sins of omission, not commission. The five foolish virgins find the door shut against them because of their negligence in not carrying extra oil. The third servant is cast out as good-for-nothing because he did nothing. Those on the left hand are punished for failing to show kindness to those in need.

Too many evangelicals are eloquent in preaching on the Ten Virgins, or even on the Talents, but neglect the implications of the Sheep and the Goats. If Christians had always given proper attention to the social implications and applications of the true gospel, the so-called "social gospel" would not have appeared.

THE REJECTED KING

DEVOTIONAL READING	Isaiah 53:1-9

ADULTS

Topic: *The Rejected King*

Background Scripture: Matthew 26–27

Scripture Lesson: Matthew 27:11, 15-23, 27-31

Memory Verse: *What shall I do with Jesus who is called Christ?* Matthew 27:22

YOUTH

Topic: *A Time for Decision*

Background Scripture: Matthew 26–27

Scripture Lesson: Matthew 27:11, 15-23, 27-31

Memory Verse: *What shall I do with Jesus who is called Christ?* Matthew 27:22

CHILDREN

Topic: *They Made Fun of Jesus*

Background Scripture: Matthew 26–27

Scripture Lesson: Matthew 27:11, 15-23, 27-31

Memory Verse: *What shall I do with Jesus who is called Christ?* Matthew 27:22

DAILY BIBLE READINGS

Mon., Apr. 5: Conspiracy Among the Leaders, Matthew 26:1-5.
Tues., Apr. 6: One Woman's Worship, Matthew 26:6-13.
Wed., Apr. 7: Preparing for the Passover, Matthew 26: 14-19.
Thurs., Apr. 8: Betrayal Foreshadowed, Matthew 26: 20-25.
Fri., Apr. 9: The Last Supper, Matthew 26:26-29.
Sat., Apr. 10: Denial Foreshadowed, Matthew 26:30-35.
Sun., Apr. 11: Jesus in Gethsemane, Matthew 26:36-46.

LESSON AIM

To seek to understand why the Jewish leaders rejected Jesus and to catch the warning for us.

LESSON SETTING

Time: April, A.D. 30

Place: Jerusalem

LESSON OUTLINE

The Rejected King

   I. **Arrested by Religious Leaders:** Matthew 26:47-56

II. **Brought Before the Sanhedrin:** Matthew 26:57-68

III. **Disowned by Peter:** Matthew 26:69-75

IV. **Condemned by the Sanhedrin:** Matthew 27:1-2

V. **Tried Before Pilate:** Matthew 27:11-26
A. Questioned by Pilate: v. 11
B. Accused by Jewish Leaders: vv. 12-14
C. Barabbas or Jesus: vv. 15-18
D. Warned by a Dream: v. 19
E. Death Demanded by the Crowd: vv. 20-23
F. Abandoned by the Governor: vv. 24-26

VI. **Mocked by the Soldiers:** Matthew 27:27-31
A. The Scarlet Robe: vv. 27-28
B. The Crown of Thorns: v. 29
C. The Cruel Abuse: vv. 30-31

VII. **Crucified and Mocked:** Matthew 27:32-44
A. The Callous Soldiers: vv. 32-37
B. The Cruel Crowd: vv. 38-40
C. The Mocking Leaders: vv. 41-44

SUGGESTED INTRODUCTION FOR ADULTS

Passion Week was the climax of the many crises through which Christ had gone. It was marked by the rejection on Sunday, the unfriendly questioning on Tuesday, the plot to kill Jesus (26:3-5), the consciousness that He would be betrayed and denied, the agony of Gethsemane, the arrest, the Jewish and Roman trials, and finally the crucifixion.

But there were two bright spots in this week of agony. One was the enthusiasm of the Galilean pilgrims, who welcomed Him as their Messiah (21:1-11). The other was the anointing at Bethany (26:6-13).

Jesus was always welcome in the home of Mary and Martha (Luke 10:38-42). It is identified here as the home of Simon the Leper (26:6). But John (12:1-8) tells us that it was where Lazarus lived with his two sisters, Martha and Mary, and that it was Mary who anointed Him. Probably Simon the Leper was their father.

How it must have cheered Jesus' saddened heart to have Mary pour the perfume on His head! No wonder He exclaimed, "She has done a beautiful thing to me" (26:10, NIV).

The main event of Thursday evening was the Last Supper, which culminated with the Lord's Supper. It was the annual Passover meal (26:17-19). At the table Jesus predicted that one of His own disciples would betray Him (vv. 20-25). Then He instituted the Lord's Supper (vv. 26-30).

The climax of those agonizing hours leading up to the crucifixion came in the Garden of Gethsemane (vv. 36-46). Jesus said, "My soul is overwhelmed with sorrow to the point of death" (v. 38, NIV; note that the quotation in v. 40 is in the form of a question). The crux of Jesus' prayer was: "Yet not as I will, but as you will" (v. 39, NIV). That is what we must pray.

SUGGESTED
INTRODUCTION
FOR YOUTH

Decisions in life are important, for our decisions determine our destiny. Sometimes young people make important decisions carelessly, thoughtlessly. But that can be fatal. The greatest decision in life is to accept Jesus as Savior and Lord.

CONCEPTS FOR
CHILDREN

1. The Jewish leaders made fun of Jesus.
2. They answered His love with mockery.
3. People still make fun of those who do right.
4. We must meet ridicule with love, knowing that Jesus suffered the same way.

THE LESSON COMMENTARY

I. ARRESTED BY RELIGIOUS LEADERS:
Matthew 26:47-56

While Jesus was still warning His disciples that His betrayer was approaching (v. 46), Judas arrived. With him was a large crowd, armed with swords and clubs, who had been sent by the "chief priests and elders of the people" (the Sanhedrin) to arrest Jesus. The depth of Judas's depravity is shown by the fact that he stepped up immediately to Jesus, said, "Greetings, Rabbi!" and kissed Him (v. 49). It was a diabolical act. Jesus' answer (v. 50) can be translated either as a question, "Friend, wherefore art thou come?" (KJV), or as a command, "Friend, do what you came for" (NIV). Then Jesus was arrested.

Looking at the large crowd that had come to seize Him, He asked a justifible question: "Am I leading a rebellion, that you have come out with swords and clubs to capture me?" (v. 55, NIV). Why hadn't they arrested Him while He was teaching daily in the temple courts? The answer is given in 23:3-5.

II. BROUGHT BEFORE THE SANHEDRIN:
Matthew 26:57-68

Jesus' captors led Him away to the house of Caiaphas the high priest.

There the members of the Sanhedrin had hastily assembled. At last they had Him in their hands!

Peter has often been condemned for following his Master "afar off" (v. 58). Perhaps he should rather be commended for following Him at all. That is more than the other disciples did; they all "forsook him, and fled" (v. 56). Peter went into the courtyard ("palace," KJV) of the high priest and sat down with the servants "to see the end." It was a melancholy prospect!

"The chief priests and the whole Sanhedrin were looking for false evidence against Jesus so that they could put him to death" (v. 59, NIV). When Jesus cleansed the temple He challenged the authority of the chief priests (21:12-13, 23). They never forgave Him for this. From that time on they spearheaded the drive to have Him killed.

At first no false evidence was forthcoming. But finally two witnesses agreed on one point: "This fellow said, I am able to destroy the temple of God, and to build it in three days" (v. 61, NIV). This was a distortion of Jesus' actual words (John 2:18-22).

When Christ made no reply to these false accusations, the high priest tried to "bully" Him into answering (v. 62). But still Jesus remained silent. Then Caiaphas said to Him: "I charge you under oath by the living God: Tell us if you are the Christ, the Son of God" (v. 63, NIV). He compelled Jesus to assert whether or not He was the Messiah.

Christ answered in the affirmative. And then He added that the Son of Man would sit at the right hand of "power"—a typical Jewish euphemistic substitute for "God"—and come on "the clouds of heaven" (v. 64).

When the high priest heard this, he "rent his clothes" (v. 65). This was forbidden in the Law under ordinary circumstances (Leviticus 10:6; 21:10). But by this time it had become the custom to do it in extreme cases. As he tore his clothes, Caiaphas said: "He has spoken blasphemy! Why do we need any more witnesses? Look, now you have heard the blasphemy. What do you think?" (NIV). They answered, "He is worthy of death" (v. 66).

What followed was contrary to all the rules of decency and justice. The members of the Sanhedrin spit in His face and "struck him with their fists" (v. 67, NIV). Some slapped Him and challenged Him to tell who it was that hit Him (v. 68). Luke (22:64) says He was blindfolded.

III. DISOWNED BY PETER:
Matthew 26:69-75

As Peter was sitting outside in the courtyard, a servant girl said to him, "You also were with Jesus of Galilee" (v. 69, NIV). The scared apostle denied the charge: "I don't know what you're talking about," he said (v. 70, NIV).

To escape further detection, Peter went out to the gateway. But there another girl spotted him and identified him as a follower of "Jesus of Nazareth" (v. 71). This time Peter denied it with an oath, saying that he did not know Jesus (v. 72).

A little later he got into trouble again. Some who were standing there declared that he must be "one of them; for thy speech bewrayeth thee" (v. 73). It goes without argument that there is no such word in English today

as "bewrayeth." The New International Version gives the correct translation: "Surely you are one of them, for your accent gives you away." Peter spoke with a distinct Galilean accent, which was different from that used in Judea. The people in Jerusalem would quickly notice this.

In response to this accusation, Peter began "to curse and to swear" (v. 74). This has often been interpreted to mean that the trapped apostle reverted to the rough, profane language of a fisherman—perhaps to prove that he was no follower of Jesus! But this is not the meaning of the Greek. The correct translation is: "Then he began to call down curses on himself and he swore to them, 'I don't know the man!' " Thus he became guilty of perjury.

Just then a rooster crowed. Peter remembered Jesus' prediction of the threefold denial (26:31-35). "And he went out, and wept bitterly" (v. 75). It was Peter's saddest hour.

IV. CONDEMNED BY THE SANHEDRIN:
Matthew 27:1-2

When morning came, "all the chief priests and the elders of the people came to the decision to put Jesus to death" (v. 1, NIV). The Sanhedrin was not legally permitted to meet at night. So the action taken at the illegal night session had to be made official by a meeting called at daybreak. Thereupon they bound Jesus as a prisoner and led Him away to Pilate, the governor (v. 2). The Roman government had taken away from the Jewish Sanhedrin the right to exercise capital punishment, except in the case of a Gentile who went beyond the Court of the Gentiles into the sacred precincts of the temple area. So the Jewish leaders had to hand Jesus over to Pilate to be executed.

There follows in Matthew (alone) the sad story of Judas's remorse at having betrayed his Master. He returned the thirty silver coins to the priests, saying, "I have sinned" (v. 4).

Their callous answer was: "What is that to us? That's your responsibility" (NIV). No wonder Judas hanged himself!

V. TRIED BEFORE PILATE: Matthew 27:11-16

A. Questioned by Pilate: v. 11

Now Jesus was standing as a prisoner before Pilate. The governor asked Him if He was the King of the Jews. His brief reply—two words in both Greek and English—was, "Thou sayest."

This has caused some debate. There are those who think the words mean, "That's what you say"—literally, "You are saying (it)." But it seems clear that it should be treated as a straightforward affirmative answer. M'Neile thinks it implies: "Thou art verbally correct, but the truth is beyond thy comprehension" (*Matthew*, p. 409).

B. Accused by Jewish Leaders: vv. 12-14

When Jesus was accused by the chief priests and elders, He gave no answer. Surprised, Pilate asked Him if He wasn't hearing all the accusations hurled at Him. "But Jesus made no reply, not even to a single charge—to the great amazement of the governor" (v. 14, NIV). It was the same perfect poise that He had maintained in the Sanhedrin (26:62-63). This made His enemies jittery.

C. Barabbas or Jesus: vv. 15-18

"Now it was the governor's custom at the Feast to release a prisoner chosen by the crowd" (v. 15, NIV). Objection has been made that his practice is not mentioned outside the Gospels. But we know that prisoners were released at certain festivals in Rome. Carr makes the helpful comment: "It is not, therefore, improbable that Herod the Great, who certainly familiarized the Jews with other usages of

Greece and Rome, introduced this custom, and that the Roman governor, finding the custom established and gratifying to the Jews, in accordance with Roman practice ... retained the observance of it" (*The Gospel According to Matthew*, p. 303). This agrees with Pilate's statement, "Ye have a custom" (John 18:39).

At that time they had a "notable" —better, "notorious"—prisoner named "Barabbas" (v. 16). This is an Aramaic word, compounded of *bar*, "son," and *abba*, "father." So it literally means "son of a father." The Jewish leaders rejected the true "Son of the Father" in favor of this false "son of a father." Both Mark (15:7) and Luke (23:19) call attention to the fact that Barabbas had committed murder in an insurrection against the Roman government. It was this that led Peter to say: "But ye denied the Holy One and the Just, and desired a murderer to be granted unto you; and killed the Prince of life" (Acts 3:14-15).

When the crowd had gathered (v. 17), alerted to the exciting things that were going on, Pilate asked the people whether they wanted him to release Barabbas or Jesus, who was called Christ (Messiah). Matthew tells us that Pilate knew it was because of envy that the Jewish leaders had handed Jesus over to him (v. 18).

D. Warned by a Dream: v. 19

While Pilate was sitting on the judge's seat—the *bema*, the only place from which he could make official pronouncements—his wife sent a message to him, urging him not to become involved in the case of "this innocent man." She had "suffered many things ... in a dream because of him." This was a merciful divine warning to Pilate, but he ignored it.

E. Death Demanded by the Crowd: vv. 20-23

During the few minutes that Pilate busied himself with the message from his wife, the chief priests and elders took advantage of the opportunity to harangue the crowd into demanding Jesus' death. In his book, *Behold the Man* (p. 302), Kagawa of Japan gives a very realistic touch. He pictures the servants of the high priests hurrying through the crowd, passing out coins and urging the recipients to yell, "Crucify him!" This seems entirely likely. Probably in this and other ways the leaders "persuaded the multitude that they should ask (for) Barabbas and destroy Jesus" (v. 20).

Once again the governor asked, "Which of the two do you want me to release to you?" (v. 21, NIV). He should have heeded his wife's warning and not put this question again. For he was soon trapped. Instigated by the chief priests, the crowd answered once more, "Barabbas." Pilate is an excellent example of a person failing to take prompt action in doing right.

Verse 22 is one of the great evangelistic texts of the New Testament: "What shall I do then with Jesus which is called Christ?" Pilate tried to evade the issue. But he was forced to give an answer. The songwriter has caught it well:

> What will you do with Jesus?
>   Neutral you cannot be;
> Some day your heart will be asking,
>   "What will He do with me?"

Christ cannot be ignored. Eventually every person has to make a crucial decision about Him.

The answer of the crowd was, "Let him be crucified." Pilate protested: "Why? What crime has he committed?" (v. 23, NIV). But the crowd was in no mood for logic or reasoning. The people simply "shouted all the louder, 'Crucify him!' " (NIV).

Pilate proved the folly of putting off a decision, for indecision usually leads to wrong decision. According to Luke (23:4, 14, 22) and John (18:38; 19:4, 6) the governor three times declared that he found no crime in Jesus. Yet he crucified Him.

F. Abandoned by the Governor: vv. 24-26

The pressure of the crowd was getting stronger, and the purpose of Pilate was getting weaker. Finally he "caved in." We read: "When Pilate saw that he was getting nowhere, but that instead an uproar was starting, he took water and washed his hands in front of the crowd. 'I am innocent of this man's blood,' he said. 'It is your responsibility!' " (v. 24, NIV).

But guilt cannot be washed away with water. And responsibility cannot be transferred by wishful thinking. The governor's symbolical act was rather a confession of guilt than exoneration from it. He had all the might of Rome behind him, and there was no excuse for his failure to administer justice.

The answer of the people was even worse: "His blood be on us, and on our children" (v. 25). The destruction of Jerusalem just forty years later (A.D. 70) is a tragic footnote to this verse.

Pilate's last act of criminal cruelty was to have Jesus scourged and then crucified. Many a man died under the Roman scourge, his back lacerated and broken by sharp pieces of bone and metal.

VI. MOCKED BY THE SOLDIERS: Matthew 27:27-31

A. The Scarlet Robe: vv. 27-28

The governor's soldiers took Jesus into the "common hall" (v. 27). This is one word in Greek, *praitorion*, from the Latin "Praetorium," which is the correct translation here. This was the term used for the official residence of the governor of a province. Pilate's main residence was at Caesarea, on the seacoast. But at the time of the Feast of the Passover, when religious feelings ran high and there was the greatest danger of riots, the governor would go up to Jerusalem to keep a watch on conditions. There is some debate as to where the Praetorium in Jerusalem was. Some scholars think it was the Roman barracks, the Tower of Antonia, overlooking the temple area on the north side. Others prefer the former palace of Herod the Great, situated inside the Jaffa Gate on the west side of the city. But Herod Antipas, son of Herod the Great and ruler of Galilee, was in Jerusalem at this time (Luke 23:7). Would not Herod be staying at his father's palace? We cannot be sure.

The word for "band" means "cohort." This was a tenth of a legion. A Roman legion ordinarily consisted of six thousand soldiers; so a cohort would be about six hundred men.

The soldiers stripped Jesus and put on Him a "scarlet robe" (v. 28). This was the outer cloak of a Roman legionnaire. Perhaps they used an old one that had faded to purple, representing the purple robe of a king. Incidentally, the purple dye of that day was derived only from a certain shellfish in the Mediterranean, and so was very scarce and expensive. That is why "wearing the purple" refers to royalty, even today.

B. The Crown of Thorns: v. 29

Having robed Jesus like a king, the soldiers wove a crown of thorns and put it on His head. Then they placed a reed in His hand. All of these were probably cheap looking substitutes for royal robe, crown, and scepter. The

---

DISCUSSION QUESTIONS

1. Why did the religious leaders reject Jesus?
2. How were they victims of their own erroneous ideas?
3. Does that abolish their moral responsibility?
4. How can we avoid the same mistake?
5. How guilty was Pilate?
6. What responsibility does a public official have in such cases?

---

whole thing was a hollow mockery. Having arrayed Him thus, they knelt in front of Him and mocked Him: "Hail, King of the Jews!" How carnal can men be?

C. The Cruel Abuse: vv. 30-31

The despicable mockery was followed by crass cruelty. The soldiers spit on Him, an act which is everywhere considered to be the ultimate insult. They took the reed out of His hand—the scepter that was the symbol of royal authority—and hit Him on the head. The last verb is in the imperfect tense, indicating repeated action: "they struck him on the head again and again" (NIV). Then they put His own clothes on Him and led Him away to crucify Him. One can only imagine how Jesus must have felt during all this time of terrible abuse and mockery. But Incarnate Love made no protest.

VII. CRUCIFIED AND MOCKED: Matthew 27:32-44

A. The Callous Soldiers: vv. 32-37

As they left the city to walk the few hundred yards to Golgotha, the soldiers impressed into service a passerby to carry the heavy cross. The man was Simon of Cyrene, a city in North Africa. He was probably not a black man, as Negroes lived mainly south of the Sahara Desert.

"Golgotha" (v. 33) is the Aramaic word for "skull" (Greek, *kranion*, "cranium"). The Latin word for this (*calvaria*) gives us "Calvary," a word found in the Bible (KJV) only in Luke 23:33, where it translates *kranion* in the Greek.

The soldiers offered Jesus "vinegar . . . mingled with gall" (v. 34). This was evidently a pain-killing drink provided by the merciful women of Jerusalem for victims on the cross. Jesus refused to drink it, because He wanted to be fully conscious for the events that would follow.

The callous soldiers gambled over

Jesus' clothes (v. 35). Then they sat down and "kept watch over him there" (v. 36, NIV). Over His head was the written charge: THIS IS JESUS THE KING OF THE JEWS (v. 37).

B. The Cruel Crowd: vv. 38-40

Jesus was crucified between two "thieves" (v. 38). The Greek word means "robbers." In fact, it was used at that time for the fanatical insurrectionists against the government. Probably these two men were followers of Barabbas. If so, he was the one who was slated for the middle cross. But Jesus, the Prince of Life, died in the place of this murderer.

Those who passed "hurled insults at him, shaking their heads" in disdain (v. 39, NIV). If He was really the Son of God, let Him prove it by coming down from the cross (v. 40).

C. The Mocking Leaders: vv. 41-44

This is the saddest picture of all.

The religious leaders of the nation taunted Him: "He saved others; himself he cannot save" (v. 42). They spoke better than they knew. He could not save Himself and also save others. He must die to become the Savior of the world. But their claim that if He came down from the cross they would believe in Him was hollow mockery and a deliberate lie. He had already amply proved His deity and Messiahship by His compassionate miracles.

Verse 43 was the worst taunt of all: If God wanted Jesus as His Son, let Him show it now by delivering Him. The cruelty of these religious leaders is impossible to explain.

The two robbers crucified with Jesus "cast the same in his teeth" (v. 44). To say the least, this is a very free paraphrase in the King James Version. The Greek has only two words, meaning "insulted Him."

CONTEMPORARY APPLICATION

Christ is our Eternal Contemporary. We cannot avoid Him; we cannot evade Him. We may run from Him at one corner, but we will find Him waiting for us at the next turn of the road. And if we run from Him all our lives we will still have to meet Him at the Judgment.

He is "The Inescapable Christ." That is what Pilate discovered in our lesson today, and what we must all realize before it is too late.

AFTER THE RESURRECTION

(Easter)

DEVOTIONAL READING	I Corinthians 15:20-28

ADULTS

Topic: *After Rejection—Resurrection*

Background Scripture: Matthew 28

Scripture Lesson: *Matthew 28:1-10, 16-20*

Memory Verse: *Go therefore and make disciples of all nations, baptizing them in the name of the Father and of the Son and of the Holy Spirit, teaching them to observe all that I have commanded you; and lo, I am with you always, to the close of the age.* Matthew 28:19-20

YOUTH

Topic: *After Rejection—Resurrection*

Background Scripture: Matthew 28

Scripture Lesson: Matthew 28:1-10, 16-20

Memory Verse: *Go therefore and make disciples of all nations, baptizing them in the name of the Father and of the Son and of the Holy Spirit, teaching them to observe all that I have commanded you; and lo, I am with you always, to the close of the age.* Matthew 28:19-20

CHILDREN

Topic: *Celebrating New Life*

Background Scripture: Matthew 28

Scripture Lesson: Matthew 28:1-10, 16-20

Memory Verse: *Go therefore and make disciples of all nations, baptizing them in the name of the Father and of the Son and of the Holy Spirit.* Matthew 28:19

DAILY BIBLE READINGS

Mon., Apr. 12: Peter at the Tomb, John 20:1-10.
Tues., Apr. 13: Mary Magdalene Outside the Tomb, John 20:11-18.
Wed., Apr. 14: Jesus Appears to His Disciple, John 20:19-23.
Thurs., Apr. 15: Doubting Thomas and Jesus, John 20:24-31.
Fri., Apr. 16: The Women at the Tomb, Luke 24:1-12.
Sat., Apr. 17: Jesus Appears to Two Disciples, Luke 24:13-35.
Sun., Apr. 18: Jesus Appears Again, Luke 24:36-43.

LESSON AIM

To discover the meaning of the resurrection for our lives today.

LESSON SETTING

Time: April, A.D. 30

Place: Jerusalem and Galilee

After the Resurrection

I. **The Women at the Sepulcher:** Matthew 28:1-8
   A. The Two Marys: v. 1
   B. The Angel at the Tomb: vv. 2-4
   C. The Message of the Empty Tomb: vv. 5-7
   D. The Messengers from the Empty Tomb: v. 8

II. **The Meeting with Jesus:** Matthew 28:9-10
   A. Greeting: v. 9
   B. Appointment in Galilee: v. 10

LESSON OUTLINE

III. **The Bribing of the Guard:** Matthew 28:11-15
   A. The Report of the Guards: v. 11
   B. The Action of the Sanhedrin: vv. 12-14
   C. The False Story: v. 15

IV. **The Meeting in Galilee:** Matthew 28:16-17
   A. The Eleven Apostles: v. 16
   B. Belief and Unbelief: v. 17

V. **The Great Commission:** Matthew 28:18-20
   A. Full Authority: v. 18
   B. Discipling and Baptizing: v. 19
   C. Teaching Obedience: v. 20a
   D. Assurance of His Presence: v. 20b

SUGGESTED INTRODUCTION FOR ADULTS

Traditionally Christmas is the most joyful day of the year. Probably that is because love brightens this day above all others. Everybody is giving, and giving makes us happy—because giving is an expression of love, and love produces joy.

But there is a real sense in which Easter ought to be the most joyful day of the year. For it was on that day that Jesus rose from the dead to become our living Lord. His birth at Bethlehem would have done us no good, had He not died at Calvary. And His death would have done nothing for us if He had not risen from the grave. Admittedly, if He had not been born He could not have died. But the resurrection was the climax of His ministry. For us it is the guarantee of His living presence with us in this life and also the assurance that we shall live with Him forever in the next. So let us be glad and rejoice on this Easter day.

SUGGESTED INTRODUCTION FOR YOUTH

He lives! He lives!
Christ Jesus lives today.

This has been a favorite chorus with Christian young people for many years. And it never wears out. Our hearts still thrill with joy and hope whenever we hear it sung.

Youth wants life. How fortunate are those who early find the secret and source of all true life in Christ. He alone is our spiritual life, its only source. In Him we are aiive—really alive! But He is also the source of intellectual life. When we accept Him as "the Truth" as well as "the Life," we have truth. And He is the Sustainer of our physical life. He is "the Way" we should live every day. In Christ we have everything we need.

CONCEPTS FOR CHILDREN

1. Jesus is not some dead God of the past.
2. He is our risen, living Lord.
3. Because He lives, we too will live.
4. The living Christ wants to live in our lives today, and His presence helps us to live each day as we should.

THE LESSON COMMENTARY

I. THE WOMEN AT THE SEPULCHER:
Matthew 28:1-8

A. The Two Marys: v. 1

"In the end of the sabbath" means "after the Sabbath" (NIV). The Jewish sabbath lasted from sunset Friday night until sunset Saturday night. "At dawn on the first day of the week" (NIV) shows that it was Sunday morning.

Mary Magdalene is a well-known person in the Gospels. We are told that Jesus had cast seven demons out of her (Luke 8:2), and she was eternally grateful for this. John tells of her coming to the tomb very early Sunday morning and being the first to see the risen Christ (John 20:1-18).

It is typical of Matthew to mention people in pairs. So here he adds "the other Mary." On Friday afternoon these two women had sat "over against the sepulcher" and watched as Jesus was buried (27:61). Mark identifies the other Mary as "Mary the mother of Joses" (Mark 15:47). She was also the mother of "James the younger" (Mark 15:40, NIV; 16:1). Adam Clarke thinks that she was the wife of Cleopas, who is mentioned in Luke 24:18.

B. The Angel at the Tomb: vv. 2-4

Matthew alone mentions the violent earthquake that accompanied the resurrection of Jesus. "For" (v. 2) would suggest that the descending angel caused the earthquake. He rolled back the heavy stone from the door and sat upon it. All four Gospels say that the women found the stone rolled back from the entrance to the tomb, but only Matthew tells us that it was an angel who did this.

"His appearance was like lightning, and his clothes were white as snow" (v. 3, NIV). "Countenance" (KJV) is too narrow a translation. The Greek word *eidea* (only here in New Testament) probably refers to his whole appearance. We have similar descriptions of angels in the Old Testament (e.g., Judges 13:6).

In Daniel 7:9 we read that the "Ancient of days" had clothes "white as snow." Adam Clarke says of the angel at the tomb: "He was clothed in garments emblematical of the *glad tidings* which he came to announce." And then he adds this interesting observation: "It would have been inconsistent with the message he brought, had the angel appeared in *black robes*, such as those preposterously wear who call themselves his successors in the ministry of a once *suffering*, but now *risen* and highly exalted, Saviour" (*The New Testament of Our Lord and Saviour Jesus Christ*, I, 282).

"The guards were so afraid of him that they shook and became like dead men" (v. 4, NIV). The verb translated "shook" is *seio*, which is the root of the noun *seismos* ("earthquake") in verse 2. This noun is used in 8:24 for a "tempest" on the Lake of Galilee. It literally means "a shaking." The verb is used in 27:51 ("the earth did quake"), where it clearly refers to an earthquake at the time of Jesus' death. But here the "earthquake" (v. 2) may have been a shaking of the guards with fear (v. 4) at the lightninglike appearance of the angel. Adam Clarke favors this interpretation and goes on to say: "God can, by one and the same means, *comfort* his *servants*, and *terrify* his *enemies*. The resurrection of Christ is a subject of *terror* to the servants of sin, and a subject of consolation to the sons of God; because it is a proof of the resurrection of both, the one to shame and everlasting contempt—the other to eternal glory and joy" *New Testament of Our Lord*, I, 282).

Where were the disciples on this first Easter morning? We read in John's account (20:1-18) that when Mary Magdalene came to the tomb early that morning and found the stone rolled away from the entrance, she ran to tell Peter and John. They hurried to the sepulcher, but finding nothing there they went back home (for breakfast?!). But Mary stayed at the empty tomb, waiting and weeping, until she saw her risen Lord.

Too often this pattern is true today. The women have greater love and devotion, greater courage and concern, greater patience and persistence than most men. The Easter story in the Gospels pays high tribute to women, and we should honor them today!

C. The Message of the Empty Tomb: vv. 5-7

The angel's message to the women is very similar to that recorded in Mark (16:6-7). The first words were, "Do not be afraid." This is in striking contrast to verse 4, where we read that the guards were shaking with fear. Frequently in the Old Testament we find God saying to His people, "Fear not." Jesus often greeted His disciples that way when they were afraid, as when

He came to them at night, walking on the water (Mark 6:50). After His resurrection His favorite greeting to His own was "Peace be with you" (Luke 24:36; John 20:21, 26).

The angel went on to say, "I know that you are looking for Jesus, who was crucified" (v. 5, NIV). These women had brought spices and were coming to anoint the body of Jesus in the tomb (Mark 16:1). What they found there was very different from what they had expected!

Verse 6 gives us the heart of "The Message of the Empty Tomb." It is twofold. First, there is "The Mystery of the Empty Tomb": "He is not here." Why not? Where had He gone? What had happened to Him? Where could they find Him? It was a haunting, harrowing mystery.

In order to appreciate the perplexity of these devoted women we have to put ourselves in their place, setting aside all our knowledge of Easter. They had followed the Prophet from Nazareth, expecting Him to set up His kingdom at Jerusalem. Instead He had been condemned and crucified. The only comfort they had left was to show their love by anointing His body with aromatic perfume. But now even that privilege was taken away; His body was gone! What should they do? The mystery of it all overwhelmed them.

Second, there was "The Miracle of the Empty Tomb"; "He is risen." We can imagine how this statement struck their ears. It was incredible, incomprehensible! How could it be? But it was! He was alive!

That is the miracle of Easter: "He lives!" How do we know He lives? "He lives within my heart." The words of that song never cease to thrill our souls. The reality of Easter is the risen, living Lord in our hearts. The resurrection is more than an article of faith; it is an abiding Presence within us today.

We might add a third note: "The Meaning of the Empty Tomb." And this, in turn, is threefold. The empty tomb first means "An Accepted Sacrifice." We read that Jesus "was delivered for our offences, and was raised again for our justification" (Romans 4:25). Without the resurrection, the crucifixion would not have brought us salvation. The resurrection of Jesus was the Father's act of validating the sacrifice that His Son had made for our sins. It is proof of the acceptance of that sacrifice, and so of our acceptance in Christ.

In the second place, the empty tomb means "An Abiding Presence." The risen Lord now comes to us, when we will receive Him to live forever in our hearts. We need more than a crucifix; we need the living Christ. And He is here!

But there is a third, solemn meaning of the empty tomb: "An Appointed Judgment." In Acts 17:31 we read: "Because he hath appointed a day, in the which he will judge the world in righteousness by that man whom he hath ordained; where of he hath given assurance unto all men, in that he hath raised him from the dead." The resurrection of Jesus is God's sure token to men that there will be a final judgment day. Those who accept the risen Lord into their hearts have "an Advocate," a lawyer or attorney, "with the Father, Jesus Christ the righteous" (I John 2:1). He is "one who speaks to the Father in our defense" (NIV). But for those who reject Him He will be the righteous Judge, who will have to condemn them for their impenitent sins. The joy of Easter is for those who accept Him now.

The women were invited to step into the open tomb and see where the body of Jesus had been placed (v. 6). Thus they could satisfy themselves that He really was not there.

Then they were commanded: "Go quickly and tell his disciples: 'He has risen from the dead and is going ahead of you into Galilee. There you will see him.' Now I have told you" (NIV).

D. The Messengers from the Empty Tomb: v. 8

With prompt obedience, the women "departed quickly from the sepul-chre with fear and great joy; and did run to bring his disciples word." This was a day of glad tidings, and they must hurry. The good news could not wait. They knew that the disciples' hearts were filled with sorrow. They must be told at once that their Lord was alive. And He had made an appointment to meet them in Galilee. This was nearly a week's walk away; so the disciples must be on the move.

II. THE MEETING WITH JESUS: Matthew 28:9-10

A. Greeting: v. 9

The first clause, "And as they went to tell his disciples," is not in the earliest Greek manuscripts. Some copyist added it as a logical sequel to the previous verse. Verse 9 properly reads: "Suddenly Jesus met them. 'Greetings,' he said. They came to him, clasped his feet and worshiped him" (NIV).

"All hail" (KJV) is one word in the Greek, chairete—literally, "Rejoice" or "Be glad." Lenski writes: "The verb chairein is used to express all manner of greetings and always conveys a wish of happiness and well being" (Interpretation of St. Matthew's Gospel, p. 1157).

B. Appointment in Galilee: v. 10

Repeating the angel's words to the women (v. 5), Jesus said, "Be not afraid." Then He confirmed the previous instructions (v. 7), telling them: "Go tell my brethren that they go into Galilee, and there shall they see me." This was in fulfillment of His promise: "But after I am risen again, I will go before you into Galilee" (26:32).

III. THE BRIBING OF THE GUARD: Matthew 28:11-15

A. The Report of the Guards: v. 11

Matthew is the only one who tells about the posting of the guard (27:62-66). After Jesus' burial, the chief priests (Sadducees) and Pharisees came to Pilate (v. 62). They reported Jesus' prediction, "After three days I will rise again" (v. 63; cf. 16:21). So they asked for security measures at the tomb, "lest his disciples come by night, and steal him away, and say unto the people, He is risen from the dead: so the last error"—belief in the resurrection of Jesus—"shall be worse than the first" (v. 64)—belief in His Messiahship. Pilate answered them, "Ye have a watch" (v. 65). This should probably be translated, "Take a guard"—of Roman soldiers. Now this guard was reporting to the chief priests all that had happened at the tomb on Sunday morning.

B. The Action of the Sanhedrin: vv. 12-14

The Sanhedrin met and "devised a plan" (NIV). A large bribe was given to the soldiers with the instructions that they were to say, "His disciples came by night and stole him away while we slept" (v. 13). Since the Roman law prescribed that sentries who slept on duty were to be put to death, the Jewish leaders promised the soldiers that they would protect them in case of trouble by "bribing" the governor—the technical meaning of the Greek words for "persuade him, and secure you" (v. 14).

C. The False Story: v. 15

The soldiers accepted the bribe and did as they were instructed. "And this story has been widely circulated among the Jews to this very day" (NIV). At the time this Gospel was written—some thirty years later—this was still the official Jewish version of the resurrection.

IV. THE MEETING IN GALILEE: Matthew 28:16-17

A. The Eleven Apostles: v. 16

"The eleven disciples"—Judas Iscariot had already committed suicide (27:3-5)—went north to Galilee, "to the mountain where Jesus had told them to go" (NIV). We are not told anywhere which mountain this was. It could have been the mount of the Beatitudes, the mount of Transfiguration, or some other hilltop made sacred by a previous session with the Twelve. In any case, the disciples knew which one it was and met their appointment.

B. Belief and Unbelief: v. 17

When Jesus put in His appearance, "they worshipped him; but some doubted." This seems to imply a larger group than the eleven apostles. Of these it is only indicated that Thomas at first doubted Jesus' appearance to the disciples on the same day as His resurrection (John 20:19-25). The following Sunday night he saw the risen Lord and believed (John 20:26-29). Both of these appearances preceded the one in Galilee, for we have already noted that the northward trip would take about a week each way. For this reason it has been suggested that the meeting in Galilee may have been the one to "above five hundred brethren at once" (I Corinthians 15:6). The eleven apostles may have gathered a large group of known followers of Jesus in Galilee to meet the Master at the appointed place. In such a gathering it would be expected that "some" would have doubts.

DISCUSSION QUESTIONS

1. How did the resurrection confirm Jesus' authority as King?
2. How does it make our religion personal?
3. How is Easter related to worship on Sunday?
4. To whom was the Great Commission given?
5. On whom is it binding today?
6. How can we help to carry it out?

V. THE GREAT COMMISSION: Matthew 28:18-20

A. Full Authority: v. 18

The Greek word for "power" (KJV) is not *dynamis* but *exousia*, which means, "right" or "privilege" or "authority." The correct translation is: "All authority in heaven and on earth has been given to me" (NIV). Adam Clarke writes: "One fruit of the sufferings and resurrection of Christ is represented to be, his having *authority* or *right* in *heaven* to send down the Holy Spirit—to raise up his followers thither—and to crown them in the kingdom of an endless glory: *in earth*, to convert sinners; to sanctify, protect, and perfect his Church; to subdue all nations to himself; and, finally, to judge all mankind." He adds: "If Jesus Christ were not equal with the Father, could he have claimed this equality of power, without being guilty of impiety and blasphemy?" (*New Testament of Our Lord*, I, 284). It is a tremendous statement that Jesus makes here.

B. Discipling and Baptizing: v. 19

The words "teach" (v. 19) and "teaching" (v. 20) are very different in the Greek. The verb in verse 19 is *matheteuo*, which means to "make a disciple." The verb in verse 20 is *didasko*, "teach." So the correct translation of the first part of verse 19 is: "Therefore go and make disciples of all nations" (NIV). On the basis of His "all authority," Jesus has given to His followers this all-inclusive command. The church has not yet carried it out in full, though nineteen centuries have passed.

What is to be done with these new disciples? "Baptizing them in the name of the Father and of the Son and of the Holy Spirit." It is usually assumed that the one and only reference here is to water baptism, and many have practiced tri-immersion on the basis of the reference to the Trinity. But the Greek word for "in" (*eis*) literally means "into," though it is sometimes used as equivalent to *en* ("in"). So we cannot rule out the possibility that Jesus meant that we are to be spiritually baptized into fellowship with Father, Son, and Holy Spirit. (See the NIV of Acts 8:16; 19:5; Romans 6:3; I Corinthians 1:13; 10:2; Galatians 3:27.) This puts the Great Commission on a higher spiritual plane.

C. Teaching Obedience: v. 20a

New Christians must be taught to obey all that Christ has commanded. He is the Head of the church and speaks with divine authority. If we acknowledge Him as our Lord, we must render Him complete and unquestioning obedience. We cannot give this to any man, but we must give it to Him.

D. Assurance of His Presence: v. 20b

Those who obey the command to "Go" have the promise: "Lo, I am with you alway, even unto the end of the world" (Greek, "age"). "Alway" is literally "all the days." While the natural meaning of this is undoubtedly the chronological span of time, one is tempted to suggest the application to all kinds of days—the bad as well as the good. Whatever happens, He is there!

CONTEMPORARY APPLICATION

The Home Moravian Church in Winston-Salem, North Carolina, is one of the great historic churches of America. As one stands on the platform he faces four beautiful stained glass windows at the rear of the sanctuary. To the left of the main entrance are portrayals of Gethsemane and the crucifixion. To the right, one sees the resurrection and the ascension depicted.

We were told that through no planning, but by happy coincidence, the two windows on the left are shaded all day long, and so are relatively dark. But in the afternoon the sun shines brightly through the other two, illuminating them with glory.

Gethsemane and Golgotha were dark hours. But the sun rose that first Easter, and the ascension bespeaks the return of our Lord.

THE CHALLENGE OF A CHRISTIAN STYLE OF LIFE

DEVOTIONAL READING | II Corinthians 5:16-21

ADULTS

Topic: *A Christian Family Life-Style*

Background Scripture: Colossians 3:1-21

Scripture Lesson: Colossians 3:1-14, 18-20

Memory Verse: *Above all these put on love, which binds everything together in perfect harmony.* Colossians 3:14

YOUTH

Topic: *Faith—Family Style*

Background Scripture: Colossians 3:1-21

Scripture Lesson: Colossians 3:1-14, 18-20

Memory Verse: *Above all these put on love, which binds everything together in perfect harmony.* Colossians 3:14

CHILDREN

Topic: *Ideals for the Family*

Background Scripture: Colossians 3:1-21

Scripture Lesson: Colossians 3:1-5, 12-17

Memory Verse: *Above all these put on love, which binds everything together in perfect harmony.* Colossians 3:14

DAILY BIBLE READINGS

Mon., Apr. 19: Jesus Teaches His Disciples, Luke 24: 44-49.
Tues., Apr. 20: Jesus Ascends, Luke 24:50-53.
Wed., Apr. 21: Wait for the Holy Spirit, Acts 1:1-5.
Thurs. Apr. 22: The Coming of the Kingdom, Acts 1:6-11.
Fri., Apr. 23: Love, Peace, and Thanks, Colossians 3:14-17.
Sat., Apr. 24: The Indwelling Christ, Ephesians 3:14-19.
Sun., Apr. 25: The Need of Prayer, Colossians 4:2-4.

LESSON AIM | To see how we should live as Christians, and specifically as members of a family.

LESSON SETTING

Time: The Epistle to the Colossians was written about A.D. 60.

Place: Paul wrote Colossians in prison at Rome.

LESSON OUTLINE

The Challenge of a Christian Style of Life

    I. Heavenly Life in Christ: Colossians 3:1-4

A. Raised with Christ: vv. 1-2
B. Hidden with Christ in God: v. 3
C. Expecting His Coming: v. 4

II. The Death of the Old Life: Colossians 3:5-11
   A. Putting to Death Immorality: vv. 5-7
   B. Putting Off the Old Life: vv. 8-9
   C. Putting On the New Life: vv. 10-11

III. The Christian in Society: Colossians 3:12-14
   A. Clothed with Compassion: v. 12
   B. Forbearing and Forgiving: v. 13
   C. Love, the Supreme Virtue: v. 14

IV. The Christian in the Church: Colossians 3:15-17
   A. Members of One Body: v. 15
   B. Encouraging Each Other: v. 16
   C. Everything in the Name of Jesus: v. 17

V. The Christian in the Home: Colossians 3:18-21
   A. Wives: v. 18
   B. Husbands: v. 19
   C. Children: v. 20
   D. Parents: v. 21

SUGGESTED INTRODUCTION FOR ADULTS

The most important unit of society is the family. And it is precisely family life that is most threatened in modern society. If we fail here, the whole social structure will collapse. So it is fitting that we now devote six lessons to a study of family life.

All of us are aware—although perhaps not sufficiently so—of the fact that family life is disintegrating today in America. This is showing up in numerous ways. The most tragic evidence is the rapid increase in divorce. In the rural society of a century ago divorce was a rather rare phenomenon. Divorced people were looked down on. But in our generation the pattern has changed rapidly. Half a dozen years ago the ratio was one divorce for every four marriages in the United States. Now it is one divorce for every three marriages, and in some places one for every two. More and more unmarried couples are living together. The concept of a family unit is being discarded.

Another evidence of the breakdown in family life is the increasing number of teen-agers that run away from home. It used to be a few boys. Now it is fifteen- and sixteen-year-old girls by the thousands. Something sad is happening to the American home. We need to do all we can to build Christian family life.

SUGGESTED INTRODUCTION FOR YOUTH

What is happening in your family? Is there a strong tie of unity? Or is it falling apart?

Christian young people can do a lot to help hold the family together. Do you have family worship in the home every day? If not, why not urge Mother and Dad to start it—after dinner each night. Everybody try to be there. It could well be a time of asking each other's forgiveness and keeping a good spirit. In many homes young people could take the lead in creating a new Christian family life-style. Why not try it?

CONCEPTS FOR CHILDREN

1. Children can help to make their home a happy one.
2. Ask your parents to have family worship.
3. Reading the Bible together draws us nearer to each other.
4. A forgiving spirit is essential to a happy family.

THE LESSON COMMENTARY

I. A HEAVENLY LIFE IN CHRIST: Colossians 3:1-4

A. Raised with Christ: v. 1-2

Since we have been raised with Christ into a new resurrection life of victory, we should seek things above, heavenly things, because Christ is now seated on His throne at the right hand of the Father. If we are to be in fellowship with Him, we must live in the atmosphere of His life.

Paul has already said in this Epistle: "Buried with him in baptism, wherein also ye are risen with him through the faith of the operation of God, who hath raised him from the dead" (2:12). We are to be identified by faith with Christ in His death and burial, in order that we may be united with Him in His resurrection. This is the only way that we can experience and live the resurrection life in Christ.

"With Christ" is basically equivalent to "in Christ," which is the key phrase in Paul's letters, especially the Christological Epistles—Colossians, Ephesians, and Philippians. It has been well said that all of Paul's theology can be summed up in the phrase "in Christ."

And so the apostle goes on to say: "Set your affection on things above, not on things on the earth" (v. 2). "Set your affection" is one word in Greek, *phroneite*, which comes from the word for "mind." So Paul is saying, "Set your minds on things above" (NIV). Think about heavenly things, not just earthly things all the time, as most people do. The Christian is a citizen of heaven, as well as a citizen of his country and community.

Adam Clarke puts it this way: "Be as much in earnest for heavenly and eternal things, as you formerly were for those that are earthly and perishing" (*The New Testament of Our Lord and Saviour Jesus Christ*, II, 526). As long as our minds are engrossed entirely with the things of this earth, we will continue to live on too low a level. We lift our lives to a higher level by thinking higher thoughts—about heavenly things. It is our thoughts that ultimately control our lives. If we think all the time about material things, we will become materialistic. To be spiritual we must think spiritual thoughts.

B. Hidden with Christ in God: v. 3

"For ye are dead" is more accurately translated, "For you died" (NIV). One of the great paradoxes of Christianity is simply this: You have to die to live. George Mueller, that great man of faith of Bristol, England, said, "There was a day when I died, utterly died!" That was the secret of his spiritual power that enabled him to trust God to care for his thousands of orphans without ever soliciting a penny of money. He belonged wholly to God.

The apostle Paul sounds this note many times in his Epistles. Just in the previous chapter he says, "if you died with Christ" (2:20, NIV). In Galatians 2:20 he writes: "I have been crucified with Christ, and no longer is it I who lives, but Christ lives in me." (That is what the Greek says; "nevertheless I live" in the King James Version is a mistranslation.) In Romans 6:6 we read: "Knowing this, that our old man is crucified with him, that the body of sin might be destroyed, that henceforth we should not serve sin." It is only as we die with Christ that we can live the resurrection life of victory in Him. We repeat: "You have to die to live!"

Once we have died with Christ to sin and self, to our own desires and wishes, then our life "is hid with Christ in God." John Nielson writes: "*Hid* indicates that this life is not knowable to the one who does not believe (II Cor. 4:3-6). However it is a reality to the believer and is realized in a new ethical awareness and power for righteousness. That life, though in a sense hidden, waits to be revealed in a far more glorious way (I Cor. 15:51ff.; I Thess. 4:13-18; I John 3:2)" (*Beacon Bible Commentary*, IX, 411).

C. Expecting His Coming: v. 4

Paul refers to Christ as "our life." (The best Greek manuscripts have "your life.") This means that Christ is the one and only source of our life; we derive all our spiritual life directly from Him. This is a mystery, but it is one of the most important truths in the New Testament.

This verse contains the only clear reference to the Second Coming in this short Epistle. When Christ appears, then we also will appear with Him in glory. What a glorious prospect! It is worth waiting for! If we suffer with Him in this life, we shall reign with Him forever in the next.

II. DEATH OF THE OLD LIFE: Colossians 3:5-11

A. Putting to Death Immorality: vv. 5-7

"Mortify" (v. 5) has a much weaker meaning today than it originally did. We speak of being "mortified" when we simply mean "embarrassed." Sometimes we even stupidly say, "I was mortified to death." Our word mortify comes from the Latin and clearly means "put to death." That is the correct translation here. And it is in the aorist tense, indicating a crucial, decisive act.

What are we to "put to death"? Paul says, "your members which are upon the earth." These are the members of "the body of sin" (Romans 6:6), the manifestations of "the law of sin" (Romans 7:23). By faith we are to reckon (account) ourselves "dead to sin" (Romans 6:11).

Paul proceeds to enumerate some of these "members" of the body of sin. He mentions five.

The first is "fornication," or "sexual immorality" (NIV) of any kind. The Greek term is used in this broad sense. The second is "uncleanness," which also takes in a lot of territory. Phillips calls it "dirty-mindedness." That is certainly one aspect of it. The third is "inordinate affection." This is one word in Greek, *pathos*, "passion." In the New Testament this is always used in a bad sense, as when we say that one's "passions" are aroused by a pornographic display. The New International Version translates it "lust."

The fourth item is "evil concupiscence." This Latinism is no longer in common use. The Greek simply says "evil desire." The fifth is "covetousness"—what we today would call "greed." It is characterized here as "idolatry," which means wanting anything else more than God. That is what a greedy person does.

All of these things, except the last, come under what we usually associate with immorality. But greediness is also immoral in God's sight.

Paul goes on to say that because of these things "the wrath of God is coming" (v. 6, NIV). These, even if curbed in their outward expression, are all serious sins in His sight and will bring divine punishment.

"Wrath" is something different from impetuous anger. Nielson says that the Greek word *orge* "means, not vindictive evil, but righteous judgment" (*Beacon*, IX, 412). It is God's settled attitude of hatred of sin. Since God is holy, His wrath against evil is inevitable. Jesus reacted with "anger" (*orge*) to the selfish, sinful attitude of the Pharisees (Mark 3:5). A person who does not experience any anger against wrong lacks moral consciousness.

Paul often uses "walk" in the sense of "live," as in Ephesians 4 and 5. But here in verse 7 they are differentiated. The apostle says, "You used to walk in these ways, in the life you once lived" (NIV). Vincent thinks the meaning here is that "their conduct and their condition agreed" (*Word Studies in the New Testament*, III, 502).

B. Putting Off the Old Life: vv. 8-9

"Put off" is literally "lay aside." The apostle again enumerates five things that the Christian must put away from himself.

The first is *orge*, which means "hot anger," boiling over (cf. "rage," NIV). We would reverse the order of "anger" and "wrath."

The third thing he mentions is "malice." Abbott-Smith defines the Greek word *kakia* as meaning "wickedness, depravity, malignity" (*Lexicon*, p. 227). It is literally "badness." The fourth, "blasphemy," translates *blasphemia*. But the original meaning of this Greek term was "slander," and that is the correct translation here. Later on it was applied to one's attitude toward God, and then it meant "blasphemy." We slander men, but blaspheme God. Here it is our relation to our fellow human beings that is being discussed.

The fifth vice is "filthy communication out of your mouth," or, as we would say now, "filthy language" (NIV). "Filthy communication" is one word in the Greek, *aischrologia* (only here in New Testament), which Abbott-Smith defines as "abusive language." But since the adjective *aischros* means "shameful," it would seem that the compound term could be applied to any talk that is suggestive or vulgar.

Over and over again we are warned in the New Testament not to "lie" to each other. This was one of the besetting sins of the Graeco-Roman culture of that day. In modern times it has been almost a national sin in some countries. We fear that now it has become almost universal in supposedly civilized countries. Honesty and truthfulness are at the top of the list of cardinal virtues in God's catalog.

"Put off" (v. 9) and "put on" (v. 10) translate Greek terms that are used regularly for taking off and putting on clothes. Here these words are employed metaphorically. We are to take off the old man and clothe ourselves with the new man.

What is meant by "the old man" (v. 9)? It is commonly interpreted as meaning "the old way of life." But Paul says in Romans 6:6 that our "old man" was crucified with Christ. Can one crucify a way of life?

It is interesting to note Adam Clarke's handling of the problem. He comments on this phrase in connection with Romans 6:6. But he holds that it has the same meaning here and in Ephesians 4:22, which is very closely parallel to the Colossian passage.

Here is what Adam Clarke says: "By the destruction of the *body of sin*, our *old man*, our wicked, corrupt, and fleshly self, is to be crucified" (*New Testament of Our Lord*, II, 77). It seems to us that the additional phrase at the end of verse 9, "with his deeds," makes "the old man" more than a pattern or way of life. It has been defined as "the unrenewed self," what the Jews called "the old Adam." (*Adam* is the Hebrew word for "man.")

C. Putting On the New Life: vv. 10-11

"The new man" is "the *renewed* self, the regenerated, sanctified self" (Nielson, *Beacon IX*, 415). It is constantly being "renewed"—the present participle of continuous action—in knowledge according to "the image of him that created him" (v. 10). The Creator is Christ, who is now, by His Spirit, renewing in us the "image" of God in which man was originally created. It is a beautiful concept of redemption. Salvation is much more than escape from hell. It is our re-creation in the image of God.

In this new society in Christ there are no distinctions of race, religion, or social caste. There is "neither Greek nor Jew"—the two divisions of the human race in the Jewish mind. There is neither "circumcision"—the Jew within the covenant—nor "uncircumcision"—all those outside. No one is a "Barbarian"—a term given by Greeks to all others, because their talk sounded to sophisticated Greek ears like "bar-bar-bar." There is no "Scythian," probably referring to a cruel, fierce people who savagely invaded Palestine in the seventh century B.C., and so a term used for the lowest dregs of society. Neither is there any distinction between "bond" (slave) or "free." This Epistle was actually taken to Colosse by a slave, Onesimus, who was now a Christian brother. No, "Christ is all, and in all." He is all that matters ultimately. To be in Him and have Him in us—that makes us Christians.

III. THE CHRISTIAN IN SOCIETY: Colossians 3:12-14

A. Clothed with Compassion: v. 12

"Put on" is again the Greek verb for putting on clothes (cf. v. 10). As God's chosen people, holy and loved by Him, we are to clothe ourselves with "bowels of mercies." The Greeks located the center of one's feelings and affections in the bowels. Today we find it in "the heart," as we call it metaphorically. The King James Version "bowels" conveys an entirely wrong idea to the modern reader.

The correct translation here is "clothe yourselves with compassion,

kindness, humility, gentleness and patience" (NIV). These are all ennobling terms that lift one's spiritual sights. These attitudes and attributes are the foundation of Christian living.

B. Forbearing and Forgiving: v. 13

We are to forgive others as Christ forgave us. How did He forgive us? Immediately, graciously, completely—undeserving as we are. And that is the way we must forgive others, if we are to be true Christians.

We can only maintain happy Christian homes as we daily practice forbearance toward each other and show a forgiving spirit. Family worship is an excellent time to ask forgiveness for anything we have said or done that has hurt another member of the family.

C. Love, the Supreme Virtue: v. 14

The figure of putting on clothes carries through this verse. On top of all the virtues previously mentioned (vv. 13-14) we are to put on love, which ties them all together in a perfect unity.

IV. THE CHRISTIAN IN THE CHURCH: Colossians 3:15-17

A. Members of One Body: v. 15

The most important concept that we can have of the true church of Jesus Christ is that it is His body and we are individual parts of it. So in "peace" and thankfulness we must fill our place and contribute to the unity of the whole.

B. Encouraging Each Other: v. 16

If we are to help others in the church, we must be diligent students of God's Word. It is not primarily a matter of studying *about* the Bible, but having God's Word *dwell in us* "richly." This comes by daily reading and meditation. "In all wisdom" should go with the following clause, rather than the preceding one; it is with all wisdom that we are to be "teaching and admonishing one another." And one of the best means of teaching and counseling is by the use of "psalms and hymns and spiritual songs."

C. Everything in the Name of Jesus: v. 17

This verse is self-explanatory. If we did everything in Jesus' name, it would keep us from doing anything displeasing to God.

V. THE CHRISTIAN IN THE HOME: Colossians 3:18-21

In 3:18–4:1 Paul addresses six groups of people in the society of that day. Since "slaves" (3:22-25) and "masters" (4:1) do not exist today, these are omitted in our lesson. All six of these are discussed at greater length in Ephesians 5:22–6:9, since Ephesians was written after Colossians.

A. Wives: v. 18

To many people today the command given here seems hopelessly out of date. But a devout woman with a strong, independent personality once said to us that she believed all Christian wives would be glad to observe the spirit of this injunction if their husbands would fulfill their orders: "Husbands, love your wives, even as Christ also loved the church" (Ephesians 5:25). This is the catch. And until husbands can love their wives with the unselfish, devoted love that Christ has for His church, they have no right to quote verse 18 to them. Amen!

B. Husbands: v. 19

Actually, unselfish love is a harder requirement than submission. If the husband is proud of his position as "head of the house," he should keep two things constantly in mind. The first is that Christ is the Head of the church, and so is in authority over both him and his wife together. The second is that Christ always asserts His authority in gentle, understanding love. The husband's responsibility is clearly stated: "Husbands, love your wives and do not be harsh with them" (NIV). (Read Ephesians 5:25-33.)

C. Children: v. 20

This verse obviously needs to be read with common sense and intelligence. Is a Christian child to obey parents' orders to renounce Christ or blaspheme God, or even to steal or lie? It is the general principle that is being laid down here. Also Paul is addressing groups within the church, and so he has Christian parents in mind. In this case, there would be very few exceptions to obedience.

D. Parents: v. 21

It is probable that by "fathers" Paul means both parents, though doubtless fathers are most in need of the admonition. They must be careful not to discourage their children by being unreasonable with them.

DISCUSSION QUESTIONS

1. What are some divisive attitudes in the home that we should put off?
2. What are some uniting ones we should put on?
3. How does the attitude of parents toward each other affect their children?
4. Can there be individual diversity within family unity?
5. What part does forgiveness play in the home?
6. How can we help our children to be obedient?

CONTEMPORARY APPLICATION

We often see the slogan: "The family that prays together stays together." But observation compels us to say that we believe this needs revising. It should read: "The family that prays *and plays* together stays together."

Praying together at church and in family worship in the home is the most vital force to keep a family intact in spirit. But the social life is also important. If the only time children see their dad is in family worship, they are going to feel cheated and robbed. But if reverent prayer can be followed by happy times of playing together, a real camaraderie of love and mutual respect will develop.

THE CHALLENGE OF MOBILITY

DEVOTIONAL READING	Psalm 139:1-10, 23-24

ADULTS

Topic: *Faith and Families on the Move*

Background Scripture: Genesis 12:1-9; Hebrews 11:1, 8-16

Scripture Lesson: Hebrews 11:1, 8-16

Memory Verse: *By faith Abraham obeyed when he was called to go out to a place which he was to receive as an inheritance; and he went out, not knowing where he was to go.* Hebrews 11:8

YOUTH

Topic: *Faith and the Family on the Move*

Background Scripture: Genesis 12:1-9; Hebrews 11:1, 8-16

Scripture Lesson: Hebrews 11:1, 8-16

Memory Verse: *By faith Abraham obeyed when he was called to go out to a place which he was to receive as an inheritance; and he went out, not knowing where he was to go.* Hebrews 11:8

CHILDREN

Topic: *The Family Moves Out*

Background Scripture: Genesis 12:1-9; Hebrews 11:1, 8-16

Scripture Lesson: Genesis 12:1-9

Memory Verse: *By faith Abraham obeyed when he was called to go out to a place which he was to receive as an inheritance; and he went out, not knowing where he was to go.* Hebrews 11:8

DAILY BIBLE READINGS

Mon., Apr. 26: A Command and a Promise, Genesis 12:1-3.
Tues., Apr. 27: Responding to God, Genesis 12:4-9
Wed., Apr. 28: Faith as a Starting Point, Hebrews 11:1-3.
Thurs., Apr. 29: A Homeland in Heaven, Hebrews 11: 13-16.
Fri., Apr. 30: Looking Ahead to God, Luke 9:57-62.
Sat., May 1: A Man with Faith in Jesus, John 4:46-54.
Sun., May 2: Following Jesus, John 8:12-20.

LESSON AIM

To see how faith can operate, even in our mobile society today.

LESSON SETTING

Time: Abraham: about 2000 B.C.; Hebrews: about A.D. 65

Place: Abraham: Haran, Shechem, Bethel; Hebrews: unknown

LESSON OUTLINE

The Challenge of Mobility

I. The Nature of Faith: Hebrews 11:1
   A. A Confidence toward the Unknown Future: v. 1a
   B. A Conviction of the Unseen Present: v. 1b

II. Pioneer Faith: Hebrews 11:8-10
   A. The Obedience of Faith: v. 8
   B. The Patience of Faith: v. 9
   C. The Expectation of Faith: v. 10

III. Persistent Faith: Hebrews 11:11-12
   A. Sarah's Miracle: v. 11
   B. Abraham's Many Descendants: v. 12

IV. Pilgrim Faith: Hebrews 11:13-16
   A. Strangers and Pilgrims: v. 13
   B. Looking for a Better Country: v. 14
   C. No Turning Back: v. 15
   D. A Heavenly Country: v. 16

SUGGESTED INTRODUCTION FOR ADULTS

Since we have already studied the story of Abraham's call and obedience in Genesis 12:1-9 (lesson for October 5, 1975), we shall concentrate today on the passage in Hebrews. This gives us a very restricted portion of Scripture, but the main object in this lesson is to see the application to our own day.

So the adult topic is "Faith and Families on the Move." Every alert person is aware of the fact that we live in a very mobile society, far different from what our grandparents knew. People used to "stay put." But today it seems that almost everyone is on the move. Now each year one out of every four or five families in the United States moves. Some of us can remember when we had the same neighbors year after year, indefinitely. Now we are getting used to greeting new neighbors and saying goodbye to old ones many times a year. It's a new way of life.

All this brings new hazards. People lose their ties with family, church, and community. Too often they simply drift, failing to seek new ties that will help to hold them in place. What can be done about it?

SUGGESTED INTRODUCTION FOR YOUTH

Families are on the move these days. Everybody knows that. But is faith moving with the family? Too often we don't know; we can only hope so.

When Christians move to a new community, the first

thing they should do is to seek out the right church and tie into it immediately. Failure to do this can easily result in a Christian family falling apart and never getting together again. Our faith is our most important possession. We must guard it!

CONCEPTS FOR CHILDREN

1. Children often suffer when the family moves.
2. Christian children should get immediately into a good Sunday school.
3. They should also seek the companionship of good children, who will help them.
4. At the same time they should try to help less fortunate children.

THE LESSON COMMENTARY

I. THE NATURE OF FAITH: Hebrews 11:1

A. A Confidence Toward the Unknown Future: v. 1a

The Greek word for "substance" is *hypostasis*, which has already occurred twice in this Epistle. In 1:3 we read that God's Son is the "express image" (one word in Greek, *character*) of His "person" (*hypostasis*). Here it means the "essence" of Deity. In 3:14 believers are said to become sharers in Christ if they hold firmly to the end the beginning of their "confidence" (*hypostasis*). In the first of these two passages the Greek word has the objective sense of "substance" or "essence." In the second it has the subjective sense of "confidence" or "assurance." Which does it mean here in 11:1?

The King James Version and the New English Bible take it the first way—"substance." The American Standard Version and the Revised Standard Version take it the second way—"assurance." F. F. Bruce writes: "But on the whole the subjective meaning 'assurance' is the more probable, especially as this meaning chimes in well with the companion word 'conviction' " (*The Epistle to the Hebrews*, p. 278). We would agree with this: "Now faith is confidence with regard to what is hoped for."

B. A Conviction of the Unseen Present: v. 1b

The word for "evidence" is *elenchos*—found only here in the New Testament. It can mean "evidence" or "proof." Bruce comments that "here it means 'conviction' in much the same sense as 'assurance' in the preceding phrase." He continues: "Physical eyesight produces conviction or evidence of visible things; faith is the organ which enables people (like Moses in verse 27) to see the invisible order" (*Hebrews*, p. 279).

Commenting on the entire verse, Westcott says: "Thus the general scope of the statement is to shew that the future and the unseen can be made real for men by Faith" (*The Epistle to the Hebrews*, p. 351). We would translate the verse: "Now faith is a confidence with regard to things hoped for, a conviction of the reality of the unseen." The New International Version reads: "Now faith is being sure of what we hope for and certain of what we do not see."

It has been suggested that Hebrews 11:1 does not give us a definition of faith, but rather describes its nature and functions. Some have thought that Romans 4:21 gives us more nearly a definition of faith: "Being fully persuaded that, what he had promised, he was able also to perform." Faith is a full persuasion that God can and will do what He has promised. Abraham had this kind of faith, Paul says, and it was credited to him for righteousness. This is the kind of faith that we must have today.

Hatch writes: "Faith is the ground of things hoped for, i.e., trust in God, or the conviction that God is good and that He will perform His promises, is the ground for confident hope that the things hoped for will come to pass. . . . So trust in God furnishes to the mind which has it a clear proof that things to which God has testified exist, though they are not visible to the senses" (quoted by Marcus Dods, *Expositor's Greek Testament*, IV, 352).

II. PIONEER FAITH:
Hebrews 11:8-10

The eleventh chapter of Hebrews has been called the "Westminster Abbey" of faith. This impressive building in London is where some of the greatest men of England's history, such as the pioneer missionary-explorer David Livingstone, are buried. In addition to this, on the walls are plaques of other such notables as John Wesley. So this chapter displays the names of many of the leading men and women of the Old Testament. The roll call is impressive: Abel, Enoch, Noah, Abraham, Sarah, Isaac, Jacob, Joseph, Moses, Rahab. Then the writer runs out of breath and out of space: "And what shall I more say? for the time would fail me to tell of Gideon, and of Barak, and of Samson, and of Jephthae; of David also, and Samuel, and of the prophets" (v. 32). Poor David gets slight notice!

A. The Obedience of Faith: v. 8

Today we concentrate on Abraham. This verse declares: "By faith Abraham, when called to go to a place he would later receive as his possession, obeyed and went, even though he did not know where he was going" (NIV). As has often been said, Abraham did not know where he was going but he knew who was leading him.

And that is all we need to know today. In the words of the song writer:

Many things about tomorrow
I don't seem to understand
But I know who holds tomorrow,
And I know who holds my hand.

That is all we need to know. It is not necessary that we have a preview of our lives, or that we even know our next step. When the time comes to move, God will show us which way to go. What a wonderful assurance. We can echo with real meaning the poet's words:

He leadeth me, O blessed thought;
O words with heavenly comfort fraught.

"When he was called" is literally "being called" (present participle). This, coupled with the aorist "obeyed"—in close proximity in the Greek text—indicates that as soon as he was called, Abraham immediately obeyed and went. Westcott says, "He obeyed the call while (so to say) it was still sounding in his ears" (*Hebrews*, p. 358). There was no hesitation, no arguing with God about the matter. Marcus Dods comments: "The faith of Abraham appeared in his promptly abandoning his own country on God's promise of another, and the strength of this faith was illustrated by the circumstance that he had no knowledge where or what that country was" (*Expositor's Greek Testament*, IV, 355).

Abraham was called to "go out." This is highlighted in the Old Testament account of the original call: "Get thee out of thy country, and from thy kindred, and from thy father's house, unto a land that I will shew thee" (Genesis 12:1). There is a sense in which each of us today is called to go out—from a life of sin, from the old associations. Beyond this, some are specifically called to leave their family and country to go to some distant nation with the gospel. Whatever God's call, it must be obeyed.

In both the Genesis account and

the Hebrews reference the fact is emphasized that Abraham knew nothing about the country to which God was calling him. Dods notes: "It was, therefore, no attractive account of Canaan which induced him to forsake Mesopotamia, no ordinary emigrant's motive which moved him, but mere faith in God's promise" (*Expositor's Greek Testament*, IV, 355). Westcott makes the point that in this act of obedience "Abraham had no example to follow" (*Hebrews*, p. 358). His was truly a "pioneer faith."

The faith of obedience was a faith of self-surrender. Abraham had to submit himself wholly to God's will.

B. The Patience of Faith: v. 9

The obedience of faith was followed by the patience of faith, as it is in our lives today. Abraham's walking was followed by his waiting. He obeyed God's call to go out to an unknown country, but when he arrived there he had to wait patiently for the fulfillment of God's promise.

We read that he "sojourned" in the promised land. The verb *paroikeo* occurs in the New Testament only here and in Luke 24:18, where it is translated "stranger." Abbott-Smith says it means "*to dwell* in a place *as a paroikos* or stranger" (*Lexicon*, p. 346).

The verse continues: "as in a strange country"—"like a stranger in a foreign country" (NIV). God had promised this land to him as his possession. Yet Abraham lived there as a stranger. Such is the paradox of the Christian's life in this world.

As with Isaac and Jacob, Abraham lived in "tabernacles." The Greek simply says "tents." These patriarchs were much like nomads, taking their flocks from one place to another. In contrast to this, Ur of the Chaldees was a great center of culture in Abraham's day, as excavations there show. If he lived in Ur when God called him, he left an advanced city civilization to be a nomad in a strange land.

Isaac and Jacob were "heirs with him of the same promise." God's promise to Abraham that all the land of Canaan would be his (Genesis 13:15) was renewed to Isaac (Genesis 26:3) and Jacob (Genesis 28:13).

C. The Expectation of Faith: v. 10

The word for "builder" is *technites*, from which we get "technician." It refers to the one who planned the city. "Maker" is *demiourgos*, found only here in the New Testament. The correct translation of these two words together is "architect and builder." God planned the city and is building it.

The Greek word for "looked" is a compound, meaning "expectantly waited for." Abraham was willing to forgo the luxury of living in a settled house, because he was expectantly waiting for a city that had foundations—quite a contrast to the tents they pitched.

What is this city? It is described in 12:22 as "the city of the living God, the heavenly Jerusalem." In Galatians 4:26 it is called "Jerusalem which is above." A city suggests a settled dwelling. Here it refers to the spiritual fellowship of the saints, at home forever with God. Looking forward to this, Abraham was willing to live in a tent down here.

H. Orton Wiley writes: "There were many cities in Canaan, ancient and wealthy, but Abraham's spiritual insight saw that these were subject to decay, as also any city would be which he himself might establish.... His faith carried him beyond the things earth might offer, to that spiritual and heavenly realm above the fleeting things of time" (*The Epistle to the Hebrews*, p. 367).

III. PERSISTENT FAITH: Hebrews 11:11-12

A. Sarah's Miracle: v. 11

"Through faith" is exactly the same in the Greek (*pistei*) as "by faith" in verses 4, 5, 7, 8, 9. 17, 20, 21, 22, 23, 24, 27, 29, 30, 31. There seems to be no justification for the

King James Version translating *pistei* "through faith" here and in verses 3 and 28.

"Also Sara" should be "even Sarah." At the least, this means "even Sarah" who was too old to bear. At the most it means "even Sarah" who laughed at the suggestion that she would have a child (Genesis 18:12). She was reproved for her laughter of incredulity and out of fear denied it (Genesis 18:13-15).

This has posed a real problem for commentators. But it does not seem unreasonable to hold that although Sarah's first reaction was that of unbelief, with the passage of time she achieved a real faith along with Abraham. R. V. G. Tasker makes this helpful comment: "Even Sarah's acceptance of a promise which at first she seemed to hear with indifference is to the mind of the *anctor ad Hebraeos* a venture into the unseen world which faith makes real" (*New Testament Studies*, II, 183).

There is another, more difficult, problem in this verse. "To conceive seed" is not what the Greek says; the original describes rather the male act of depositing seed. There is no evidence of the phrase here ever being used for female conception.

F. F. Bruce in his volume on *The Epistle to the Hebrews* in *The New International Commentary on the New Testament* suggests this translation of the verse: "By faith he (Abraham) also, together with Sarah, received power to beget a child when he was past age, since he counted him faithful who had promised" (p. 302). This is basically the same as the translation adopted in the New International Version of the New Testament. (It should perhaps be noted that F. F. Bruce is usually considered to be the leading evangelical New Testament scholar in the British Isles today.)

B. Abraham's Many Descendants: v. 12

As Dr. Bruce notes, this verse follows very naturally from verse 11

when it (v. 11) is translated in this way. It is all a discussion of Abraham's strong faith, which Sarah came to share with him as his partner in carrying out God's promise.

Though he was "as good as dead," yet from Abraham there "came descendants as numerous as the stars in the sky and as countless as the sand of the seashore" (NIV). This language is reminiscent of God's promises to Abraham (Genesis 22:17). One is tempted to suggest that the "stars in the sky" refer to Abraham's spiritual descendants and the "sand of the seashore" to his physical seed. But perhaps the distinction was not intended.

IV. PILGRIM FAITH: Hebrews 11:13-16

A. Strangers and Pilgrims: v. 13

The Old Testament saints never received the complete fulfillment of God's promises to them. For instance, verse 12 includes Abraham's spiritual descendants in this age. Many Old Testament promises look forward to Christ and His salvation made possible by His death on the cross. The heroes of faith died too soon for this. But they died in faith—"still living by faith when they died" (NIV).

Though these men only saw "afar off" the fulfillment of the promises given them, they "welcomed them" (NIV)—literally "saluted them" or "greeted them." ("And were persuaded

---

DISCUSSION QUESTIONS

1. Is God limited to one geographical location?
2. Are there some places where His presence is more easily found than in others?
3. What are some of the perils of a mobile society?
4. What can churches do to help?
5. What precautions must Christian families take?
6. How can we maintain our faith today?

THE CHALLENGE OF MOBILITY

of them" is not in the early Greek manuscripts.) They confessed that they were "strangers and pilgrims on the earth." Philippians 3:20 tells us that our "citizenship"—not "conversation" (KJV)—is in heaven. So we are "foreigners and strangers" (NIV) on earth. This was what Abraham called himself (Genesis 23:4). The three patriarchs (v. 9) did not even see the fulfillment of the promise that the land would be theirs. But they believed it to the end.

B. Looking for a Better Country: v. 14

Though they doubtless enjoyed their sojourn in Canaan and their living in tents, the fact that they called themselves foreigners and pilgrims shows that they looked for a better country eventually. So it is with us. We are to enjoy the good things that God has given us in this life. But we must always remember that we are only pilgrims here, on our way to an eternal realm.

C. No Turning Back: v. 15

This is the refrain of a chorus that has become popular in the last twenty years. We first heard it in 1953 from the lips of the great Presbyterian missionary, Dr. Lambie, near Bethlehem. Retired from active service in the Sudan, he devoted his last days to building a hospital in the Valley of Berachah ("blessing") for the Arab refugees. We, like the ancient patriarchs, are free to turn back—but determined not to!

D. A Heavenly Country: v. 16

The key word of Hebrews is "better." We read in this Epistle that Christ is a better Messenger (chaps. 1–2), a better Leader (chap. 3), a better Rest (chap. 4), a better High Priest (chaps. 5–7), the Maker of a better covenant (chap. 8) and a better Sacrifice (chaps. 9–10). Now we learn that He provides a better country. And "better" is defined as meaning "heavenly."

The example of Abraham, Isaac, and Jacob teaches us that wherever we go, or how often we move, we should be sure that God goes with us. We must always put Him first, taking time to worship Him and seeking to obey Him in everything. Like them, we must live "by faith." This is the key phrase of this chapter.

CONTEMPORARY APPLICATION

Many years ago we knew some brothers whose father had taken his family to a frontier town in the West. They had not been there long when he discovered that drinking and gambling were the life-style of that community. He began to think about the possible consequences for his boys.

At considerable financial loss he decided to take his family back to a place that was far more Christian. The result was that all his boys turned out well and some of them went into the ministry. Did it pay?

THE CHALLENGE OF RELATIONSHIPS

DEVOTIONAL READING

Ephesians 4:25–5:2

ADULTS

Topic: *Living in the Christian Family*

Background Scripture: Ruth; Ephesians 4:25–6:4; I Peter 3:1-12

Scripture Lesson: Ephesians 5:21–6:4

Memory Verse: *Have unity of spirit, sympathy, love of the brethren, a tender heart and a humble mind.* I Peter 3:8

YOUTH

Topic: *Getting Along with My Family*

Background Scripture: Ruth; Ephesians 4:25–5:2; 6:1-4; I Peter 3:1-12

Scripture Lesson: I Peter 3:1-7; Ephesians 6:1-4

Memory Verse: *All of you have unity of spirit, love of the brethren, a tender heart and a humble mind.* I Peter 3:8

CHILDREN

Topic: *Growing in Family Relationships*

Background Scripture: Ruth; Ephesians 4:25–5:2 6:1-4; I Peter 3:1-12

Scripture Lesson: Ephesians 4:25-32

Memory Verse: *Let all bitterness and wrath and anger and clamor and slander be put away from you, with all malice: and be kind to one another, tenderhearted, forgiving one another, as God in Christ forgave you.* Ephesians 4:31-32

DAILY BIBLE READINGS

Mon., May 3: Constancy in Friendship, Ruth 1:16-22.
Tues., May 4: Blessings of a New Friendship, Ruth 2:7-12.
Wed., May 5: Beginning of the Messianic Line, Ruth 4:13-22.
Thurs., May 6: Unity in Christ, Ephesians 4:25-32.
Fri., May 7: Encouragement in Christian Living, Ephesians 5:1-10.
Sat., May 8: Counseling Married Couples, I Peter 3:1-10.
Sun., May 9: Divine Hearing, I Peter 3:11-12.

LESSON AIM

To suggest some guidelines for living in a Christian family.

LESSON SETTING

Time: The Epistle to the Ephesians was written about A.D. 60.

Place: It was written in prison at Rome.

The Challenge of Relationships

I. Walking in Love: Ephesians 5:1-7

II. Walking as Children of Light: Ephesians 5:8-14

III. Walking Carefully: Ephesians 5:15-21

IV. The Duty of Wives: Ephesians 5:22-24

LESSON OUTLINE

V. The Duty of Husbands: Ephesians 5:25-33
   A. Example of Christ's Love for the Church: vv. 25-27
   B. Love Wives as Themselves: v. 28-30
   C. Be Joined to the Wife: v. 31
   D. The Mystery of Christ and the Church: v. 32
   E. Mutual Love and Respect: v. 33

VI. The Duty of Children: Ephesians 6:1-3
   A. Obedience to Parents: v. 1
   B. Honoring Parents: v. 2-3

VII. The Duty of Parents: Ephesians 6:4

SUGGESTED INTRODUCTION FOR ADULTS

The Epistle to the Ephesians divides itself very naturally into two main sections. The first three chapters describe the Christian's *worship;* the last three chapters present the Christian's *walk.*

In the first half of the book we are taken up in the airplane of prayer. The key phrase of this part is "in the heavenlies [in Christ]" (1:3, 20; 2:6; 3:10). From this elevated fellowship we catch glimpses of God's great eternal purpose in Christ for us.

Then Paul brings us abruptly down to earth and seems to say: "Now get out and walk in the light of the vision you have seen of life in Christ." Five times in chapters 4 and 5 he says, "Walk" (4:1, 17 5:2, 8, 15). The last three are a part of today's lesson.

We must first worship well if we are going to walk satisfactorily. That is why we begin each week with Sunday worship and why we need to begin each day with private devotions. Our walk will depend on our worship.

SUGGESTED INTRODUCTION FOR YOUTH

How do you get along with your family? You may be tempted to ask, "What difference does it make?" In Bible language we would answer, "Much every way!"

Where there is a breakdown in family life, all of life is apt to go to pieces. There never was a time when family fellowship was more needed than now. There are too many attractions outside the home to lure young people away. If we stay close together as a family, it will help us to stay close to God. For the family is the divinely ordained unit of human society.

CONCEPTS FOR
CHILDREN

1. Quarrels are common in most families.
2. Quarreling can become a habit, but it destroys happiness.
3. We should ask God to help us to have love and patience for each other.
4. We should be quick to ask forgiveness.

THE LESSON COMMENTARY

I. WALKING IN LOVE:
Ephesians 5:1-7

The Greek word for "followers" (v. 1) is *mimetai*, "imitators." As God's children we are to imitate Him in our lives. Since God is love, imitating Him means that we "walk in love" (v. 2)—that is, "live a life of love" (NIV). This is our highest responsibility as Christians.

Why should we walk in love? Because "Christ loved us and gave himself up for us as a fragrant offering and sacrifice to God" (NIV). This parallels what Paul says in II Corinthians 2:15.

If we are going to walk in love we must avoid all immorality, for lust is a negation of love. Hollywood love is mere lust, and unfortunately this is the concept of love that is most widely publicized today. So much is this true that one almost hesitates to use the word "love" in public, lest it provoke a snicker.

Westcott points out the connection of verse 3 with verse 2. He writes: "Love answers to holiness, and honours and cherishes the highest in all. All sins of self-indulgence therefore, in which a man sacrifices another to himself, or his own higher nature to the lower, are diametrically opposed to love" (*Epistle to the Ephesians*, p. 76).

"Fornication" takes in all sexual immorality. "Uncleanness" is a more general term, but of course is to be taken in a moral sense. "Covetousness" or "greed," is widely condemned in both the Old and New Testaments. These vices are not even to be named among Christians, because they are improper for saints.

In verse 4 the apostle warns against three other evils. "Filthiness" refers to something that is shameful; it may be translated "obscenity" (NIV). "Jesting" means "coarse joking." These are not "convenient," or "fitting" for a Christian.

Paul makes it clear that "no immoral, impure, or greedy person" (NIV) will have any part in the Kingdom (v. 5). Rather, God's wrath will be poured out on those who conduct themselves in this way (v. 6). "Therefore do not be partners with them" (v. 7, NIV).

II. WALKING AS CHILDREN OF LIGHT:
Ephesians 5:8-14

Every sinner dwells in darkness. As Christians we should "walk as children of light." We do this by obeying the light of God's Word and the light of human conscience.

In verse 9 the best Greek text reads "the fruit of the light" rather than "the fruit of the Spirit." It is light which Paul is emphasizing at this point. The fruit of light consists in living a life of goodness, righteousness, and truth. Walking in sin means walking in darkness. But the three things mentioned here all flood our lives with light.

Westcott makes this helpful comment on verse 9: "The life in light is not rigid and monotonous. It is shewn *in every form of goodness and righteousness and truth*, in all moral duties reckoned under the familiar classification, the good, the right, the true. The first includes personal character, the second social dealings, the third ruling principles, marking generally our obligation to self, our neighbours, God" (*Ephesians*, p. 78).

"Proving" (v. 10) may be translated "testing." We must weigh our actions carefully "and find out what pleases the Lord" (NIV). This is the central responsibility of every Christian.

Still pursuing the theme of walking in the light, the apostle goes on to say: "Have nothing to do with the fruitless deeds of darkness, but rather expose them" (v. 11, NIV). We are not only to avoid indulging in them, but we are to expose them. Jesus said that we are the light of the world (Matthew 5:14). The light of God's holiness in us should expose the world's dark deeds for what they are. Paul declares that it is a shame even to talk about the evil deeds that sinners perform in secret (v. 12). Instead we should have enough divine light to show them up in all their ugliness (v. 13). To do this we must keep awake and alert (v. 14).

III. WALKING CAREFULLY:
Ephesians 5:15-21

This is the crowning admonition of the five exhortations to "walk." It gathers up all the others. To "walk carefully" is to walk in love and in the light, being constantly careful how we walk day by day. Only fools live carelessly. Wise people live carefully. One of the most important of the A, B, C's of life is: "Always Be Careful!" It is the supreme safety slogan. Just because we are God's children and so in His care does not relieve us of the responsibility to live carefully.

"Redeeming" (v. 16) is literally "buying up." Time is the most valuable commodity of life, and we need to prize it highly. The idea is that of "making the most of every opportunity" (NIV). The word translated "time" here is not *chronos*, which means the passage of time, but *kairos*, "opportune time." Often such times are quickly gone.

Why do we need to buy up the time? Because "the days are evil"— "and the season for action is brief and precarious and precious" (Westcott, *Ephesians*, p. 81). In view of all this we are not to be foolish, "but understand what the will of the Lord is" (v. 17).

Christians are not to be drunk with wine, "which leads to debauchery" (NIV), but "be filled with the Spirit" (v. 18). This is one of the great commands of the New Testament. It is not enough to avoid evil; we must be filled with good. And only being constantly filled with the Spirit can keep us that way.

We are admonished to speak to each other with "psalms and hymns and spiritual songs" (v. 19). The first of these should probably be taken literally. The Jews chanted the Psalms of the Old Testament, and the early Christians naturally followed that custom. "Hymns" are properly songs addressed to Deity. Because they turn our minds to God, they should be what we normally use in Sunday worship. "Spiritual songs" would take in the rest of what we sing—songs of praise, testimony, and devotion. We are to sing and make music in our hearts to the Lord. Music is not only an essential part of worship, but it also cheers our hearts and deepens our love for God and for each other.

Verse 20 is a challenging command. Do we give thanks always for all things? In Christ's name we can and should.

Paul is everlastingly, insistently practical. And so he proceeds to discuss the relationships of six groups in the church: wives, husbands, children, parents, slaves, masters. Since the last two (6:5-9) do not exist in modern society, they are omitted from the lesson. Of the other four, the longest space is given to the relationships between husbands and wives (5:22-33).

But first Paul gives a general admonition to all Christians: "Submitting yourselves one to another in the fear of the Lord" (v. 21). Each of us has his place and part in the body of Christ. As we submit to each other in humility, we live and work together harmoniously. It is pride that makes us want to have our own way rather than submitting to others in the church.

IV. THE DUTY OF WIVES:
Ephesians 5:22-24

This duty can be summed up in one word: submission. The apostle compares the relationship of husband and wife to that of Christ and the church. That is the figure which dominates the entire discussion from verse 22 through verse 33.

It must be recognized, of course, that the place of women in ancient oriental society was very different from what it is in modern occidental society. Culture and customs change. But basic principles remain the same.

The dominant motive here is love. True love will make us want to please our companion and to do what is best for him or her. In order that the family may have unity in love it is necessary to have some authority. If there is bickering between husband and wife, this authority breaks down and the children are damaged. For their sake there must be a central authority figure.

V. THE DUTY OF HUSBANDS:
Ephesians 5:25-33

A. Example of Christ's Love for the Church: vv. 25-27

Lest any husband should exult in the idea that his wife is to be in submission to him, let us hasten to point out that a far higher, more difficult demand is placed on the husband. For the husbands are commanded to love their wives even as Christ loved the church. Before any husband quotes verse 22 to his wife, he had better be sure that he is obeying verse 25. As the popular saying goes, "That will stop him in his tracks!" For what husband could honestly look his wife in the eye and say, "I love you as Christ loves His church." Obeying verse 25 will keep any Christian husband on his toes

throughout his married life! It is the greatest challenge given to any human being. Totally unselfish love is what it demands.

Christ "gave himself" for the church. While the husband cannot give himself redemptively for his wife, he should have sacrificial love for her.

Verse 26 reads literally: "That he might sanctify her [the church], having cleansed her with the washing of water by the word." This is what is referred to in Titus 3:5 as "the washing of regeneration." In salvation, regeneration comes first, then sanctification. We have to be made alive in Christ by the New Birth before God's sanctifying grace can bring us into the image of Christlikeness.

The purpose of all this is expressed in verse 27: "That he might present it to himself a glorious church, not having spot, or wrinkle, or any such thing; but that it should be holy and without blemish." This is the final fruit of redemption. The church will be presented to Christ as His bride, glorious and blameless. Westcott suggests that "without spot or wrinkle" means "without one trace of defilement or one mark of age." Of the last two adjectives, "holy" refers primarily to the inner life of the spirit and "blameless" (or, "without blemish") to the outward life.

B. Love Wives as Themselves: vv. 28-30

After this magnificent passage about Christ and His bride, the church, Paul comes right down to earth again and says, "So ought men to love their wives as their own bodies" (v. 28). Westcott insists that this means "*as being their own bodies,* not 'as they love their own bodies.' As the Church is Christ's body, so in a true sense the wife is the husband's body. Through her he extends his life" (*Ephesians,* p. 85). But this seems a bit extreme, though both interpretations may well be true. In either case it means "as oneself." So Paul adds: "He that loveth his wife loveth himself." This

makes good sense philosophically in
the light of verse 31. But it also makes
good sense psychologically and practically. The husband who hurts his
wife hurts himself, because he destroys
his own happiness. But the husband
who keeps his wife happy reaps rich
benefits from that condition. Looked
at even from a selfish point of view, it
simply isn't smart for a husband to
make his wife unhappy.

The apostle enforces this idea in
verse 29: "After all, no one ever hated
his own body, but he feeds and cares
for it, just as Christ does the church"
(NIV). If the husband and wife are
joined into one, the husband should
no more be unkind to his wife than he
would be to himself.

Paul adds: "For we are members of
his body" (v. 30). As such we are the
constant recipients of His love and
care, and we should extend the same
kind of love and care to our wives. "Of
his flesh, and of his bones" (KJV) is a
meaningless gloss added by some late
scribe; it is not in the earliest Greek
manuscripts.

C. Be Joined to the Wife: v. 31

This verse is a quotation of Genesis
2:24. This is God's ordained relationship of husband and wife, beginning
with Adam and Eve in the Garden of
Eden. One man and one woman are to
be joined into one flesh for life.

Many a marriage is wrecked because the man does not "leave his

DISCUSSION QUESTIONS

1. How are we to "walk in love"?
2. How may authority be maintained in the home?
3. How can the church minister to
   families?
4. How can the lines of communication be kept open?
5. What is the greatest hindrance
   to family fellowship?
6. What special resources does the
   Christian have?

father and mother." It is misery for
the wife whose husband keeps running
back to his mother's apron strings, acting like a baby instead of a grown
man. The husband must "leave" his
mother before he can be truly
"joined" to his wife. The Greek word
for "joined" literally means "be
glued." What is needed in modern marriage is more glue—the glue of sincere,
strong love—to hold them together.

Some have spiritualized "one
flesh." But this expression has a physical as well as a spiritual significance.

D. The Mystery of Christ and the Church: v. 32

Paul was greatly intrigued with the
relationship of the church to Christ as
His bride—as well as His body (v. 30).
Both figures are full of fruitful meaning. There is no richer mystery for the
Christian to meditate on than this twofold truth.

E. Mutual Love and Respect: v. 33

In addition to being intriguingly
mystical, Paul is incisively and insistently practical. So after his flight into
the heavenlies, meditating on Christ
and His bride, he comes right down to
earth again and says: "However, each
one of you must also love his wife as
he loves himself, and the wife must
respect her husband" (NIV).

VI. THE DUTY OF CHILDREN: Ephesians 6:1-3

A. Obedience to Parents: v. 1

The main duty of children is that
of obeying their parents. This is the
basis of a happy home. And children
must first learn to obey those who are
in authority over them before they can
assume their places as adults and have
authority over their own children.
Young people have to be disciplined
by loving parents before they can
achieve self-discipline.

This obedience is to be "in the

Lord." Divine authority is above parental authority. Every relationship of the Christian must put Christ first. He is supreme Lord.

B. Honoring Parents: v. 2-3

This is the fifth of the Ten Commandments (Exodus 20:12). Paul calls it "the first commandment with promise" and quotes that promise in verse 3. The nations of earth that have had the longest continuous history have proved this promise true.

VII. THE DUTY OF PARENTS: Ephesians 6:4

"Fathers" are mentioned as the head of the house, but both parents are probably implied. "Provoke to wrath" is one word, meaning to "make angry." Parents must not make their children angry, but raise them in the "nurture"—more correctly, "discipline"—and "admonition" (or, "instruction") of the Lord. The burden of initiative throughout this section of Scripture lies with the husbands and fathers.

CONTEMPORARY APPLICATION

In the present breakdown of the home life no teaching is more relevant than what we find in our lesson. The worst trouble spot is in the relation of husbands and wives. This must be given first attention. The second area of difficulty is in the relation of parents and children. These must all be worked out prayerfully in love.

THE CHALLENGE OF CONFORMITY

DEVOTIONAL READING	Psalm 24

ADULTS

Topic: *Pressures on the Christian Family*

Background Scripture: Joshua 24:1-18; Romans 12

Scripture Lesson: Romans 12:1-10, 14-18

Memory Verse: *Do not be conformed to this world but be transformed by the renewal of your mind, that you may prove what is the will of God, what is good and acceptable and perfect.* Romans 12:2

YOUTH

Topic: *Pressures on the Christian Family*

Background Scripture: Joshua 24:1-18; Romans 12:1-21

Scripture Lesson: Romans 12:1-10, 14-18

Memory Verse: *Let love be genuine; hate what is evil, hold fast to what is good.* Romans 12:9

CHILDREN

Topic: *The Family, Loyal to God*

Background Scripture: Joshua 241-18; Romans 2:1-21; I Corinthians 10:6-15

Scripture Lesson: Joshua 24:1-18

Memory Verse: *Do not be conformed to this world but be transformed by the renewal of your mind, that you may prove what is the will of God, what is good and acceptable and perfect.* Romans 12:2

DAILY BIBLE READINGS

Mon., May 10: Paul's Teaching of Love, Romans 12:1-8.
Tues., May 11: Christian Humility, Luke 14:10-14.
Wed., May 12: The Christian Spirit, Romans 12:9-13.
Thurs., May 13: Christian Concerns, Romans 12:17-21.
Fri., May 14: God's Benefits to a Nation, Joshua 24:1-18.
Sat., May 15: A Covenant, Genesis 28:20-22.
Sun., May 16: Social Pressures, Romans 13:1-8.

LESSON AIM

To see that as individuals and families we must not allow ourselves to be pressured into conforming to the ways of the world.

LESSON SETTING

Time: Romans was written about A.D. 56.

Place: The Epistle was written at Corinth.

The Challenge of Conformity

LESSON OUTLINE

SUGGESTED INTRODUCTION FOR ADULTS

As Moses' successor, Joshua had led the Israelites in their conquest of Canaan. Then he had supervised the division of the land to the various tribes. Now he was old and soon would be gone. So he called the people together for his last message to them (Joshua 24:1-15).

First he gave a resumé of the history of God's dealings with the chosen people. He reminded the people that their ancestors were idolaters (v. 2). But God called Abraham from "the other side of the flood" (v. 3)—that is, beyond the Euphrates River—and led him into the land of Canaan (Palestine).

Later, God selected Moses to deliver the people from Egyptian bondage (v. 5). Miraculously they were saved at the Red Sea (vv. 6-7). The Lord brought them safely through the wilderness (vv. 8-10) and gave them the land of Canaan (vv. 11-13).

On the basis of all this, Joshua pleaded with the people to renounce all idolatry and serve the Lord, the true God, with sincerity and truth (v. 14). He challenged them to choose what god they would serve, and ended by declaring firmly his own position: "But as for me and my house, we will serve the Lord" (v. 15). This must be our settled decision in each home.

SUGGESTED INTRODUCTION FOR YOUTH

The pressure to conform is especially strong among young people. Teen-agers find the pressure of their peers almost irresistible. "Well, everybody does it" is the favorite alibi for questionable conduct or customs.

Today's lesson tells us that as Christians we are not to conform to the world but to be transformed as citizens of another world. It takes courage to be a nonconformist, but that is taking up our cross to follow Christ.

CONCEPTS FOR CHILDREN

1. We have to stand by our convictions, as Joshua did.
2. We have to be willing to be different as Christians.
3. It doesn't matter if "Everybody does it!"
4. We must try to live as Jesus would live in our circumstances.

THE LESSON COMMENTARY

I. THE BASIC CHRISTIAN PATTERN:
Romans 12:1-3

A. Commitment to God: v. 1

Rather than saying, "I command as an apostle," Paul says, "I beseech you therefore, brethren, by the mercies of God." These mercies of God he has been describing in the previous eleven chapters. There was God's mercy in the forgiveness of sin (chaps. 1–5). Then God's mercy extended further in the sanctifying of the Christian (chaps. 6–8). God's mercy has also been shown in His dealing with disobedient Israel (chaps. 9–11).

On the basis of all these mercies, Paul pleads for his readers to present their bodies as a living sacrifice to God. "That ye present" is one word in Greek, *parastesai*. It is the aorist infinitive, "to present"—right here and now, as a decisive act of complete commitment.

It is generally agreed that the word *bodies* here stands for the whole being. So it means "to present yourselves," all there is of you.

The apostle here is not asking us to give ourselves to a martyr's death. What God needs and wants is a "living sacrifice." We must be willing, if necessary, to die for Him. But it is a far greater challenge to live for Him day by day, doing His will.

Our sacrifice is to be "holy." Much has been made of the idea that the adjective *hagios* means "set apart to God, sacred." But this is the minimal meaning. That which is set apart to God must be holy, for God is holy and can only associate with holy people. While there is a strong emphasis on ceremonial holiness in the Old Testament, the moral concept becomes more and more prominent in the Prophets, and it is the moral sense of *holy* that is dominant in the New Testament. If we are to be a sacrifice "acceptable unto God," we must be holy in heart and life.

The Greek word for "reasonable" is *logicos*, from which we get "logical." The most reasonable thing we can do is to serve God.

The word for "service" is *latreia*, which also means "worship." That is why we speak of having a "worship service" at church. Actually worship and service cannot be separated. When we are serving, we are worshiping; and when we are worshiping we are serving. All our service for the Lord should be "divine service," which is the real meaning of this word.

B. Nonconformity to the World: v. 2

The apostle continues: "And be not conformed to this world" (or, "this age"). J. B. Phillips' translation of this has become justly famous: "Don't let the world squeeze you into its mold." This is very meaningful. The world constantly puts pressure on all of us, seeking to squeeze us into its pattern of living. We have to keep resisting this pressure and maintain our integrity as God's people.

But there is a positive side that is just as important as the negative. It is not enough to avoid conforming to the world; we must be transformed into Christian character.

The word for "transformed" is *metamorphousthe*, from which we get "metamorphosis," a change from one state to another. This verb occurs in only three other places in the New Testament. In the King James Version it is rendered "transfigured" in Matthew 17:2 and Mark 9:2, in connection with the transfiguration of Jesus on the mountain. In II Corinthians 3:18 it is translated "changed." We are to have our lives transfigured into Christlikeness by the presence and power of the indwelling Holy Spirit. God wants us not to live in conformity to the world, but to live transfigured by His grace.

How are we to be transfigured? "By the renewing of your mind." We can transform our personalities by changing our thinking. If we think mean, ugly, miserly thoughts, our faces become hard and harsh in appearance. If we think low, sensual thoughts, the animal desires cause us to look more and more like animals. But if we think high and holy thoughts, our faces take on a clean, noble look. If we think kind, loving thoughts, it shows unmistakably in our countenance. And when we see a person with a happy, smiling face, we instinctively know that that person is thinking happy thoughts.

What you think reveals what you are and makes you what you will be. Some people say, "I try to be careful what I say, but it's nobody's business what I think." But that's not true. There is a very real sense in which our thoughts are written on our faces. Charles Reznikoff, as quoted in the *Reader's Digest* some years ago, put it very well: "The fingers of your thoughts are molding your face ceaselessly." We can't escape giving away what we are thinking.

This leads us to note that while "present" in the first verse is in the aorist tense of a decisive act of commitment, "transformed" is in the present imperative of continuous action. The second verse literally says, "Stop being conformed to this world, but go on (day by day, more and more) being transformed by the renewing of your mind. Make your thoughts new and you will eventually make a new personality. You are what you think!"

One other point might be made. The first verb here, "conformed," is *suschematizo*. *Schema*, from which we get "scheme," referred to the outward "fashion" of a thing. The second verb, *metamorphoo*, "transformed," is compounded of *meta*, "across," and *morphe*, essential "form." The first is outer, the second inner. That is why *Good News for Modern Man* (TEV) translates this passage: "Do not conform outwardly to the standards of this world, but let God transform you inwardly by a complete change of your mind."

It is only as we commit ourselves fully to God and allow Him to transform our thinking that we can know ("prove" or discern) what is the will of God—good and well-pleasing and perfect.

C. Humility Toward Self: v. 3

Every person is to avoid thinking of himself more highly than he ought to think. "To think more highly" is one word in Greek, *hyperphronein* (only here in the New Testament). It means to be overproud, high-minded. "To think soberly" is likewise one word, *sophronein*. Abbott-Smith defines this as "to be temperate, discreet, self-controlled" (*Lexicon*, p. 438).

To overrate oneself is stupid. It will only get a person into trouble with himself, with others, and with God. Neither are we to underrate ourselves, speaking in a deprecating fashion. True humility is honest self-appraisal, and that will keep any intelligent person humble!

II. THE CHRISTIAN IN THE CHURCH:
Romans 12:4-10

A. The Body of Christ: vv. 4-5

One of Paul's favorite figures is the church as the Body of Christ. He begins here by drawing the analogy of the human body. He writes: "We have many parts in the one body, and all these parts have different functions" (v. 4, TEV). This is a familiar fact. The eye has one function, the ear another, the nose another, the hand another, and the foot another.

In the same way, says Paul, "we, being many, are one body in Christ, and every one members [parts] one of another" (v. 5). All the parts ("members") of the body are in a real sense interrelated. The body is not complete, and cannot function efficiently, without all its parts. Each one has a function, and each one is needed for some purpose. Even the so-called "appendix" is now thought to have a basic function in the body. So we should recognize all other members of the Body of Christ as functioning with us.

B. Varying Functions: vv. 6-8

The apostle refers to these functions in the church as "gifts" from God. We are to exercise these gifts "according to the grace that is given to us" (v. 6).

He then proceeds to enumerate these gifts or functions. The first is "prophecy." In the New Testament this means "preaching." Our word *prophet* comes directly from the Greek *prophetes*, which means "one who speaks for another." Prophecy, then, is giving God's message to the people. This gift is to be exercised "according to the proportion of faith." The Greek word for "proportion" is *analogia* (only here in the New Testament), from which we get "analogy." We must use the faith we have, and God will give us more.

The second gift is "ministry" (v. 7). The Greek word, *diaconia*, simply means "service." Its earliest usage was for waiting on tables, serving meals. So it may apply especially to the pastor who feeds his flock. But it could also take in every other form of service in the church. The one who has this function assigned to him should busy himself in service.

The third gift is "teaching." This would apply not only to the pastor, who teaches the Word of God from the pulpit, but also to all Sunday school teachers. Everyone who has this assignment in the church should ask God to give him (or her) a special gift for teaching, and then should do his best in carrying out this function.

The fourth gift is "exhortation" (v. 8). "Exhorting"—the Greek word also means "comforting" or "encouraging"—is something different from teaching. But both functions are essential in the church. We not only need to be taught from God's Word what we should do, but we need someone to exhort us to do it.

The fifth gift belongs to the one "that giveth." The Greek verb means to "share." The one who shares should do it "with simplicity." Probably a better translation is "generously" or "liberally." We are told that God loves a liberal giver. One of the best ways to dry up our Christian experience is to be stingy or miserly in our giving.

The sixth gift belongs to one "that ruleth." The verb means to "preside" or "govern." The one who has this responsibility must exercise it with "diligence." The Greek word means "zeal" or "earnestness." It is a real challenge: "Whoever has authority, must work hard" (TEV).

The seventh and last gift is showing mercy. The recipient of this gift must exercise it with "cheerfulness." The Greek word (only here in the New Testament) is *hilarotes*, from which we get *hilarity*. We should show mercy not grudgingly or sparingly, but joyfully.

Are we always cheerful and joyful in the work of the Lord? This is a real test of our Christian character. And it affects greatly our effectiveness in what we do.

C. Sincere Love: v. 9

"Without dissimulation" is one word in Greek, *anhypocritos*—literally "un-hypocritical." In Greek a *hypocrites* was one who wore a mask, who had a false face. True love is not something put on to impress people. It is sincere love, coming from the heart that God has filled with His love.

The next part of the verse seems at first glance to be unrelated to the first part. But we cannot have sincere love in our hearts unless we hate evil. Only the pure heart can be the love-filled heart.

"Abhor" is a strong compound in Greek, *apostygeo*. It means to hate a thing so that one turns completely away from it and "cleave" literally means "be glued." We cannot "cleave" to the good until we "abhor" the evil. To be cemented to what is good we must first be separated from what is bad. If we are unwilling to forsake evil, we can never be good.

D. Brotherly Love: v. 10

"Be kindly affectioned" is one word in Greek, *philostorgoi* (only here in the New Testament). It is an adjective meaning "tenderly loving." True Christians all belong to one family, and so they should have tender love toward each other.

This tender love is to be shown in "brotherly love" (Greek, *philadelphia*). In Paul's day, Philadelphia was the name of the city that is now Amman, capital of the Jordan Kingdom. In modern times the name was optimistically given to a city in Pennsylvania (Penn's Woods). But the high hopes of the Quaker colonist, William Penn, have hardly been fulfilled in the twentieth century. Granted! But how about "brotherly love" in our local churches, as well as in our homes?

"In honour preferring one another." How many of us really prac-

tice this? It is a constant challenge to our Christian love.

III. THE CHRISTIAN'S SPIRITUAL LIFE:
Romans 12:11-13

In these three verses, which come between the two sections of our printed lesson, we have a series of brief, epigramatic commands or exhortations. Due to lack of space, we can only glance at them.

A. Fervent in Spirit: v. 11

"Not slothful in business" is literally "not hesitating in earnestness." The adjective "fervent" is *zeontes*, literally, "boiling hot." We are not to be lukewarm in our spirits, as was the church at Laodicea. In everything we are to be serving the Lord as His "love-slaves."

B. Persistent in Prayer: v. 12

We can only rejoice in hope and hold steady in tribulation—as the Greek says—if we are persevering in prayer. "Continuing instant" is one word, meaning "continue steadfastly."

C. Generous in Giving: v. 13

"Distributing" basically means "sharing," *koinoneo*. "Fellowship" and "sharing" are the same in the Greek,

---

DISCUSSION QUESTIONS

1. How can one make a complete commitment to Christ?
2. How can we be "a living sacrifice"?
3. How can we renew our thinking?
4. What does the transfigured life involve?
5. What responsibility do we have to fellow Christians?
6. How do we demonstrate our Christianity to those outside?

koinonia. A spirit of sharing, both materially and spiritually, builds fellowship. Hospitality was more needed then than now, but it still has a place in the church.

IV. THE CHRISTIAN AND OTHERS: Romans 12:14-18

A. Kindness and Concern: vv. 14-15

Verse 14 echoes Jesus' command in the Sermon on the Mount (Matthew 5:44). It takes God's grace in the heart to do this. How do we react to persecution?

Verse 15 presents a basic principle of Christian love and fellowship. We get closer to people when we enter into their joys and sorrows with them. This builds Christian unity and mutual support.

B. Unity and Humility: vv. 16-17

The first clause of verse 16 is literally "thinking the same thing toward each other." Instead of parading our differences and making a sharp issue of them, we should seek unity of thought and purpose, subordinating our own desires to those of our fellow Christians in humble love. Humility is an essential foundation for unity.

"Condescend to men of low estate" can just as accurately be translated, "Be content with simple things" (or, "lowly duties"). The problem is that we cannot tell whether the Greek is masculine or neuter, as the form here is used for both. Since we have no way of being sure as to which meaning was intended, why not accept both interpretations? They both have meaningful applications. We should be willing to associate with humble people and we should also be content with simple things.

We are not to "recompense" (pay back) evil for evil. But we are to "pro-vide good things before all men" (literal Greek).

C. Peace with All Men: v. 18

This verse has often been abused by professing Christians. When confronted with it they say, "Yes, but it doesn't lie in me to live at peace with so-and-so!"

We cannot hide behind this selfish alibi. Actually, the Greek does not say "as much as lieth in you," but "whatever is from you." The correct meaning, then, is that no quarreling is to come from our side. We cannot keep people from fussing and even fuming at us. But we can refuse to add fuel to the flames by replying in the same way.

V. THE CHRISTIAN AND HIS ENEMIES: Romans 12:19-21

Again Paul warns against seeking revenge on those who hurt us. Rather, he says, "give place unto wrath." This statement can easily be misunderstood. To "give way to anger" is our idiom for expressing anger. Just the opposite is meant here. There is almost universal agreement that this passage means "make way for *God's* wrath." The quotation at the end of the verse (from Deuteronomy 32:35) proves that this is the correct meaning. It is God's business to punish, not ours.

Instead we are to be kind and generous toward our enemies. But we should watch out that we do not take unholy delight in heaping "coals of fire" on their heads!

Verse 21 gives one of the greatest secrets of victorious Christian living. Instead of being overcome by evil, we should overcome evil by good. Whenever Satan tries to fill our minds with unclean or unkind thoughts, we should immediately begin to think of something good, beautiful, and uplifting.

CONTEMPORARY APPLICATION

Some years ago Queen Elizabeth of Britain was finishing a long day of public appearances. For hours she had stood in her high heels, with no chance to rest.

Finally came the last appointment.

It was at a school for deaf mutes. Weary, she sagged a bit. Prince Philip looked over at her and said encouragingly, "Perk up, my cabbage."

Immediately the children broke into gales of laughter. They had read the prince's lips!

That became a slogan at our house, when either of us felt a bit "down." How about perking each other up?

May 23, 1976

THE CHALLENGE OF DRUGS AND ALCOHOL

(Temperance)

DEVOTIONAL READING	Psalm 1
ADULTS	Topic: The Problem of Drugs and Alcohol Background Scripture: I Corinthians 6:9-20; Galatians 5:13-26 Scripture Lesson: I Corinthians 6:9-20 Memory Verse: *Do you not know that your body is a temple of the Holy Spirit within you, which you have from God? You are not your own; you were bought with a price. So glorify God in your body.* I Corinthians 6:19-20
YOUTH	Topic: *Taking Care of Yourself* Background Scripture: I Corinthians 6:9-20; Galatians 5:13-26 Scripture Lesson: I Corinthians 6:9-20 Memory Verse: *"All things are lawful for me,"* ... *but I will not be enslaved by anything.* I Corinthians 6:12
CHILDREN	Topic: *Growing in Self-Control* Background Scripture: Galatians 5:13-26; Philippians 4:8 Scripture Lesson: Galatians 5:13-26 Memory Verse: *Whatever is true, whatever is honorable, whatever is just, whatever is pure, whatever is lovely, whatever is gracious, if there is any excellence, if there is anything worthy of praise, think about these things.* Philippians 4:8
DAILY BIBLE READINGS	Mon., May 17: Christian Circumspection, Ephesians 5:18-21. Tues., May 18: Not Retaliation but Kindness, I Peter 3:8-12. Wed., May 19: Justified by Faith, Galatians 3:21-26. Thurs., May 20: Sanctity of the Body, I Corinthians 3:16-20. Fri., May 21: Christian Calling, I Corinthians 7:22-24. Sat., May 22: Exhortation to Holiness, I Peter 1:13-19. Sun., May 23: Fruits of the Spirit, Galatians 5:22-26.
LESSON AIM	To gain a Christian concept of the body as intended to be a temple of the Holy Spirit.

LESSON SETTING

Time: I Corinthians was written about A.D. 55.

Place: It was written at Ephesus.

The Challenge of Drugs and Alcohol

I. **The Unrighteous and the Redeemed:** I Corinthians 6:9-11
   A. Sexual Immorality: v. 9
   B. Criminal Immorality: v. 10
   C. The Redeemed: v. 11

II. **Answering Opponents:** I Corinthians 6:12-13
   A. All Things Are Lawful: v. 12
   B. Food for the Stomach: v. 13

LESSON OUTLINE

III. **The Sacredness of the Body:** I Corinthians 6:14-18
   A. Joined to Christ: vv. 14-17
   B. The Seriousness of Immorality: v. 18

IV. **The Body as the Temple of the Spirit:** I Corinthians 6:19-20
   A. A Sacred Sanctuary: v. 19
   B. For the Glory of God: v. 20

V. **Life in the Spirit, Not the Flesh:** Galatians 5:13-26
   A. Liberty, Not License: vv. 13-15
   B. Walking in the Spirit: vv. 16-18
   C. The Works of the Flesh: vv. 19-21
   D. The Fruit of the Spirit: vv. 22-23
   E. Life in the Spirit: vv. 24-26

SUGGESTED INTRODUCTION FOR ADULTS

What can adults do about drugs and alcohol? This question has been discussed considerably in recent years.

Let's take alcohol first. As long as parents drink alcoholic beverages in the home, they have no right to complain if their children become cynical and go on drugs. Drinking is causing the death of about thirty thousand people on our highways each year. It is responsible for countless millions of dollars being spent on welfare for families with drunk fathers. How can children have respect for drinking parents, when they know what alcohol is doing to our nation? To them it is all hypocrisy.

What about drugs? Perhaps some parents should take a look at their own drug habits—daily doses of aspirin, sleeping tablets, etc. If we would all give more attention to proper eating and exercise, we could eliminate some of this and set a better example to our children.

These are days that call for honesty, understanding, common sense, and prayerful seeking for guidance in our life patterns. We must lead our young people in the right way.

SUGGESTED
INTRODUCTION
FOR YOUTH

Why do young people go on drugs? Probably there is a variety of reasons—boredom, curiosity, desire for thrills, effort to find "kicks," etc. But every informed person knows that the end of the drug trail has been disaster and destruction.

The only safe way for young people is to make a firm, unchangeable resolve that they will never touch drugs or alcohol. If one never takes a glass of liquor, he will never get drunk. If one never touches drugs, he will never be "hooked." Let's lock the door on it all!

CONCEPTS FOR
CHILDREN

1. To live happy lives we have to discipline ourselves.
2. We must learn to say No to temptation.
3. Glue-sniffing may seem harmless, but it can be fatal.
4. It's better to be safe than sorry.

THE LESSON COMMENTARY

I. THE UNRIGHTEOUS AND THE REDEEMED:
I Corinthians 6:9-11

A. Sexual Immorality: v. 9

Paul makes a flat statement: "The unrighteous shall not inherit the kingdom of God." He is a righteous God and only righteous people—those who are right with Him and live upright lives—can be in His kingdom.

Then the apostle lists some of the forms of unrighteous living that will bar a person from the Kingdom. All those named in this verse are related to sexual immorality. Today we would say: "the sexually immoral . . . idolaters . . . adulterers . . . male prostitutes . . . homosexual offenders" (NIV). It is a dark picture, but one that correctly represents too much of our society today. In these days when leading denominations are ordaining to the ministry men who openly claim to be homosexuals, it is time we took a fresh look at God's Word. Both the Old and New Testaments firmly condemn homosexuality as sin. For practicing homosexuals to claim to be children of God, as many do, is sheer blasphemy. This sin was very common in the first century, when Christ first came, and its startling increase in the

twentieth century could well be one of the signs of the Second Coming.

B. Criminal Immorality: v. 10

Unfortunately, the sins mentioned in verse 9 have pretty well ceased to be crimes in the United States and Europe. But in God's sight they are just as serious as are those we read about in this verse.

Today we would call these people "thieves . . . greedy . . . drunkards . . . slanderers . . . swindlers" (NIV). The first class and the last two classes are considered criminals. And their number is increasing today, as recent events have revealed.

C. The Redeemed: v. 11

The apostle reminds his readers: "And that is what some of you were" (NIV). The city of Corinth, where these people lived, was notoriously wicked. In fact, the Greeks had coined a word, the equivalent of "Corinthianize," which meant to corrupt morally. Corinth was a great center of trade, the main port between Ephesus (Asia) on the east and Italy on the west. Its streets were filled with sailors and merchantmen from all over the Mediterranean. As usually happens in such situations, too many houses were filled with sin. That is why Paul had to speak so pointedly on these matters in writing to the Corinthian church. A bad case of immorality was being tolerated within its membership (5:1). The situation called for stern, rugged morality (5:3-5). Paul warns his readers against all kinds of immorality.

Though some of the Corinthian Christians had been victims of their surroundings, Paul could now assure them: "But you were washed, you were sanctified, you were justifed in the name of the Lord Jesus Christ and by the Spirit of our God" (NIV).

"Sanctified" (*hegiasthete*) and "justified" (*edikaiothete*) are inverted from their usual order. J. J. Lias makes this helpful suggestion: "It is best to take *hegiasthete* in the sense of *dedicated to a holy life* (*halowed*, Wiclif) . . . and *edikaiothete* as referring to the actual righteousness of life which is brought about by union with Christ through the operation of the Holy Spirit" (*First Epistle to the Corinthians*, p. 75). Perhaps Paul puts "sanctified" first to emphasize the strong contrast with their former life of immorality.

II. ANSWERING OPPONENTS: I Corinthians 6:12-13

A. All Things Are Lawful: v. 12

The words "All things are lawful unto me" should be put in quotation marks. Paul is not expressing his own opinion but quoting his opponents. This was a typical libertine attitude: "Everything is permissible for me" (NIV). It was what many of the Corinthians were saying so long ago, but it sounds hauntingly familiar in our modern permissive society, where "everything goes."

Paul twice quoted this false statement, only to repudiate it. First he declared, "But not everything is beneficial" (NIV). Then he went a step further and said, "But I will not be brought under the power of any." The apostle acknowledged only Christ as Lord of his life. He refused to be enslaved by anything in this world that would threaten Christ's complete lordship.

B. Food for the Stomach: v. 13

In this verse the apostle quoted another carnal, materialistic slogan of his opponents. They were saying, "Food for the stomach, and the stomach for food" (NIV). His rejoinder to this was, "But God will destroy them both."

Then he zeroed in on the besetting sin of the Corinthians: "Now the body is not for fornication, but for the Lord; and the Lord for the body." It must be remembered that "fornication" includes adultery and all other forms of sexual immorality, as well as what is technically called "fornication."

Our bodies are given to us to use only in ways that will please the Lord, not for breaking His laws and bringing disgrace to His name. Christ must be Lord of our bodies, or He is not Lord of all. There is a very real sense in which man's soul and body cannot be divorced; they form one personality.

III. THE SACREDNESS OF THE BODY: I Corinthians 6:14-18

A. Joined to Christ: vv. 14-17

The apostle now relates the body—created and owned by Christ—to the resurrection. Just as God raised up His Son, so He will also raise us. Vincent comments: "The body being destined to share with the body of Christ in resurrection, and to be raised up incorruptible, is the subject of a higher adaptation, with which fornication is incompatible" (*Word Studies in the New Testament*, III, 216).

Charles W. Carter writes: "In verse 14 Paul clinches his argument of the preceding verse with reference to the resurrection of Christ as the assurance of man's resurrection. It is not the stomach, or the physical nature of man, that will live on, but rather the spiritual person who is immortal. Thus the perishable physical nature of man can never be equated with the imperishable spiritual personality" (*Wesleyan Bible Commentary*, V, 163).

Still attacking the loose, prevalent immorality of Corinth, Paul reminds his readers: "Your bodies are the members of Christ" (v. 15). We belong to Christ and are united to Him—in both body and soul. Should we then "take the members of Christ, and make them the members of an harlot?"

Emphatically the apostle answers, "God forbid." The Greek *me genoito* literally means, "May it not be!" It is a strong exclamation and may be translated, "By no means" or simply, "Never!" (RSV, NIV).

Paul goes on to say, "Do you not know that he who unites himself with a prostitute is one with her in body?" (v. 16, NIV). To support this statement he quotes from Genesis 2:24: In the marriage relation the husband and wife become "one flesh." So the man who has sexual relations with a prostitute becomes one with her in body. A Christian, who is united to Christ, cannot do this. In fact, no married man can do it without in a real sense breaking his marriage. Contrary to the popular attitude today, adultery is one of the most serious sins that a man can commit. Yet it has ceased to be a crime in "civilized" countries.

The Christian is united to the Lord and so becomes "one spirit" with Him (v. 17). The word for "joined" in verses 16 and 17 is literally "glued." It suggests a strong, firm attachment. We must not get "stuck" by allowing ourselves to be glued to the wrong person or thing. Rather, we should be strongly glued to the Lord by a love of full loyalty.

B. The Seriousness of Immorality: v. 18

Urgently Paul admonishes his readers: "Flee fornication" (v. 18). Why? Because while other sins, such as lying and stealing, are "without" (that is,

"outside") the body, sexual immorality involves the physical and so is a sin against one's body.

IV. THE BODY AS THE TEMPLE OF THE SPIRIT: I Corinthians 6:19-20

A. A Sacred Sanctuary: v. 19

This is one of the most important verses in this Epistle. It gives the highest possible concept of the human body: It is the "temple"—*naos*, "sanctuary"—of the Holy Spirit who dwells in us. One who faces up honestly to this fact could never prostitute his body to low living. Our body is a sacred trust from God. As the sanctuary of His Spirit it must be kept clean and holy. Temples are sacred buildings, and so our bodies must be treated as sacred.

The one who accepts this concept of his body is not going to poison it with alcohol or nicotine. He will not take drugs that he knows will do it harm. Nor will he defile it with immoral conduct. To do any of these things is to deny the fact that we belong to God as His holy temple. We need to keep this constantly in mind.

B. For the Glory of God: v. 20

"Ye are not your own" (v. 19) should go with this verse: "You are not your own; you were bought at a price" (NIV). Since we do not belong to ourselves but to God, we must do what He wants with our bodies, not what we might wish.

So Paul admonishes us: "Therefore glorify God in your body," since it is His sacred property. The rest of the verse, "and in your spirit, which are God's" (KJV), is not in any of the early Greek manuscripts. It was added in the Middle Ages, when Gnosticism had pervaded the church with the heretical teaching that all matter is evil; only spirit is good. Therefore the body is essentially evil and always will be. So the true command of this verse was "toned down" by adding, "and in your spirit." But we are to glorify God in our bodies, which are His sacred temple, and so must be kept holy.

V. LIFE IN THE SPIRIT, NOT THE FLESH:
Galatians 5:13-26

A. Liberty, Not License: v. 13-15

As Christians we have liberty in Christ. But we are not to use this liberty "for an occasion to the flesh," to do as we please. Our liberty must be controlled by love. For all the law, Paul says, is fulfilled in one command, "Love your neighbor as yourself." If Christians keep on biting and devouring each other, they will be destroyed by each other.

B. Walking in the Spirit: vv. 16-18

The only way to keep from fulfilling the desires of the flesh is to keep on walking in the Spirit. Walking in the Spirit means obeying the Spirit's promptings and prohibitions.

The King James Version suggests that the Holy Spirit "lusts." This sounds almost blasphemous. The Greek says: "For the flesh longs against the Spirit, and the Spirit against the flesh." The flesh longs to do what is contrary to God's will, while the Spirit longs to free us from what the flesh would have us do.

C. The Works of the Flesh: vv. 19-21

Paul declares that "the works of the flesh are manifest"—and they certainly are in these 1970s! Then he enumerates them.

This long list of the deeds of the flesh may be divided into four parts, as indicated by the punctuation in the New International Version. The first part consists of matters of sex: "sexual immorality, impurity and debauchery." The second relates to superstition: "idolatry and witchcraft." The third describes wrong attitudes: "hatred, discord, jealousy, fits of rage, selfish ambition, dissensions, factions and envy." The fourth describes too much of the life of that day and our day: "drunkenness, orgies, and the like."

Every one of these "works of the flesh" is divisive—divisive of countries, communities, churches, homes, and hearts. The sinful "flesh" is the ultimate source of all the evils in the world.

D. The Fruit of the Spirit: vv. 22-23

It would be hard to conceive of a greater contrast than one finds here between "the works of the flesh" and "the fruit of the Spirit." The former bring division; the latter brings unity.

John Wesley makes the cogent observation that the first item here, "love," is "the root of all the rest" (*Explanatory Notes*, p. 697). That is, love is the root that produces all the fruit. This makes good Scriptural sense, for the Holy Spirit is God, and "God is love" (I John 4:8, 16). If our hearts are filled with the Holy Spirit, they are filled with love. That is what will generate joy, peace, and the other fruit named here. Perhaps that is why the verb here is singular. "The fruit of the Spirit is love," which manifests itself in joy, peace, etc.

Someone has said that "joy is the echo of God's life within us" and that "joy is the reflection of spiritual

---

DISCUSSION QUESTIONS

1. How can we keep our young people from drugs and alcohol?
2. In what ways can the church minister to this problem?
3. How do we avoid living fleshly lives?
4. What does it mean to "walk in the Spirit"?
5. Why is negativism alone not enough?
6. What are some conditions of fruit-growing?

health in the soul." The Old Testament says, "The joy of the Lord is your strength" (Nehemiah 8:10). A joyless Christian is a weak Christian.

What is "peace"? It has been defined as "the consciousness of adequate resources to meet all the emergencies of life." When one knows that he has adequate resources for whatever may happen, he is not nervous or jittery; he is at peace.

"Longsuffering" is something that all of us will need as long as we live or work with other people. The best of people differ so much in tastes and temperament that they have to be patient with each other.

"Gentleness" is symbolized by the dove, and it was in the form of a dove that the Holy Spirit descended on Jesus at His baptism. The Gentle Dove will make us gentle, if we allow Him to. The Greek word here may also be translated "kindness."

"Goodness" is a central virtue in Christian character. But goodness is more than the absence of evil. A person is not good because of what he does not do or does not say. It is not a negative, but a positive virtue. Charles R. Erdman has given an excellent definition. He says, " 'Good-

ness' is love in action" (*Epistle of Paul to the Galatians*, p. 112).

"Faith" should be "faithfulness." The Holy Spirit will help us to be faithful to our rightful responsibilities.

"Meekness" isn't weakness. It is strength under control. Erdman writes of this: "It does not necessarily denote a low conception of one's own abilities, but it is the state of mind which is submissive to the will of God and is unselfish in view of the needs and claims of others" (*Galatians*, p. 113).

"Temperance" should be translated "self-control." This is one of the most important factors in successful Christian living.

E. Life in the Spirit: vv. 24-26

Paul goes on to say that those who belong to Christ "have crucified the flesh with the affections and lusts" (v. 24)—Greek: "its passions and desires."

In verse 25 the apostles says, "If we live in the Spirit, let us also walk in the Spirit." The Greek word for "walk" here is not the one that Paul usually has, *peripateo*. Rather, it is *stoicheo*, which means to "go step by step." So the second clause is best translated, "Let us keep in step with the Spirit."

CONTEMPORARY APPLICATION

It goes without saying that we live in a day of alcohol, drugs, and sex. But it is not enough to avoid all these evils in our lives. If we are going to be fully Christian we must live in the Spirit, letting Him grow in our hearts the

fruit of the Spirit. As the nine virtues enumerated here appear in our lives their true worth will be seen. They are Christ's substitutes for drugs and alcohol.

THE HEALING COMMUNITY

DEVOTIONAL READING	James 5:7-20

ADULTS

Topic: *The Greater Family*

Background Scripture: Romans 14:13—15:6; Galatians 6:1-10

Scripture Lesson: Galatians 6:1-10

Memory Verse: *We who are strong ought to bear with the failings of the weak, and not to please ourselves; let each of us please his neighbor for his good, to edify him.* Romans 15:1-2

YOUTH

Topic: *Youth in the Community of Faith*

Background Scripture: Romans 14:13—15:6; Galatians 6:1-10

Scripture Lesson: Galatians 6:1-10

Memory Verse: *We who are strong ought to bear with the failings of the weak, and not to please ourselves; let each of us please his neighbor for his good, to edify him.* Romans 15:1-2

CHILDREN

Topic: *Caring for One Another*

Background Scripture: Romans 13:8-10; Galatians 6:1-10

Scripture Lesson: Galatians 6:1-7, 10

Memory Verse: *Owe no one anything, except to love one another; for he who loves his neighbor has fulfilled the law.* Romans 13:8

DAILY BIBLE READINGS

Mon., May 24: Support the Weak, I Peter 4:8-10.
Tues., May 25: Be Sympathetic, Galatians 6:2-5.
Wed., May 26: Be Children of the Light, Ephesians 5:6-13.
Thurs., May 27: Do Not Be Weary in Well-doing, Galatians 6:9-10.
Fri., May 28: Be Alert, Strive for Perfection, II Timothy 3:13-17.
Sat., May 29: Stewardship of the Gospel, I Timothy 6:18-21.
Sun., May 30: Be Concerned, Romans 14:13-21.

LESSON AIM

To see how the church can be a healing community.

LESSON SETTING

Time: Galatians was written about A.D. 48 or 54.

Place: Unknown

LESSON OUTLINE

The Healing Community

I. The Practice of Christian Charity: Romans 14:13-23

II. Living for Others, Not Self: Romans 15:1-6
   A. Helping the Weak: v. 1
   B. Pleasing Our Neighbor: vv. 2-4
   C. Maintaining Unity: vv. 5-6

III. Compassion for Fellow Christians: Galatians 6:1-5
   A. Restoring the Fallen: v. 1
   B. Bearing Other's Burdens: v. 2
   C. Keeping Humble: v. 3
   D. Testing Our Own Work: v. 4
   E. Carrying Our Own Load: v. 5

IV. Supporting the Ministry: Galatians 6:6

V. Reaping What We Sow: Galatians 6:7-8
   A. The Warning: v. 7
   B. The Encouragement: v. 8

VI. Doing Good to All: Galatians 6:9-10
   A. Reaping in Due Season: v. 9
   B. Caring Especially for Fellow Christians: v. 10

SUGGESTED INTRODUCTION FOR ADULTS

Too often we think of the church as a place where people come to hear preaching and get saved so that they will avoid hell and get to heaven. But this is too narrow a concept.

The church should be a community of the concerned. It should be a place where people come to find comfort and strength, and go away helped.

If the church is going to be a healing community, the greatest need is for compassionate, understanding love. The pastor cannot do it all. If the members are criticizing each other and are unconcerned about the spiritual and social needs of those who attend, the church will fail in its function as the body of Christ in this world.

We have hospitals for physical healing and counseling centers for emotional and mental healing. But the church fulfills a unique role as a place where people can find spiritual healing. And for its own members the church should be a place where hurts are healed and hearts are helped—week by week. Let's help to make our own church a healing community.

SUGGESTED INTRODUCTION

What does your church mean to you? Do you find help in the fellowship of the church for the hard places you hit during the week? Is the church a healing community for you?

There is still one more question: Are you helping to make it more of a healing community for others? We must give as well as take. We all have a part to play in making our church what it ought to be. So let's get involved in healing as well as being healed.

1. As Christians we should care for each other.
2. We should try to find ways to show our concern.
3. The church should be one big family.
4. As members of that family we should seek to help.

THE LESSON COMMENTARY

I. THE PRACTICE OF CHRISTIAN CHARITY:
Romans 14:13-23

In the Sermon on the Mount Jesus said, "Don't judge, in order that you may not be judged" (Matthew 7:1, literal translation). Paul echoes this here: "Let us not therefore judge one another any more." Judgment belongs to the great Judge of all the earth, and we should not presume to take over His prerogatives.

Instead of judging others, we are to be careful not to put a "stumbling block" or "an occasion to fall" in our brother's way. The first expression is *proscomma*, which refers to something that causes us to stumble. The second (one word in Greek) is *scandalon*, which means "a snare." We should never do or say anything that will cause a brother to stumble or fall or be caught in a snare. This is a solemn responsibility. We are to be helping people in their Christian life, not hindering them.

Verse 14 harks back to the first part of this chapter. There Paul says that one church member thinks it all right to eat all kinds of food; another—whom he labels as "weak"—is a vegetarian (v. 2). Now he expresses his own conviction that the distinction between clean and unclean foods has been done away in Christ. But then he goes on to say: "If your brother is distressed because of what you eat, you are no longer acting in love. Do not by your eating destroy your brother for whom Christ died" (v. 15, NIV). This is the practice of Christian charity.

Then the apostle states an important principle: "For the kingdom of God is not a matter of eating and drinking, but of righteousness, peace and joy in the Holy Spirit" (v. 17, NIV). True religion is in the spiritual realm, not the material. It is not a matter of outward observance of certain rules and regulations. Rather it is an inward work of the Holy Spirit in our hearts, giving us righteousness, peace, and joy. The curse of false religion, both inside and outside Christianity, is the emphasis on the material rather than the spiritual. This is the snare of legalism.

And so Paul exhorts: "Let us therefore follow after [Greek, "pursue"] the things which make for peace, and things wherewith one may edify [build up] another" (v. 19). We are not to tear each other down with criticism (v. 13) or selfish conduct (v. 15) but to build each other up in love.

And so the apostle says we should avoid doing anything that will cause our brother to fall (v. 21). We must always act in "faith" (v. 23), or we shall be condemned.

II. LIVING FOR OTHERS, NOT SELF:
Romans 15:1-6

A. Helping the Weak: v. 1

"We then that are strong ought to bear the infirmities of the weak, and not to please ourselves." Literally the first part reads: "We the capable ones ought to bear the weaknesses of the incapable ones." Instead of looking down on the weaker members of the church with contempt, or even condescension, we ought to look at them with eyes of compassion and concern. We should put up with their failings and help to strengthen them.

B. Pleasing Our Neighbors: vv. 2-4

Instead of pleasing ourselves, we should seek to please our neighbor "for his good, to build him up" (v. 2, NIV). The Greek word for "edification" is used for the building of a house. To "edify" a person means to "build him up." This should be the goal of all our relationships with others—primarily giving rather than taking.

"For even Christ pleased not himself" is a challenging statement to every Christian. A young fellow who sold Bibles and mottoes to put himself through school told us how he showed to a lady a motto with those words on it. Immediately she reacted with, "No, I don't want that! It would make me feel uncomfortable to have that hanging in my house." She wanted to continue to please herself.

After quoting (v. 3) from Psalm 69:9, Paul reminded his readers that the Old Testament Scriptures were written "to teach us, so that through endurance and the encouragement of the Scriptures we might have hope" (v. 4, NIV). Christ found strength and comfort in the Scriptures, and so can we.

C. Maintaining Unity: vv. 5-6

But this is not an individual matter alone. Paul breaks spontaneously into a prayerful wish: "May the God who gives endurance and encouragement give you a spirit of unity among yourselves as you follow Christ Jesus" (v. 5, NIV). And all this is "that ye may with one mind and one mouth glorify God, even the Father of our Lord Jesus Christ" (v. 6). A spirit of unity in the church brings glory to God. Disunity brings reproach on His name.

III. COMPASSION FOR FELLOW CHRISTIANS:
Galatians 6:1-5

A. Restoring the Fallen: v. 1

In this passage in Galatians, Paul is likewise dealing with the relationships of people in the church. So he addresses his readers as "brethren" and poses a problem: "If a man be overtaken in a fault." The verb here means "detect, overtake, surprise" (Arndt and Gingrich, Lexicon, p. 715). The word for "fault" literally means "a falling beside (the path)." It signifies a "false step, transgression, sin" (p. 627). Paul recognizes the possibility of a Christian falling by the wayside.

What is to be done in such a case? Kick him clear over into the gutter? No! The spiritual ones in the church are to "restore such an one in the spirit of meekness." The Greek word for "restore," katartizo, was used for setting broken bones and mending broken nets. It means to restore something to its former condition. Remember, the church is to be "the healing community." This is one area in which it can fulfill its function. We should not only seek to win the lost to Christ, but we should also be much concerned about restoring an erring brother.

This must be done "in the spirit of meekness," that is, in a gentle manner. Why? "Considering thyself, lest thou also be tempted." The word for "considering" literally means "watching" or "looking out." Everyone of us is subject to temptation. We are warned in the Scriptures: "Let him that thinketh he standeth take heed lest he fall" (I Corinthians 10:12). The realization of our own constant danger should cause us to deal gently with those who err.

B. Bearing Other's Burdens: v. 2

"Bear ye one another's burdens," says Paul, "and so fulfill the law of Christ." That is the law of love, of always seeking to do what is best for others.

The word for "burdens" carries the idea of a heavy weight that is burdensome. That is what temptations are, especially to a new convert. We should help to bear these crushing burdens that threaten to get a young Christian down. We need to stoop and help to lift the pressing weight with him.

The Greek word is also used in the sense of "oppressiveness" or "heaviness" (Liddell-Scott-Jones, *Lexicon*, p. 307). There are times when a spirit of heaviness comes on some Christians. On such occasions we should be quick to help lift the burden with prayerful concern and encouraging words. We are to act as partners in the Christian life, concerned for others as much as we are concerned for ourselves.

C. Keeping Humble: v. 3

This verse states a self-evident truth: If anyone thinks he is something when he is nothing, he is just fooling himself! E. D. Burton notes that the "for" links this with the previous verse and "implies that conceit, thinking one's self to be something more than one really is, tends to make one unwilling to share another's burdens. Conceiving ourselves to have no faults, we have no sympathy with those who have faults and refuse to make their shortcomings any concern of ours" (*Epistle to the Galatians*, p. 330).

When we recall that it is only by the grace of God that we are saved and kept, we realize that there is no place for pride in the Christian life. It is "all of God," all from Christ. "Apart from me you can do nothing," said Jesus to His disciples (John 15:5). And He still says that to us today. Where, then, does pride come in? It is excluded!

D. Testing Our Own Work: v. 4

"But let every man prove his own work." The Greek word for "prove" is the verb *dokimazo*. It was used primarily to describe the testing of metals, to see how good they were. That is the meaning here: "Each man should test his own actions."

Doing that, he will "have rejoicing in himself alone, and not in another." The expression "rejoicing" is literally "his glorying." Burton writes: "The self-deceived man may boast of his superiority to the man who has fallen into a fault, not perceiving his own real condition. He has in reality ground of glorying only in respect to his fellow and his shortcomings. But the man who tests himself has his ground of glorying, whatever that be, in respect to himself" (*Galatians*, p. 332).

E. Carrying Our Own Load: v. 5

At first glance it would seem that this verse conflicts with verse 2. There we are told to bear each other's burdens; here we are told that everyone must bear his own burden.

But the seeming contradiction disappears at once when we realize that two very different Greek words for "burden" are used in these two places. In verse 2, as we have noted, the word for burden, *baros*, meant a crushing weight. The word here, *phortion* comes from the verb *phero*, which means to "carry." So it simply indicates what one normally carries. It was used in classical Greek for a soldier's "pack."

So the proper translation of verse 5 is, "For each man should carry his own load" (NIV). Verse 2 emphasizes the importance of helping those who are overburdened. Verse 5 underscores the responsibility of every man to carry his own proper load in life, not to shirk.

IV. SUPPORTING THE MINISTRY: Galatians 6:6

The word *communicate* in this verse in the King James Version doesn't communicate! To put it plainly, the Greek original has no relation whatever to the current sense of "communicate." The Greek verb simply means to "share."

So the correct rendering is, "Anyone who receives instruction in the word must share all good things with his instructor" (NIV). That is, the one who is being taught spiritual truths should share his material goods with his teacher.

This fits in perfectly with Jesus' words: "The labourer is worthy of his hire" (Luke 10:7). Paul also states this principle clearly: "Even so hath the Lord ordained that they which preach the gospel should live of the gospel" (I Corinthians 9:14). In both of these Epistles it is clearly taught that the minister should be supported by those to whom he ministers.

V. REAPING WHAT WE SOW: Galatians 6:7-8

A. The Warning: v. 7

Earnestly the prophet warns, "Be not deceived!" Then he declares, "God is not mocked." The Greek verb is a strong word. Literally it means "to turn up one's nose," and so "to sneer at." If we think we can sneer at God and win out in the end, we are only fooling ourselves. No man mocks God and gets away with it—permanently.

The second half of the verse enunciates an important principle of life: "For whatsoever a man soweth, that shall he also reap." The figure here suggests two statements of fact. The first is: We reap what we sow. If we sow wheat in one field, we know that we will reap wheat. If we sow oats in another field, we know that we will reap oats. And if we sow wild oats in life, we will reap wild oats—and the reaping will be bitter! We cannot escape reaping what we sow.

But there is also another fact, which is even more significant: We reap more than what we sow. If we sow a bushel of wheat, we expect several bushels in return. If we sow a bushel of oats, we look for large returns. And if we sow our wild oats, the crop will be unendurably great. Using a slightly different figure, Hosea said, "They have sown the wind, they shall reap the whirlwind" (Hosea 8:7).

But there is a good side to this. If we sow good deeds in love, we shall also reap a bountiful harvest—and it will be a glorious reward. In the ninth chapter of II Corinthians Paul is pleading with the church at Corinth to give a generous offering for the poor saints at Jerusalem. He makes this observation: "He which soweth sparingly shall reap also sparingly; and he which soweth bountifully shall reap also bountifully" (II Corinthians 9:6). If we are stingy with God, we only cheat ourselves. If we want abundance of blessing from God, we should give generously to His work.

B. The Encouragement: v. 8

Sowing can be of two kinds, and we choose which it will be. If we sow to the flesh, we will reap corruption. But if we sow to the Spirit, He will give us life everlasting.

This should be an encouragement

DISCUSSION QUESTIONS

1. What should be our attitude toward a weak brother?
2. What attitudes are harmful? helpful?
3. What are some "burdens" of others that we should carry?
4. What are some ways in which a church can become a healing community?
5. Why should ministers be supported?
6. What obligations do we have to our fellow Christians?

to us. We can spend our lifetime sowing good seed by the help of the Holy Spirit, and reap an abundant crop of blessing. And the best part of it is that we shall keep on reaping a reward from it throughout eternity. For we don't see all the results of our labors while we are in this life. The sowing ends at death, or the Second Coming, but the reaping lasts forever.

VI. DOING GOOD TO ALL: Galatians 6:9-10

A. Reaping in Due Season: v. 9

Paul urges us not to "be weary in well doing." Why not? Because "in due season we shall reap, if we faint not"—"if we do not give up" (NIV). It will pay us to persist in well doing, for the rewards will be far beyond anything we can imagine down here. So we must not get discouraged and quit; we must keep on to the end. "In due season," in God's appointed time, we will reap an abundant reward.

B. Caring Especially for Fellow Christians: v. 10

As opportunity affords, we are to do good to all men for we have an obligation to all men as our brothers in the human race. But we have a special responsibility toward our brothers in Christ, for they belong to our family— the family of God. We should try to reach out a helping hand to anyone in need. But we should especially seek to give a healing touch to those "who are of the household of faith"—"those who belong to the family of believers" (NIV). It is an accepted principle of society that each person has a primary obligation to his own family.

CONTEMPORARY APPLICATION

There is a real sense in which we are either helping or harming each person that we meet in a vital way. We either have a healing influence or a hurting influence. If we scowl at people and take a harsh, judgmental attitude toward them, we are hurting them. If we smile at them and speak a pleasant, encouraging word, we are helping to heal them. Which are we doing?

THE BIBLE AND CHURCH HISTORY

DAYS OF BEGINNING

DEVOTIONAL READING	Joel 2:28-32
ADULTS	Topic: *Days of Beginning* Background Scripture: Matthew 16:18; Luke 1:1-4; Acts 1–2 Scripture Lesson: Acts 1:1-2; 2:22-32 Memory Verse: *On this rock I will build my church, and the powers of death shall not prevail against it.* Matthew 16:18
YOUTH	Topic: *Starting Point!* Background Scripture: Matthew 16:18; Luke 1:1-4; Acts 1–2 Scripture Lesson: Acts 1:1-2; 2:22-32 Memory Verse: *On this rock I will build my church, and the powers of death shall not prevail against it.* Matthew 16:18
CHILDREN	Topic: *The Church Begins* (see lesson for February 22, 1976) Background Scripture: Matthew 16:16-20; Acts 1–2 Scripture Lesson: Acts 2:37-42 Memory Verse: *You are the Christ, the Son of the Living God.* Matthew 16:16
DAILY BIBLE READINGS	Mon., May 31: The Departure of Jesus, Acts 1:6-11. Tues., June 1: Appointment of a New Apostle, Acts 1:15-26. Wed., June 2: Ancient Promise of the Spirit, Joel 2:28-32. Thurs., June 3: Arrival of the Spirit, Acts 2:1-4. Fri., June 4: The Miracle of Tongues, Acts 2:5-13. Sat., June 5: Peter's Explanation, Acts 2:14-21. Sun., June 6: The Church Begins to Grow, Acts 2:41-47.
LESSON AIM	To seek to recapture some of the spirit of the early church in its dependence on the Holy Spirit.
LESSON SETTING	Time: June of A.D. 30 Place: Jerusalem

Days of Beginning

LESSON OUTLINE

SUGGESTED INTRODUCTION FOR ADULTS

The general topic of the lessons this quarter is "The Bible and Church History." The study is divided into three units corresponding to the three major periods of church history in the West.

Unit I covers the Apostolic Age (first century), as recorded in the New Testament, and the next four centuries of Christian history. It was a period of the development of both doctrine and organization, together with the settlement of the canon of the New Testament.

Unit II covers the Medieval Period (A.D. 500-1500). There was some missionary expansion, the rise of the monastic system, and a few pre-Reformation attempts to reform the church. But it was the least fruitful thousand years of church history.

Unit III deals with the Modern Period, from the Reformation to the present. Here we have the Protestant Reformation in the sixteenth century, the Evangelical Reformation of the eighteenth century, and the great expansion of world missions and Bible translation in the nineteenth and twentieth centuries.

SUGGESTED INTRODUCTION FOR YOUTH

How did the church start? That is what we study about in today's lesson. We have first the declaration of Jesus: "On this rock [Peter's confession of His deity] I will build my church." Then we find that the four Gospels were written as records of Christ's redeeming ministry. Finally we find the beginning of the church described in the first two chapters of Acts.

In later lessons this quarter we shall glance at the church's development down across the centuries. It will help us to understand our church today.

CONCEPTS FOR
CHILDREN

1. The church was founded by Jesus Christ, the Son of God.
2. It actually began with the coming of the Holy Spirit on the Day of Pentecost.
3. It began with prayer in an upper room.
4. It grew with the power of the Holy Spirit.

THE LESSON COMMENTARY

I. CHRIST THE FOUNDER OF THE CHURCH:
Matthew 16:18

We have already looked at this verse in our lesson for February 22. So we shall glance at it only briefly at this time.

At Caesarea Philippi the apostle Peter had confessed: "Thou art the Christ [the Messiah], the Son of the Living God" (v. 16). Jesus commended him (v. 17) and then said: "Upon this rock I will build my church" (v. 18). The rock foundation of the church is the deity of Jesus, which Peter had just confessed. Christ is both the Founder and the Foundation of the church.

II. ORIGIN OF THE GOSPEL OF LUKE:
Luke 1:1-4

Luke is the leading historian of the apostolic church. And so he follows the pattern of Greek historians in telling us why he wrote and how he made his preparation for the task.

He begins by saying that many had already undertaken to write an account of the ministry of Jesus (v. 1). Evidently he was not satisfied with these and felt that a more thorough job should be done.

Luke intimates that he himself had not seen and followed Jesus. For he says that the facts had been handed down to him by those who were eyewitnesses from the beginning (v. 2). The tradition is that Luke was a Greek, perhaps the only Gentile writer of a book of the Bible, and so had received his information from those who knew Jesus. Like Paul, he came into the church after Pentecost.

"Having had perfect understanding of all things from the very first" (v. 3, KJV) misses the real point here. The correct translation of the Greek is: "Since I myself have carefully investigated everything from the beginning" (NIV). He did not have firsthand knowledge of Jesus' life. So he carefully investigated what had happened, talking with eyewitnesses who had known Jesus.

Having gathered his information, he says: "It seemed good also to me to write an orderly account for you, most excellent Theophilus, so that you may know the certainty of the things you have been taught" (vv. 3-4, NIV).

The title "most excellent" was that ordinarily given to high Roman officials (Acts 23:26). Since one of Luke's evident purposes was to present to the Roman government a defense of Christianity, it may well be that Theophilus was a Roman of rank.

Theophilus, whose name—perhaps given at his baptism—means "friend of God," had been "taught" or "instructed" (KJV) in the Christian way. The Greek says "catechized." The earliest form of instruction was given by the question and answer method.

It was the custom of Greek writers of that day to dedicate their work to a wealthy patron, who would pay for its publication. Apparently Luke was doing this with Theophilus.

III. INTRODUCTION TO THE BOOK OF ACTS:
Acts 1:1-2

A. Jesus' Works and Words: v. 1

"The former treatise" very clearly refers to the Gospel of Luke. This is shown by the fact that both books are addressed to Theophilus, and it is supported by the very close similarity of style and vocabulary in these two writings. Many Greek words occur in both Luke and Acts, and nowhere else in the New Testament.

Luke says that in his former volume he told of all that Jesus "began to do and teach"—that is, His works and *words*. And that is what we find in the Gospel of Luke. It records many of the miracles that Jesus performed, and especially His healing of the sick. Paul calls Luke "the beloved physician" (Colossians 4:14). Luke was interested in Jesus as the Great Physician, but he also has long sections of Jesus' teaching.

The word "began" here is significant. It implies that Luke is going to tell, in his second volume (Acts), what Jesus *continued* "to do and teach" through His disciples by the power of the Holy Spirit. And that is exactly what we have in the Book of Acts.

B. His Ascension: v. 2

Luke's Gospel carries us right up to the time when Jesus "was taken up." This is the incident with which the Gospel closes (Luke 24:50-53) and with which the Book of Acts practically opens (1:9-11). These are the only two places in the New Testament where the Ascension is described—both times by Luke.

Before He ascended Jesus gave commandments to the apostles he had chosen. Luke says that He did this through the Holy Spirit. All three Synoptic Gospels tell how the Holy Spirit came down in the form of a dove on Jesus at His baptism. Luke says that Jesus "being full of the Holy Spirit returned from Jordan" (Luke 4:1). Later he says that after temptation, "Jesus returned in the power of the Spirit into Galilee." Now we find that "full of the Holy Spirit" is the key phrase of the Book of Acts.

IV. THE FORTY DAYS OF MINISTRY:
Acts 1:3-11

A. The Command: vv. 3-5

After His suffering ("passion") Jesus showed Himself alive to His disciples by many "infallible proofs." This is one word in Greek, a strong term that was used at that time for convincing evidence that would stand up anywhere. The resurrection of Jesus is a well-attested fact, which cannot be denied (I Corinthians 15:3-8).

After His resurrection Jesus appeared to His followers now and then over a period of "forty days." This is the only place where the length of His postresurrection ministry is indicated. From this figure we get ten days in the upper room before Pentecost, which was the Old Testament Feast of Weeks (Exodus 34:22). By the time of Christ it was called by a Greek name, Pentecost ("fiftieth"), because it came fifty days after the Feast of Firstfruits, which symbolized the resurrection.

The command is given in verse 4. The disciples were not to leave Jerusalem but wait there for "the promise of the Father" that Jesus had told them about. This is defined in verse 5: "For John baptized with water, but in a few days you will be baptized with the Holy Spirit" (NIV). The Jews baptized Gentiles who became proseltyes to Judaism, as a sign that their Gentile uncleanness was washed away. John baptized Jews with water, which was a confession that they were unclean before God. But the distinctive baptism that Christ brought was the baptism with the Holy Spirit (cf. Matthew 3:11).

B. The Ascension: vv. 9-11

When Jesus was taken bodily up to heaven, the announcement of His second coming was made: "This same Jesus, which is taken up from you into heaven, shall so come in like manner as ye have seen him go into heaven." That is our blessed hope.

V. THE TEN DAYS OF WAITING: Acts 1:12-26

A. The Upper Room: vv. 12-14

From the Mount of Olives, where the Ascension took place, the disciples went back to Jerusalem, "a sabbath day's journey"—that is, about half a mile. There they went into an upper room where the eleven apostles were living (v. 13). Jesus' mother and brothers joined them there, and they all "continued with one accord in prayer and supplication" (v. 14).

B. The Election of Matthias: vv. 15-26

The number of those waiting prayerfully for the Holy Spirit reached a total of about 120. Finally Peter, as the main spokesman of the apostles, stood up and suggested that they elect a successor to Judas Iscariot, to fill the vacancy in the Twelve. So they nominated two men and by casting lots elected Matthias as apostle.

VI. THE MEANING OF PENTECOST: Acts 2:1-21

The promise of Jesus to His disciples was fulfilled on the day of Pentecost, when "they were all filled with the Holy Ghost" (2:4). This most important event in the Book of Acts—without which that book would never have been written—was accompanied by three symbols. The first was "a sound from heaven as of a rushing mighty wind" (v. 2). The second was "tongues like as of fire" that came to rest on each of the 120 in the upper room (v. 3). The third was the speaking in tongues, "as the Spirit gave them utterance" (v. 4).

These were all signs and symbols of the ministry of the Holy Spirit, who had filled their hearts. The roaring sound was a symbol of *power*. The fire was a symbol of *purity*. Both of these take place when one is filled with the Holy Spirit. The speaking in tongues was a symbol of *proclamation*.

It should be noted that these men did not speak in unknown tongues. In the vast crowd that had assembled for the Feast of Pentecost, "every man heard them speak in his own language" (v. 6). Amazed, the people exclaimed, "How hear we every man in our own tongue, wherein we were born?" (v. 8). But the word here for "tongue" is *dialectos*, "language," the same as in verse 6. After naming fifteen language areas from which they had come (vv. 9-11), the people said, "We do hear them speak in our tongues the wonderful works of God" (v. 11). It is stated very clearly that the disciples on the Day of Pentecost spoke in at least fifteen intelligible languages of that day. These were known languages, not unknown tongues.

When the people asked, "What does this mean?" (v. 12, NIV), Peter said: "This is what was spoken by the prophet Joel" (v. 16). He then quoted Joel 2:28-32. Here "the last days" is taken in its wider sense of the whole Messianic era, reaching from the first coming of Christ to His second coming. God said that He would pour out His Spirit on "all flesh"—Jews and Gentiles, young and old, men and women. Christianity is for all races and classes of people. It is the universal offer of salvation to all who will accept. For "whosoever shall call on the name of the Lord shall be saved" (v. 21). That is the gospel in a nutshell.

VII. THE MESSAGE OF PETER: Acts 2:22-24

A. Jesus' Life: v. 22

Peter declared that Jesus of Nazareth was a man "approved"—"attested" (RSV) or "accredited" (NIV)—to them by "miracles" and "wonders" and "signs." The first of these is *dynameis*, "powerful works." This emphasizes the nature of the miracles. "Wonders" indicates the effect produced; the people were amazed. "Signs" underscores the purpose of the miracles as demonstrating Jesus' deity and signifying some spiritual truth. For instance, Jesus declared, "I am the light of the world" (John 8:12). Then He healed the man born blind as a demonstration of this fact (chap. 9). At the same time, the miracle was symbolical of the fact that Christ brings us out of the darkness of spiritual blindness into His kingdom of light.

Peter asserted that his hearers knew about these miracles—"as ye yourselves also know." So they were without any excuse for rejecting Jesus.

DISCUSSION QUESTIONS

1. Why is the deity of Jesus essential to Christianity?
2. How can we help Christ build His church?
3. Why did the disciples need to be filled with the Spirit?
4. What did this experience do for them?
5. Why was the Resurrection important?
6. What was the significance of the miracles of Jesus?

B. His Death: v. 23

This verse highlights the combination of divine sovereignty and human freedom in actual life. Anyone who denies either one of these is shutting his eyes to what is going on. Jesus was "delivered by the determinate counsel and foreknowledge of God." At the same time, "ye have taken [Him], and by wicked hands [literally, "through the hand of lawless ones," that is, the Romans] have crucified and slain [Him]." God ordained the death of His Son for our salvation. But the leaders who condemned Him to death exercised their freedom of choice in doing so. Otherwise they could not justly be punished for their crime.

C. His Resurrection: v. 24

Men put Jesus to death, "but God raised him from the dead, freeing him from the agony of death, because it was impossible for death to keep its hold on him" (NIV). Even in His incarnation He was God's eternal Son. So the powers of death could not hold Him in the grave. On the third day He rose, triumphant over death.

VIII. THE PROPHECY OF THE RESURRECTION: Acts 2:25-32

A.   David's Words: vv. 25-28

The quotation is from Psalm 16: 8-11. David is rejoicing because the Lord is always before him, at his right hand, so that he will not be shaken ("moved"). Because of this his heart is glad and his tongue rejoices, so that his body lives in hope. Why? "Because you will not abandon me to the grave, nor will you let your Holy One undergo decay" (v. 27, NIV). The Greek word translated "hell" is *Hades*, which means the place of departed spirits, not eternal hell fire. It is the equivalent of the Hebrew *Sheol*, which is translated "grave" sometimes in the Old Testament (KJV). That seems to be the meaning here. So David rejoices:

"You have made known to me the
paths of life;
you will fill me with joy in
your presence"
(v. 28, NIV).

These verses quoted from the
Psalms are beautiful poetry and should
be lined off in poetical form, as they
are in most modern versions. They are
good examples of the main feature of
Hebrew poetry—that is, parallelism of
thought.

B. Their Significance: vv. 29-32

Peter now applies these words of
David to Christ, the Messiah. He calls
attention to the fact that David actually died and was buried and his tomb
was near Jerusalem. So the full import
of these words did not apply to him.
Rather, David was looking forward
prophetically to his great descendant,
the Messiah (v. 30). So he predicted
Christ's resurrection (v. 31).

Then Peter made the contemporary application: "This Jesus hath God
raised up, whereof we all are witnesses" (v. 32). Jesus of Nazareth was
the Messiah of Israel, crucified but resurrected.

One proof of the resurrection was
the fulfillment of Christ's promise that
He would send them the Holy Spirit.
"Shed forth" (v. 33) is not a good
translation. The Greek says, "poured
out." The people were now seeing and
hearing the evidence that the Holy
Spirit had come.

David had not ascended to heaven.
But in Psalm 110:1 he prophesied
that the Father would say to the Son,
"Sit thou on my right hand, until I
make thy foes thy footstool" (vv. 34-
35).

Then Peter reached the conclusion
of his sermon: "Therefore let all the
house of Israel know assuredly, that
God hath made that same Jesus, whom
ye have crucified, both Lord and
Christ" (v. 36). The crucified, resurrected, ascended Christ is now at the
right hand of the Father in glory. He is
the Messiah, the Savior of the world.

Three thousand souls were saved at
the close of Peter's sermon. It was a
great beginning for the Christian
church. Pentecost is usually thought of
as the birthday of the church, and it
was born alive and strong!

CONTEMPORARY APPLICATION

There is a tremendous contrast between the first two chapters of Acts.
In the first chapter the disciples are in
the upper room praying, and Peter, for
better or worse, is conducting an election. But in the second chapter, filled
with the Spirit, they are witnessing

powerfully and Peter is preaching a
sermon that resulted in three thousand
conversions.

What the church of Jesus Christ
most needs today is a fresh outpouring
of the Holy Spirit. That alone will
meet the need of the hour.

June 13, 1976

THE CHURCH ORGANIZES

DEVOTIONAL READING	Ephesians 4:1-16

ADULTS

Topic: *The Church Organizes*

Background Scripture: Acts 6:1-6; Romans 16:1-6; Ephesians 4:11-16; I Timothy 3:1-13

Scripture Lesson: I Timothy 3:1-13

Memory Verse: *His gifts were that some should be apostles, some prophets, some evangelists, some pastors and teachers, for the equipment of the saints, for the work of ministry, for building up the body of Christ.* Ephesians 4:11-12

YOUTH

Topic: *Getting Organized*

Background Scripture: Acts 6:16; Romans 16:1-6; Ephesians 4:11-16; I Timothy 3:1-13

Scripture Lesson: I Timothy 3:1-13

Memory Verse: *His gifts were that some should be apostles, some prophets, some evangelists, some pastors and teachers, for the equipment of the saints, for the work of ministry, for building up the body of Christ.* Ephesians 4:11-12

CHILDREN

Topic: *Everyone Has a Job*

Background Scripture: Acts 6:1-6, 8-15; Romans 16:1-6· Ephesians 4:11-16; I Timothy 3:1-13

Scripture Lesson: Ephesians 4:11-16

Memory Verse: *And his gifts were that some should be apostles, some prophets, some evangelists, some pastors and teachers, for the equipment of the saints, for the work of ministry, for building up the body of Christ.* Ephesians 4:11-12

DAILY BIBLE READINGS

Mon., June 7: The Church Appoints Seven Deacons, Acts 6:1-6.

Tues., June 8: The Lord Calls Another Messenger, Acts 9:1-9.

Wed., June 9: Paul Is Received by the Disciples, Acts 9:10-19.

Thurs., June 10: Two Missionaries Are Appointed, Acts 13:1-5.

Fri., June 11: Additional Missionaries Are Recruited, Acts 15:36-41.

Sat., June 12: Paul Greets Various Workers, Romans 16: 1-6.

Sun., June 13: Diverse Roles in One Body, Ephesians 4:1-16.

LESSON AIM

To see the importance of good organization in the church.

LESSON SETTING

Time: The incident recorded in Acts 6 occurred about A.D. 33. Romans was written in A.D. 56, Ephesians in A.D. 60 and I Timothy about A.D. 63.

Place: Jerusalem. Romans was written in Corinth and Ephesians in Rome. I Timothy, uncertain.

The Church Organizes

I.   Appointment of Seven Helpers: Acts 6:1-6
     A. The Problem: v. 1
     B. A Suggested Solution: vv. 2-4
     C. The Chosen Seven: vv. 5-6

II. Some of Paul's Helpers: Romans 16:1-6

III. Various Workers in the Church: Ephesians 4:11-16
     A. Different Functions: vv. 11-12
     B. All One Body: vv. 13-16

LESSON OUTLINE

IV. Qualifications of an Overseer: I Timothy 3:1-7
     A. High Character: vv. 1-3
     B. Ability to Discipline: vv. 4-5
     C. Mature Experience: v. 6
     D. A Good Reputation: v. 7

V.   Qualifications of Deacons: I Timothy 3:8-13
     A. Good Conduct: vv. 8-9
     B. Experience: v. 10
     C. Godly Wife: v. 11
     D. Ability to Discipline: vv. 12-13

SUGGESTED INTRODUCTION FOR ADULTS

In the ultimate sense, the church of Jesus Christ is an organism. Every part of the organism must be functioning properly if the body is to be healthy.

But the church is also an organization. No new movement can become strong and effective unless it organizes well. It takes organization to have any group of people functioning smoothly and efficiently.

At first there was no organization, no leaders except the apostles whom Jesus had appointed. But in the first part of the lesson today we find that the church had to organize further to meet needs that arose with the passing of time. Later we find a group of elders in every church.

As the church organized properly under the guidance of the Holy Spirit, things ran smoothly and the church was more effective in carrying out its mission. Organization is essential to permanent growth.

SUGGESTED INTRODUCTION FOR YOUTH

Getting organized—that's the need! Many a good idea has disappeared because its sponsors lacked the organization to carry it out.

It's the old story of horse and harness. If there's too much harness and not enough horse, nothing moves. If there's too much horse and not enough harness, the horse may jump around but he doesn't get much work done.

If we are going to have efficient performance, we must have both enthusiasm and organization. This is the winning combination.

CONCEPTS FOR CHILDREN

1. The early church gained by having a division of labor.
2. We should each one find some responsibility in the church.
3. Children can help in many ways.
4. "Everyone has a job"—that's the ideal.

THE LESSON COMMENTARY

I. APPOINTMENT OF SEVEN HELPERS:
Acts 6:1-6

A. The Problem: v. 1

The first problem that confronted the early church was persecution, coming from the outside. This was met by prayer and the power of the Holy Spirit (chaps. 4–5).

But now came a more serious problem, because it was an internal one. The church solved this one effectively by prayer and wise planning. Different problems require different solutions. But always prayer is the key to success.

The membership of the church was growing rapidly. This always creates problems. We are told that "there arose a murmuring." The noun is *gongysmos*, a word whose sound suggests its sense. It was like the buzzing of bees. And when bees begin to swarm noisily, something needs to be done about it before somebody gets stung!

In this case it was Greek-speaking Jews complaining against the Aramaic-speaking community because their widows were being neglected in the daily distribution of food. This was not so much a racial conflict as a cultural one. But it was a delicate situation that needed to be handled carefully, lest the church be split in two.

B. A Suggested Solution: vv. 2-4

Fortunately the apostles had their ears to the ground and heard the murmuring. They took quick action, which was essential. Calling the crowd of disciples together, they said, "It would not be right for us to neglect the ministry of the word of God in order to wait on tables" (v. 2, NIV).

So they suggested that seven men be chosen to take care of this need. (Perhaps there were seven sections in the city.) The apostles, meanwhile, would give themselves to conducting public worship and preaching the Word.

It is very interesting to note the three qualifications they specified for these men: (1) "of honest report," or "of good reputation"; (2) "full of the

Holy Spirit"; (3) full of "widom," or tact. It may seem strange that men who were waiting on tables should have to meet such high qualifications. But the first is obviously essential for all workers in the church. And these men would need to be filled with the Spirit and very tactful in order to take care of the complaining members.

Anyone who has been engaged for a considerable length of time in church work knows that most internal problems come from members who are not filled with the Spirit but are selfish, self-willed, and self-seeking. They do and say things and show bad attitudes that cause division and strife. Happy is the church that has Spirit-filled men and women in places of responsibility.

C. The Chosen Seven: vv. 5-6

The whole church was pleased with the suggestion of the apostles. So they chose seven. The first was Stephen, a man full of faith and of the Holy Spirit. He becomes the central figure in chapters 6 and 7. He was the first Christian to receive the martyr's crown—his name means "victor's crown."

The second man chosen was Philip. He is the main character in chapter 8, holding a great revival in Samaria and then leading the Ethiopian eunuch to Christ. So the church was wise in its selection of such men.

The church held a sort of ordination service for these humble servants. They brought them to the apostles, who prayed for God's blessing and then laid their hands on them (v. 6).

These seven are often referred to as "deacons." While they are not called that here, their function was similar to that of the later ordained deacons.

II. SOME OF PAUL'S HELPERS: Romans 16:1-6

Paul wrote the Epistle to the Romans during his last recorded visit in Corinth. The sixteenth chapter consists almost entirely of greetings to or from some thirty friends of his.

First he writes: "I commend unto you Phebe our sister, which is a servant of the church which is at Cenchrea." The word for "servant" is *diaconos* and perhaps means "deaconess." Cenchrea was the eastern port of Corinth, which was situated on a narrow isthmus.

Paul urges his readers to receive Phoebe in the Lord and give her whatever assistance she needs, "for she has been a great help to many people, including me" (v. 2, NIV). Women played an important part in the work of the early church. Across the centuries (particularly the last one) they have made up a large part of the missionary force. It is high time that the church honored them with greater appreciation.

The apostle also asks his readers to "greet Priscilla and Aquila my helpers in Christ Jesus" (v. 3). Paul always names her first. It is obvious that she was a more outstanding Christian worker than her husband—a situation that is sometimes seen today.

Paul first met this couple at Corinth, where he joined them in making tents for a living (Acts 18:1-3). When he went to Ephesus, they accompanied him there (Acts 18:18-19). Partly because of this, some scholars have suggested that the sixteenth chapter of Romans was actually a separate, short letter sent to Ephesus. But Claudius had driven them, with all the Jews, out of Rome (Acts 18:2), and there is no reason why they might not have returned to their old establishment after the death of Claudius.

The apostle speaks very highly of Priscilla and Aquila. He said that they had risked their lives for him (v. 4)— probably at Corinth or Ephesus, perhaps in both places. Not only is he grateful for this, but "also all the churches of the Gentiles." Paul sends greetings to the church that was meeting at their house. Here was a couple that was an ideal example of "lay" workers in the church.

The apostle likewise extends greetings to Epaenetus, "who was the first convert to Christ in the province of Asia" (v. 5, NIV). Then he writes: "Greet Mary, who worked very hard for you" (v. 6, NIV). This list of names, running through verse 16, reminds us that God is keeping a record of all His helpers in the church, and they will receive an abundant reward at the end.

III. VARIOUS WORKERS IN THE CHURCH:
Ephesians 4:11-16

A. Different Functions: vv. 11-12

Five groups of workers in the church are mentioned here. The first was "apostles." Apparently this group was restricted to the first century. Next came "prophets," or preachers. The third was "evangelists"—our English word comes directly from the Greek. They were the bearers of the good news of salvation. The fourth was "pastors," or "shepherds"—our English word *pastor* is the Latin word for "shepherd." The fifth was "teachers," instructing people in the Word of God.

As is well known now, probably the comma should be dropped after "saints" in verse 12. The first part would then read: "for equipping the saints for the work of the ministry"— "to prepare God's people for works of service" (NIV). That is, the work of the church is not to be done only, or even mostly, by ordained ministers. Rather, they are to act as leaders, training the "laity" for the work of winning souls and strengthening fellow Christians. The purpose of it all is "the edifying [building up] of the body of Christ." All are to work together at this job.

B. All One Body: vv. 13-16

Just as the human body has many organs and yet is one organism, so it is with the church, the body of Christ. The purpose of all the various ministries is that we might finally come to be a complete unity, "unto the mea-sure of the stature of the fulness of Christ" (v. 13). What a prospect, and what a challenge!

So we are not to be tossed about by every wind of doctrine, or caught by the craftiness of deceitful men (v. 14). Instead, speaking the truth in love, we are to grow up into Christ, who is the Head of the body, His church. "From him the whole body, joined and held together by every supporting ligament, grows and builds itself up in love, as each part does its work" (v. 16, NIV).

Here is the true concept of the church. It must be a unity, as the human body is, or it cannot live. Each part (member) must carry out his (or her) appointed function. And always the Head must be obeyed.

IV. QUALIFICATIONS OF AN OVERSEER:
I Timothy 3:1-7

A. High Character: vv. 1-3

"The office of a bishop" (v. 1) is one word in Greek, *episcopos*, from which we get "episcopacy." The New International Version translates this verse: "Here is a trustworthy saying: If anyone sets his heart on being an overseer, he desires a noble task." Why "overseer" rather than "bishop"? Simply this: In the early church (first century) there were several "bishops" in each local congregation, whereas the "bishop" we know today is a diocesan official, over a large group of churches. So the term "bishop" connotes to us something quite different from what it meant in the first century. For instance, Paul addresses "the bishops and deacons" in the church at Philippi (Philippians 1:1). Actually the word *episcopos* simply meant overseer and was used for a "foreman" over a group of workers.

The first qualification of the overseer is that he must be "blameless" (v. 2), or "above reproach" (NIV). The strong Greek compound is found only in I Timothy (see 5:7; 6:14).

He must be "the husband of one

wife." Some leaders in the early church interpreted this as meaning "married only once" and so opposed second marriage by a widower. But it probably means having only one wife at a time.

The overseer must also be "sober" or "temperate" and "self-controlled" or "sober-minded." He must be "of good behavior"—one word, *cosmion.* Newport White comments: "perhaps *dignified* is the best sense of the term" (*Expositor's Greek Testament*, IV, 112). He must be "hospitable," an important characteristic in that ancient culture. Also he must be "apt to teach," which probably means both capable of teaching and willing to teach.

Because of the prevalence of heavy drinking in the Graeco-Roman world of that day, Paul mentions "not given to wine." The Greek *paroinos* suggests staying beside (*para*) wine (*oinos*).

The overseer must not be a "striker," one who gets angry and hits people. "Not greedy of filthy lucre" is not in the earliest Greek manuscripts.

Instead he must be "patient," or "gentle," not a "brawler" (a contentious person). He is not to be "covetous"—literally, "a lover of money."

B. Ability to Discipline: vv. 4-5

This is a very reasonable requirement. An overseer should be one who has managed his own family well, "having his own children in subjection with all gravity"—"with the strictest regard to propriety" (*Expositor's Greek Testament*, IV, 113). Logically Paul argues: "For if a man know not how to rule his own house, how shall he take care of the church of God?" (v. 5). This is a fair test.

C. Mature Experience: v. 6

The overseer must not be a "novice" (Greek, *neophyton*)—that is, "a recent convert." Sometimes much damage is done by placing an inexperienced new convert in a responsible place of leadership. Paul points out the

danger. Such a person might be "lifted up with pride" and "fall into the condemnation of the devil"—"he may become conceited and fall under the same judgment as the devil" (NIV). Pride is one of the most subtle temptations. It caused Satan's fall, and it has wrecked many a person in every age.

Leaders must be people of experience, who have proved themselves before they are chosen. The welfare of the church is too important to allow any risks at this point.

D. A Good Reputation: v. 7

"A good reputation with outsiders" (NIV) is an essential qualification for every church worker. The devil's trap is set for unwary feet.

V. QUALIFICATIONS OF DEACONS:
I Timothy 3:8-13

A. Good Conduct: vv. 8-9

Deacons were apparently those who took care of the material affairs of the church, such as handling finances. They must be "grave." The Greek word is *semnos.* William Barclay writes beautifully of this word. He notes that it has in it "all the majesty of kingship and royalty" (*More New Testament Words*, p. 142). He concludes: "The Christian should be *semnos;* he should ever display in his life the majesty of Christian living" (p. 145).

DISCUSSION QUESTIONS

1. Why is it wise to handle problems promptly?
2. What is the importance of division of labor?
3. Should a church allow its pastor to do all the work?
4. How can we all become helpers?
5. Why does a worker need to be Spirit-filled?
6. How important is family discipline?

Deacons must not be "double-tongued," speaking out of both sides of their mouths. Rather they must be "sincere" (NIV). They must not be "given to much wine," a common fault of that day—and ours. "Not greedy of filthy lucre" is genuine here. When church leaders are "pursuing dishonest gain" (NIV), the church will soon be in a bad way, and the leader will lose his own soul.

All Christians, but especially leaders, must be honest and sincere in their faith, keeping a clear conscience (v. 9). This is an important requirement, binding on all of us.

B. Experience: v. 10

Candidates for the diaconate must "first be tested; and then if there is nothing against them, let them serve as deacons." Again we say, "This is fair enough." And it is certainly an important protection for the church.

The verb *dokimazo* has three stages in its usage: (1) *test*, (2) *prove* by testing, and (3) *approve* as the result of testing. Probably all three ideas could be applied here. Only those who have been tested, proved, and finally approved should be placed in responsible places of leadership in the church. Too much is at stake.

C. Godly Wife: v. 11

Similar requirements are made of the "wives." Since the same word is used in Greek for "wife" and "woman," some scholars feel that it is "deaconesses" that are meant here. But in the next verse (12) Paul reverts to the "deacons." So it would seem most natural to take this as their wives.

They, like their husbands, are to be "grave" (*semnos*). On "slanderers" White makes this comment: "While men are more prone than women to be *dilogoi*, double-tongued, women are more prone than men to be slanderers" (*Expositor's Greek Testament*, IV, 116).

D. Ability to Discipline: vv. 12-13

This logical requirement is repeated for the deacons. They must prove their ability to control those under their care. Paul concludes: "Those who have served well gain an excellent standing and great assurance in their faith in Christ Jesus" (NIV). It is also true that those who fail had better never have sought or accepted the position.

CONTEMPORARY APPLICATION

Christ wants all of us to be His helpers in the church. It is only as we all work together that the job can be done satisfactorily.

But it is still true: "What's everybody's business is nobody's business." Every organization must have selected leaders if it is going to function effi-ciently. And the church is no exception.

The church should be very careful in choosing its leaders, for much depends on them. Carelessness at this point can be costly. Prayer and wise planning are both needed in church work.

STRUGGLE AND GROWTH

DEVOTIONAL READING	Ephesians 6:10-20
ADULTS	**Topic:** *Struggle and Growth* **Background Scripture:** Acts 11:11-18; 15:1-35; 19:23-27; Galatians 2:11-16 **Scripture Lesson:** Galatians 2:11-16; Acts 11:11-18 **Memory Verse:** *Then to the Gentiles also God has granted repentance unto life.* Acts 11:18
YOUTH	**Topic:** *Struggle and Growth* **Background Scripture:** Acts 11:11-8; 15:1-35; 19:23-27; Galatians 2:11-16 **Scripture Lesson:** Galatians 2:11-16; Acts 11:11-18 **Memory Verse:** *Then to the Gentiles also God has granted repentance unto life.* Acts 11:18
CHILDREN	**Topic:** *Overcoming Differences* **Background Scripture:** Acts 15:1-35; 19:23-27; Galatians 2:11-16 **Scripture Lesson:** Acts 15:1, 2, 6, 12-14, 19-20, 22, 30-31 **Memory Verse:** *The same Lord is Lord of all and bestows his riches upon all who call upon him.* Romans 10:12
DAILY BIBLE READINGS	**Mon., June 14:** The Apostles Are Arrested, Acts 5:12-20. **Tues., June 15:** The Apostles Are Tried and Beaten, Acts 5:33-40. **Wed., June 16:** Dissension Among the Brethren, Acts 15:1-5. **Thurs., June 17:** Peter Stresses God's Grace, Acts 15:6-11. **Fri., June 18:** The Assembly Sends a Letter, Acts 15:22-29. **Sat., June 19:** The Word Is Proclaimed, Acts 15:30-35. **Sun., June 20:** The Christian's Armor, Ephesians 6:10-20.
LESSON AIM	To see how the church has survived in spite of doctrinal controversy.
LESSON SETTING	**Time:** In the A.D. 40s **Place:** Antioch (in Syria) and Jerusalem

309

Struggle and Growth

LESSON OUTLINE

SUGGESTED INTRODUCTION FOR ADULTS

As Christians we shrink from controversy, and rightly so. But we must face the fact that there were doctrinal and even personality conflicts in the early church. People's hearts may be right and yet their heads wrong.

We are all to a certain extent the products of our past. Even Christians continue to be influenced by their earlier training. In the case of Peter and most of his associates, this training was in the Mosaic law. It is no wonder that they were slow to see that being a Christian did not involve being under the Law. So we must look at them with generous, understanding eyes.

It is also true that equally devoted believers may differ considerably in their thinking. We do not see all things alike. To a certain extent we must think and let think. What is needed is the ability to distinguish between what is central and what is peripheral. What is essential must be retained and defended at all costs. But there must be liberty with regard to nonessentials.

SUGGESTED INTRODUCTION FOR YOUTH

It is easy to idealize the early church and criticize the contemporary church. But this is unrealistic. The first generation Christians had their faults, too. Of course, we ought to profit by the mistakes of the past and improve the present. But we are all still human. As such, we are fallible—liable to mistakes.

Sometimes conflict leads to growth, as undesirable teachings are weeded out. But our differing opinions must always be expressed in love.

CONCEPTS FOR CHILDREN

1. Discussion of differences may be helpful, if carried on in a loving spirit.

2. But we should emphasize our agreements rather than our disagreements.
3. The nearer we draw to Christ the nearer we are to each other.
4. We need to listen as well as talk.

THE LESSON COMMENTARY

I. PETER AND PAUL IN ANTIOCH:
Galatians 2:11-16

A. Peter's Bad Action: vv. 11-12

Probably the first ten verses of this chapter are a description of the council at Jerusalem (Acts 15, discussed at the end of this lesson). So Peter's visit to Antioch came after this.

The Antioch mentioned here was in the northern part of Syria. It was the home base for all three of Paul's missionary journeys and the chief center of Gentile Christianity at the middle of the first century.

When Peter came to Antioch, Paul withstood him to his face. Why? "Because he was to be blamed." Paul felt that Peter had done what was actually wrong.

Then he tells us what had happened. At first Peter ate freely with the Gentile Christians (v. 12). This was contrary to the custom of that day. The Pharisees considered it a sin for any Jew to eat with Gentiles.

Then "certain came from James." This is James the brother of Jesus, who was the head pastor of the Jewish Christian congregation at Jerusalem (cf. Acts 12:17). It is supposed that he was the author of the Epistle of James, which is very Jewish in tone. Josephus, the leading Jewish historian of the first century, refers to him as "James the Just"—that is, a careful observer of the Mosaic law.

When these men from the Jerusalem church appeared, Peter "withdrew and separated himself, fearing them which were of the circumcision." The old taboos were deeply ingrained. Though he had already eaten with Gentiles in the house of Cornelius at Caesarea and had defended his action in doing so (Acts 11:1-18), yet when he found himself surrounded by strict Jews from Jerusalem he weakened and gave in to their pressure. Old customs die hard! He doubtless did not realize the serious wrong of his action.

B. Peter's Bad Influence: v. 13

"The other Jews"—Jewish Christians in the Antioch church—"dissembled likewise with him; insomuch that Barnabas also was carried away with their dissimulation." The verb "dissembled" is *synhypecrithesan*, "played the hypocrite with." And the noun "dissimulation" is *hypocrisis*, "hypocrisy." Peter and Barnabas were acting like hypocrites. Why so? Because they had both been eating freely with their Gentile brothers in Christ. For them now to separate themselves, just because some Jerusalem Jewish Christians were present, was hypocritical.

Of course they were not consciously disobeying God. They simply failed to face up intelligently to the implications of what they were doing. They were guilty of disfellowshiping Christian brothers. Though unconscious, it was nevertheless a very serious sin against love. But this sin has been repeated many times in the church.

C. Paul's Rebuke: v. 14

"Walked . . . uprightly" is one word in Greek, *orthopodousin*. The verb means to "walk straight." At this point, Peter and Barnabas were wobbling out of line.

It took Paul, himself a Jew, to assess the situation correctly and administer a needed rebuke. Right in front of everybody present he reproved the leading apostle, the one who had preached at Pentecost so successfully that three thousand were saved. But Paul realized that the issue was crucial to the continuance of Christianity as a universal religion.

So he said to Peter publicly: "You are a Jew, yet you live like a Gentile and not like a Jew. How is it, then, that you force Gentiles to follow Jewish customs?" (NIV). The last four words in English are one word in Greek—*ioudaizein*, "to Judaize." Peter had been associating with Gentiles, not observing the Jewish law. What right, then, had he to make the Gentile believers conform to Judaism?

D. Justification by Faith: vv. 15-16

Those who were Jews "by nature" ("by birth," NIV) considered all Gentiles to be "sinners" (v. 15). But Paul declares we "know that a man is not justified by observing the law, but by faith in Jesus Christ. So we, too, have put our faith in Christ Jesus that we may be justified by faith in Christ and not by observing the law, because by observing the law no one will be justified" (v. 16, NIV).

This verse sounds the keynote of the Epistle to the Galatians—justification by faith. It was the discovery of this truth in Galatians that made Martin Luther the pioneer of the Protestant Reformation in the sixteenth century. This great evangelical doctrine had been lost sight of during the so-called Dark Ages of the church. Luther's rediscovery of it was revolutionary.

Why did the light of the church go so far into eclipse during the Middle Ages? Part of the reason, at least, is to be found in the doctrinal controversies of the fourth and fifth centuries. Instead of missionary conferences and conferences on evangelism, which have marked the twentieth century, there were church councils that argued endlessly over single words in theological creeds. Meanwhile the millions of earth lived and died without ever hearing the gospel of Jesus Christ. This has been the repeated tragedy of Christendom.

An important thing, however, happened at the end of the fourth century. In A.D. 397 the Council of Carthage fixed the limits of the New Testament canon. Several books of doubtful value, that had been used in some places as sacred Scripture, were excluded. Exactly our twenty-seven books of the New Testament were authorized to be read as Scripture in the churches. So the church was saved from the danger of false teachings being introduced through new "revelations" offered by men.

II. PETER IN JERUSALEM: Acts 11:11-18

The tenth chapter of Acts tells how an angel appeared to the Roman centurion Cornelius in Caesarea and told him to send to Joppa for Peter. Just before the messengers arrived at the house where Peter was staying, the Lord prepared His apostle by giving him a vision on the rooftop, where he had gone to pray. The purpose of the vision was to show him that in God's sight the Gentiles were no more "unclean" than Jews—all were the same.

When the messengers reached the house, the Holy Spirit told Peter to go with them. He did so, walking the thirty miles to Caesarea. There he preached the gospel to Cornelius and his assembled friends. While Peter was speaking, the Holy Spirit fell on the whole group of Gentiles, as He had come on the Jews in the upper room at Pentecost. Peter proceeded to baptize these Gentiles as members of the Christian church (10:48).

But when Peter got back to Jerusalem he found himself in trouble. "They that were of the circumcision contended with him" (11:2). The Jewish Christians at Jerusalem were still observing the custom of avoiding ceremonial defilement by associating with Gentiles. So they voiced their criticism to Peter: "You went into the house of uncircumcised men and ate with them" (v. 3, NIV).

If one knows that he is in the right, the best defense he can make is simply to relate the pertinent facts. This Peter proceeded to do. He told of his vision on the housetop at Joppa. It was the voice from heaven that said to him, "Do not call anything impure that God has made clean" (v. 9, NIV). The vision was repeated twice more, for emphasis (v. 10).

A. Peter Led by the Spirit: vv. 11-12

Continuing his defense, Peter related the fact that "right then" (NIV), as soon as the vision was finished, the three men who had been sent from Caesarea by Cornelius appeared at the outer gate of the house. God's timing is always perfect!

Then Peter said, "The spirit bade me go with them, nothing doubting" (v. 12). The last two words may be translated "making no distinction" (RSV) or "without hesitation" (Twentieth Century New Testament; cf. NIV).

Fortunately for Peter, six Christian "brothers," all Jews, went with him to Caesarea. They could now give ample testimony to confirm the truth of the amazing story that the apostle told. It was extremely providential that these men had accompanied Peter, for no one could doubt the combined testimony of six Jewish Christians. They were eyewitnesses.

B. Cornelius's Report: vv. 13-14

The centurion Cornelius told Peter and the men with him how an angel had appeared to him in his house and had instructed him to send to Joppa for Simon Peter—"who shall tell thee words, whereby thou and all thy house shall be saved" (v. 14). While Cornelius was a devout worshiper of God, he was not a part of the Christian community before Peter's visit. This is shown by the fact that Peter had him and his associates "baptized in the name of the Lord" (10:48).

It is also supported by the content of Peter's preaching (10:34-43). He ended his message by saying: "To him give all the prophets witness, that through his name whosoever believeth in him shall receive remission of sins" (v. 43). It is obvious that Peter understood his assignment to be that of telling Cornelius how to be saved (see *Beacon Bible Commentary*, VII, 383).

C. Coming of the Holy Spirit: vv. 15-17

While Peter was speaking (cf. 10:44) the Holy Spirit fell on the people, "as on us at the beginning"— that is, at Pentecost. There it was on Jews in the upper room. Here it was on Gentiles in the house of Cornelius. Peter makes this same connection in Acts 15:8-9.

The apostle went on to say that when this happened he remembered Jesus' words ("the word of the Lord"): "John baptized with water, but you will be baptized with the Holy Spirit" (v. 16, NIV).

Then Peter scored his winning point: "Forasmuch then as God gave the like gift as he did unto us, who believed on the Lord Jesus Christ; what was I, that I could withstand God?" (v. 17). He wasn't to blame for what happened; God did it!

D. A New Understanding: v. 18

"When they heard these things, they held their peace [Peter's critics were at last silenced!] and glorified God." After all, these men were sincere Christians, but they had strong, deep-seated prejudices. When they were finally convinced, they made no more complaint. They went further: they praised God for what He had done.

Still amazed, they said, "Then hath God also to the Gentiles granted repentance unto life." It was hard to believe! All their lives they had been taught that the Israelites were the people of God; the Gentiles were unclean and outside the covenant. That Gentiles could be saved apart from the Mosaic law was a revolutionary idea, to say the least. It is difficult for us today to appreciate the situation as it was then.

III. THE JERUSALEM COUNCIL: Acts 15:1-29

A. The Reason for It: vv. 1-5

It all started in this way: "Some men came down from Judea to Antioch and were teaching the brothers: 'Unless you are circumcised according to the custom taught by Moses, you cannot be saved'" (v. 1, NIV). Paul and Barnabas immediately reacted against this Judaistic teaching and entered into "sharp dispute and debate with them" (v. 2, NIV).

It was decided that these leaders in the church at Antioch should "go up to Jerusalem unto the apostles and elders about this question." The Christians in far-off Antioch felt that they should refer the matter to the mother church for a decision. In particular, it was felt that the apostles there possessed special authority conferred on them by Jesus.

But when Paul and Barnabas reached Jerusalem and gave a report of how God had used them on the first missionary journey (Acts 13-14) in the salvation of the Gentiles, they ran into difficulty. Some believers who belonged to the party of the Pharisees stood up and contended that the Gentile believers must be circumcised and required to keep the law of Moses (v. 5).

This was a very serious issue. If this view had prevailed, Christianity would have been just another sect within Judaism. It would have suffocated in the swaddling clothes of that national faith and could never have become a world religion. This was the most significant problem that had yet confronted the Christian church. It must be settled right.

B. Peter's Speech: vv. 6-11

The apostles and elders called a special meeting to consider the matter (v. 6). After much argument, Peter got up and reminded the group that God had used him to employ the keys (cf. Matthew 16:19) to open the kingdom of heaven to the Gentiles (v. 7). Then he equated what had happened to the Gentiles in the house of Cornelius with what had happened to Jews on the day of Pentecost (vv. 8-9). In both cases two things took place simultaneously—they were filled with the Holy Spirit and their hearts were purified. Sanctification and Spirit-filling are the same experience.

So Peter appealed to his fellow Jews not to "put a yoke upon the neck of the disciples, which neither our fathers nor we were able to bear" (v. 10). Then he made the significant assertion: "But we believe that through the grace of the Lord Jesus Christ we shall be saved, even as they" (v. 11). The Jews can only be saved the same way the Gentiles are being saved—"through the grace of the Lord Jesus Christ."

C. Paul and Barnabas: v. 12

Peter's speech had the desired effect. The "much disputing" (v. 7)

DISCUSSION QUESTIONS

1. What doctrinal controversies are especially important in our time?
2. Why was Peter's conduct so blameworthy?
3. What part did Paul play in the early development of Christianity?
4. What are some harmful results of doctrinal debate?
5. What are some vital issues in the church today?
6. In what spirit should doctrinal discussion be carried on?

stopped; "the whole assembly became silent" (NIV). The people were now ready to listen to Barnabas and Paul, as these reported their miraculous ministry among the Gentiles.

D. James's Conclusion: vv. 13-21

James, the brother of Jesus, was the head pastor of the Jewish Christian congregation at Jerusalem. As such, he acted as moderator of this first church council (A.D. 48). He referred to Peter's report of how God had used him to introduce the Gentiles for the first time to the gospel. Then he quoted from Amos 9:11-12 to show that God had always purposed to include Gentiles in the people who would be saved (vv. 16-18).

Thereupon he declared the decision of the council: "It is my judg-ment, therefore, that we should not make it difficult for the Gentiles who are turning to God. Instead we should write to them, telling them to abstain from food polluted by idols, from sexual immorality, from the meat of strangled animals and from blood" (vv. 19-20, NIV). If people wanted to know the law of Moses, they could hear it read every sabbath day (Saturday) in the synagogues (v. 21).

E. The Council's Letter: vv. 22-29

These four "decrees" were put into a letter to Gentile churches, suggesting only these restrictions. Very significant are the words in verse 28: "It seemed good to the Holy Spirit and to us" (NIV). The leaders of the church at Jerusalem felt that they had found the mind of the Spirit.

CONTEMPORARY APPLICATION

We should be very grateful that Christianity was freed promptly (within twenty years of Jesus' death) from the shackles of legalistic Judaism. It could never have swept around the world, winning many millions of people, if this had not happened. The council at Jerusalem was one of the most significant moments in the nearly two thousand years of Christian history.

THE CHURCH AND CIVIL AUTHORITIES

DEVOTIONAL READING

Philippians 3:12-21

ADULTS

Topic: *The Church and Civil Authorities*

Background Scripture: I Kings 22:1-28; Acts 5:21b-29; Romans 13:1-10; Revelation 13:11-18

Scripture Lesson: Romans 13:1-10

Memory Verse: *We must obey God rather than men.* Acts 4:29

YOUTH

Topic: *Giving Allegiance*

Background Scripture: I Kings 22:1-28; Acts 5:21b-29; Romans 13:1-10; Revelation 13:11-18

Scripture Lesson: Romans 13:1-10

Memory Verse: *We must obey God rather than men.* Acts 5:29

CHILDREN

Topic: *The Church Obeying God*

Background Scripture: Acts 5:12-42; Romans 13:8-10

Scripture Lesson: Acts 5:17-29

Memory Verse: *We must obey God rather than men.* Acts 5:29

DAILY BIBLE READINGS

Mon., June 21: The Kings Inquire of the Prophets, I Kings 22:1-12.
Tues., June 22: The Prophet Seeks to Avoid Punishment, I Kings 22:13-18.
Wed., June 23: The Lord Directs the Prophets, I Kings 22:19-23.
Thurs., June 24: The Prophet Is Punished, I Kings 22:24-28.
Fri., June 25: The Apostles Before the Council, Acts 5:21-32.
Sat., June 26: Honor the Authorities, Romans 13:1-7.
Sun., June 27: Our Commonwealth Is in Heaven, Philippians 3:12-21.

LESSON AIM

To discover our responsibility as citizens in relation to civil authority.

LESSON SETTING

Time: The events of Acts 5: soon after A.D. 30. Romans was written in A.D. 56, Revelation in about A.D. 95.

Place: Jerusalem; Corinth; Isle of Patmos

316

The Church and Civil Authorities

LESSON OUTLINE

I. The Church Under Persecution: Acts 5:21b-29

II. Subjection to Civil Government: Romans 13:1-5
    A. Governments Divinely Ordained: vv. 1-2
    B. Security for Good People: vv. 3-4
    C. Subjection for Consciences' Sake: v. 5

III. Duty of Paying Taxes: Romans 13:6-7
    A. Payment for Services: v. 6
    B. Paying Each His Due: v. 7

IV. Duty of Love: Romans 13:8-10
    A. The Inescapable Debt of Love: v. 8
    B. The Supreme Social Commandment: v. 9
    C. The Fulfilling of the Law: v. 10

SUGGESTED INTRODUCTION FOR ADULTS

The relation of the Christian to his government is a very vital matter today. Within the broad spectrum of Christendom we find many different attitudes taken.

Looking at the extreme right for a moment, we see almost a blind devotion to governmental authority. It is "my country, right or wrong." Patriotism—a much needed virtue today—may be perverted into obeying men rather than God.

On the extreme left we find quite a different picture. Here we see the demonstrators, the dissidents, the protesters. We are treated to the unedifying spectacle of religious leaders promoting protest that sometimes turns into mad hatred, with violent destruction of life and property—all in the name of Christianity!

As in many other relationships of life, the Biblical believer will find himself in a middle-of-the-road position somewhere between these extremes. His supreme loyalty will always be to God. But he will also recognize his Christian responsibility to be in subjection to governmental authority. This is the teaching of the New Testament.

SUGGESTED INTRODUCTION FOR YOUTH

On university campuses in recent years there have been violent clashes between students and the forces of law. What is the proper attitude of Christians toward those in authority?

The New Testament is clear at this point. Jesus enforced the rule of paying taxes to the ruling government (Matthew 22:21). Today's lesson teaches us that we are to be in subjection to those who are over us.

CONCEPTS FOR CHILDREN

1. The early apostles gave supreme loyalty to God.
2. They risked their lives to obey God.
3. Love is the highest principle in life.
4. Children should obey parents, teachers, and other authorities.

THE LESSON COMMENTARY

I. THE CHURCH UNDER PERSE-CUTION:
Acts 15:21b-29

The first problem that confronted the Christian church was that of persecution. In the second chapter of Acts we read of the conversion of three thousand people at the close of Peter's sermon on the day of Pentecost. Peter healed the lame man at the Beautiful Gate of the temple and then preached a second sermon when a large crowd gathered (see chap. 3). Things were moving ahead in fine shape.

But then the blow came. The chief priests resented the apostolic preaching on the resurrection (4:1-2), as well as the large influx of Jews into the Christian church. So they arrested the apostles and put them in prison (4:3).

The next day the Sanhedrin (the Supreme Court of Israel) met, summoned the apostles, and demanded to know by whose authority and in whose name they had healed the cripple (vv. 5-7). Peter declared boldly that it was in the name of Jesus (v. 10). Then he made an assertion that must have "rocked" these religious leaders: "Neither is there salvation in any other: for there is none other name under heaven given among men, whereby we must be saved" (v. 12).

Amazed at the holy boldness of Peter and John, the Sanhedrin held a secret session (vv. 13-17). Then the apostles were summoned again and commanded "not to speak at all nor teach in the name of Jesus" (v. 18).

What was the reaction of Peter and John? They answered: "Whether it be right in the sight of God to hearken unto you more than unto God, judge ye. For we cannot but speak the things which we have seen and heard" (v. 20). Obedience to God must always take the highest priority.

In the fifth chapter of Acts we find the story of the second persecution. Again it was the success of the church that provoked it. We read in verse 14:

"And believers were the more added to the Lord, multitudes both of men and women." And again it was the chief priests who headed the opposition (v. 17). They arrested the apostles and put them in prison (v. 18). During the night an angel of the Lord released them from prison and told them to preach salvation in the temple courts (vv. 19-20). Obediently the apostles entered the temple area early in the morning and taught (v. 21a).

Soon the Sanhedrin met and summoned the apostles from prison (v. 21b). To their amazement, the officers found the prison empty—even though the doors were locked and the sentries were on duty (vv. 22-23). About that time the report came: "Behold, the men whom ye put in prison are standing in the temple, and teaching the people" (v. 25).

This time the captain of the temple guard went with his officers. They brought the apostles "without violence," because they were afraid the people would stone them (v. 26).

When the apostles again stood before the Sanhedrin, the high priest said sternly to them: "We gave you strict orders not to teach in this name. . . . Yet you have filled Jerusalem with your teaching and are determined to make us guilty of this man's blood" (v. 28, NIV).

It was a threatening moment for the apostles. What was their reply? Essentially the same as before: "We ought to obey God rather than men" (v. 29). This must always be the basic principle of operation for every Christian. God's will is the only supreme authority.

II. SUBJECTION TO CIVIL GOVERNMENT:
Romans 13:1-5

A. Governments Divinely Ordained: v. 1-2

The two greatest passages in the New Testament on the Christian's relationship to civil authorities are in Romans 13 and in I Peter 2.

Here Paul says: "Everyone must submit himself to the governing authorities, for there is no authority except that which God has established. The authorities that exist have been established by God" (v. 1, NIV). The apostle asserts that governmental authority is not a human notion; it is divinely ordained. Unquestionably there have often been bad governments in power. But it still remains true that "any government is better than no government." For where there is no governing authority there is anarchy, and even the worst monarchy is better than anarchy. When no government rules the lives of the citizens are not safe.

Paul does not say that every person in power was ordained by God to rule. To affirm that it was God's will for Hitler to dominate Europe would be sheer blasphemy. God has ordained government, but the personnel is often man's choice. Still, we should respect the authority of those who are over us.

Why does Paul write so strongly on this subject to the Roman church in A.D. 56? There may be some connection between this and the expulsion of all Jews from Rome in A.D. 49 by the decree of Emperor Claudius (cf. Acts 18:2). Suetonius, in his *Life of Claudius* writes: "He expelled the Jews from Rome because they kept rioting at the instigation of Chrestus." Most scholars feel that "Chrestus" is a variant spelling for "Christus," or Christ. It is thought that when Christianity was introduced into the Jewish synagogues in Rome it caused so much conflict that Claudius told all Jews, including Christian Jews, to leave the city. That is why Aquila and Priscilla were in Corinth when Paul arrived there on his second journey.

So the apostle sounds a warning: "Whosoever therefore resisteth the power, resisteth the ordinance of God: and they that resist shall receive to themselves damnation" (v. 2). But the word "damnation" here is totally un-

justifiable. The Greek simply has *krima*, "judgment." The New International Version gives the correct translation: "Consequently, he who rebels against the authority is rebelling against what God has instituted, and those who do so will bring judgment on themselves." That is, they will be punished by the government. Even if it be argued that Paul is talking about divine judgment, it is not "damnation."

In their excellent commentary on Romans, Sanday and Headlam put the matter well: "The logical result of this theory as to the origin of human power is that resistance to it is resistance to the ordering of God; and hence those who resist will receive *krima*—a judgment of condemnation which is human, for it comes through human instruments, but Divine as having its origin and source in God. There is no reference here to eternal punishment" (p. 367).

B. Security for Good People: vv. 3-4

It is obvious that Paul is speaking in generalities here when he says, "For rulers are not a terror to good works, but to evil." The apostle had already suffered at the hands of unscrupulous Roman authorities, as at Philippi (Acts 16:22-24). But many other times the Roman governors protected him from Jewish fanatics who tried to kill him. Paul appreciated the fact that, in general, governmental authorities protect the good people and punish the bad. That is their divinely given responsibility, and they usually operate that way. We are reminded of the old saying, "There are exceptions to every rule"—which is in itself an over-generalization.

With regard to the word "rulers," Sanday and Headlam say: "The plural shows that the Apostle is speaking quite generally. He is arguing out of the duty of obeying rulers on general principles, deduced from the fact that 'the state' exists for a beneficent end: he is not arguing from the special condition or circumstance of any one state."

If we want to live without fear of those in authority, "do that which is good, and thou shalt have praise of the same."

In verse 4 the apostle bolsters his argument a bit: "For he is God's servant to do you good. But if you do wrong, be afraid, for he does not bear the sword for nothing. He is God's servant, an agent of justice to bring punishment on the wrongdoer" (NIV). Sanday and Headlam comment: "The sword is the symbol of the executive and criminal jurisdiction of a magistrate, and is therefore used of the power of punishing inherent in the government" (pp. 367-68).

The first three verses of this chapter find a striking parallel in I Peter 2:13-14: "Submit yourselves to every ordinance of man for the Lord's sake: whether it be to the king, as supreme; or unto governors, as unto them that are sent by him for the punishment of evildoers, and for the praise of them that do well." Also in I Peter 3:13 we read: "And who is he that will harm you, if ye be followers of that which is good."

C. Subjection for Consciences' Sake: v. 5

"Therefore, it is necessary to submit to the authorities, not only because of possible punishment but also because of conscience" (NIV). In his commentary on Romans, Godet says:

"If the state were only armed with means of punishing, it would be enough to regard it with fear; but it is the representative of God to assert justice among men; and hence it is from a principle of *conscience* that submission must be given to it" (p. 444).

Here we have the outward incentive (punishment) and the inward incentive (conscience). Taken together, they should keep us in line! Subjection to civil government is clearly the duty of every Christian.

This idea of submission to government must, of course, be handled in a reasonable fashion, not with fanatical extreme either way. C. W. Quimby makes this helpful suggestion: "Today under our different form of government, in case of injustice, this teaching of Paul cannot be made to mean: Never object to any law, never agitate for repeal or change, never seek reforms. But it meant then, and it still means most properly: Never flout decent public order! Along that path lies anarchy and chaos. It is anti-God, for God is the God of order" (*The Great Redemption*, p. 183).

After noting the words of Peter and John in Acts 5:29, Dr. William Greathouse writes: "Even so, the conscientious objector must be prepared to suffer the punishment which the state dictates, for as a Christian he believes that even an evil state is better than anarchy" (*Beacon Bible Commentary*, VIII, 251, note 58).

III. DUTY OF PAYING TAXES: Romans 13:6-7

A. Payment for Services: v. 6

"This is also why you pay taxes, for the authorities are God's servants, who give their full time to governing" (NIV). That is, we are paying for the services that the government renders to us.

Any thoughtful person will recognize the logical validity of this. What do we get for our city taxes? The most obvious and necessary services are the protection afforded by the police and

---

DISCUSSION QUESTIONS

1. How did the Roman government differ from ours today?
2. Does one's obedience to law depend on the type of personnel engaged in law enforcement?
3. Why is government necessary?
4. What methods should be used to effect reforms?
5. What example did Jesus set?
6. What was Paul's practice?

fire departments. Provided individually, these services would cost us far more. Then there are such things as paved streets and parks. In spite of the annoyance of some waste of money by the government, modern society could not exist without governmental authority.

And this goes for the state and federal governments as well. We all derive innumerable benefits that we could not purchase individually and directly.

Verse 6 is an echo of Jesus' words. The Pharisees and Herodians asked Him the question, "Is it right to pay taxes to Caesar or not?" After pointing out the fact that their money carried the name and portrait of the reigning emperor, Tiberius, He said to them: "Give to Caesar what is Caesar's, and to God what is God's" (Matthew 22:21, NIV). The importance of this statement is shown by the fact that it occurs in all three Synoptic Gospels (cf. Mark 12:17; Luke 20:25). Anyone who refuses to pay taxes is rejecting both the words of Jesus and the inspiration of Paul's writings.

Constructive criticism is always in order. But a rebellious spirit is of Satan, not of God. As Paul goes on to say a few verses later, all we do must be governed by love. That is the final criterion.

B. Paying Each His Due: v. 7

"Give everyone what you owe him: If you owe taxes, pay taxes; if revenue, then revenue; if respect, then respect; if honor, then honor" (NIV). If we try to distinguish between the first two (KJV: "tribute . . . custom"), it may be that the first refers to direct taxes and the second to indirect taxes.

But Knox wisely comments: "Perhaps Paul has no particular distinction in mind; certainly he does not think of *respect* and *honor* as separately due to two distinct classes of men. The form of the sentence is in large part determined by rhetorical considerations. The point is that whatever one truly owes another (i.e., *their dues*), whether it is money or respect, one must fully pay" (*Interpreter's Bible*, IX, 605). It is by fulfilling this command that we maintain proper relationships to our fellowmen.

IV. DUTY OF LOVE:
Romans 13:8-10

A. The Inescapable Debt of Love: v. 8

"Let no debt remain outstanding, except the continuing debt to love one another, for he who loves his fellow man has fulfilled the law" (NIV). Our debt of love we can never pay in full; we shall always be in debt.

B. The Supreme Social Commandment: v. 9

Paul quotes the seventh, sixth, eighth, ninth, and tenth commandments in that order. Then he declares that whatever other commandments there are can be summed in one rule: "Love your neighbor as yourself." This includes and comprehends all our duties to our fellow human beings.

C. The Fulfilling of the Law: v. 10

One of the great statements of Scripture is this: "Love is the fulfilling of the law." The only way we can fulfill the demands of God's law is to have sincere, unselfish love for everyone. This is true religion.

CONTEMPORARY APPLICATION

There has been a great deal of irresponsible talk in recent years about

Jesus being a "revolutionary," giving the impression that He agitated revolt against governmental authority. As this lesson shows, exactly the opposite is true. Jesus told His fellow Jews to pay taxes to the foreign, hated Roman government. And Paul and Peter echoed His words, amplified them, and enforced them. Revolt is not Jesus' solution.

THE SPREAD OF THE CHURCH

DEVOTIONAL READING	Isaiah 40:3-8

ADULTS

Topic: *The Spread of the Church*

Background Scripture: Matthew 28:16-20; Luke 10:1-24; Acts 1:6-8; II Corinthians 5:16-20; Ephesians 2

Scripture Lesson: Acts 1:6-8; II Corinthians 5:16-20

Memory Verse: *God was in Christ reconciling the world unto himself ... and entrusting to us the message of reconciliation. So we are ambassadors for Christ, God making his appeal through us.* II Corinthians 5:19-20

YOUTH

Topic: *New Worlds for Christ*

Background Scripture: Matthew 28:16-20; Luke 10:1-12; Acts 1:6-8; II Corinthians 5:16-20

Scripture Lesson: Acts 1:6-8; II Corinthians 5:16-20

Memory Verse: *God was in Christ reconciling the world unto himself ... and entrusting to us the message of reconciliation. So we are ambassadors for Christ, God making his appeal through us.* II Corinthians 5:19-20

CHILDREN

Topic: *The Church Grows*

Background Scripture: Matthew 28:16-20; Acts 13; 14; 16; 17; 18; 19; 28; II Corinthians 5:16-20

Scripture Lesson: Matthew 28:12-60; II Corinthians 5:16-20

Memory Verse: *Go therefore and make disciples of all nations.* Matthew 28:19

DAILY BIBLE READINGS

Mon., June 28: The Calling of the Fishermen, Mark 1:14-20.
Tues., June 29: The Calling of Philip and Nathanael, John 1:43-49.
Wed., June 30: The Mission of the Seventy, Luke 10:1-12.
Thurs., July 1: The Return of the Seventy, Luke 10:17-24.
Fri., July 2: The Great Commission, Matthew 28:16-20.
Sat., July 3: The Call to Mission, Luke 24:44-53.
Sun., July 4: The Nature of True Freedom, John 8:31-36.

LESSON AIM

To see how quickly the church spread throughout the world in the first century, and how it is spreading today.

LESSON SETTING

Time: Jesus' words in Acts 1:6-8 in A.D. 30, between His resurrection and ascension. II Corinthians was written in A.D. 55, Ephesians about A.D. 60.

Place: Near Jerusalem; Macedonia; Rome

LESSON OUTLINE

The Spread of the Church

I. The Power and Program of the Church: Acts 1:6-8
   A. The Question of the Disciples: v. 6
   B. The Warning of Jesus: v. 7
   C. The Promise of Power and Propagation: v. 8

II. The Ministry of Reconciliation: II Corinthians 5:16-20
   A. The Divine Christ: v. 16
   B. A New Creation: v. 17
   C. Reconciliation in Christ: vv. 18-19
   D. Ambassadors for Christ: v. 20

SUGGESTED INTRODUCTION FOR ADULTS

The spread of the church was the consequence of the Great Commission of Jesus found in Matthew 28:18-20. First He said, "All authority in heaven and on earth has been given to me" (NIV). (The King James Version has "power," but the Greek word is *exousia*, "authority," not *dynamis*, "power.") Because Jesus has all authority He can commission His disciples to evangelize the world.

So He said to them: "Therefore go and make disciples of all nations, baptizing them in the name of the Father and of the Son and of the Holy Spirit, and teaching them to obey everything I have commanded you" (vv. 19-20a, NIV). Jesus was speaking to "the eleven disciples" (v. 16), who had followed Him in His earthly ministry. Now that He was about to go back to heaven, He told them to go and make disciples around the world, baptizing them and teaching them. It was a big assignment. How could they carry it out?

The answer is found in the last part of verse 20: "And, lo, I am with you alway, even unto the end of the world" (Greek, "age"). Only with the presence and power of Christ could they succeed; and with Him they would not fail.

SUGGESTED INTRODUCTION FOR YOUTH

"New Worlds for Christ." That is a thrilling challenge—enough to stir the mind and imagination of any red-blooded young person.

There are "new worlds" beyond the ocean waiting for those who will accept God's call to overseas services. For those who do not receive this assignment there are new worlds at our doorstep, people who need to be contacted by an outreach program. Christ has promised to go with us if we go.

CONCEPTS FOR CHILDREN	1. The church began with 120 believers in Jerusalem. 2. Soon it had thousands of members there. 3. Within a generation it had spread around the Roman Empire. 4. The church is still expanding in the world today.

THE LESSON COMMENTARY

I. THE POWER AND PROGRAM OF THE CHURCH: Acts 1:6-8

A. The Question of the Disciples: v. 6

The disciples had expected Jesus to set up His Messianic kingdom in Jerusalem. Three times He had told them that it was not a throne that awaited Him in Jerusalem, but a cross—He was going there to die.

In spite of these repeated warnings, His death was a shattering experience to them. But after what seemed an endless time of sorrow, with all hope gone, the risen Christ had appeared to them the next Sunday evening. Then (why not sooner?) they remembered that all three times He had predicted His death He had also promised that He would rise on the third day.

Now that He was with them again, in greater power and glory, the old question came up. And so they asked it: "Lord, wilt thou at this time restore the kingdom of Israel?"—(Greek, "to Israel"). Surely the One who had defied and overcome the powers of death could overthrow the Roman domination and free Israel, as Moses had done long ago!

The trouble was that the disciples, in common with the devout Jews of that day, expected that the Messiah would set up an earthly, political kingdom. The fact that Jesus had confined His ministry almost entirely to Israel would seem to point in that direction.

In his volume on Acts in the *Harper's New Testament Commentaries*, C. S. C. Williams writes: "They awaited a material kingdom, for the

Spirit was not yet poured out on them to give them a more enlightened conception of it" (p. 56). And in his commentary on Acts in the *Cambridge Greek Testament* J. Rawson Lumby says: "The change from the spirit which dictated the question in this verse, to that in which St. Peter (Acts ii. 38, 39) preached repentance and forgiveness to all whom the Lord should call, is one of the greatest evidences of the miracle of Pentecost" (p. 83).

The saddening thing is the probable reason for their asking this question. On the way up to Jerusalem the disciples had been quarreling as to who would have first place in the Kingdom. James and John had actually requested the seats of highest honor on either side of Jesus. Were they still concerned about their place in the Messianic kingdom? Was this why they were anxious to know how soon it would be set up? We hope that they had higher, unselfish motives.

B. The Warning of Jesus: v. 7

Jesus' reply was direct and reproving: "It is not for you to know the times or the seasons, which the Father hath put in his own power." Again we note that the word translated "power" here, as in Matthew 28:18 is not *dynamis* but *exousia*, "authority."

The word for "times" is *chronos*, from which we get "chronology." It refers to the passing of time. But the word for "seasons" is *kairos*, which signifies time "in the sense of a fixed and definite period" (Abbott-Smith, *Lexicon*). In his book, *Synonyms of the New Testament*, R. C. Trench says that "seasons" means "the critical epoch-making periods foreordained of God" (p. 211). F. F. Bruce gives the distinction between the two Greek words this way: "*Chronous* refers to the time that must elapse before the final establishment of the Kingdom; *kairous* to the critical events accompanying its establishment" (*The Acts of the Apostles*, p. 66). And Albert C. Winn puts it succinctly when he says that the disciples could know neither "the length of time nor the key moments" (*Layman's Bible Commentary*, XX, 22).

The New International Version has caught it well: "It is not for you to know the times or dates the Father has set by his own authority." This is in line with what Jesus had already told His disciples about the time of His second coming: "But of that day and hour knoweth no man, no, not the angels of heaven, but my Father only" (Matthew 24:36).

C. The Promise of Power and Propagation: v. 8

This is the key verse of the Book of Acts. It gives us both the *power* and the *program* of the church of Jesus Christ. The *power* is the Holy Spirit; the *program* is world evangelization. These go together. Just as Jesus said in the Great Commission (see introduction for adults), "Go . . . and lo, I am with you," so the power of the Holy Spirit is not given to us for our personal enjoyment but so that we may evangelize the world.

Acts 1:8 also gives us the logical outline of the book. We find in Acts the propagation of the gospel (1) in Jerusalem, chaps. 1–7; (2) in all Judea and Samaria, chaps. 8–12; (3) to the ends of the earth, chaps. 13–28. Anyone who reads the Book of Acts with this outline in mind will find that it fits perfectly.

In the seventh chapter all the events take place in or near Jerusalem. In chapter 8 we read how Philip took the gospel to Samaria. In chapter 9 Peter ministers at Lydda and Joppa,

and in chapter 10 he is in Joppa and Caesarea—all on the Judean coast of the Mediterranean. In chapter 11 he is in Jerusalem, defending what he did in Caesarea. And in chapter 12 we find the deliverance of Peter (in Jerusalem) and the death of Herod (in Caesarea).

In chapters 13–28 we see the gospel spread to Cyprus and Asia Minor (chaps. 13–14), to Macedonia in Europe (chap. 16), to Greece (chaps. 17–18). Finally Paul carries the message to Rome (chap. 28), which for the people of Palestine was "the uttermost part of the earth."

"Witnesses unto me" is, in the best Greek text, "my witnesses" (*mou* instead of *moi*). This makes it a bit more personal. We are to be Christ's own witnesses.

II. THE MINISTRY OF RECONCILIATION: II Corinthians 5:16-20

A. The Divine Christ: v. 16

At first sight this verse seems a bit difficult to understand. What is meant by "after the flesh"?

In his volume on II Corinthians in the *International Critical Commentary* Alfred Plummer suggests that it means "according to external distinctions," that is, "by what he is in the flesh." He would translate the first part of this verse: "We value no one because of his external attributes" (p. 176).

In his excellent volume on II Corinthians in *The New International Commentary on the New Testament* Philip E. Hughes writes: " 'Henceforth' doubtless means from the time when he formed the judgment or conclusion expressed in the two preceding verses, that is, the time of his conversion and enlightenment by the Holy Spirit" (p. 197). He explains the first part as meaning: "Typically worldly distinctions, such as those of race, social status, wealth, and title, should no longer govern the Christian's estimate of his fellow-men."

But what about the second part of the verse? In what way had Paul known Christ "after the flesh"? P. Gardner comments: "This reference is not to the human life of Jesus, which Paul had probably not witnessed, but to the kind of knowledge which is only of the senses, and has not become a process of the spirit" (*The Religious Experience of St. Paul*, p. 200). Hughes puts it in rather general terms: "Prior to his conversion his knowledge of Christ had been after the flesh, formed in accordance with external and mistaken standards; but his conversion had meant the transformation of his knowledge of Christ" (*Commentary on New Testament*, p. 199).

The last part of this verse is a good example of how we need to use our intelligence and common sense in reading the Bible. In the King James Version it reads: "Yet now henceforth know we him no more." The Greek says literally: "But now no longer we know." Taken absolutely, this would be a declaration by Paul that he didn't any longer know Christ—which is obviously untrue!

The New International Version gives a good rendering of the whole verse: "So from now on we regard no one from a worldly point of view. Though we once regarded Christ in this way, we do so no longer." That is, Paul now knew Jesus not only as a historical figure, but as the Son of God and Savior. And it was experiential, not just intellectual, knowledge.

B. A New Creation: v. 17

"Therefore, if anyone is in Christ, he is a new creation; the old has gone, the new has come!" (NIV). It should perhaps be noted that "all things" (KJV) is not in the earliest Greek manuscripts. The Greek tenses in the last part indicate that the passing away of the old was a crisis experience, whereas the presence of the new is a permanent state. We have become a new creation in Christ.

"Creation" is a better translation than "creature." J. H. Bernard says of this: "The expression 'a new creation' was a common Rabbinical description

of a converted proselyte" (*Expositor's Greek Testament*, III, 71).

"Therefore" ties this verse in with the previous verses. Plummer comments: "It no longer matters whether a man is by birth a Jew or a Gentile, bond or free; the one thing that is of weight is whether he has the right spiritual relation to Christ" (*Critical Commentary*, p. 180).

For the Jews of the first century this verse had an obvious application. Plummer puts it this way: "The Apostle calls to mind that the narrowness and exclusiveness of Judaism, the intolerable burden of the Law, and the still more intolerable burden of sin, have passed away from those who believe in Christ, and that a dispensation of comprehension, freedom, and peace has taken their place. This is no longer the hope of a prophet, or the guess of an apocalyptic dreamer, but an abiding fact" (*Critical Commentary*, p. 180).

As has often been said, the phrase "in Christ" sums up the heart of Paul's theology. He clearly and beautifully shows in his Epistles that our redemption is all "in Christ." And all the blessings we receive from God come to us in Christ Jesus.

The last clause of this verse begins with "behold" (Greek, *idou*, represented by an exclamation point in the New International Version). Hughes comments: "The exclamation 'behold!' sounds an unmistakable note of spontaneous jubilation. In its 'sudden note of triumph,' says Denney, 'we feel, as it were, one throb of that glad surprise with which he (Paul) had looked out on the world after God had reconciled him to Himself by His Son.' This response of delight and wonderment cannot fail to be evoked in the hearts of those to whom the miracle of God's new creation is revealed" (*Commentary on New Testament*, p. 203).

Isaiah predicted this: "Remember ye not the former things, neither consider the things of old. Behold, I will do a new thing" (43:18-19). In Revelation we read: "The former things are passed away.... Behold, I make all things new" (21:4-5).

C. Reconciliation in Christ: v. 18-19

This is one of the greatest theological passages in the Bible. It gives us the heart of the gospel.

Paul first reminds us that "all" the wonderful "things" he has been talking about—"all this," NIV—come to us from God. The Greek is strong here— "out from God" (*ek tou theou*), as its source. God is the inexhaustible source of all the good things we enjoy in this life, and especially our salvation.

God has reconciled us to Himself "by Jesus Christ"—Greek, "through Christ." And He has given to us "the ministry of reconciliation."

"Reconciled" and "reconciliation" are great terms with great meanings. Commenting on the middle clause of this verse, Plummer writes: "This is the usual language of N.T., in which the change which brings about the reconciliation between God and men is regarded as taking place in them rather than in Him. Greeks thought of God as estranged from men, and it was He who needed to be won over. Jews thought rather that it was men who by their sins were estranged from God, and the sins had to be 'cleansed,' or 'purged,' or 'covered,' in order to bring about reconciliation. St. Paul follows Jewish rather than Hellenistic thought. It is man who is reconciled to God, rather than God to man" (*Critical Commentary*, p. 181). Yet Plummer goes on to show that there is a sense in which God, who has been deeply offended by our sin, has to be reconciled to us. This takes place as we repent.

Our "ministry of reconciliation" is that of giving the message that "God was in Christ, reconciling the world to himself" (v. 19). From the time of the early church there has been a widespread difference of opinion as to whether this is the correct translation, or whether it should be: "In Christ God was reconciling the world to himself." In the *Expositor's Greek Testament* J. H. Bernard argues forcefully that the grammar of the sentence demands the second rendering. But not all agree. Actually the meaning is only slightly different. The emphasis for us to catch is the close identity of Father and Son in the work of our redemption.

The gospel is "the word of reconciliation." Socrates used the Greek term for "word" (*logos*) as indicating what is true and trustworthy, not a fictitious myth. The gospel is not fiction; it is fact. Christ died on the cross to reconcile us to God and save us from our sins.

"The world" means all mankind. Plummer observes: "God did all that on His side is necessary for their being reconciled to Him; but not all men do what is necessary on their side" (*Critical Commentary*, p. 183)—which is repentance and faith.

D. Ambassadors for Christ: v. 20

An ambassador is the official representative of his government. The position carries high status. To be "Christ's ambassadors" (NIV) is the greatest honor that could come to any human being. But it also carries grave responsibility. We must properly represent Him whose ambassadors we are.

As ambassadors our message is "Be reconciled to God." It is a word that every man needs to hear. What a privilege—and what a responsibility—to proclaim this word of salvation!

DISCUSSION QUESTIONS

1. What is the cause of perennial date-setting for the Second Coming?
2. How did Jesus relate knowledge and power?
3. How does Acts 1:8 still apply today?
4. What does it mean to be "in Christ"?
5. What is meant by "a new creation"?
6. What is the meaning of "reconciliation"?

CONTEMPORARY APPLICATION

Gypsy Smith was once asked, "What is the greatest need of Christendom?" Three times he answered, "Another Pentecost."

For those of us who knew Gypsy Smith, with his shaggy white hair and commanding figure, this carries a genuine challenge. We need a fresh outpouring of the Holy Spirit.

VARIETY OF LIFE-STYLES

DEVOTIONAL READING | I Corinthians 12:1-13

ADULTS

Topic: *Variety of Life-styles*

Background Scripture: Matthew 16:24-26; 19:16-30; II Corinthians 6:14—7:1; Colossians 2:16-23

Scripture Lesson: Matthew 19:16-30

Memory Verse: *There are varieties of working, but it is the same God who inspires them all in every one.* I Corinthians 12:6

YOUTH

Topic: *Variety of Life-styles*

Background Scripture: Matthew 16:24-26; 19:16-30; II Corinthians 6:14—7:1; Colossians 2:16-23

Scripture Lesson: Matthew 19:16-30

Memory Verse: *There are varieties of working, but it is the same God who inspires them all in every one.* I Corinthians 12:6

CHILDREN

Topic: *Living the New Life*

Background Scripture: Matthew 16:24-26; 19:16-30; II Corinthians 6:14—7:1; Colossians 2:16-23

Scripture Lesson: Matthew 19:16-30

Memory Verse: *Whatever is true, whatever is honorable, whatever is pure, whatever is lovely, whatever is gracious, if there is any excellence, if there is anything worthy of praise, think of these things.* Philippians 4:8

DAILY BIBLE READINGS

Mon., July 5: Prayer for the Church, John 17:6-19.
Tues., July 6: A Life of Commitment, Matthew 16:24-28.
Wed., July 7: A Life of Holiness, II Corinthians 6:14—7:1.
Thurs., July 8: A Life of Discipline, Colossians 2:16-23.
Fri., July 9: A New Life in Christ, Colossians 3:1-11.
Sat., July 10: A Life of Devotion, Colossians 3:12-17.
Sun., July 11: Equipping for Ministry, Ephesians 4:11-16.

LESSON AIM | To discover how we may imitate Christ without necessarily imitating each other.

LESSON SETTING

Time: Matthew 19: about A.D. 29; II Corinthians: A.D. 55; Colossians: A.D. 60.

Place: Galilee; Macedonia; Rome.

Variety of Life-styles

I. **The Rich Young Man:** Matthew 19:16-22
   A. The Man's Question: v. 16
   B. Jesus' Reply: v. 17
   C. Keeping the Commandments: vv. 18-19
   D. "What Lack I Yet?" v. 20
   E. The Counsel of Perfection: v. 21
   F. The Young Man's Failure: v. 22

II. **The Danger of Riches:** Matthew 19:23-26
   A. The Handicap of Being Rich: vv. 23-24
   B. The Disciples' Surprise: v. 25
   C. The Divine Possibility: v. 26

III. **The Rewards of Discipleship:** Matthew 19:27-30
   A. Peter's Question: v. 27
   B. The Future Status of the Apostles: v. 28
   C. A Hundredfold Reward: v. 29
   D. The First and the Last: v. 30

What does it mean to be separate from the world? This has been a perennial problem in the church.

For the monks of the Middle Ages it meant almost complete isolation from society. Monasteries had high walls around them to keep out the public. The monks wore a distinct "habit"—a long robe. Some orders of monks were enjoined to complete silence most of the time.

Was this imitating Christ? Anyone who reads the Gospels knows that the answer is No. Jesus moved almost constantly among the multitudes, ministering to their needs (cf. Matthew 19:1-2).

In modern times many groups have emphasized "the separated life." This is a much-needed Christian note. Jesus said: "If any man will come after me, let him deny himself, and take up his cross, and follow me" (Matthew 16:24).

But even this Scriptural emphasis on separation can be "run into the ground." When it means uniformity in dress and conduct, it can be more of an external conformity to certain rules and standards than an internal change of heart. It is the spiritual life that is supremely important.

What does it mean to be "in the world but not of the world"? Our separation from the world must be primarily a matter of spirit. There must be a complete devotion to Christ, an unconditional submission to His lordship in our lives.

But this does not mean that we must all adopt exactly the same life-style. Regimentation is the military way, but not the Christian way. We are to be ourselves—but "in Christ."

<table>
<tr><td>CONCEPTS FOR
CHILDREN</td><td>
1. The rich young man was living for self.
2. Being a Christian means that we live for Christ and others.
3. Love and concern should mark the Christian.
4. We serve Christ when we serve others (Matthew 25:40).
</td></tr>
</table>

THE LESSON COMMENTARY

I. THE RICH YOUNG MAN: Matthew 19:16-22

A. The Man's Question: v. 16

One of the characteristics of Matthew's Gospel is that he often generalizes whereas Mark and Luke are more specific. Matthew simply says here that "one" came to Jesus. In this case Mark (10:17) uses the same designation, though he has the man running and then kneeling before Christ. But Luke (18:18) calls him "a certain ruler." This evidently means that he was the ruler of a synagogue (cf. Jairus, Mark 5:22). Under the foreign rule of Rome the Jews had no political power.

Matthew describes this seeker as young and very wealthy (v. 22). So he is often referred to as "the rich young ruler."

Addressing Jesus as "Teacher" (KJV, "Master"), he asked, "What good thing shall I do, that I may have eternal life?" His question betrays his legalistic background as a Pharisee. He thought he had to "do" certain things in order to be saved or "have eternal life."

Having said this, we should note the earnestness and eagerness with which this young man came. We read in the previous verse that Jesus "departed thence." It would seem that this synagogue ruler hurried to see Jesus before He left that area. For him to kneel down before this Teacher showed genuine humility for a man of his position. And his question was certainly commendable; he wanted to know how to have eternal life. He was not a blind materialist, but one who believed in a future life and was concerned about preparing for it.

It should also be noted that here was a man who sought out the Master. As far as we know, he had not been approached. He had enough desire to come himself.

B. Jesus' Reply: v. 17

The answer given here in the King James Version is: "Why callest thou me good?" We find the same thing in Mark (10:18) and Luke (18:19). But the best Greek text in Matthew has: "Why do you ask me concerning the good?" As a synagogue ruler, this young man had been carefully instructed in the sacred Scriptures. He was supposed to know what was good in God's sight.

And so Jesus went on to say, "There is none good but one, that is, God." And He has shown us in His Word what is good, what His will is.

The heart of God's covenant with Israel at Sinai was the Ten Commandments. Moses received them from God's hand on the top of the mountain. They contained the essential requirements that God would make of man. And they have not been revoked. They are the foundation of all good society.

So Jesus said to the young man, "If thou wilt enter into life, keep the commandments." These were the conditions of the covenant. If the people kept the commandments, God would keep His covenant with them. This note is sounded frequently in the Old Testament, from Genesis to Malachi. And the survival of civilization today depends on adherence to the basic principles set out in the Ten Commandments.

C. Keeping the Commandments: v. 18-19

The young man was still full of questions. So he asked, "Which?"

The Greek literally means, "Of what kind?" So Carr comments as follows: "What commandments? written or unwritten? human or divine? the law of Moses or the traditions of the elders? or perhaps the young ruler expected a specimen of the rules with which this new Rabbi would instruct his disciples to 'fence around' the law" ("The Gospel According to St. Matthew," *The Cambridge Greek Testament*, p. 230). The Mosaic law had a multitude of commandments. Which ones did Jesus have in mind?

In reply the Master cited the sixth, seventh, eighth, ninth, and fifth of the Ten Commandments, in that order. The first of the two stone tablets at Sinai contained four commandments, setting out at some length man's duties toward God. The second tablet had the other six commandments, which consisted of man's duties toward his fellowman.

We cannot be certain as to why Jesus did not mention the first four commandments. Perhaps it was because it is more difficult to test one's relationship to God than one's relationship to his fellowman. Again, it may have been that the Master wanted this young man to face the lesser, lower requirements before He probed him on the primary matter of his devotion to God.

In place of the tenth commandment, Jesus quoted from the Old Testament: "Thou shalt love thy neighbour as thyself" (Leviticus 19:18). This requirement sums up the six commandments on the second tablet—duties toward man.

D. "What Lack I Yet?" v. 20

After listening to Jesus' enumeration of these commandments, the young man replied, "All these things have I kept from my youth up." He was doubtless sincere in saying this. But was he telling the truth?

If "these things" refers only to the specific five items cited from the Ten Commandments, the answer would probably be Yes. We have every reason to believe that this conscientious young Pharisee had not committed murder or adultery, that he had not stolen material things, that he had not given false testimony, and that he had honored his father and mother. He was probably a model of what a young Jew was supposed to be. He was proud of the strict, religious life he had lived.

But what about "Thou shalt love thy neighbour as thyself"? As the subsequent narrative shows, he was not fulfilling this requirement. For if we really love our neighbors as ourselves we will be willing to share with them whatever God asks. There was a deep-seated selfishness in this "pious" man's heart.

We must respect him, however, for adding, "What lack I yet?" Here was a young man who didn't want to fail, to fall short. He was conscious of a need, but didn't know how to identify it. Incidentally, this reveals the poverty of legalism. It can never really satisfy the human heart. It does not bring joy or peace. Taken by itself, a sense of *duty* can be depressing and discouraging. It takes *love* to lift duty to a higher level of joyful fulfillment.

It is that inner lack that haunts people today, as it did this young man. No matter what the circumstances, no matter what material resources a person may have, no matter what external righteousness he may exhibit in his life—if his heart is not filled with love he is not happy.

E. The Counsel of Perfection: v. 21

The young man asked for it, and Jesus gave it to him! He threw out to him the greatest challenge that can be given to any person: "If you want to be perfect" (NIV).

In any and every area of life perfection is costly. Not many are willing to pay the price for perfection in the arts and sciences. That is why we have so much shabby, shoddy work.

But it is in the spiritual realm that perfection is most expensive. For, as Jesus indicated here, it means expenditure of one's all. That is the cost of following Him.

To the young man Jesus said, "Go, sell your possessions and give to the poor, and you will have treasure in heaven. Then come, follow me" (NIV). Is this the universal path to perfection, Christ's requirement for all His followers today?

Those who have gone into convents and monasteries have taken Jesus' words literally. They have taken the three vows of poverty, chastity, and obedience. By "poverty" is meant the renunciation of all rights to private property. By "chastity" is meant celibacy, renouncing marriage. By "obedience" is meant full submission—not to God, but to the superior of the order.

Jesus apparently was poor and owned no property—He had no place "to lay his head" (Matthew 8:20). Is He to be our example in this?

When one faces the total picture of the New Testament it seems clear that the answer is No. There is no hint, for instance, that Lydia at Philippi sold her property and quit her business. Rather, she took care of the missionaries and gave generously to love offerings sent to Paul. If all Christians sold all they had and gave the proceeds to the poor, who would pay the bills to carry on the work of the church?

Why then did Jesus make this sweeping demand of the rich young ruler? The answer is plain. This man had allowed money to become his god. Actually he had broken the first and supreme commandment: "Thou shalt have no other gods before me" (Exodus 20:3). He was guilty of idolatry, worshiping his money. Jesus knew that this man could never be a true follower of His until he destroyed this idol by getting rid of his money.

What is the price of perfection for us today? It is that of surrendering everything to the lordship of Christ. It means giving "our all" to Him. First, it is the surrender of our will, our heart. Then all we have is put at His disposal, to use as He wishes.

F. The Young Man's Failure: v. 22

When the young man heard Jesus' challenge, he turned his back on Christ, and so on eternal life. We read that "he went away sorrowful: for he had great possessions."

The challenge was too great for him, the choice too difficult. He weighed the matter, and decided to hold on to his wealth. It was a tragic decision. How long could he keep his riches? Only till death! And then what? Ah, yes, what then?

Not surprisingly, some have suggested that Jesus may have had this young man in mind when He told the Parable of the Rich Fool (Luke 12:13-21). It certainly furnishes a dramatic postlude, if not an actual sequel. We wonder how many times the rich young ruler may have regretted his choice. One never regrets the decision to follow Jesus.

II. THE DANGER OF RICHES: Matthew 19:23-26

A. The Handicap of Being Rich: vv. 23-24

'When the young man had left, Jesus turned to His disciples—with a sad face, we may be sure—and said to them, "I tell you the truth, it is hard for a rich man to enter the kingdom of heaven" (v. 23, NIV). Why? Because money has a way of getting a stranglehold on those who hoard it.

Then Jesus declared, "It is easier for a camel to go through the eye of a needle, than for a rich man to enter into the kingdom of God" (v. 24). Christ was fond of using hyperbole, as when He talked about those who strain a tiny unclean gnat out of their drinking water and at the same time swallow a camel whole. So here we should not try to reduce the "camel" to "rope," as George Lamsa does. Nor should we think of a supposed "needle's-eye gate" in Jerusalem. Jesus purposely exaggerated for dramatic effect.

B. The Disciples' Surprise: v. 25

The twelve disciples were amazed at Jesus' statement. Their reaction was, "Who then can be saved?"

To appreciate their astonishment, we must remember that in the Old Testament material prosperity is often equated with God's blessing. God promised Solomon great wealth, although it seems to have contributed to his spiritual downfall. But the Book of Job should have alerted the rabbis, who taught the people the Scriptures in the synagogue on the sabbath, that loss of property was no sign of divine disfavor. Yet there again, we have to recognize that the Lord restored to Job double what he had.

C. The Divine Possibility: v. 26

There are many things impossible to man, such as a rich person being saved. But "with God all things are possible." He can bestow enough grace on a wealthy man to help him to be fully dedicated and unselfish.

III. THE REWARDS OF DISCIPLESHIP: Matthew 19:27-30

A. Peter's Question: v. 27

Peter always had something to say—before Pentecost too often at the wrong thing. So here he answered for the whole group: "We have left everything to follow you! What then will there be for us?" (NIV).

It sounds mercenary, selfish, self-seeking. We ought to be serving God in love, out of gratitude for all He has done for us. We can never repay the boundless debt we owe Him. All we can do is to seek to pay back a little of it in loving service to others. It is a carnal heart that asks, "What am I going to get out of this?"

B. The Future Status of the Apostles: v. 28

Patiently and lovingly Jesus answered Peter's selfish question by saying: "I tell you the truth, at the renewal of all things, when the Son of Man sits on his throne in heavenly glory, you who have followed me will also sit on twelve thrones, judging the twelve tribes of Israel" (NIV). It is obvious that the "renewal" (KJV, "regeneration") refers to the time when God will say, "Behold, I make all things new" (Revelation 21:5). At that time His apostles—not Judas Iscariot—will reign with Him.

C. A Hundredfold Reward: v. 29

The heavenly reward extends to all those who forsake everything to follow Christ. They will receive a "hundredfold"—10,000 percent dividend the investment of their lives in God's service. Is it worth it?

On top of all the rewards for faithful service will come the unmerited free gift of "everlasting life." This we cannot earn; we can only receive it as a gift of God's grace.

But even in this life those who sacrifice to serve Christ will be abundantly repaid. Many a missionary who has left relatives behind can testify that he has found hundreds of brothers and sisters, and fathers and

DISCUSSION QUESTIONS

1. What does it mean to be separate from the world?
2. What is common to all Christians?
3. What variations may there be?
4. In what ways are we to imitate Christ?
5. How far may we imitate others?
6. What does it mean to give up all to follow Jesus?

mothers, in the Lord. This is one of the great recompenses for Christian service.

D. The First and Last: v. 30

Jesus sounded a warning against Peter's greedy spirit and selfish ambi-tion. He said that many who came "first" would end up "last." On the other hand, many who came last would finally be first. The least, humble saint may be first in God's sight.

CONTEMPORARY APPLICATION

What each of us must do is to find God's will for *our* life. We have often heard the motto: "Others may; you cannot." God may seem to ask more from some in a material way than from some others. Our responsibility is to obey His instructions to us.

STORMS WITHIN THE CHURCH

DEVOTIONAL READING	I Timothy 4:6-16

ADULTS

Topic: *Storms Within the Church*

Background Scripture: Matthew 7:15-29; I John 4:1-12

Scripture Lesson: I John 4:1-12

Memory Verse: *Jesus began to say to them, "Take heed that no one leads you astray."* Mark 13:5

YOUTH

Topic: *Internal Storms*

Background Scripture: Matthew 7:15-29; I John 4:1-12

Scripture Lesson: I John 4:1-12

Memory Verse: *Jesus began to say to them, "Take heed that no one leads you astray."* Mark 13:5

CHILDREN

Topic: *Good and Bad Leaders*

Background Scripture: Matthew 7:15-29; I John 4:1-12

Scripture Lesson: Matthew 7:15-29.

Memory Verse: *And Jesus began to say to them, "Take heed that no one leads you astray."* Mark 13:5

DAILY BIBLE READINGS

Mon., July 12: Jesus Faces Rejection, Luke 4:24-30.
Tues., July 13: The Controversy at Jerusalem, Acts 15:1-11.
Wed., July 14: Paul's Disagreement with Barnabas, Acts 15:36-41.
Thurs., July 15: Dissension at Corinth, I Corinthians 3:1-9.
Fri., July 16: Disagreement at Philippi, Philippians 4:1-7.
Sat., July 17: Deception at Crete, Titus 1:5–2:1.
Sun., July 18: Warning Against False Prophets, Matthew 7:15-23.

LESSON AIM

To see what our attitude should be toward differences of opinion within the church.

LESSON SETTING

Time: Jesus' words: about A.D. 28; writing of I John: about A.D. 95.

Place: Galilee; Ephesus.

LESSON OUTLINE

Storms Within the Church

    I. False Prophets: Matthew 7:15-20

A. Wolves in Sheep's Clothing: v. 15
B. Recognized by Their Fruits: vv. 16-20

II. False Profession: Matthew 7:21-23

III. False and True Foundations: Matthew 7:24-29
A. Building on the Rock: vv. 24-25
B. Building on the Sand: vv. 26-27
C. Reaction of the Crowd: vv. 28-29

IV. False Prophets: I John 4:1-6
A. Testing the Spirits: v. 1
B. The Test of Truth: vv. 2-3
C. The Spirit of Truth and of Error: vv. 4-6

V. Fruit of Love: I John 4:7-12
A. Love as Proof of Godliness: vv. 7-8
B. Love Shown in Redemption: vv. 9-10
C. Love for Each Other: vv. 11-12

SUGGESTED INTRODUCTION FOR ADULTS

There have always been false prophets in the church. Jesus, in the Sermon on the Mount, predicted that there would be. John, in his First Epistle, said that there were already many by the end of the first century. The second century was marked by struggles with Gnosticism, the leading heresy that plagued the early church.

Since then there have been dozens of heresies that have risen to lead people astray. The third and fourth centuries were times of turbulent strife over doctrines. The Middle Ages produced less frequent doctrinal debate, but it had its share of false prophets.

When Martin Luther launched the Protestant Reformation in the sixteenth century, immediately he encountered distortions of his teachings. The eighteenth and nineteenth centuries saw the rise of extreme, destructive criticism, undermining the authority of the Bible. The first half of the twentieth century saw the consequences of this in a widespread denial of the deity of Jesus and His blood atonement for sin. And in the second half of the century we have been treated to a "death of God" theology.

SUGGESTED INTRODUCTION FOR YOUTH

Internal storms—that is what the church has encountered from the beginning. How are we going to test what is true? The first test must always be: Is it Biblical?

But we have to recognize the fact that the Bible is sometimes interpreted differently by different people. And so we have to apply two other tests: Jesus' test of the fruit—what are the moral consequences?—and John's test of love. Any doctrine that produces wrong living is bad. And always there must be the spirit of love.

CONCEPTS FOR CHILDREN

1. Even in the church there are false prophets.
2. We should test all teachings by the Bible.

3. We should also note the results of any teaching.
4. Love is the supreme test.

THE LESSON COMMENTARY

I. FALSE PROPHETS:
Matthew 7:15-20

A. Wolves in Sheep's Clothing: v. 15

Near the beginning of His ministry, Jesus told His disciples to look out for "false prophets." This is a compound word in Greek, *pseudopropheton*. It occurs three times in Matthew (cf. 24: 11, 24); once each in Mark, Luke, Acts, II Peter and I John; and three times in Revelation—for a total of eleven times. The word *pseudochristoi*, "false Christs," occurs only twice (Matthew 24:24; Mark 13:22)—both in the Olivet Discourse. There have been many false prophets in church history but only a few false messiahs.

Jesus said that these false prophets would appear in sheep's clothing, as though they were innocent lambs, or belonged to the true flock of God. But inwardly they would be "ravening" wolves. This adjective would naturally be taken by us as equivalent to "ravenous"—that is, hungry for food. But the earliest meaning of both "ravening" and "ravenous" in English was "taking by force"; that is the way wild animals often get their food. And this is the meaning of the Greek word here— *harpages*, "seizing by force." So "rapacious" or "ferocious" (NIV) is a better translation than "ravenous."

One of the marks of false prophets is that they do everything for self. They show an intense interest in getting a large following and making a lot of money. This is one of the surest evidences of their falseness. The true prophet of God is not seeking fame or fortune.

B. Recognized by Their Fruits: vv. 16-20

In verse 1 of this chapter Jesus said, "Judge not, that ye be not judged." We are not to judge others. But here Jesus declares, "By their fruit you will recognize them" (v. 16, NIV). It is not a matter of judging, but of recognizing the obvious, when we say that one tree is bearing oranges or peaches, while another is producing lemons or persimmons. So we can easily recognize the fact that some people's lives are sweet and loving, while others' personalities are sour and critical. If we come across a man who is staggering down the sidewalk, reeking of alcohol, it is not judgmental to say that he is drunk. That is simply recognizing a fact.

So Jesus said, "Do people pick grapes from thornbushes, or figs from thistles?" (NIV). Making the application, He continued: "Likewise every good tree bears good fruit, but a bad tree bears bad fruit" (v. 17, NIV). Which kind of a tree are we? Our fruit of daily living furnishes the answer. And we cannot escape revealing in our lives the real nature of our hearts. A bad heart will show itself in bad attitudes and actions. And so will a good heart reveal its nature. Eventually people will recognize us for what we are. For, "a good tree cannot bring forth evil fruit, neither can a corrupt tree bring forth good fruit" (v. 18).

Verse 20 recapitulates: "Wherefore by their fruits ye shall know them" (cf. v. 16a). False prophets can be recognized by their aims and actions.

II. FALSE PROFESSION:
Matthew 7:21-23

The Master now sounded a serious note of warning: "Not every one that saith unto me, Lord, Lord, shall enter into the kingdom of heaven; but he that doeth the will of my Father which is in heaven" (v. 21). It is not enough to call Jesus "Lord." We must show that He has become Lord of our lives by living in constant obedience to the will of God. It must be more than profession; it must be demonstration.

Obedience is the test of true discipleship. Not even preaching and working miracles will compensate for a lack of obedience to God's will. Jesus declared that many would say to Him in "that day [that is, the last day] Lord, Lord, did we not prophesy in your name, and in your name drive out demons and perform many miracles?" (v. 22, NIV).

Certainly all this would prove that one was a true follower of Christ! "Not so," said Jesus. Instead we have the ominous words: "And then will I profess unto them, I never knew you: depart from me, ye that work iniquity" (v. 23).

The final judgment day will be a terrible "moment of truth." All false profession will be exposed for what it is. Only those who have been living in humble obedience will pass the test. The All-knowing One will make no mistake in judgment.

III. FALSE AND TRUE FOUNDATIONS: Matthew 7:24-29

A. Building on a Rock: vv. 24-25

Doing, not saying, will be the test. Jesus used the illustration of two kinds of houses, one built on a rock and the other on sand.

First He said: "Therefore, everyone who hears these words of mine and puts them into practice is like a wise man who built his house on the rock" (NIV)—the Greek suggests a solid ledge of rock. Of course, for us that is the Rock of Ages, Christ Jesus. This Scripture passage is the basis for the well known lines:

On Christ the solid Rock I stand;
All other ground is sinking sand.

Jesus went on to describe what happened: "The rain came down, the streams rose, and the winds blew and beat against that house; yet it did not fall, because it had its foundation on the rock" (v. 25, NIV). "I've anchored to the Rock of Ages"—those words we sing must be our actual experience if we are going to stand firm when the storms of life assail us.

B. Building on the Sand: vv. 26-27

The one who hears Jesus' words but does not put them into practice will be like a foolish man who builds his house on the sand. The winds will topple it—"it fell with a great crash" (NIV). We cannot afford to build our theology on the shifting sands of men's opinions, but rather on the Gibraltar of God's Word. And we must not build our lives on the oozy-woozy nonsense of "situation ethics." The Bible is our foundation for living.

C. Reaction of the Crowd: vv. 28-29

When Jesus had finished His message, the crowds were amazed at His "teaching" (not "doctrine," KJV). Why? Because He "taught them as one having authority, and not as the scribes" (v. 29). The scribes ("teachers of the law," NIV) were in the habit of quoting previous rabbis. But Jesus taught with absolute divine authority.

IV. FALSE PROPHETS: I John 4:1-6

A. Testing the Spirits: v. 1

John warned his readers not to believe every spirit, "but test the spirits to see whether they are from God" (NIV). What is meant by "spirits" here? It has been suggested that it means "spiritual influences," such as come to us from many directions and sources.

Writing in "The Epistles of St. John" (*Cambridge Greek Testament*), Alfred Plummer says: "But besides ordinary spiritual influences, St. John probably has in his mind those extraordinary and supernatural powers which at various periods of the Church's history persons have claimed to possess. Such claims exhibit them-

selves in professed revelations, prophecies, miracles and the like. About all
such things there are two possibilities
which must put us on our guard:
(1) they may be unreal; either the de-
lusions of fanatical enthusiasts, or the
lies of deliberate imposters; (2) even if
real, they need not be of God. Miraculous powers are no absolute guarantee
of the possession of truth" (p. 94).

In line with this, Dr. Harvey
Blaney writes: "There is a diabolic
supernatural power, as well as a righteous supernatural power, working in
the world and in the lives of men.
There are also false prophets who
make evil out of good. Some are to be
found in the church—those who substitute institutionalized religion for the
vitality of the Spirit of Christ, and
those who substitute a humanism for
the gospel of Christ" (*Beacon Bible
Commentary*, X, 387).

B. The Test of Truth: vv. 2-3

How can we know that what is said
comes from the Spirit of God? John
gives first a positive test (v. 2) and
then a negative test (v. 3).

He writes, "Every spirit that ac-
knowledges that Jesus Christ has come
in the flesh is from God" (v. 2, NIV).
The first and supreme test of orthodoxy is the Incarnation (cf. John
1:14), the confession that the Son of
God has "come in the flesh"—that is,
in a true physical body. Unless He was
human, Christ could not have died in
our place. And unless He was divine,
His death could not atone for our sins.
From Matthew to Revelation, the New
Testament emphasizes this twofold
truth of the true deity and real humanity of Jesus Christ. This is the
touchstone of orthodoxy.

Then comes the negative side:
"But every spirit that does not acknowledge Jesus is not from God" (v.
3, NIV). "Christ is come in the flesh"
(KJV) is not in the best Greek text,
but is implied from verse 2.

From this and other passages in
this Epistle it is evident that John is
combating Docetic Gnosticism. The

term *docetic* means "seeming."
Gnosticism, a heresy condemned by
the church in the second century, held
that all spirit is good, all matter is evil.
So if Christ was the true Son of God,
He could not have had a physical
body; He just seemed to have. Thus
the Docetic Gnostics denied the real
humanity of Jesus.

John labels this false teaching as
"that spirit of antichrist, whereof ye
have heard that it should come; and
even now already is it in the world." It
is interesting to note that the word
"antichrist" occurs only in I John (2:
18, 22; 4:3) and II John 7. In 2:18 he
says that there are "many antichrists"
—those who oppose Christ. But as
early as the second century, Irenaeus
identified the "man of lawlessness" (II
Thessalonians 2:3, NIV) and "the
Beast" of Revelation as *the* antichrist
of the end of this age.

C. The Spirit of Truth and of Er-
ror: vv. 4-6

In Christ the child of God is an
overcomer, because Christ, the one
who dwells in him, is greater than the
spirit of the world. This is the affirmation of verse 4.

John addresses his readers as "little
children." In the first verse of this
chapter he calls them "beloved." Both
of these are favorite expressions of the
aged apostle in this Epistle. They reveal the tenderness and warm love of
his heart.

John declares that his readers are
"of God"—more literally "from God,"
as the source of their spiritual life. In
contrast to this, "they" (the false
prophets) are "of the world" (v. 5), as
the source of their thinking. Because
of that, they speak "of the world"—
not about the world, but "from the
world" as the source of their thinking
and talking. So the world listens to
them.

"The world" is a favorite expression of John's, occurring seventy-nine
times in his Gospel and twenty-three
times in his First Epistle. Paul uses it
twenty-one times in I Corinthians. But

it is used very sparingly in the other books of the New Testament. For John, "the world" comprises what is opposed to God—a selfish, self-seeking spirit of disobedience and rebellion against divine authority. It has often been remarked that in John's view there was no gray; everything was black or white. He saw "the world" as all black.

Including himself now, John says, "We are of God" (v. 6)—that is, "from God." Just as the world listens to the false prophets, so those who know God listen to John and his associates. The rest refuse to listen to God's message through His true prophets.

"The spirit of truth" is the Holy Spirit, who reveals truth. "The spirit of error" (only here in the New Testament) is the spirit of Satan, the father of lies (John 8:44).

V. FRUIT OF LOVE:
I John 4:7-12

A. Love as Proof of Godliness: vv. 7-8

"Beloved, let us love one another." What a beautiful combination! John's readers were loved by God and by the apostle. So they were to love one another.

Obviously John is thinking primarily about the loving fellowship of believers. Just as we have a special love

for our own "loved ones," so Christians should have a special love for those who belong to the family of God.

Why should we love one another? Because "love is of God"—better, "from God." If we have been born of God spiritually, we should have love in our hearts. If we "know" Him experientially, we share His love.

Verse 8 contains a solemn warning: "Whoever does not love does not know God" (NIV). Why? Because "God is love." If we have Him in our hearts, we have love. It's just as simple as that. For a person not to show love when he claims to have Jesus in his heart is a denial of his profession.

"God is love" is the simplest, and yet profoundest, statement in the Bible. Very few nouns are equated with God. But love is absolute, infinite, eternal. This truth should be a constant challenge to us. We find this statement repeated in verse 16.

B. Love Shown in Redemption: vv. 9-10

"In this was manifested the love of God toward us [Greek, "in us" or "among us"] because that God sent his only begotten Son into the world, that we might live through him" (v. 9). Christ had to die in order that we might live. That is the heart of the gospel.

The true meaning of love is illustrated in verse 10. We did not first love God; He first loved us. And He demonstrated that love by giving His Son to be the propitiatory sacrifice for our sins—to atone for our sins. Love is always giving, outgoing, outflowing. True love is always unselfish.

The Greek word for "propitiation" (hilasmos) refers us back to the "mercy-seat" in the holy of holies in the ancient tabernacle and temple. It was where the blood of the sin offering was sprinkled by the high priest once a year on the Day of Atonement (Yom Kippur). Christ, our High Priest, gave His own blood as a once-for-all atonement for our sins.

DISCUSSION QUESTIONS

1. What are some of the false teachings of our day?
2. What are some examples of wolves in sheep's clothing?
3. How can we know whether a teaching is false?
4. What are some of the sands on which people build their lives?
5. What place does love play in the Christian life?
6. How can we best express our love to others?

C. Love for Each Other: vv. 11-12

The logic of verse 11 is inescapable: "If God so loved us, we ought also to love one another." God always takes the initiative. But we are to respond in love to Him and follow His example in love to others.

"No one has ever seen God" (v. 12, NIV)—that is, with physical eyes, because God is spirit. But if we love one another, it is evidence that God lives in us. His purpose is that His love may be "perfected," or "made complete," in us. John was the great apostle of love.

CONTEMPORARY APPLICATION

Today "love" is a much used and much abused term. Hollywood has dragged it down into the dirt of low living until for many people it simply means sex.

But *agape* is a great word, occurring 116 times in the New Testament. Even though I John is one of the shorter books, this term occurs 27 times.

What is true love? It is not merely physical attraction or even psychological attachment. Neither of these is strong enough to hold. Rather, it is essentially a spiritual attachment. Since "God is love," we can only know love at its highest level as we know Him.

SCRIPTURE ALONE

DEVOTIONAL READING	Jeremiah 36:27-32

ADULTS

Topic: *Scripture Alone*

Background Scripture: II Kings 22:1-13; Luke 4:16-21; Romans 1:16-17; 15:4; Galatians 2:15-21; 3:23-29

Scripture Lesson: Galatians 2:15-21; 3:23-29

Memory Verse: *Whatever was written in former days was written for our instruction, that by steadfastness and by the encouragement of the scriptures we might have hope.* Romans 15:4

YOUTH

Topic: *Scripture Alone*

Background Scripture: II Kings 22:1-13; Luke 4:16-21; Romans 1:16-17; 15:4; Galatians 2:15-21; 3:23-29

Scripture Lesson: Galatians 2:15-21; 3:23-29

Memory Verse: *Whatever was written in former days was written for our instruction, that by steadfastness and by the encouragement of the scriptures we might have hope.* Romans 15:4

CHILDREN

Topic: *Love—God's Gift*

Background Scripture: Romans 1:16-17; Galatians 2:15-21; 3:23-29

Scripture Lesson: Galatians 2:15-21

Memory Verse: *For God so loved the world that he gave his only Son, that whoever believes in him should not perish but have eternal life.* John 3:16

DAILY BIBLE READINGS

Mon., July 19: Discovering the Book of the Law, II Kings 22:3-13.

Tues., July 20: Reform Under King Josiah, II Kings 23:1-8.

Wed., July 21: Keeping God's Law, II Kings 23:21-25.

Thurs., July 22: Jesus' Concern for Scripture, Luke 4:16-21.

Fri., July 23: An Old Testament Affirmation, Habakkuk 2:1-4.

Sat., July 24: A New Testament Confirmation, Romans 1:8-17.

Sun., July 25: The Encouragement of the Scriptures, Romans 15:1-6.

LESSON AIM
| To understand why we say that the Bible is our final authority for doctrine and practice.

LESSON SETTING
| **Time:** Luke's Gospel was written probably about A.D. 60; Galatians, A.D. 48 or 55; and Romans about A.D. 56.

| **Place:** Luke, uncertain; Romans, Corinth

Scripture Alone

I. **Prophetic Scripture:** Luke 4:16-21
   A. Jesus in His Home Synagogue: v. 16
   B. The Lesson from Isaiah: vv. 17-19
   C. The Fulfillment of Scripture: vv. 20-21

II. **Revelation in Scripture:** Romans 1:16-17
   A. The Power of the Gospel: v. 16
   B. The Revelation of Divine Righteousness: v. 17

LESSON OUTLINE

III. **The Purpose of Scripture:** Romans 15:4

IV. **Redemption in Scripture:** Galatians 2:15-21
   A. Justification by Faith: vv. 15-16
   B. Dead to the Law: vv. 17-19
   C. Crucified with Christ: vv. 20-21

V. **The Function of the Law:** Galatians 3:23-24

VI. **The Function of Faith:** Galatians 3:25-26

VII. **One in Christ:** Galatians 3:27-29

SUGGESTED
INTRODUCTION
FOR ADULTS

It is generally agreed that one of the important revivals in the Old Testament was that under King Josiah in 621 B.C. And it started with the rediscovery of the neglected sacred Scriptures.

Josiah was only eight years old when he began his reign of thirty-one years in Jerusalem (II Kings 22:1). "In the eighth year of his reign [when he was only fifteen or sixteen years of age] he began to seek after the God of David his father," and in the twelfth year, at twenty years of age, he began to purge Judah and Jerusalem of its idolatry (II Chronicles 34:3). "In the eighteenth year of King Josiah" (II Kings 22:3)—that is, "in the eighteenth year of his reign" (II Chronicles 34:8)—he undertook the repairing of the temple at Jerusalem.

Hilkiah the high priest discovered in the temple a forgotten copy of the law, and he gave it to Shaphan the scribe (II Kings 22:8). When Shaphan read it to the king, Josiah tore his own clothes in consternation. He realized that according to the Word of God, Jerusalem was under divine wrath for its many sins and especially its neglect of the Law. The result was a crusade against idolatry in Judah (II Kings 23). No other king had turned to the Lord with his whole heart, soul, and might as did young Josiah (II Kings 23:25). And it was all because of the Word of God.

SUGGESTED
INTRODUCTION
FOR YOUTH

It was a young king in his middle teens who began to seek after the Lord (II Chronicles 34:3). As he was finishing his teen years, the discovery of a copy of the Law (perhaps Deuteronomy) made him a zealous reformer of his nation. "Josiah's revival," as it is called, was begun by an earnest young man who wanted all of God's will.

CONCEPTS FOR
CHILDREN

1. Martin Luther rediscovered the main emphasis of the New Testament and started the Protestant Reformation.
2. He was opposed by the church but remained faithful.
3. Our supreme allegiance must be to God.
4. If we are true, God will see us through.

THE LESSON COMMENTARY

I. PROPHETIC SCRIPTURE:
    Luke 4:16-21

A. Jesus in His Home Synagogue: v. 16

After Jesus' baptism by John and His temptation by Satan in the desert, He "returned in the power of the Spirit into Galilee" (v. 14) and began a teaching ministry in the synagogues there.

Finally He reached Nazareth, His home town in the hills of southern Galilee. Bethlehem was His birthplace, but Nazareth was "where he had been brought up" (v. 16). Then we read that "as his custom was, he went into the synagogue on the sabbath day." He had been brought up in a godly home, where attendance at the synagogue services was the regular practice.

The first Scripture lesson in a typical sabbath service was always from the Torah, the Law. This was followed by a lesson from the Prophets. Perhaps someone else read first from one of the five books of Moses, and then Jesus was asked to read from the Prophets—or He may have volunteered. At any rate, He stood up to

read, as the Jews always did, out of reverence for their sacred Scriptures.

B. The Lesson from Isaiah: vv. 17-19

"The scroll of the prophet Isaiah was handed to him" (NIV) by the synagogue attendant. "Unrolling it, he found the place where it was written. ..." There were no printed books at that time, of course. Each individual book consisted of a leather scroll on a roller. The Dead Sea Scroll of Isaiah, from about 125 B.C., is nearly twenty-four feet long, and very well preserved. For years it was fully unrolled and on exhibition in the Shrine of the Book at Jerusalem. Now it is stored in darkness to preserve it more carefully.

"He found the place where it was written" suggests that He may have chosen this Scripture, that it was not an assigned lesson for that day. Later on the lessons were carefully specified.

Jesus read from Isaiah 61:1-2. He probably read in Hebrew, which He had learned at the synagogue school. Someone would interpret it into Aramaic for the congregation. It appears that the common people had lost their knowledge of Hebrew during the Babylonian exile.

Jesus read: "The Spirit of the Lord is upon me, because he hath anointed me to preach the gospel to [Greek verb *euangelizo*, "evangelize"] the poor." This was His highest mission. The reading ended with the words "to preach ["proclaim"] the acceptable year of the Lord."

C. The Fulfillment of Scripture: vv. 20-21

"Then he rolled up the scroll, gave it back to the attendant and sat down" (v. 20, NIV). It was the Jewish custom to stand while reading the Scriptures but to sit while teaching or preaching. Again we note that Jesus conformed to the customs of that day.

With the eyes of all those in the synagogue fastened on Him, He said to the people, "This day is this scripture fulfilled in your ears" (v. 21). Now we can see why He stopped His reading in the middle of the sentence. If He had read the next line—"and the day of vengeance of our God"—He could not have said, "This day is this scripture fulfilled." The first coming of Christ was "the acceptable day" of salvation. The second coming will be a time of judgment on sinners.

Verse 18 describes beautifully the varied ministry of Jesus. The most important thing He did was to announce to the poor the good news of salvation. The rest of the language has primarily a metaphorical, spiritual application as illustrating what salvation is. But He did literally give sight to the blind. "To heal the broken hearted" (KJV) is not in the earliest Greek manuscripts.

II. REVELATION IN SCRIPTURE: Romans 1:16-17

A. The Power of the Gospel: v. 16

Paul had just asserted that he was eager to preach the gospel in Rome (v. 15). Now he affirms: "I am not ashamed of the gospel because it is the power of God for the salvation of everyone who believes: first for the Jew, then for the Gentile" (NIV). ("The gospel of Christ" [KJV] is simply "the gospel" in the early manuscripts.)

The gospel is more than words, more than a creed. It is "the power of God unto salvation." Many writers have commented that we have in this verse the main thrust of this Epistle. W. H. Griffith Thomas broadens this a bit. Combining verses 16 and 17, as in our main heading above, he says, "These two verses should be carefully studied, for they contain practically all the leading thoughts of the entire Epistle" (*St. Paul's Epistle to the Romans,* p. 60).

The Greek word for "power" is *dynamis*, from which we get "dynamite" and "dynamic" and "dynamo." The gospel is like dynamite in blasting us free from sin. It takes real power to do that. Then it puts a dynamo in our souls that furnishes light, heat, and power to meet all our needs. And if we really let the gospel possess us, it will make us dynamic personalities. A Spirit-filled individual should certainly be dynamic. We have seen weak people become powerful witnesses and workers when the gospel actually got hold of them.

But it is not wasted power. It is power for a purpose—for "salvation." This is a bigger term than our little definitions can encompass. But basically and primarily it means deliverance from sin.

This salvation comes only to those who believe. It is provided for all and proffered to all. But only those who accept it by faith are actually saved.

B. The Revelation of Divine Righteousness: v. 17

The Greek says "a righeousness" (no definite article). So some scholars have suggested that the expression refers to a special righteousness that God has prepared for believers, rather than "the righteousness of God" as a divine attribute. But why not both? It is

God's own righteousness which He both imputes and imparts to us when we are justified by faith in Christ. We have no righteousness of our own. The only genuine righteousness that we will ever have is what we receive from God. Actually, Christ is our righteousness (I Corinthians 1:30).

Sanday and Headlam give an excellent discussion of this point. They write: "The righteousness of which the Apostle is speaking not only proceeds from God but *is* the righteousness of God Himself: it is this, however, not as inherent in the Divine Essence but as going forth and embracing the personalities of men" (*Epistle to the Romans*, p. 25).

This righteousness is revealed "from faith to faith." Sanday and Headlam say that the phrase means "starting from a smaller quantity of faith to produce a larger quantity" (*Romans*, p. 28).

The keynote of Romans is found in the quotation at the end of this verse: "The just shall live by faith"— taken from Habakkuk 2:4. "Justification by faith" is really the theme of the Epistle. It is by faith that we are saved and by faith that we live.

III. THE PURPOSE OF SCRIPTURE: Romans 15:4

The New International Version represents the original Greek of this verse more accurately than does the King James Version. It reads: "For everything that was written in the past [Paul obviously means "in the Scriptures"] was written to teach us, so that through endurance and the encouragement of the Scriptures we might have hope."

So here we see the purpose of the Old Testament. Griffith Thomas comments: "It was written to uphold believers in their life of patient hope. They were to learn, and from learning to derive endurance and comfort, which in turn would lead to hope" (*Romans*, p. 381).

Every devout Christian knows that it is the thoughtful, prayerful reading of the Bible which gives him strength and courage for each day. What would we do without the Bible to read?

IV. REDEMPTION IN SCRIPTURE: Galatians 2:15-21

A. Justification by Faith: vv. 15-16

Paul was a Jew "by nature"; that is, he was born that way, of Jewish parents. All Jews considered the Gentiles to be "sinners," separated from God, unclean.

The King James Version uses "of" constantly where the proper English translation is "by" or "from" or "in." This verse is a good example. Twice it speaks of the faith "of" Christ, where clearly the meaning is faith "in" Christ. We are not justified by observing the Law but by faith in Jesus Christ. Paul ends this important verse by saying, "for by the works of the law shall no flesh be justified." It is obvious that in this context "flesh" means "person."

It was in his study of Romans and Galatians that Martin Luther came to a clear understanding of the New Testament teaching on justification by faith and made this the watchword of the Protestant Reformation in the sixteenth century. He had to fight much the same battle with the Roman Catholic Church that Paul had fought with the Judaizers in the first century.

B. Dead to the Law: vv. 17-19

Verse 17 is difficult to understand at first reading. Paul is answering an accusation of the Judaizers that by ignoring the Law in depending on Christ for his salvation, he was making himself a "sinner" like the Gentiles. He accepts the accusation—with that meaning of "sinner." But he rejects the deduction that this makes "Christ the minister of sin." He answers this idea with an emphatic *me genoito*— translated in the King James Version as "God forbid." Literally it means

"May it not be," and so "Absolutely not!" (NIV).

On the contrary, Paul says, "If I build again the things which I destroyed, I make myself a transgressor" (v. 18). That is, if I go back to observing the Law, then I *do* become a sinner.

So he concludes, "For through the law I died to the law so that I might live for God" (v. 19, NIV). Because of Paul's experience of the folly of dead legalism ("through the law"), which he describes in the seventh chapter of Romans, he had severed all relations to it ("I died to the law"), so that he now might be alive in his new-found faith in Christ. This was Paul's glorious experience of the grace of God.

C. Crucified with Christ: vv. 20-21

There is no basis in the Greek for the "nevertheless" (KJV). The correct translation of verse 20 is: "I have been crucified with Christ and I no longer live, but Christ lives in me. The life I live in the body, I live by faith in the Son of God, who loved me and gave himself for me" (NIV).

One of the great paradoxes of Christianity is simply this: You have to die to live. Unless Christ had died on the cross He could not have been resurrected to live in our hearts as the risen, living Lord. And until we have been crucified with Christ we cannot know fullness of life in Him. George Mueller of Bristol said, "There was a day when I died, utterly died." It was this that made him so fully alive in Christ that he became one of the greatest men of faith in all the history of Christianity. We have to die to self and sin in order to live the resurrection life of victory in Christ.

Paul goes on to say: "I do not set aside the grace of God, for if righteousness could be gained through the law, Christ died for nothing!" (v. 21, NIV). For Paul it was definitely law or grace; there was no compromise. He had proved in his own experience the futility of trying to find righteousness by observing the Law. Only the grace of God could bring justification and life.

What is meant by "righteousness"? Abbott-Smith defines the Greek word as: "conformity to the Divine will in purpose, thought, and action" (*Lexicon*, p. 116).

V. THE FUNCTION OF THE LAW: Galatians 3:23-24

The Mosaic law given at Sinai did have a purpose. Paul puts it this way: "Before this faith came, we were held prisoners by the law, locked up until faith should be revealed" (v. 23, NIV). The function of the Law was to guard God's people until, in the fullness of time, Christ should come to make atonement for sin.

Then Paul uses an interesting figure. He says: "Wherefore the law was our schoolmaster to bring us unto Christ, that we might be justified by faith" (v. 24, KJV).

The Greek word for "schoolmaster" is *paidagogos*, which gives us our word *pedagogue*, a "schoolteacher" (cf. *pedagogy*, which means "the art or profession of teaching"). But the Greek word had a somewhat different meaning. In his monumental volume on Galatians in the *International Critical Commentary* series, E. D. Burton writes: "A *paidagogos* was a slave employed in Greek and Roman

---

DISCUSSION QUESTIONS

1. Why is it necessary to hold to the sole authority of the Bible?
2. What happens when *I* become my final authority?
3. What theme unites the Bible as one book?
4. How is "salvation by works" taught today?
5. Why do we need to study our Bibles more?
6. Who is the final interpreter of the Bible to us?

families to have general charge of a boy in the years from about six to sixteen, watching over his outward behaviour and attending him whenever he went from home, as e.g. to school" (p. 200). Arndt and Gingrich define the word as: *"attendant (slave), custodian, guide,* literally 'boy-leader,' the man, usually a slave . . . whose duty it was to conduct the boy or youth . . . to and from school and to superintend his conduct generally; he was not a 'teacher' (despite the present meaning of the derivative 'pedagogue')" (*Lexicon,* p. 608).

VI. THE FUNCTION OF FAITH:
Galatians 3:25-26

God had always intended that the Law should be a temporary provision for His people: "Now that faith has come, we are no longer under the supervision of the law" (v. 25, NIV). Instead we are "children of God by faith in Christ Jesus" (v. 26). Faith in Christ brings us into the family of God.

It should be obvious by now that the main purpose of the Epistle to the Galatians is to show that all we get from God, including especially our salvation, comes to us through faith in Jesus Christ. It is all of faith.

VII. ONE IN CHRIST:
Galatians 3:27-29

The Greek word for "put on" (v. 27) means to put on clothes. So the passage means: "For all of you who were united with Christ in baptism have been clothed with Christ" (NIV). Burton comments: " 'To put on Christ' is to become as Christ, to have his standing; in this context to become objects of the divine favour, sons of God, as he is the Son of God" (*Critical Commentary*, p. 203). To be clothed with Christ implies that we display Christ to the world that would otherwise not see Him. For the first thing that people usually notice about us is our clothes. Do they immediately think of Christ when they look at us? Do they?

The gospel does away with all distinctions of race, status, and sex: Gentiles are just as welcome as Jews; slaves, as free men; women, as men. Paul says, "You are all one in Christ" (v. 28). In the family of God all these differences disappear.

If we belong to Christ, we are "Abraham's seed, and heirs according to the promise" (v. 29). The Judaizers were telling the Galatians that only those who came by way of Judaism were the seed of Abraham, and so heirs to the promises God gave to him. Paul assured them that because they belonged to Christ, all this was theirs.

CONTEMPORARY APPLICATION

The Roman Catholic Church holds that Scripture and Tradition (decrees of councils and papal dogmas) form the twofold authority for its doctrine. The Protestant declaration, beginning with Martin Luther, is that the Bible is our sole authority for doctrine and practice—"Scripture Alone." Today many Liberals discount the divine authority of the Bible, resulting in moral chaos.

TRANSLATING THE BIBLE

DEVOTIONAL READING	Psalm 119:105-112

ADULTS

Topic: *Making the Message Plain*

Background Scripture: Psalm 1:1-3; Jeremiah 31:31-34; Nehemiah 8:1-8; Acts 8:26-39; II Corinthians 3:1-3

Scripture Lesson: Acts 8:26-39

Memory Verse: *Write the vision;*
make it plain upon tablets,
So he may run who reads it.
Habakkuk 2:2

YOUTH

Topic: *God's Word in Man's Language*

Background Scripture: Psalm 1:1-3; Jeremiah 31:31-34; Nehemiah 8:1-8; Acts 8:26-39; II Corinthians 3:1-3

Scripture Lesson: Acts 8:26-39

Memory Verse: *Write the vision;*
make it plain upon tablets,
So he may run who reads it.
Habakkuk 2:2

CHILDREN

Topic: *Telling the Story of Jesus*

Background Scripture: II Kings 23:1-14; Psalm 1:1-3; Acts 8:26-39; I Corinthians 1:26-31; 3:10-15; 4:1-13; I John 5:1-5

Scripture Lesson: Acts 8:26-39

Memory Verse: *Jesus said, "You shall be my witnesses in Jerusalem and in all Judea and Samaria and to the end of the earth." Acts 1:8*

DAILY BIBLE READINGS

Mon., July 26: Delight in the Law, Psalm 1.
Tues., July 27: Walking by God's Word, Psalm 119:1-8.
Wed., July 28: Remembering God's Word, Psalm 119:9-16.
Thurs., July 29: Written on Our Hearts, Jeremiah 31:31-34.
Fri., July 30: Written by the Spirit, II Corinthians 3:1-6.
Sat., July 31: Fulfilling the Law of Christ, Galatians 5:22–6:2.
Sun., Aug. 1: A Light for Our Path, Psalm 119:105-112.

LESSON AIM

To see how the Word of God has been communicated to man in many languages.

LESSON SETTING

Time: Nehemiah, about 440 B.C.; Acts 8, about A.D. 33; II Corinthians, A.D. 55

Place: Jerusalem; Samaria; Macedonia

Translating the Bible

LESSON OUTLINE

I. Public Reading of the Word: Nehemiah 8:1-8
    A. Request of the People: v. 1
    B. Response of Ezra: vv. 2-3
    C. Reverence for the Word: vv. 4-6
    D. Reading with Explanation: vv. 7-8

II. Private Reading of the Word: Acts 8:26-39
    A. Philip Guided by the Lord: v. 26
    B. Ethiopian Eunuch Reading the Word: vv. 27-28
    C. Philip's Question: vv. 29-30
    D. The Eunuch's Answer: v. 31
    E. Passage in Isaiah: vv. 32-34
    F. Explanation of the Scripture: v. 35
    G. Baptism of the Eunuch: vv. 36-39

III. Presentation of the Word in Life: II Corinthians 3:1-3

SUGGESTED INTRODUCTION FOR ADULTS

The Bible is God's Word to man. We should forever be grateful that God has not left us in the dark, to grope our way through life. The psalmist declared, "Thy word is a lamp unto my feet, and a light unto my path" (Ps. 119:105). Those who read the Bible carefully and prayerfully find that it guides them safely in their daily walk.

The very first Psalm emphasized the importance of reading the Word. The "blessed" man is one of whom it is said, "His delight is in the law of the Lord; and in his law doth he meditate day and night" (v. 2).

We say that our Bible is divided into the Old Testament and the New Testament. We get this from the Latin *testamentum*, which means a "will." Actually, the correct expressions are the "Old Covenant" and the "New Covenant." That is what the Hebrew and Greek words mean.

One of the most significant passages in the Old Testament is Jeremiah 31:31-34. There the Lord declares that the time will come when He will make a new covenant with His people; He will write His law on their hearts. This refers to the experience of the indwelling Holy Spirit causing us to want to do God's will.

SUGGESTED INTRODUCTION FOR YOUTH

We live in a day when thousands of new books are being written and multiplied millions of copies are being sold. This means that we have to be selective in our reading.

Recently it was stated that the top nonfiction best seller was *The Living Bible,* which has sold eighteen million copies in the last three years. We rejoice over the fact that more young people are reading the Bible these days. May God's Word increase in power!

CONCEPTS FOR CHILDREN

1. Many people need help in understanding the Bible.
2. New versions make its meaning clearer.
3. The Bible is being translated into many languages.
4. We should encourage others to read the Bible.

THE LESSON COMMENTARY

I. PUBLIC READING OF THE WORD:
Nehemiah 8:1-8

A. Request of the People: v. 1

It was in 444 B.C. that Nehemiah, who was cupbearer to the Persian king Artaxerxes, returned to Judea to rebuild the walls of Jerusalem. He had a willing spiritual ally in Ezra the scribe.

This verse tells how all the people in Jerusalem "gathered themselves together as one man into the street that was before the water gate." There they asked Ezra to bring "the book of the law of Moses" and read it to them.

B. Response of Ezra: vv. 2-3

This deeply devoted man of God, whose book precedes Nehemiah's in our Bibles, was glad enough to comply. He brought the scroll of sacred Scripture on "the first day of the seventh month," at the time of the Feast of Trumpets, to read to the congregation composed of both men and women.

He stood in the "street"—better "broad place"—and read "from the morning until midday," probably from nine o'clock till twelve. This shows how eager the people were to hear the Word of God. We read that "the ears of all the people were attentive unto the book of the law" (v. 3). Would that this were always so!

C. Reverence for the Word: vv. 4-6

In order to be heard by the large crowd, Ezra stood on a high wooden platform ("pulpit," KJV) especially made for the occasion. He was flanked on either side by leaders of the people, showing their appreciation of what was taking place (v. 4).

"Ezra opened the book in the sight of all the people ... and when he opened it, all the people stood up" (v. 5). It is a good custom still today to have the congregation stand reverently for the reading of the Scripture. And the preacher should handle the Bible in a reverent manner. People notice the attitude that we take toward the Word of God. As God's message to His people, it deserves to be treated as sacred.

Before starting to read, "Ezra blessed the Lord, the great God. And all the people answered Amen, Amen, with lifting up their hands: and they bowed their heads, and worshipped the Lord with their faces to the ground" (v. 6). It was an impressive occasion. Perhaps these people had not heard the Word of God read in a long time. Today we can all have Bibles, usually several of them, in our homes. New Testaments cost less than a hamburg sandwich. But in those days, when all copies of the sacred books were made laboriously by hand, very few people could have them in their homes. The only time when they would hear the Word of God was when it was read in public. How thankful we ought to be that we can all read and mark our own Bibles in our private devotions. We take for granted many of our wonderful blessings and opportunities.

D. Reading with Explanation: vv. 7-8

The Levites, who were familiar with the Law, "caused the people to understand the law" (v. 7). Bible teaching is of paramount importance.

Verse 8 is a most significant passage. It says: "So they read in the book in the law of God distinctly [the Bible should never be read any other way!], and gave the sense, and caused them to understand the reading." The statement that they "gave the sense" probably means that they paraphrased the Hebrew text into Aramaic, since the returned captives had largely lost their knowledge of the Hebrew language. These Aramaic paraphrases are called Targums. In the time of Christ they were recited orally (see lesson 8). Some centuries later they were put in written form. Today scholars find them helpful for the understanding of some Old Testament passages.

There is nothing more important than giving people everywhere the Bible in a language that they can clearly understand. If we believe that the Bible is the Word of God, then we should seek to communicate it as clearly and effectively as possible. For the Bible only becomes actually God's Word to people when they understand it. This is the compelling reason behind all modern-speech versions.

As far as English-speaking people are concerned, it started back near the end of the fourteenth century. The only Bible available was the Latin Vulgate, the official Bible of the Roman Catholic Church. But only the learned could read it. To the common people it was a closed book.

A man named Wyclif became concerned about this situation. So he produced the first English Bible in 1382. This was before the invention of printing, and so all copies had to be made by hand. It is on record that a man gave a load of hay for just a few pages of this Bible. The Word of the Lord was precious in those days.

In the middle of the fifteenth century one of the greatest aids to civiliza-tion came in the invention of printing. It is significant that the first book to appear from the press was a Bible—the Gutenberg Bible, about 1456. But it was the Latin Vulgate.

The first printed English New Testament was that of Tyndale (1525-26). Whereas Wyclif's Bible was a translation of the Latin Vulgate, Tyndale's New Testament was translated directly from the original Greek. But Tyndale paid for this with his life. In 1536 he was condemned for heresy and burned at the stake.

The first printed English Bible was issued by Coverdale in 1535. He used Tyndale's translation for the New Testament and part of the Old Testament.

The Great Bible appeared in 1539. It is sometimes referred to as the Chained Bible, because in each church in England a copy of this large Bible was chained to a lectern. People would stand for hours to hear someone read from the Scriptures, because they still did not have any Bibles in their homes.

The Geneva Bible (1560), made in Geneva, Switzerland, was too "Protestant" to suit the bishops of the Church of England. So they issued their own "Bishop's Bible" in 1568. The great King James Version (1611) is a revision of the Bishop's Bible. Unfortunately it retains some of the Latinisms of that version, such as "charity" (Latin, *caritas*) for "love." But the King James Version was done so well that it has been the most widely used English Bible for the past three centuries.

Today, however, the King James Version does not communicate the Word of God adequately, because of its somewhat antiquated language. Over eight hundred words in that version have changed their meaning since 1611, over two hundred of these rather radically. In addition to that fact, we have a better Greek text today than did the King James translators. Their Greek text was based on a few late medieval manuscripts, none of them earlier than the tenth century. Today we have over five thousand Greek manuscripts of the New Testament (in whole or in part), reaching back to the fifth, fourth, and even early third centuries.

So in 1885 the English Revised Version appeared. The American Standard Edition of the Revised Version (ASV) came out in 1901. But the Revised Version lacked the literary qualities of the King James Version and never became popular. In 1952 the Revised Standard Version sought to remedy this situation. It was a revision of the American Standard Version "in the direction of the King James Version." From the literary point of view it succeeded well.

But many Evangelicals were not happy with it. So in 1971 the New American Standard Bible appeared. It was likewise a revision of the American Standard Version (1901), but done entirely by Evangelicals. It is the best study Bible available in English today.

In 1973 the New Testament of the New International Version (NIV) was published. It also was done entirely by committed Evangelicals. But it is in more contemporary English style than the New American Standard Bible. It is hoped that the New International Version Old Testament will be published in 1978.

In addition to these, there have been many Bible translations produced by individuals in this century. One thinks of Moffatt, Weymouth (New Testament), Goodspeed, *Good News for Modern Man* (TEV) and the most popular of them all, *The Living Bible*. The last, as the title page indicates, is a paraphrase, not an exact translation.

Any and all of these can be used with great profit by sincere Christians who want to understand God's Word better. It can be said without hesitation that one who reads half a dozen or a dozen new translations of the New Testament will gain many fresh insights into its true meaning. In fact, these translations make a good commentary on the original text.

By reading a chapter a day a person can go through the New Testament in less than a year. An excellent plan is to read through each year a new translation.

II. PRIVATE READING OF THE WORD: Acts 8:26-39

A. Philip Guided by the Lord: v. 26

Philip was one of the seven men chosen to take care of the daily distribution of food in the church at Jerusalem (6:1-6). When that Jewish Christian church was scattered by the violent persecution that followed Stephen's death, Philip went down to a city of Samaria and "preached Christ" there (8:1-5). The result was that many people were saved, "and there was great joy in that city" (v. 8). A little later Peter and John were sent from Jerusalem. They laid their hands on the new converts, who then received the Holy Spirit (vv. 14-17).

But now an angel of the Lord spoke to Philip and gave him a new assignment: "Go south to the road—the desert road—that goes down from Jerusalem to Gaza" (v. 26, NIV). It seemed like a strange order. Why should he leave the great revival in Samaria and go out into the desert? But God never makes a mistake.

Gaza was about sixty miles southwest of Jerusalem, the southernmost city of Palestine, almost on the border of Egypt. The "Gaza Strip" has figured in the news in recent years in the negotiations between Egypt and Israel.

B. Ethiopian Eunuch Reading the Word: vv. 27-28

In spite of the seeming incongruity of the call, Philip didn't argue or protest. Instead, as the Greek forcefully indicates by the aorist tense, he obeyed immediately. Because he started out at once, he met his man. If he had hesitated, or stopped to argue, he would have missed him! It always pays to obey the Lord promptly.

For there was a man on the Gaza road that needed spiritual help, and

Philip was the one to minister to him. This man was an important figure—"an eunuch of great authority under Candace queen of the Ethiopians, who had charge of all her treasure" (v. 27). In other words, he was the Chancellor of the Exchequer, the highest position under the queen.

"Candace" was a title for the Ethiopian queens, like Pharoah of Egypt or Caesar of Rome. It was the custom of that day for royal families to have eunuchs serving them in the palace.

This eunuch had been to Jerusalem "to worship." The phrase here means "on a pilgrimage." He had evidently been attracted by the superiority of Judaism over the pagan religion of his country.

Now he was returning home (v. 28). As befitted his high position, he had the best transportation those times afforded: He was "sitting in his chariot." To while away the long hours of the journey, he was reading from a scroll of the prophet Isaiah. (Being a man of wealth, he was able to purchase this expensive scroll.) And he was following the advice of the Jewish rabbis that the Law should be read aloud by one who was traveling.

C. Philip's Question: vv. 29-30

The Spirit said to Philip, "Go near, and join thyself to this chariot" (v.

29). In the same way the Holy Spirit can guide us today in doing personal work. It is physically impossible for us to witness to everybody. But the Spirit will lead us to speak to those whose hearts are open to receive the Word.

Again obeying promptly, Philip "ran up to the chariot and heard the man reading Isaiah the prophet" (v. 30, NIV). It is claimed by scholars that all reading in that day was done aloud —no one read silently. Even today in Moslem mosques one hears men reading the Koran out loud.

Then Philip asked the Ethiopian eunuch a very pertinent question: "Do you understand what you are reading?" (NIV). In the Greek there is an interesting play on words: *ginoskeis ha anaginoskeis*. This question has universal application and relevance. How much of what we read do we really understand?

D. The Eunuch's Answer: v. 31

Almost plaintively—possibly even brusquely, in keeping with his office— the eunuch replied, "How can I, unless someone explains it to me?" (NIV). "So he invited Philip to come up and sit with him" (NIV).

There are thousands of people today who are reading the Bible without understanding it properly. We thank God for every helpful teaching of the Word that is going on in churches and over radio. And many people are being helped by Bible study groups meeting in private homes—provided there is a competent person to lead the discussion.

E. Passage in Isaiah: vv. 32-34

The eunuch was reading from the fifty-third chapter of Isaiah, verses 7 and 8 (quoted in verses 32-33). Puzzled by what he read, the eunuch said to Philip: "Tell me, please, who is the prophet talking about, himself or someone else?" (v. 34, NIV). This was an intelligent, legitimate question. The eunuch was seeking light.

DISCUSSION QUESTIONS

1. Why is it important that people understand the Word of God?
2. What is the significance of the public reading of the Scriptures?
3. What is the importance of Bible translation?
4. How may we all contribute to it?
5. Why do we need new English translations of the Bible?
6. How can we translate the Bible into our lives?

F. Explanation of the Scripture: v. 35

"Then Philip began with that very passage of Scripture and told him the good news [the Greek verb is *euangelizo*, "announce good news"] about Jesus" (NIV). There is no better place in the Old Testament from which to preach Christ. For here we have the outstanding passage prophesying Christ's atoning death for sinners. He was the Lamb of God, who takes away the sin of the world (John 1:29).

The first clause of verse 33 should read: "In his humiliation he was deprived of justice" (NIV). This was true of both His Jewish trial by the Sanhedrin and His Roman trial before Pilate.

G. Baptism of the Eunuch: vv. 36-39

The eunuch accepted the message of salvation through Jesus Christ and was ready to receive Christian baptism. Just then they came to an oasis, where there was water—possibly the place now called "Philip's Fountain," on the road between Bethlehem and Hebron. So the eunuch said: "See, here is water; what doth hinder me to be baptized?" (v. 36). He was eager to go all the way.

Verse 37 is not in the oldest Greek manuscripts and so is rightly omitted in modern versions. It was added by later scribes.

The eunuch ordered his driver to stop the chariot. Right then and there Philip baptized this new convert (v. 38).

When they came up out of the water, "the Spirit of the Lord caught away Philip" (v. 39). He was not needed any more. But the eunuch "went on his way rejoicing" in his new faith in Christ. It is always this way with those who experience a genuine conversion.

III. PRESENTATION OF THE WORD IN LIFE: II Corinthians 3:1-3

This passage suggests that we are to translate the Bible into our lives, so that people can read the Word of God by watching us. This puts on us a great responsibility to present God's Word correctly by exemplifying its teachings.

CONTEMPORARY APPLICATION

The Bible, in whole or in part, has now been translated into some thirteen hundred languages of the world. Yet as recently as the beginning of the nineteenth century only seventy-one languages and dialects had even a portion of the Bible. Then the Bible societies were formed and a veritable explosion of new translations took place. In 1938 it reached a thousand languages, and the number now increases rapidly. So the Word goes forth.

Along with this forward thrust of translation have come the great conferences on evangelism. The world *can* be evangelized in our generation, so that Christ may return (Matthew 24:14).

EVANGELICAL EXPERIENCES

DEVOTIONAL READING	I John 1

ADULTS

Topic: *Evangelical Experiences*

Background Scripture: Acts 8:4-19; 10:1-48; 19:8-20; Romans 8:1-9a; I John 3:1-3

Scripture Lesson: Acts 10:30-44

Memory Verse: *By grace you have been saved through faith; and this is not your own doing, it is the gift of God.* Ephesians 2:8

YOUTH

Topic: *Happenings Now*

Background Scripture: Acts 8:4-19; 10:1-48; 19:8-20; Romans 8:1-9a; I John 3:1-3

Scripture Lesson: Acts 10:30-44

Memory Verse: *By grace you have been saved through faith; and this is not your own doing, it is the gift of God.* Ephesians 2:8

CHILDREN

Topic: *Being Children of God*

Background Scripture: Acts 10; 16:25-34; I John 3:1-3; James 1:22—2:26

Scripture Lesson: Acts 16:25-34

Memory Verse: *Beloved, we are God's children now.* I John 3:2

DAILY BIBLE READINGS

Mon., Aug. 2: Salvation Available for All, Romans 3: 21-26.
Tues., Aug. 3: A Gentile Believes, Acts 10:34-48.
Wed., Aug. 4: Lydia Believes, Acts 16:11-15.
Thurs., Aug. 5: The Ministry of Apollos, Acts 18:24-28.
Fri., Aug. 6: Life in the Spirit, Romans 8:1-6.
Sat., Aug. 7: Born of God, I John 3:1-9.
Sun., Aug. 8: Abiding in Christ, I John 3:19-24.

LESSON AIM

To see the nature and importance of an evangelical experience of conversion.

LESSON SETTING

Time: Sometime between A.D. 35 and 40

Place: Joppa and Caesarea, both on the Mediterranean coast of Palestine

358

Evangelical Experiences

I. **Cornelius's Vision:** Acts 10:1-8
   A. The Character of Cornelius: vv. 1-2
   B. The Message of the Angel: vv. 3-6
   C. The Obedience of Cornelius: vv. 7-8

II. **Peter's Vision:** Acts 10:9-23a
   A. No Distinction Between Jew and Gentile: vv. 9-16
   B. The Assurance of the Spirit: vv. 17-20
   C. The Message from Cornelius: vv. 21-23a

LESSON OUTLINE

III. **Peter at Cornelius's House:** Acts 10:23b-33
   A. Cornelius's Greeting: vv. 23b-26
   B. Peter's Response: vv. 27-29
   C. Cornelius's Report: vv. 30-33

IV. **Peter's Message:** Acts 10:34-43
   A. No Divine Partiality: vv. 34-35
   B. The Earthly Ministry of Jesus: vv. 36-38
   C. The Death and Resurrection of Jesus: vv. 39-43

V. **The Results:** Acts 10:44-48
   A. The Outpouring of the Spirit: v. 44
   B. The Astonishment of the Jews: vv. 47-48
   C. The Baptism of Gentiles: vv. 47-48

SUGGESTED INTRODUCTION FOR ADULTS

Evangelicals are those who emphasize salvation through grace by faith, rather than by good works or the sacraments. The word *evangelical* is almost equivalent to "gospel" used as an adjective.

The Book of Acts is full of evangelical experiences. Saul's experience on the road near Damascus was an evangelical conversion (chap. 9). In Acts 8:5-8 (see background Scripture) we find evangelical conversions taking place on a large scale in Samaria under the preaching of Philip. The Ethiopian eunuch's conversion (last week's lesson) was an evangelical experience.

The background Scripture of today's lesson also describes this experience coming to a large number of people in the city of Ephesus (Acts 19:8-20). Paul began in the synagogue, speaking there each sabbath day. When Jewish opposition drove him out, he continued preaching and teaching for two years in the lecture hall of Tyrannus, with many people converted. The proof that they had turned from their superstitious beliefs was shown in a bonfire in which they burned ten-thousand-dollars worth of magic scrolls (v. 19). Paganism went up in flames.

SUGGESTED INTRODUCTION FOR YOUTH

Being brought up in a Christian home does not make one a Christian. Nor does being baptized and joining a church. One has to experience a genuine evangelical conversion. This involves confessing one's sins, asking God's forgiveness, and then accepting Jesus as Savior and Lord. We have to be born again in order to become the children of God.

CONCEPTS FOR CHILDREN	1. The Philippian jailer asked the most important question in the world (Acts 16:30).
	2. The answer was clear and simple (v. 31).
	3. We are not born as children of God.
	4. We become children of God by the New Birth.

THE LESSON COMMENTARY

I. CORNELIUS'S VISION: Acts 10:1-8

A. The Character of Cornelius: vv. 1-2

Caesarea was a magnificent city on the Mediterranean coast of Palestine, about sixty miles from Jerusalem. Herod the Great (37-4 B.C.) had built it as his capital and named it in honor of the Caesar at Rome. At this time it was the seat of the Roman government of Judea.

Stationed there was a man named Cornelius. He was a "centurion"—the officer in charge of a century (a hundred soldiers). His group was a part of the Italian "band," or cohort, which was a tenth of a legion. Since the Roman legion was made up of six thousand men, the cohort would normally contain about six hundred soldiers.

Cornelius is described as a devout man and one who feared God. He was also generous in his gifts to the poor, and he prayed to God always. It is clear that he was worshiping in the Jewish synagogue.

B. The Message of the Angel: vv. 3-6

The Jews offered sacrifices in the temple twice a day—the morning and evening sacrifices, at 9:00 A.M. and 3:00 P.M. The "ninth hour" would be three o'clock in the afternoon. Devout Jews made this their hour of prayer (3:1).

Cornelius saw an angel of God, who came to him and called his name.

Struck with fear, he asked, "What is it, Lord?" (v. 4). He was assured by the angel that his prayers and his giving to the poor had not gone unnoticed in heaven. He was also instructed to send messengers to Joppa and bring Simon Peter from there.

C. The Obedience of Cornelius: vv. 7-8

When the angel had disappeared, "Cornelius called two of his servants and one of his military aides who was a devout man" (v. 7, NIV). He told them all that had happened and sent them off to Joppa.

II. PETER'S VISION: Acts 10:9-23a

A. No Distinction Between Jew and Gentile: vv. 9-16

"About noon the following day as they were approaching the city, Peter went up on the roof to pray" (v. 9, NIV). Practically all the homes in Palestine still have flat roofs, with a low railing around them. This was the place for meditation and prayer.

While waiting for the noon meal to be prepared, Peter became very hungry and fell into a trance (v. 10). "He saw heaven opened and something like a large sheet being let down to earth by its four corners" (v. 11, NIV). This contained all kinds of four-footed animals, reptiles, and birds. A voice ordered him to "kill and eat" (v. 13).

Peter protested: "Not so, Lord; for I have never eaten any thing that is common or unclean" (v. 14). The Jews used the word "common" for Gentiles and careless Jews, with the sense of "unclean."

This apostle of Christ was reproved for his attitude of discrimination. The voice spoke again: "Do not call anything impure that God has made clean" (v. 15, NIV). The vision was repeated twice again to enforce this important lesson (v. 16).

The significance of the vision is clear. The old distinctions between "clean" and "unclean" foods was done away in Christ. Likewise there was to be no distinction between Jews and Gentiles. Both could become children of God equally through faith in Jesus Christ. It was an epochal revelation from heaven.

B. The Assurance of the Spirit: vv. 17-20

"While Peter was wondering about the meaning of the vision, the men sent by Cornelius found out where Simon's house was and stopped at the gate" (v. 17, NIV). They called out to inquire if Simon Peter was staying there (v. 18).

Meanwhile, Peter was still thinking about the vision. Then the Spirit disclosed to him the fact that three men were looking for him (v. 19). "So get up and go downstairs. Do not hesitate to go with them, for I have sent them" (v. 20, NIV). It probably took both the vision and the direct command of the Holy Spirit to make Peter willing to go with these men to the home of a Gentile.

The striking lesson we learn from this is the way God can work things at both ends of a situation and bring them together with perfect timing. Cornelius had his vision first, and that initiated the action. But it was not until two days later, when the messengers from Cornelius were approaching Joppa, that Peter had his vision—at just the right time!

God still works things out with equally miraculous provision. If we are fully submitted to His leading, He will arrange things perfectly.

C. The Message from Cornelius: vv. 21-23a

Peter went down to the men and said to them: "I'm the one you're looking for. Why have you come?" (v. 21, NIV). After his vision and the assuring words of the Holy Spirit, Peter was prepared to go with these men. But he wanted further information as to why they were looking for him.

In reply the messengers told him of the vision that Cornelius had seen and of the angel's instructions to send for Peter. Thus informed, Peter invited the men to come into the house as his guests.

III. PETER AT CORNELIUS'S HOUSE: Acts 10:23b-33

A. Cornelius's Greeting: vv. 23b-26

The three messengers stayed overnight with Peter at Joppa. This is shown by the statement here that he started out with them the next day (v. 23b).

Fortunately, "some of the brothers from Joppa went along" (NIV). For when Peter was "called on the carpet" on his return to Jerusalem because he had eaten with Gentiles in Cornelius's house, he could say, "These six brothers also went with me" (11:12, NIV).

On the following day they arrived in Caesarea. They found that "Cornelius was expecting them and had called together his relatives and close friends" (v. 24, NIV).

When Peter started to enter the house, Cornelius met him at the door and fell at his feet in reverence (v. 25). Peter remonstrated with him: "Stand up; I myself also am a man" (v. 26). We can easily understand why Cornelius wanted to worship him.

B. Peter's Response: vv. 27-29

When Peter got inside he found that a large number of people had assembled. By way of introduction he said: "You are well aware that it is against our law for a Jew to associate with a Gentile or visit him. But God has shown me that I should not call any man impure or unclean" (v. 8, NIV). This must have relieved the minds of his hearers of any lingering fears they had. Now both sides were ready for God to minister to them.

When Peter asked why they had sent for him (v. 29), Cornelius gave a full explanation. He started out by saying, "Four days ago I was in my house praying at this hour, at three in the afternoon" (v. 30, NIV). ("Fasting" [KJV] is not in the early Greek manuscripts.)

The mention of "four days" fits in perfectly with the distances involved. Caesarea was thirty miles north of Joppa, both of them on the Mediterranean coast. The average day's travel at that time was not more than twenty miles.

The logical reconstruction seems to be something like this. Suppose that Cornelius had his vision about three o'clock Monday afternoon. It would be late for his messengers to start out that day; so they waited till the next morning, walking some twenty miles on Tuesday. "The following day" (v. 9)—that is, on Wednesday—they arrived in Joppa shortly after noon. By the time they had eaten and rested, it was again too late to start out. So Peter kept them overnight. "The next day" (v. 23b)—Thursday—he started out with them. They walked about twenty miles and stopped overnight. "The following day" (v. 24), which would be Friday, they covered the remaining ten miles and arrived in Caesarea fairly early in the afternoon. This was exactly "four days" since Cornelius's vision.

Cornelius now went on to tell how a man in shining clothes suddenly stood in front of him, commending him for his piety and generosity (v. 31), and instructing him to send to Joppa for Simon Peter (v. 32).

Graciously Cornelius went on: "So

I sent for you immediately, and it was good of you to come" (v. 33). The attitude of the waiting congregation is expressed very well in his next words: "Now we are all here in the presence of God to listen to everything the Lord has commanded you to tell us." Peter had a receptive audience.

IV. PETER'S MESSAGE: Acts 10:34-43

A. No Divine Partiality: vv. 34-35

As a result of his vision, plus Cornelius's account of the vision he had had, Peter could say: "I now realize how true it is that God does not show favoritism but accepts men from every nation who fear him and do what is right" (vv. 34-35, NIV).

As a Jew, Peter had been taught all his life that only the physical descendants of Abraham were the people of God. The Gentiles were outside the divine covenant—unclean, condemned, forever doomed. It took some fast and drastic readjustment of his thinking to welcome the idea that Cornelius was just as acceptable with God as Abraham, or David, or any contemporary Jew. Racial pride was crucified at Calvary. In Christ all men are equal before God, regardless of race, creed, culture, or intellectual background.

B. The Earthly Ministry of Jesus: vv. 36-38

That is where it started. God sent a "word" to the people of Israel, "the good news of peace through Jesus Christ, who is Lord of all" (v. 36, NIV). Actually, Christ was Himself "the Word," as John tells us in the prologue to his Gospel. The message was not simply *about* Him. He was Himself God's message of love, bringing peace to those who would accept that love. We can say that Jesus Christ was at the same time both God's Messenger and God's Message. For the message of love and peace was embodied in Him. To see Him was to hear that message from the heart of God.

Peter then proceeded to recapitulate in capsule form the ministry of Jesus. He reminded his hearers that they were familiar with reports about Christ's earthly career. It began after His baptism by John, when He was anointed with the Holy Spirit and power. The center of His ministry was in Galilee, where He went about doing good and healing those who were oppressed by the devil (v. 38).

C. The Death and Resurrection of Jesus: vv. 39-43

Peter declared that he was a witness of everything Jesus did during His earthly ministry in Galilee. Then it had narrowed down to Jerusalem, where "they killed him by hanging him on a tree" (v. 39, NIV). This would be an especially vivid memory for Peter, for the crucifixion took place only a few hours after the leading apostle had denied his Lord three times. It must have hurt to recollect those awful hours.

But the story didn't end there: "God raised him from the dead on the third day and caused him to be seen" (v. 40, NIV). Not by all the people, "but by witnesses whom God had already chosen—by us who ate and drank with him after he rose from the dead" (v. 41, NIV).

It has been pointed out that Peter's message thus far is almost a brief outline of Mark's Gospel. And the early church was unanimous in saying that Mark's Gospel gives us the preaching of Peter.

Then Peter went beyond the resurrection to the Great Commission: "He commanded us to preach to the people and to testify that he is the one whom God appointed as judge of the living and the dead" (v. 42, NIV). In the King James Version "quick" is obsolete English for "living."

Peter's conclusion was that the Old Testament prophets foretold that "whosoever believeth in him shall receive remission of sins" (v. 43). One such reference would be Joel 2:32.

So Peter ended his message on a clear, strong evangelistic note. Salvation was for all men—Jews or Gentiles —who would believe on Jesus. It is a "whosoever" gospel.

V. THE RESULTS: Acts 10:44-48

A. The Outpouring of the Spirit: v. 44

"While Peter was still speaking these words, the Holy Spirit came on all who heard the message" (NIV). Why did this take place so quickly, so suddenly? The answer is to be found in the beautiful spirit of eagerness, obedience, and receptivity shown by Cornelius and his friends. The centurion spoke for the whole group when he said, "Now we are all here in the presence of God to listen to everything the Lord has commanded you to tell us" (v. 33, NIV). The stage was perfectly set for an outpouring of the Holy Spirit. These people wanted all that God had for them, and He did not disappoint them.

How often we have seen that happen in our own day! When people come into God's presence—in a church sanctuary, or in small group for Bible study or prayer—the place can become permeated with the Spirit's presence and blessing.

DISCUSSION QUESTIONS

1. Why did the first Jewish Christians have such a narrow, nationalistic outlook?
2. How did God help them to overcome this?
3. What narrow attitudes do some Christians have today?
4. What is the remedy for this?
5. What is an "evangelical conversion"?
6. What attitude should we take toward such movements as the "Jesus People"?

B. The Astonishment of the Jews: vv. 45-46

"The circumcised believers [the six Jewish Christians who had accompanied Peter (11:12)] ... were astonished that the gift of the Holy Spirit had been poured out even on the Gentiles" (v. 45, NIV). They could hardly believe what they saw. Surely God's promises were only for the Jews!

"For they heard them speak with tongues and magnify God" (v. 46). Why this recurring phenomenon? Evidently in order to prove to these Jewish believers with Peter that the Holy Spirit had really come to the Gentiles. On the day of Pentecost the "tongues" were intelligible, known languages of that day (Acts 2:4, 6, 8-11). It follows logically that the "tongues" in the house of Cornelius were known languages, not "unknown tongues," or the Jews present would not have been convinced that the same thing was happening here that had happened to them on the Day of Pentecost.

C. The Baptism of Gentiles: vv. 47-48

The action that Peter took was perfectly logical. If these Gentiles had received the Holy Spirit just as the Jews had at Pentecost, "Can anyone keep these people from being baptized with water?" (v. 47, NIV). Evidently there was no objection raised, and so these new believers were "baptized in the name of Jesus Christ" (v. 48, NIV)—so the best Greek text. They became an accepted part of the Christian community. As could be expected, the new converts asked Peter to stay with them for a few days, so that they might receive further instruction.

One of the greatest spiritual movements since the first century was the Evangelical Revival of the eighteenth century. It began with John Wesley. As a devout young Anglican priest, he had sought earnestly to please the Lord by fasting, prayers, and good deeds. But he found no peace of soul, no relief from legal bondage.

After ten years of self-effort—between the ages of twenty-five and thirty-five—he went one evening to a society meeting in an upper room on Aldersgate Street in London. Here is how he describes in his *Journal* what happened: "In the evening I went very unwillingly to a society in Aldersgate Street, where one was reading Luther's preface to the Epistle to the Romans. About a quarter before nine, while he was describing the change which God works in the heart through faith in Christ, I felt my heart strangely warmed. I felt I did trust in Christ, Christ alone for salvation: and an assurance was given me, that he had taken away *my* sins, even *mine*, and saved *me* from the law of sin and death" (*Works of John Wesley*, I, 103).

That was May 24, 1738. This experience is called Wesley's "evangelical conversion." It resulted in his winning 150,000 to Christ and infusing new spiritual life into the church of his day.

CONTEMPORARY APPLICATION

What about the new Christian youth movements of our day and the so-called charismatic movement? We should rejoice that so many people have been "turned on" for Jesus.

There are two tests that should be applied to all of these. The first is: Do they exalt Jesus Christ as Lord of all? The second is: Do they produce high moral results in holy living? Where a work is genuinely of the Holy Spirit, these two characteristics will be found.

THE BIBLE AND SOCIAL ACTION

DEVOTIONAL READING	Isaiah 58:6-12

ADULTS

Topic: *Doers of the Word*

Background Scripture: Exodus 5—6:9; Jeremiah 34:8-17; James 1:22—2:20

Scripture Lesson: James 2:1-7, 14-20

Memory Verse: *Be doers of the word, and not hearers only, deceiving yourselves.* James 1:22

YOUTH

Topic: *Doers of the Word*

Background Scripture: Exodus 5—6:9; Jeremiah 34:8-17; James 1:22—2:20

Scripture Lesson: James 2:1-7, 14-20

Memory Verse: *Be doers of the word, and not hearers only, deceiving yourselves.* James 1:22

CHILDREN

Topic: *Helping Others*

Background Scripture: Exodus 5—6:9; Jeremiah 34:8-17; James 2:1-20

Scripture Lesson: James 2:1-7, 14-20

Memory Verse: *Be doers of the word, and not hearers only.* James 1:22

DAILY BIBLE READINGS

Mon., Aug. 9: Loving in Deed and Truth, I John 3:11-18.
Tues., Aug. 10: Love for Others, I John 4:13-21.
Wed., Aug. 11: The Oppression of Slavery, Exodus 5:1-9.
Thurs., Aug. 12: The Call for Social Justice, Amos 5: 12-15, 21-24.
Fri., Aug. 13: Being Doers of the Word, James 1:22-27.
Sat., Aug. 14: The Royal Law, James 2:8-13.
Sun., Aug. 15: God's Concern for the Needy, Isaiah 58: 6-12.

LESSON AIM To see what the Bible has to say about social action.

LESSON SETTING

Time: The Epistle of James was probably written about A.D. 60.

Place: It was written in Jerusalem.

365

The Bible and Social Action

I. A Breach of Faith: Jeremiah 34:8-17
    A. Zedekiah's Covenant with the People: vv. 8-11
    B. God's Covenants with Israel: vv. 12-16
    C. Judgment for Breaking the Covenant: v. 17

II. Doers of the Word: James 1:22-27
    A. Doers, Not Just Hearers: vv. 22-25
    B. Vain Religion: v. 26
    C. True Religion: v. 27

III. Warning Against Favoritism: James 2:1-13
    A. Favoritism Forbidden: vv. 1-4
    B. Favoritism Illogical: vv. 5-7
    C. Favoritism a Sin: vv. 8-13

IV. Faith and Deeds: James 2:14-24
    A. The Folly of Empty Faith: vv. 14-17
    B. True Faith Demonstrated by Deeds: vv. 18-19
    C. Example of Abraham: vv. 20-24

SUGGESTED INTRODUCTION FOR ADULTS

Today there is a great deal of debate as to the relative merits of individual salvation and social action. Evangelicals have emphasized the New Testament doctrine of salvation from sin as a personal spiritual experience. Liberals have tended to say that social action is the main responsibility of the church, not the saving of souls. Which is right?

As is so often true, it is not a case of either/or but of both/and. The fundamental need of every human being is not physical but spiritual. But, as James declares in our lesson today, we cannot neglect the physical needs of those about us. The ministry of the church should always be first of all spiritual, meeting the needs of individual hearts. But the church should also be interested in the whole man, concerned about the individual's social and psychological, as well as spiritual needs.

In our background Scripture today we see that God was interested in the oppression of the Israelites in Egypt. He called Moses to deliver His people from physical slavery as well as from the slavery of sin. The Red Sea and Sinai were both divine events.

SUGGESTED INTRODUCTION FOR YOUTH

We are told that the church should be concerned about "social action." But what do we mean by that expression? If it means contributing money to arm guerillas to kill and plunder, is that Christian? Yet that is the kind of "Christian" social action that is being carried on in some circles today.

We need social action. But it must be thoroughly Christian, done in the spirit of Christ—that is, the spirit of love. It must always seek the *highest* good of those to whom it ministers.

1. We are not to show favoritism to individuals.
2. God is kind to all, and so should we be.
3. Our Christian faith must be demonstrated in deed.
4. True faith shows itself in love.

THE LESSON COMMENTARY

I. A BREACH OF FAITH:
Jeremiah 34:8-17

A. Zedekiah's Covenant with the People: vv. 8-11

The thirty-fourth chapter of Jeremiah deals with "broken covenants." The first was that between King Zedekiah and the people of Jerusalem during the Babylonian siege. The second was the one made between God and Israel at Sinai. Both covenants had been broken by a disobedient, selfish people.

When the armies of Nebuchadnezzar, king of Babylon, surrounded Jerusalem, Jeremiah was told to warn the wicked King Zedekiah that the city would be taken by the Babylonians and burned with fire (v. 2). Also, Zedekiah would be captured and taken to Babylon (v. 3).

Aroused at long last—but too late—the king made a covenant with the people of Jerusalem that every man would set his Jewish slaves free—both men and women servants (vv. 8-9).

The princes and people obeyed and let their slaves go (v. 10). It was an emergency measure because of the outside military threat, not an act of genuine repentance.

This was shown by the fact that when the Babylonian armies temporarily left Jerusalem, these wicked people forced their former servants back into slavery (v. 11). It was this brutal selfishness and spirit of rebellion that finally brought about their captivity in Babylon.

B. God's Covenant with Israel: vv. 12-16

The Lord reminded these rebels that He had made a covenant with their fathers when He rescued them from Egyptian bondage (v. 13). One of the conditions of that covenant was observance of the sabbatical year. A Hebrew slave could not be made to serve more than six years; he must be released on the seventh year. But this command had been ignored for years (v. 14).

When the people of Jerusalem had made their "covenant before me in the house which is called by my name" (v. 15), God was pleased. He said, "Ye were now turned, and had done right in my sight, in proclaiming liberty every man to his neighbour." It was a long-overdue reform.

Sadly, it didn't last. The people had turned back and "polluted" God's name by bringing back into subjection the slaves they had set free (v. 16).

This was too often the pattern followed by the Israelites, as we see in the books of Judges, Samuel, and Kings. A century before Jeremiah's day, Hosea had written to the people of Israel: "Your goodness is as a morning cloud, and as the early dew it goeth away" (Hosea 6:4).

But this has been true in the history of the Christian church as well. There have been many generations and even centuries when there was little spiritual life in the churches.

C. Judgment for Breaking the Covenant: v. 17

The people of Jerusalem would pay a high price for the criminal way they had broken the pledge they solemnly made in God's house. Their doom is spelled out in detail. Because they had disobeyed the Lord in refusing to give permanent freedom to their slaves, God says: "Behold, I proclaim a liberty for you . . . to the sword, to the pestilence, and to the famine; and I will make you to be removed into all the kingdoms of the earth."

All this happened within a short time. The Babylonian army returned and besieged the city. Food became so scarce in Jerusalem that we read: "The famine was sore in the city, so that there was no bread for the people of the land" (52:6). When the city walls were breached, Zedekiah tried to flee. But he was captured, his sons slain, and then his own eyes put out (52:8-11).

II. DOERS OF THE WORD: James 1:22-27

A. Doers, Not Just Hearers: vv. 22-25

James had just referred to "the engrafted [better, "planted"] word, which is able to save your souls" (v. 21). Now he warns: "But be ye doers of the word, and not hearers only, deceiving your own selves." That is a good literal translation of the Greek.

The Greek word for "hearers" occurs only here in the New Testament. It was used in classical Greek for those who attended lectures of philosophers but did not become learners or disciples. Today we would call them "sermon-tasters." A. T. Robertson describes them this way: "Some people have a sort of religious dissipation in attending revival services and imagine that they have accomplished a great deal if they simply go. People easily acquire itching ears that love to be tickled with some sensation. The word takes no root in the hearts of such men. They run from church to church to get a new word, a sort of soda-water habit" (*Studies in the Epistle of James*, p. 97).

In a similar vein, C. L. Mitton writes: "This section is an emphatic warning against sentimental and unpractical religion. There is a kind of religious man who can enjoy listening to a preacher, and being present at a public act of prayer, but fails to trans-

late his faith into effective action in daily life, fails to make obedience to Christ in the common acts of life the essential feature of his religion which it ought to be" (*The Epistle of James*, p. 66). Later he comments: "To listen to a sermon on humility or forgiveness may seem a commendable religious act, but the truly religious act begins when the listener turns what he has heard into deeds, and, in obedience to Christ, acts self-effacingly and forgivingly" (p. 67).

Jesus projected the same emphasis in the closing illustration of the two houses in the Sermon on the Mount (Matthew 7:24-27). James has many parallels to that sermon.

James goes on to say that one who is a hearer of the word and not a doer is like a man who sees his face in a "glass," but goes on his way and forgets what he looks like (v. 24). (The word "glass" should be "mirror," for the mirrors of that day were made of metal, not glass.)

On the other hand, the man who looks into the perfect law of liberty and is not a forgetful hearer, but a doer of the word, this man will be blessed (v. 25).

It is a wonderful thing to read and study the Bible. But doing this puts us under heavier responsibility to put it into action in our daily lives.

B. Vain Religion: v. 26

In the third chapter of this Epistle we find the most eloquent passage on the tongue to be found in all literature. In this verse James anticipates his later extended discussion by saying: "If anyone considers himself religious and yet does not keep a tight rein on his tongue, he deceives himself and his religion is worthless" (NIV). This is a hard saying; who can hear it!

C. True Religion: v. 27

The Greek word for "religion" in verses 26 and 27 can be translated "worship." So these verses tack right on to the preceding discussion about hearers and doers. Our worship must extend beyond the sanctuary and show itself in loving service to the needy.

We should note the combination of two aspects of true religion in this verse. There are those who emphasize only the first part: "to visit the fatherless and widows in their affliction." In other words, their religion is social action. But they fail to be concerned about personal holiness of life.

On the other hand, there are many who emphasize "the separated life." They keep themselves "unspotted from the world," but some of them are not concerned to "look after orphans and widows in their distress" (NIV).

True religion has both emphases. It is concerned about purity of heart and life. But it also cares for the needy.

III. WARNING AGAINST FAVORITISM: James 2:1-13

A. Favoritism Forbidden: vv. 1-4

"My brothers, as believers in our glorious Lord Jesus Christ, don't show favoritism" (v. 1, NIV). Then James gives a dramatic illustration of what he means. He says: "Suppose a man comes into your meeting wearing a gold ring and fine clothes, and a poor man in shabby clothes also comes in. If you show special attention to the man wearing fine clothes and say, 'Here's a good seat for you,' but say to the poor man, 'You stand there,' or, 'Sit on the floor by my feet,' have you not discriminated among yourselves and become judges with evil thoughts?" (vv. 2-4, NIV).

This description is so clear (especially in the NIV) that it hardly calls for comment. We might note, however, that the Greek word James uses for "meeting" (KJV, "assembly") is *synagoge*, "synagogue." This is the only place where this term is used for a Christian gathering; elsewhere the term used is *ecclesia*. This highlights the Jewishness of James.

B. Favoritism Illogical: vv. 5-7

In strong and forceful language James shows the folly of discriminating against the poor in favor of the rich. First, he notes that God has "chosen the poor of this world rich in faith" to be "heirs of the kingdom" (v. 5). If God has chosen the poor people, why should we reject them?

Then James becomes stern. He asserts: "But you have insulted the poor" (v. 6, NIV). He goes on: "Is it not the rich who are exploiting you? Are they not the ones who are dragging you into court? Are they not the ones who are slandering the noble name of him to whom you belong?" (vv. 6-7, NIV).

How utterly unreasonable and unfair it is, then, to "kowtow" to the wealthy and treat the poor with contempt. It is an ungodly attitude, James declares. Why should we honor those who oppress us?

In any case, favoritism is wrong. To show partiality is to act unethically.

C. Favoritism a Sin: vv. 8-13

What is the "royal," kingly law? "Thou shalt love thy neighbour as thyself." It is kingly because the King of kings *is* love—Love Incarnate. Those who love—with holy, sincere, unselfish love—are kingly in their character and conduct.

Then James returns to his theme. He declares: "But if you show favoritism, you sin and are convicted by the law as lawbreakers" (v. 9, NIV). For the heart of the law is love, and favoritism is a denial of love.

James uses a further argument. He calls attention to the obvious fact that one only has to break one commandment in order to be a lawbreaker. You don't have to commit adultery or murder to be convicted of wrongdoing. Just one transgression makes you subject to sentence.

On first thought verse 10 seems too strong and absolute. But it must be interpreted in terms of verse 11, and then it makes sense.

IV. FAITH AND DEEDS:
James 2:14-24

A. The Folly of Empty Faith: vv. 14-17

James moves on now to one of the major themes of his Epistle. We have already noted in a previous lesson that the main thrust of Galatians and Romans is "justification by faith." Some people were making this an excuse for "antinomianism"—literally, "against law."

So James asks, "What good is it, my brothers, if a man claims to have faith but has no deeds? Can such a faith save him?" (v. 14, NIV). The translation of the last sentence is especially important. We are saved by faith. But we are not saved by "such a faith" as that described in the first part of the verse—a faith that has no deeds to demonstrate it. The faith that saves us is obedient faith. There is no such thing as really believing without obeying. A genuine faith will show itself in deeds of obedience—such as the "royal law." Again James illustrates vividly what he means. He writes: "Suppose a brother or sister is without clothes and daily food. If one of you says to him, 'Go, I wish you well; keep warm and well fed,' but does nothing about his physical needs, what good is it?" (vv. 15-16, NIV).

Real faith issues in love; because faith brings God into our lives, and God is love. If we do not show love in our lives, it is clear that we do not have genuine faith.

There is a very real sense in which we must love *people*, not just their souls. To say, "I love that person's soul and I'm praying for his salvation, but I don't *like* him," is a dangerous attitude. It borders on hypocrisy. And if people sense that attitude, we can't help them spiritually.

James sums up the thrust of this paragraph by saying, "In the same way, faith by itself, if it is not accompanied by action, is dead" (v. 17, NIV). It proves to be dead, for it produces no fruit.

B. True Faith Demonstrated by Deeds: vv. 18-19

Suppose a man says, "You have faith, and I have works." James answers, "Shew me thy faith without thy works, and I will shew thee my faith by my works" (v. 18). The last part might be misunderstood as meaning "my faith that comes from my works." To avoid that totally unbiblical point of view, it may be better to transpose the words: "and I by my works will show you my faith." That is, good deeds are a demonstration of faith.

"Thou believest that there is one God; thou doest well: the devils also believe, and tremble" (v. 19). We have noted before that the Greek text of the New Testament clearly indicates that there are many demons, but only one devil (*diabolos* always singular). The word here is *daimonia*, "demons."

James is trying to jolt his hearers. It is not enough to be orthodox in our minds; the demons are that—and also diabolical. We must believe in our hearts and demonstrate our faith in our daily lives. We must have orthopraxy as well as orthodoxy.

John Wesley once preached a sermon with the title "Almost a Christian." He shocked his Oxford hearers by asserting that faith in the orthodox doctrines was, in itself, no more than the faith of demons.

DISCUSSION QUESTIONS

1. What is the penalty for breaking our covenant with God?
2. What does it mean to be "doers of the Word"?
3. How does James define true religion?
4. Why is favoritism wrong?
5. How do good deeds demonstrate our faith?
6. What social action should concern the church?

C. Example of Abraham: vv. 20-24

Again James emphasizes the point that "faith without works is dead" (v. 20). Then he cites the case of Abraham and asks the question, "Was not Abraham our father justified by works, when he had offered Isaac his son upon the altar?" (v. 21). That is, his act of utter devotion proved his faith. By his works his faith was "made complete" (v. 22, NIV).

Verse 24 seems like a flat contradiction of Paul's teaching in Romans and Galatians that a man is justified by faith, not by works. James says that "by works a man is justified, and not by faith only." Again, he means an empty faith that is not fruitful in good deeds. Unless we have genuine faith that shows itself in a life of love, we shall not ultimately be saved. By "faith" James means mental assent, Paul means moral assent. By "works" James means deeds of love, Paul means deeds of law. Paul is thinking of initial justification, James of final justification. When we recognize these differences in emphases, there is no contradiction between Paul and James.

Martin Luther emphasized the doctrine of justification by faith alone. He found the Epistle of James unsatisfactory because it seemed to deny this. But in his later sermons we can discover far greater emphasis on the necessity of works as an evidence of faith. This is because Luther found to his consternation that antinomianism was threatening to destroy the Protestant Reformation. Had he rightly understood James earlier, it would have helped him.

CONTEMPORARY APPLICATION

Social action rightly understood, is a vital part of Christianity—but only when the action is fully Christian. Much that goes under the banner of "social action" is contrary to the spirit of Christ. And social action can never take the place of individual salvation. There can be no adequate reformation without regeneration.

THE CHURCH TEACHES

DEVOTIONAL READING	Deuteronomy 11:18-23

ADULTS

Topic: *The Church Teaches*

Background Scripture: Deuteronomy 11:18-23; Proverbs 1:7; I Timothy 4:1-16; 6:2c-10; II Timothy 3:14-15

Scripture Lesson: I Timothy 4:11-16; 6:2c-10

Memory Verse: *The fear of the Lord is the beginning of knowledge; fools despise wisdom and instruction.* Proverbs 1:7

YOUTH

Topic: *Learning Together*

Background Scripture: Deuteronomy 11:18-21; Proverbs 1:7; I Timothy 4:1-16; 6:2c-10; II Timothy 3:14-15

Scripture Lesson: I Timothy 4:11-16; 6:2c-10

Memory Verse: *The fear of the Lord is the beginning of knowledge; fools despise wisdom and instruction.* Proverbs 1:7

CHILDREN

Topic: *Teaching and Learning Together*

Background Scripture: Deuteronomy 11:18-21; Proverbs 1:7; I Timothy 4:1-16; 6:2c-10; II Timothy 3:14-15

Scripture Lesson: *Deuteronomy 11:18-21*

Memory Verse: *Listen to advice and accept instruction, that you may gain wisdom for the future.* Proverbs 19:20

DAILY BIBLE READINGS

Mon., Aug. 16: Teaching God's Word, Deuteronomy 11: 18-23.

Tues., Aug. 17: Need for Teaching and Understanding, Psalm 119:129-136.

Wed., Aug. 18: The Beginning of Knowledge, Proverbs 1:2-7.

Thurs., Aug. 19: Proper Instruction, I Timothy 4:1-10.

Fri., Aug. 20: The Christian's Aim, I Timothy 6:11-16.

Sat., Aug. 21: The Value of Scripture, II Timothy 3:10-17.

Sun., Aug. 22: The Purpose of Teaching, Colossians 1:28–2:7.

LESSON AIM

To see the importance of the teaching ministry of the church.

Time: Between A.D. 62 and A.D. 67

Place: I Timothy: uncertain; II Timothy: Rome

The Church Teaches

I. False Teachings: I Timothy 4:1-5
   A. Demonic Teachings: v. 1
   B. Hypocritical Teachings: v. 2
   C. Ascetic Teachings: vv. 3-5

II. Good Teaching: I Timothy 4:6-10
   A. A Good Minister of Jesus Christ: v. 6
   B. Spiritual Training: vv. 7-8
   C. Trustworthy Teaching: vv. 9-10

III. A Good Teacher: I Timothy 4:11-16
   A. Exemplary Life: vv. 11-12
   B. Full-orbed Ministry: vv. 13-14
   C. Diligent Worker: vv. 15-16

IV. Marks of a False Teacher: I Timothy 6:3-10
   A. Love of Controversy: vv. 3-5
   B. Love of Money: vv. 6-10

V. A Godly Heritage: II Timothy 3:14-15
   A. Godly Teachers: v. 14
   B. Training in the Scriptures: v. 15

The importance of teaching cannot be overemphasized. The continuance of civilization depends on the careful instruction of our youth.

This was enforced strongly by Moses in speaking to the Israelites before they entered Canaan. And the Jews today give primary emphasis to the religious teaching of their children. A Jewish child is supposed to go certain hours each week to the synogogue school, as well as attending public school.

In Deuteronomy Moses, the founder and first leader of the nation of Israel, is giving his parting instructions to the people. He says to them: "Therefore shall ye lay up these my words in your heart and in your soul, and bind them for a sign upon your hand, that they may be as frontlets between your eyes" (11:18). As we noted in our study of Matthew, the Jews of Jesus' day took these words literally and bound phylacteries on their arms and foreheads. What Moses meant was that the Scriptures should be our daily companion and guide.

The constant teaching of the Bible to children is urged in verses 19 and 20. Careful attention to this would result in long continuance in the land (v. 21). If they obeyed

God's commands, he would give them the land of Canaan. Obedience to God's Word always brings blessing.

There are two functions that are essential to growth in the Christian life: prayer and Bible reading. They are equally important.

Young people are reading their Bibles today, and this is cause for great gratitude. But we all need guidance in our study of the Word, such as we get in Sunday school and perhaps in Bible study groups. *The Living Bible*, as its name indicates, makes the Bible come alive. The New International Bible Version (New Testament now available) is a more accurate translation. It will be found especially helpful.

1. The most important book for children to read is the Bible.
2. Good children's Bibles are available today.
3. Illustrated Bible story books are very helpful.
4. We learn as we listen carefully to good teaching.

THE LESSON COMMENTARY

I. FALSE TEACHINGS:
I Timothy 4:1-5

A. Demonic Teachings: v. 1

"The Spirit clearly says that in later times some will abandon the faith and follow deceiving spirits and things taught by demons" (NIV). These "later times," or "last days" (II Timothy 3:1) have definitely arrived. During the last few years Satan worship has grown alarmingly in the United States. The unfortunate popularity of the film, *The Exorcist*, has caused a morbid interest in demons. Young people's lives have been badly damaged. Demon-possession has become far more common.

This comes only when people willfully turn away from the sincere worship of the true God. Since they refuse to follow Him, the Lord allows them to be deceived into following false teachers.

B. Hypocritical Teachings: v. 2

"Hypocritical liars," Paul calls them; men whose consciences had been "seared as with a hot iron," so that they no longer felt any compunctions against wrongdoing.

Recently a "Christian" preacher with a gold-plated church and Rolls-Royces for his own personal pleasure, a man who spends as much as a thousand dollars a week on clothes, said it was nobody's business how many mistresses he had, nor was he concerned about his wife's affairs. It looks as though the "later times" are here!

C. Ascetic Teachings: vv. 3-5

Asceticism came out of Gnosticism, with its false teaching that all spirit is good, all matter is evil. This heresy in the early church, condemned in the second century, led people to go in opposite directions. Some said, "Since my spirit is good and my body is inherently evil, it makes no difference what my body does—that will not harm my soul." This, of course, led to immorality. But other people took the opposite road of asceticism: "Since my body is evil, I must punish and suppress it by severe self-denial."

Paul here treats two prohibitions enforced by ascetics. The first was "forbidding to marry." The Roman Catholic Church is still guilty of this false practice that Paul labels as heresy. They forbid their priests and nuns to marry. The idea that celibacy is more holy than marriage is clearly denied in God's Word, from Genesis to Revelation. God instituted "holy matrimony" in the Garden of Eden, and this was when man was pure and holy.

The second prohibition of the ascetics was: commanding to "abstain from certain foods" (NIV). The Catholic ban on eating meat on Friday—recently modified—is a case in point. Vegetarianism for religious reasons is another.

Paul evidently thought this matter to be of some importance, for he discussed it at considerable length (vv. 3-5). He says that God has created these falsely forbidden foods to be received with thanksgiving by those who believe and know the truth. This supposedly superior piety is not from God, but from Satan. Incidentally, the devil doesn't care whether he ditches us on the right side of the road in asceticism or on the left road in immorality, so long as he can get us stuck so that we don't go up the road enjoying life as God intended for us to live it—holy and happy!

Paul goes on to say: "For every creature of God is good, and nothing to be refused, if it be received with thanksgiving: for it is sanctified by the word of God and prayer" (vv. 4-5).

This passage gives a beautiful basis for "saying grace" before each meal—what we also call "asking God's blessing on the food" or "offering thanks." Especially these days, when thousands are starving to death, we ought never to eat without thanking God for the food. And it is a good custom to read just a few verses from the Word of God at the breakfast table, especially for children going to school. This consecrates our food.

II. GOOD TEACHING:
I Timothy 4:6-10

A. A Good Minister of Jesus Christ: v. 6

"If you point these things out to the brothers, you will be a good minister of Christ Jesus, brought up in the truths of the faith and of the good teaching that you have followed" (NIV). It will be remembered that the Greek word for "minister," *diaconos*, literally means "servant." But Timothy was a minister in the modern sense. Paul is emphasizing here the fact that teaching is one of the most important functions of the ministry.

B. Spiritual Training: vv. 7-8

"Have nothing to do with godless myths and old wives' tales; rather, train yourself to be godly" (v. 7, NIV). The word "fables" (KJV) comes from the Latin *fabulum* (cf. "fabulous"). The Greek word is *mythous*, which we have taken over into English and should use here. The Greek verb for "train" (KJV, "exercise") is *gymnazo*, from which we get "gymnastics." We need to get spiritual exercise.

"For bodily exercise profiteth little [Greek, "for a little," perhaps meaning for a little time, that is, for this life] but godliness is profitable unto all things, having promise of the life that now is, and of that which is to come" (v. 8). The word for "exercise" is *gymnasia* from which we get "gymnasium." All of life should be for us a gymnasium in which we take spiritual exercise every day. This is not only in our private devotions and public worship, but just as truly out in the "give and take" of daily living.

C. Trustworthy Teaching: vv. 9-10

"This is a trustworthy saying that deserves full acceptance" (v. 9, NIV) is a key expression in the Pastoral Epistles (cf. 1:15). The reference here is probably to his previous statement that spiritual exercise is more important than physical exercise—because it has eternal value, whereas physical exercise benefits us only in this life.

Paul declares that the living God is "the Saviour of all men, specially of those that believe" (v. 10). This is a very significant statement. Provisionally and potentially, because of Christ's atoning death on the cross, God is the Savior of all people. The New Testament teaches "universal salvation" in this sense. But God is actually and effectively the Savior of only those who believe. This truth is clearly indicated by such passages as John 3:16.

III. A GOOD TEACHER:
I Timothy 4:11-16

A. Exemplary Life: vv. 11-12

Timothy is urged to "command and teach these things" (v. 11, NIV). Then comes a favorite verse with young people's societies (v. 12). The first clause says, "Don't let anyone look down on you because you are young" (NIV). We should hasten to say that Timothy, to whom this Epistle was written, was definitely not a teen-ager at this time. Paul had taken him on at Lystra as an attendant, early on his second missionary journey (Acts 16:1-3). This was in A.D. 48 or early 49. Probably Timothy was about twenty years old at the time. Now it was about A.D. 63, some fifteen years later. So Timothy would be about thirty-five years old. Paul had left him as the head pastor of the important church at Ephesus (1:3). But the facts are that in Roman society "young man" meant a person between the ages of thirty and forty-five. So Timothy was still in his "youth."

Paul admonishes Timothy to be "an example of the believers, in word, in conversation, in charity, in spirit, in faith, in purity." But the Greek word for "conversation" (anastrophe) literally means "a turning about," which is also the literal meaning of the Latin derivative, "conversation." Both the Greek and Latin terms meant "manner of life, behaviour, conduct" (Abbott-Smith, Lexicon, p. 34). But our word "conversation" has narrowed down to "talk." Actually, there are three Greek words in the New Testament that are translated "conversation" in the King James Version, and not one of them means what that word now signifies. One who uses the 1611 version should cross out the word "conversation" wherever it occurs (18 times) and write "conduct" above. That will give him the correct translation. A simpler way would be to use the New International Version (1973) and get a more accurate translation throughout the New Testament. It reads here: "But set an example for the believers in speech, in life, in love, in faith and in purity."

B. Full-orbed Ministry: vv. 13-14

"Until I come, devote yourself to the public reading of Scripture, to preaching and to teaching" (v. 13, NIV). These are the three main functions of the pastor in the pulpit. Too many nonliturgical churches neglect reading the Bible in public. But this is an essential part of worship.

"Exhortation" (KJV) is one type of "preaching" (NIV) that should be balanced with "teaching." Unfortunately, these two are not always combined in one man. But the people need both kinds of ministry in the pulpit.

Paul admonished Timothy (v. 14) not to neglect the gift that was given him "by prophecy"—probably a prophetic message, perhaps indicating something of the future importance he would have in the ministry, or at least confirming his call. This came "with the laying on of hands of the presbytery" (Greek, presbyterion). "Presbyter" (Greek, presbyteros) means "an elder." So Timothy was ordained by a group of elders. This is still the common way of ordination to the ministry in nonepiscopal churches. It appears to have been the custom prevailing in the early church. It helps to build a community of concern and responsibility among the ministers.

C. Diligent Worker: vv. 15-16

The word "meditate" (KJV) does not convey to us today the meaning of the Greek verb here (*epecho*), which means "give attention to." So a better translation is this: "Be diligent in these matters; give yourself wholly to them, so that everyone may see your progress" (NIV).

Diligence is the price of success in every field of endeavor. We know this to be true in secular affairs. How much more in the work of the Kingdom—preeminently for the pastor but also for every member of the church.

"Watch your life and doctrine closely" (v. 16, NIV). This is the twofold price one must pay if he is going to save his own soul, as well as the souls of his listeners.

It is an awesome responsibility to be a teacher, whether in the pulpit or in a Sunday school classroom. Every teacher should make careful and prayerful preparation, and should watch his or her own life—both in attitude and conduct.

IV. MARKS OF A FALSE TEACHER: I Timothy 6:3-10

A. Love of Controversy: vv. 3-5

After saying, "These are the things you are to teach and urge on them" (v. 2c, NIV), Paul continues: "If anyone teaches false doctrines and does not agree to the sound instruction of our Lord Jesus Christ and to godly teaching, he is conceited and understands nothing. He has an unhealthy interest in controversies and arguments..." (vv. 3-4, NIV).

This last sentence describes many people in the religious world. They have a morbid fondness for theological argument. But it is only carnal hearts that love controversy. A Spirit-filled heart is full of love. And love promotes unity and fellowship, not controversy and strife. "By their fruits ye shall know them."

People are not won to Christ through theological argument. They are won by love and understanding, by sympathy and concern. There is enough strife already without our adding to it.

The fruits of this argument and controversy are spelled out here. They "result in envy, quarreling, malicious talk, evil suspicions and constant friction between men of corrupt mind" (vv. 4-5, NIV). This is the sort of thing that comes from endless arguing. These false teachers are further described as those who suppose "that gain is godliness" (KJV)—better, "who think that godliness is a means to financial gain" (NIV). When men become pious in order to improve their finances, their hearts are far from God. They are false not only intellectually but also spiritually.

B. Love of Money: vv. 6-10

The last part of verse 5 ("from such withdraw thyself" [KJV] is not in the early Greek manuscripts) introduces this second mark of false teachers, their love for money. Paul counteracts this by saying, "But godliness with contentment is great gain" (v. 6).

The logic of the matter is set out simply and yet strikingly in verse 7: "For we brought nothing into this world, and it is certain we can carry nothing out." Why, then, waste one's

---

DISCUSSION QUESTIONS

1. What is responsible for the growth in demon worship in Western countries?
2. What forms does religious asceticism take today?
3. What are the marks of a good teacher?
4. What are several marks of a false teacher?
5. Why and how does the love of money ruin people's lives?
6. In what ways may the teaching function of the church be carried out?

life trying to accumulate money, which must all be left behind?

So, "having food and raiment, let us be therewith content" (v. 8). The two most important things for material life are food and clothing. For millions of people in the world these bare necessities are all they crave. They would feel wealthy if they had plenty of these two items. In our modern affluent society we take them for granted. But half the world does not.

In a very real sense it can be said that our attitude toward money is a touchstone of our character. If we use it for what it is intended to be—a medium of exchange—it can be a blessing. But if we crave and hoard it, it can become a curse. Paul writes: "People who want to get rich fall into temptation and a trap and into many foolish and harmful desires that plunge men into ruin and destruction" (v. 9, NIV). Money has been a snare and trap to countless numbers of people.

We sometimes hear the assertion that money is the root of all evil. But the Bible does not say that. It declares that "the love of money is a root of all kinds of evil" (v. 10, NIV). Many specific evils are caused by other factors than the love of money. But all kinds of evil result from the selfish, greedy desire to get money. It has been the cause of more than one person wandering away from the faith and piercing himself through with many griefs.

John Wesley had the right philosophy of money: (1) Make all you can; (2) save all you can; (3) give all you can. This attitude will keep us from falling snare to the love of money.

V. A GODLY HERITAGE: II Timothy 3:14-15

A. Godly Teachers: v. 14

Timothy was fortunate in having a godly Jewish mother and grandmother (1:5). They had brought him up carefully in the Scriptures. Then, as a young man, Timothy had heard Paul preach and had been converted under his ministry. He had a wonderful heritage.

B. Training in the Scriptures: v. 15

From childhood Timothy had known the Holy Scriptures. This is a reference to the Old Testament, for none of the New Testament had been written when he was a child. But even the older Scriptures were able to make him "wise for salvation through faith in Christ Jesus" (NIV).

The greatest heritage we can give our children is what we teach them. This will be twofold: first, the example of our lives, and second, instruction in the Word of God. The home, the church, and the Sunday school all need to give this teaching.

CONTEMPORARY APPLICATION

False teachers abound in the twentieth century. The interest in religion engendered by two world wars has provided a fertile field to be exploited by these quacks.

The thing that marks most false teachers is the love of money. Billy Graham wisely put himself on salary many years ago, so that he cannot be accused of wanting big crowds to make more money. When men get wealthy preaching the gospel, something is wrong.

IN MISSION TOGETHER

DEVOTIONAL READING	Philippians 2:1-13
ADULTS	Topic: *In Mission Together* Background Scripture: John 10:1-18; I Corinthians 1:10-31; 3:5-9 Scripture Lesson: I Corinthians 1:10-17; 3:5-9 Memory Verse: *I have other sheep, that are not of this fold; I must bring them also, and they will heed my voice. So there shall be one flock, one shepherd.* John 10:16
YOUTH	Topic: *Toward a Common Goal* Background Scripture: John 10:1-18; I Corinthians 1:10-31; 3:5-9 Scripture Lesson: I Corinthians 1:10-17; 3:5-9 Memory Verse: *I have other sheep, that are not of this fold; I must bring them also, and they will heed my voice.* John 10:16
CHILDREN	Topic: *Working Together* Background Scripture: John 10:1-18; I Corinthians 1:10-31; 3:5-9 Scripture Lesson: I Corinthians 3:5-9 Memory Verse: *For we are fellow workmen for God.* I Corinthians 3:9
DAILY BIBLE READINGS	Mon., Aug. 23: Concern for the Sheep, John 10:7-18. Tues., Aug. 24: Feed My Sheep, John 21:15-19. Wed., Aug. 25: We Preach Christ Crucified, I Corinthians 1:18-25. Thurs., Aug. 26: Consider Your Call, I Corinthians 1:26-31. Fri., Aug. 27: Ambassadors for Christ, II Corinthians 5:17-21. Sat., Aug. 28: Workers Together, II Corinthians 6:1-10. Sun., Aug. 29: Proclaiming Jesus Christ, II Corinthians 4:1-6.
LESSON AIM	To see our part in the world mission of the church.
LESSON SETTING	Time: John's Gospel was written about A.D. 95, I Corinthians in A.D. 55. Place: Both of these books were written in Ephesus.

In Mission Together

LESSON OUTLINE

SUGGESTED INTRODUCTION FOR ADULTS

In the business world the name of the game is competition. This can become so keen and sharp, so cruel and selfish, that it is called "cut-throat competition."

But in the biggest business in the world, the work of the Kingdom, the guiding motive should not be competition, but cooperation. We are all "in mission together." And we are all working for the same Master. We should rejoice in the victories and accomplishments of our fellow Christians, doing our best, but thanking God when others do better.

Our first loyalty must be to Christ, the Head of the church, not to any human leaders or institutions. Common loyalty breeds unity. Divided loyalty breeds disunity. If we are all really working for Christ, we can work together.

The besetting sin of the Corinthian church was pride. This brought division. Humility brings unity. When we exalt ourselves we build barriers. When we humble ourselves we build bridges. The church desperately needs more bridge-builders.

SUGGESTED INTRODUCTION FOR YOUTH

If we are all working "toward a common goal," we ought to work together. The church is no place for political parties. We are all to be one fellowship, one community in Christ.

This is a case where separation is sin. Holiness demands love, and love demands unity. "We are not divided, all one body we" should be more than a sad bit of sarcasm.

CONCEPTS FOR CHILDREN	1. The church at Corinth was divided into cliques. 2. Paul pleaded for unity in Christ. 3. We are to be partners with God and with each other in the work of the Kingdom. 4. Workers together—that is what we should be.

THE LESSON COMMENTARY

I. THE SHEPHERD AND HIS SHEEP:
John 10:1-18

A. Sheep Following the Shepherd: vv. 1-6

In the United States, especially in the Far West, one can see droves (not "flocks") of sheep numbering as many as three thousand. They are not being led by a shepherd, but are being driven by men on horseback and by clever sheep dogs.

Quite different is the case in the Middle East. There one still sees today small flocks of sheep with a dozen, or a score or two, in each—following their shepherds. Sometimes a rather large group will be grazing together on a hillside. Then one shepherd calls, and a few sheep separate from the others and follow him. Another shepherd calls, or blows his flute, and another little flock follows him. Finally there may be three or more flocks, each following its own shepherd.

That is what Jesus meant when He said of the true shepherd: "And when he putteth forth his own sheep, he goeth before them and the sheep follow him: for they know his voice" (v. 4). He went on: "And a stranger will they not follow, but will flee from him: for they know not the voice of strangers" (v. 5). This means that if we are the true sheep of Christ we will not follow the voices of false prophets, but will follow Christ alone.

This is called a "parable" (v. 6, KJV). The Greek word, however, is not *parabole* but *paroimia*, which properly means "a proverb" or, as here, "an allegory." The people did not understand what the allegory meant.

B. The Gate for the Sheep: vv. 7-10

One of the outstanding features of John's Gospel is the great I AMs of Jesus. Two of them occur in John 10. The first is here: "I am the door of the sheep" (v. 7), repeated in verse 9: "I am the door." Christ is the only entrance to the fold of God. We either come through Him, or we do not get in at all.

C. The Good Shepherd: vv. 11-14

This is the second I AM in this chapter. Jesus went on: "The good shepherd giveth his life for the sheep" (v. 11) Christ's sacrificial death on the cross was the supreme demonstration that He was the Good Shepherd.

In verse 14 the statement is repeated: "I am the good shepherd." This time Jesus added, "and know my sheep, and am known of mine."

D. Other Sheep: vv. 15-18

What did Jesus mean by His "other sheep"? Since He was speaking to Jews, it doubtless meant Gentiles. For us today it means the people of other continents and countries.

The phrase "there shall be one fold" (v. 16) has been misused by the Roman Catholic Church to mean that all must be in the Catholic fold. The Greek says "one flock"—the followers of Jesus.

II. DIVISIONS IN THE CHURCH:
I Corinthians 1:10-17

A. Four Cliques: vv. 10-12

The church at Corinth was full of problems. In his First Epistle to that church Paul deals with no less than nine of these problems. The first three (chaps. 1–6) they had written to him about, asking for advice.

The one to which he devotes the most space is that of divisions in the church congregation (chaps. 1–4). He introduces his discussion of it by saying: "Now I beseech you, brethren, by the name of our Lord Jesus Christ, that ye all speak the same thing, and that there be no divisions among you" (v. 10). The Greek word for "divisions" is *schisma*, "schism." Paul was so concerned about this crucial problem that he got right to the point.

How had he heard about it? Some people belonging to Chloe, who was evidently a member of the church in Corinth, had come across the Aegean Sea to Ephesus—probably on business, since these were the two main seaports in that part of the world. They had perhaps stayed over the weekend and attended the new church in Ephesus, where Paul was preaching. Doubtless he asked how things were back in Corinth, and they reported that there were serious "contentions" in the congregation. Deeply disturbed, the apostle wrote to his recent converts, who were now quarreling with one another.

The matter had progressed to the point that there were four cliques in the church (v. 12). Some said, "I belong to Apollos," others, "I belong to Cephas," and still others, "I belong to Christ." The Greek has: "*Ego . . . Ego . . . Ego . . . Ego.*" That was the trouble at Corinth: too much ego! It is always pride that leads to division—in the individual heart, in the home, and in the church.

Those who said, "I belong to Paul," looked back to the year and a half that the apostle had spent at Corinth (A.D. 50-51). They had been converted under his ministry. He had been the founder of the church and its first pastor. Even though four years had gone by since he left, they still (in A.D. 55) could think only of him.

This is still a problem that plagues many churches. Some people never get weaned from their first pastor, under whom they began their Christian life. The attachment is so strong that they do not relate to the new pastor. He, poor fellow, has to hear them talk about how wonderful Brother So-and-So was! Such a selfish, carnal attitude breeds division.

Then there were those who said, "I belong to Apollos." We are first introduced to this man in Acts 18:24, at Ephesus. He is described as "an eloquent man, and mighty in the scriptures." Soon after that he moved to Corinth and ministered there (Acts 19:1).

This cues us in as to why some people preferred Apollos. They were sermon-tasters, and Apollos was an eloquent preacher. In this respect, he far surpassed Paul, who was not interested in oratory (cf. II Corinthians 10:10). Paul was more the teacher, Apollos the preacher. We still have people today who will run from church to church, just to hear eloquent preaching, instead of facing up to the demands of God's Word. They would rather have their ears tickled than their consciences stirred.

What about "Cephas"? This was the Aramaic word for "stone" and was the equivalent of the Greek *petros* (Peter). Jesus had given Simon this name when he first met him (John 1:42).

How can we identify those who said, "I am of Cephas"? We can hear them saying: "Paul was a late comer, and Apollos only a recent convert. But Cephas was the leading one of Jesus' twelve apostles, with Him from the beginning. He was the one who preached that great sermon on the day of Pentecost, when three thousand were saved. Yes, Cephas is our man!"

The fact that they called him by his Aramaic name "Cephas," rather than his Greek name "Peter," would suggest that they were Jews. If not, they at least belonged to the Judaizing party at Corinth, for Peter was recognized as the apostle to the Jews (Galatians 2:7-8).

Last were those who said, "I belong to Christ." This sounds very pious. But it was probably a false humility. They may well have been the most contentious party of the four. They were the super-saints, who prided themselves on the fact they did not submit to any human leaders; they followed Christ. Probably they gave the impression that they were the only true saints left, the only ones who had the real thing. The rest of the church was backslidden.

We still have members of this tribe with us, and they can be very obnoxious. What they don't realize is that spiritual pride is the worst pride of all. Deep spirituality always means deep humility. Those who place themselves on pedestals as super-saints are exhibiting the most offensive pride in the sight of God and man.

B. Christ, Not Paul: vv. 13-16

As far as the Greek is concerned, "Is Christ divided?" can just as well be translated "Christ is divided!" The Twentieth Century New Testament reads: "You have rent the Christ in pieces!"

While this translation is appealing (cf. *Living Bible*), the context seems against it. For the apostle goes on to ask two further questions: "Was Paul crucified for you? or were ye baptized in the name of Paul?" The answer to all three questions is an emphatic "No!" The true body of Christ, His church, is always a unity in Him. It was He who was crucified for us, not Paul: and the converts at Corinth were baptized in the name of Jesus, not in the name of Paul.

The apostle thanked God that while he was in Corinth he had not baptized any of his converts except two men and one family—"lest any should say that I had baptized in mine own name" (v. 15). He wanted his converts attached to Christ, not to himself.

C. Paul's Main Mission: v. 17

Paul's commission from Christ was not to baptize, but to preach the gospel. He had his associates do the actual baptizing so that people would not be attached to him.

Baptism is no substitute for preaching. It is said that Francis Xavier went through India baptizing people by the thousands, saying, "I make Christians." But too few of his "converts" had any change of heart or life. We can admire his zeal, but not his method.

Paul went on to say that his preaching was "not with wisdom of words, lest the cross of Christ should be made of none effect." The people of Corinth prided themselves on their superior intellectualism and eloquent speech. They tried to outdo Athens. But scholars agree that the culture and learning at Corinth was a rather thin veneer; Athens was the real center of philosophical knowledge.

III. CHRIST THE WISDOM AND POWER OF GOD: I Corinthians 1:18-31

A. The Message of the Cross: vv. 18-19

Paul eschewed all this pride of learning, this false superiority of knowledge. He recognized that it was a real snare in which some of the Christians at Corinth were being caught.

So he wrote: "For the message of the cross is foolishness to those who are perishing, but to us who are being saved it is the power of God" (v. 18, NIV). The word for "preaching" (KJV) is *logos*, "word." It does not refer to the act of preaching but to the message given.

To the intellectual, philosophical Greeks the message of the cross seemed ridiculous, utter foolishness. We are saved by knowledge, they claimed, by freeing ourselves from error in thinking. This is the main emphasis of Christian Science today. Sin, sickness, and death are just errors, and when we recognize that they don't exist, we are free. But the message of the cross is that Christ died for our sins; He alone can save us. It is a message that is still scorned by "eggheads."

B. Worldly Versus Divine Wisdom: vv. 20-25

Paul challenges his readers with a series of questions: "Where is the wise man? Where is the scholar? Where is the philosopher of this age? Has not God made foolish the wisdom of the world?" (v. 20, NIV). Where were Plato and Aristotle now? What had their "wisdom" done for Greece? Had it saved them morally and spiritually?

By its own "wisdom" (pride of false knowledge) the world did not know God (v. 21). And so "it pleased God by the foolishness of preaching to save them that believe." This has often been interpreted as saying that though preaching seems to be a foolish way of reaching the lost, it is God's chosen way of doing it. But the Greek word for "preaching" here is *kerygma*, which has been taken over into English. It does not mean the *method* of preaching but the *message* preached. This is what was "foolishness" to the Greeks; and it is foolishness to the "intellectuals" of our day also.

Verse 22 indicates two different kinds of culture, two attitudes of mind: "Jews demand miraculous signs and Greeks look for wisdom" (NIV). The gospel is neither; it is "the power of God unto salvation" (Romans 1:16).

In contrast to both the Jewish and Greek approaches to religion, Paul declares: "But we preach Christ crucified: a stumbling block to Jews and foolishness to Gentiles" (v. 23, NIV). This is not all: "But unto them which are called, both Jews and Greeks, Christ the power of God, and the wisdom of God" (v. 24). It is not signs or wisdom that the world needs. It is Christ who is God's power and God's wisdom. For Paul, Christ is all.

Again Paul throws out a challenge to these proud Corinthians, saying that God's "foolishness" (the message of the cross) is wiser than men's wisdom; and God's "weakness" (the death of His Son) is stronger than men's strength. (v. 25). Paul magnifies God, not men.

C. Boasting Only in God: vv. 26-31

The Christians at Corinth needed to come down "off their high horse" and face reality. So Paul reminds them that when they were called to follow Christ, "not many of you were wise by human standards; not many were influential; not many were of noble birth" (v. 26, NIV). God had chosen "the foolish things of the world to shame the wise" and "the weak things of the world to shame the strong" (v. 27, NIV). (The verb is the same in both clauses in the Greek; contra KJV.) Yes, God has even chosen "things that are not" (v. 28)—people who are considered "nobodies"—to bring to nothing "things that are."

The purpose of all this is "that no flesh should glory in his presence" (v. 29). It was pride that was causing the divisions in the church at Corinth; humility was needed.

Verse 30 (KJV) seems to say that God has made Christ four things to us. But the Greek clearly says: "Christ Jesus, who has become for us wisdom from God—that is, our righteousness, holiness and redemption" (NIV). His "wisdom" is displayed in these three ways.

DISCUSSION QUESTIONS

1. What are some implications of the figure that we are Christ's sheep?
2. What "other sheep" are at our doorstep?
3. What is the main cause of church divisions?
4. In what way can church splits ("schisms") be avoided?
5. Why is the message of the cross "foolishness"?
6. What should be our attitude toward "fellow workers"?

IV. UNITY IN SERVICE:
I Corinthians 3:5-9

A. Human Servants: v. 5

The Corinthian Christians boasted that they were the spiritual ones. But Paul said: "You are still worldly" (v. 3, NIV). This was proved by their "envying, and strife, and divisions." Verse 4 reads: "For while one saith, I am of Paul; and another, I am of Apollos; are ye not carnal?" Divisiveness is always a carnal trait.

B. Assigned Tasks: vv. 6-8

The Corinthians were magnifying human leaders. Paul says: "I planted the seed, Apollos watered it, but God made it grow" (v. 6, NIV). All the work of these two men would have accomplished nothing if God had not, in His creative power, brought spiritual life to the ones at Corinth to whom Paul and Apollos had ministered. So no credit belonged to them; it all belonged to God.

The apostle states this truth emphatically in verse 7: "So neither he who plants nor he who waters is anything, but only God, who makes things grow" (NIV). Paul asserts: Apollos and I are nothing; God is everything.

Then he makes a very important statement: "Now he that planteth and he that watereth are one" (v. 8). This is Paul's answer to those who claimed to belong to him or to Apollos. He is saying: "Your divisions in Corinth are unreasonable. Apollos and I are not divided; we are one." It was an effective answer to the divisions in the church.

C. Fellow Workers: v. 9

"For we are God's fellow workers; you are God's field, God's building" (NIV). Paul and Apollos were only workers in the field, but "workers together," in unity. It was God's field, not theirs. And they were also workers together on God's building, the church (cf. Matthew 16:18). And that is what all of us should be.

CONTEMPORARY APPLICATION

In a world torn by strife and division, the church should tower above it all as a symbol of unity—a unity in love under one common Lord. Unfortunately, as we all know, this is not the case.

We should be "in mission together." The fact is that we are thus overseas more than we are at home.

Denominational lines tend to fade out on the foreign fields, as most certainly they should. Fellow missionaries have close fellowship across these manmade boundaries.

The church should present a united front to the world. This would glorify God and impress the unsaved.

BIBLIOGRAPHY

Genesis

Clarke, Adam. *The Holy Bible with a Commentary and Critical Notes*, vol. 1. Nashville: Abingdon Press, n.d.
Griffith-Thomas, W. H. *Genesis*. Grand Rapids: Wm. B. Eerdmans Publishing Co., 1946 (reprint).
Haines, Lee. "Genesis," *Wesleyan Bible Commentary*, vol. 1. Grand Rapids: Wm. B. Eerdmans Publishing Co., 1967.
Henry, Matthew. *Commentary on the Whole Bible*, vol. 1. New York: Fleming H. Revell Co., n.d.
Kevan, E. F. "Genesis," *The New Bible Commentary*. Grand Rapids: Wm. B. Eerdmans Publishing Co., 1963.
Lange, John Peter. *Commentary on the Holy Scriptures*, vol. 1. Grand Rapids: Zondervan Publishing House, n.d.
Leupold, H. C. *Exposition on Genesis*. Grand Rapids: Baker Book House, 1958.
Livingston, George H. "Genesis," *Beacon Bible Commentary*, vol. 1. Kansas City: Beacon Hill Press, 1969.
Pfeiffer, C. F. *The Book of Genesis*. "Shield Bible Study Series." Grand Rapids: Baker Book House, 1958.
Whitelaw, Thomas. "Genesis," *The Pulpit Commentary*, vol. 1. Grand Rapids: Wm. B. Eerdmans Publishing Co., 1958 (reprint).
Yates, Kyle M. "Genesis," *The Wycliffe Bible Commentary*. Chicago: Moody Press, 1963.

The Gospel of Matthew

Albright, W. F., and Mann, C. S. "Matthew." *The Anchor Bible*. Garden City, NY: Doubleday & Co., 1971.
Atkinson, B. F. C. "Gospel According to Matthew," *New Bible Commentary*, 2nd ed. Grand Rapids: Wm. B. Eerdmans Publishing Co., 1954.
Barclay, William. "The Gospel of Matthew," 2 vols. *The Daily Study Bible*. Philadelphia: Westminster Press, 1956-57.
Barnes, Albert. *Notes on the New Testament: Matthew and Mark*. Grand Rapids: Baker Book House, 1949.
Clarke, Adam. *The New Testament of Our Lord and Saviour Jesus Christ*, vol. 1. New York: Abingdon Press, n.d.
Davies, J. N. "Matthew," *Abingdon Bible Commentary*. New York: Abingdon Press, 1929.
De Dietrich, Suzanne. "The Gospel According to St. Matthew," *The Layman's Bible Commentary*, vol. 16. Richmond: John Knox Press, 1961.
Earle, Ralph. "Matthew," *Beacon Bible Commentary*, vol. 6. Kansas City: Beacon Hill Press, 1964.
_____ "Matthew," *Wesleyan Bible Commentary*, vol. 4. Grand Rapids: Wm. B. Eerdmans Publishing Co., 1964.
Erdman, Charles R. *The Gospel of Matthew*. Philadelphia: Westminster Press, 1920.
Hendriksen, William. "Matthew," *New Testament Commentary:* Grand Rapids: Baker Book House, 1973. The best available commentary on Matthew.
Hobbs, Herschel H. *An Exposition of the Gospel of Matthew*. Grand Rapids: Baker Book House, 1965.

Kent, Homer A., Jr. "Matthew," *Wycliffe Bible Commentary*. Chicago: Moody Press, 1962.
Lenski, R. C. H. *The Interpretation of St. Matthew's Gospel*. Columbus, OH: Wartburg Press, 1943.
M'Neile, Alan H. *The Gospel According to St. Matthew*. London: Macmillan and Co., 1909.
Morgan, G. Campbell. *The Gospel According to Matthew*. New York: Fleming H. Revell Co., 1929.
Morison, James. *A Practical Commentary on the Gospel According to St. Matthew*. London: Hodder & Stoughton, 1899.
Ryle, J. C. *Expository Thoughts on the Gospels: Matthew-Mark*. Grand Rapids: Zondervan Publishing House, n.d.
Tasker, R. V. G. "Commentary on the Gospel According to St. Matthew." *Tyndale New Testament Commentaries*. Grand Rapids: Wm. B. Eerdmans Publishing Co., 1961.

Acts and Epistles

Bruce, F. F. "Commentary on Acts of the Apostles," *New International Commentary on the New Testament*. Grand Rapids: Wm. B. Eerdmans Publishing Co., 1954.
Hendriksen, William. "Galatians," *New Testament Commentary*. Grand Rapids: Baker Book House, 1968.
_____. "I–II Timothy and Titus," *New Testament Commentary*. Grand Rapids: Baker Book House, 1957.
Hughes, Philip E. "Commentary on the Second Epistle to the Corinthians," *New International Commentary on the New Testament*. Grand Rapids: Wm. B. Eerdmans Publishing Co., 1962.
Lenski, R. C. H. *The Interpretation of St. Paul's First and Second Epistle to the Corinthians*. Columbus, OH: Wartburg Press, 1946.
Ramsay, William M. *A Historical Commentary on St. Paul's Epistle to the Galatians*. Grand Rapids: Baker Book House, 1965 (reprint).
Stott, J. R. W. "Commentary on the Johannine Epistles," *Tyndale Bible Commentaries*. Grand Rapids: Wm. B. Eerdmans Publishing Co., 1964.
Tasker, R. V. G. "Commentary on General Epistle of James," *Tyndale Bible Commentaries*. Grand Rapids: Wm. B. Eerdmans Publishing Co., 1957.
Thomas, W. H. Griffith. *Commentary on St. Paul's Epistle to the Romans*. Grand Rapids: Wm. B. Eerdmans Publishing Co., 1946 (reprint).